T0382190

LIVY
BOOK XXII.

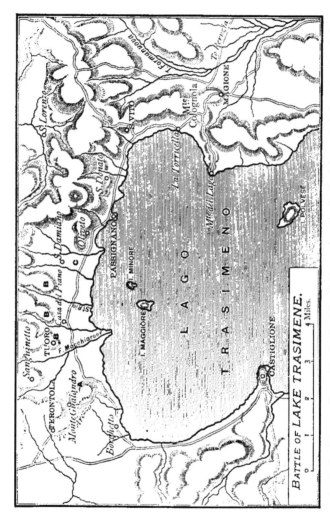

BATTLE OF LAKE TRASIMENE.

0   1   2   3   4 Miles.

A. Carthaginian cavalry.   B. Carthaginian light armed.   C. Carthaginian main body under Hannibal.

Livy xxii.

LIVY

BOOK XXII

EDITED BY

MARCUS S. DIMSDALE

CAMBRIDGE
AT THE UNIVERSITY PRESS
1953

CAMBRIDGE UNIVERSITY PRESS
Cambridge, New York, Melbourne, Madrid, Cape Town,
Singapore, São Paulo, Delhi, Mexico City

Cambridge University Press
The Edinburgh Building, Cambridge CB2 8RU, UK

Published in the United States of America by Cambridge University Press, New York

www.cambridge.org
Information on this title: www.cambridge.org/9781107683044

First published 1889
First edition 1889
Reprinted 1893, 1896, 1899, 1907, 1912, 1917, 1920, 1922, 1929, 1930, 1953
First paperback edition 2013

A catalogue record for this publication is available from the British Library

ISBN 978-1-107-68304-4 Paperback

PREFACE.

THE plan of this edition is the same as that of Bk XXI. (Cambridge University Press, 1888). I have again to acknowledge my very large debt to the edition of Weissenborn[1]. I have also consulted the notes of Wölfflin (Wlf.), of Capes (C.), and Dowdall (D.) published by Deighton and Bell, 1888.

The text is that of Weissenborn (seventh edition by Müller).

KING'S COLLEGE, CAMBRIDGE,
1889.

---

[1] The acknowledgments in the notes (W.) do not represent the extent of my debt to Weissenborn.

INTRODUCTION. I.[1]

Sources of Livy's Narrative.

AS it is Livy's practice to follow one authority in particular for a section of his work and then to turn to another, the trustworthiness of his narrative varies with that of the authority whom he is using at the time, and it would be useful if it were possible to refer each portion of his history to the source whence it is drawn. Livy's authorities for the third decade appear to have been as follows.

1. Q. Fabius Pictor wrote annals of Rome in Greek from the earliest times down to his own. He fought in the Gallic war 225 B.C., and the description of the Battle of Telamon in Polybius, which seems to be drawn from the account of an eye-witness, may be due to him. He is twice referred to in the present book. In c. 7. 4 Livy, referring to the battle of Trasimene, or to the estimates of the slain, says *Fabium aequalem temporibus huiusce belli potissimum auctorem habui.* In c. 57. 5 Fabius is mentioned as being sent to consult the oracle of Delphi after the Battle of Cannae. Being, as appears from this, in a fairly prominent position, he must have had facilities for acquiring information. On the other hand Polybius accuses him of partiality to the Romans. As a kinsman of

---

[1] The idea of this Introduction was suggested to me by the second Introduction in Livy XXIII.—IV., Macmillan, 1885, edited by Mr Macaulay, with whose conclusions with regard to Livy and Polybius I agree.

Q. Fabius Maximus he would not be disposed to underrate his exploits, and perhaps those passages in this book which tend to magnify them (e.g. 24. 11—14. 30) may be due to Fabius Pictor.

2.   L. Cincius Alimentus, another annalist, was Praetor in Sicily in 209 B.C., and was taken prisoner by Hannibal (cf. XXI. 38. 3 *qui captum se ab Hannibale scribit*).

3.   Silenus of Calatia wrote a work called Σικελικὰ and another on Roman history, in Greek. He accompanied Hannibal during his Italian campaigns (Nepos, *Hann.* 13 *duo qui cum eo in castris fuerunt, simulque vixerunt, Silenus et Sosilus Lacedaemoniensis.* Of Sosilus we know nothing). Cicero says (*de Div.* I. 2. 4) *res Hannibalis diligentissime persecutus est.* Livy cites him once, XXVI. 49, but probably did not use him directly.

4.   C. Acilius Glabrio, quaestor in 203 B.C., wrote annals in Greek. He is referred to once in this book 61. 5 (cf. Cic. *de Off.* III. 115), but not by name, and once by name XXV. 39. 12.

5.   Far more important is Polybius, son of Lycortas, born at Megalopolis in Arcadia. He wrote a history of the period 220—146 B.C., being a record of the subjugation of the Mediterranean nations by Rome. Five of the 40 books of which it consisted remain entire. Of the first 3 books, which are introductory, the 3rd corresponds to the 21st and 22nd of Livy. After the conquest of Macedonia he was brought to Rome among 1000 Achaeans to answer the charge of having assisted Perseus. He remained in Italy 167—151 B.C., and was an intimate friend of Scipio Africanus minor. He had thus an opportunity of conversing with the men, or the sons of the men, who had been principal actors in the events he described (III. 48. 12). He has deservedly won a name for impartiality; still he may have received from men of the Scipionic circle an unfair impression with regard to such a popular leader as Flaminius. With a view to the writing of his history he travelled in Sicily, Spain, Gaul, and even beyond the pillars of Hercules, III. 59. Although a careful enquirer he had not a 'geographical eye', and personal investigations on the scene of an action may in some cases have confirmed him in a mistaken conception with regard

to it. (See Appendix on the battle of Trasimene.) Livy cites
him only once by name in this decade, XXX. 45. 5, as *Polybius,
haudquaquam spernendus auctor*, but this gives no idea of
the extent of his obligations to him.

 6. L. Calpurnius Piso, consul 133 B.C., wrote annals of
Rome from its foundation down to his own time, in a meagre
style (Cic. *Brutus* 27). He is once cited by Livy.

 7. L. Coelius Antipater was a contemporary of the
Gracchi, circ. 120 B.C. He was the first of the annalists who
aimed at rhetorical ornament. *Addidit historiae maiorem
sonum, De or.* II. 54. *Paulo inflavit vehementius, De Legg.*
I. 2. 6. His seven books were devoted wholly to the Second
Punic War, and, according to Cic. *de Div.* I. 49, he used Silenus
(*in Sileni quem Coelius sequitur Graeca historia*). Livy cites
him by name only once in this work, but three times in Bk. 21,
and ten times altogether in the second decade. Probably he
used him pretty constantly.

 8. Q. Claudius Quadrigarius wrote annals from the de-
struction of Rome by the Gauls down to the time of Sulla.
Livy refers to him once in the decade as the translator of
Acilius, XXV. 39. 12.

 9. Valerius Antias lived in the former half of the last
century B.C. He wrote a history of Rome from the earliest
times down to his own in 75 books. Livy used him a good
deal in the first decade, but then seems to have become suspicious of his veracity. He reproves him on several occasions
for exaggeration, especially in the matter of numbers, e.g. XXVI.
49. 4 *adeo nullus mentiendi modus est.* XXXVI. 38. 7 *ubi ut in
numero scriptori parum fidei est, quia in augendo eo non alius
quis intemperantior est.* There is probably an allusion to him
in this sense, 7. 4. He is cited seven times in the third decade.

 10. There is a single reference to another annalist Clodius
Licinius (XXIX. 22), whom Cicero calls the successor of Coelius
Antipater.

 It is impossible to decide exactly what parts of Livy's

narrative are due to each of these authorities, as with one exception their works no longer exist. But it is possible and important to form an opinion as to the relations of Livy and Polybius, the second half of whose third book covers the same period as Livy's 22nd. In the 4th decade, where he is dealing with the affairs of Greece and Asia, Livy undoubtedly takes Polybius as his chief authority. He paraphrases or even translates large sections of Polybius' work, and only leaves him in order to note points in which the Roman annalists differ from him. But in the 3rd decade the case is different. Much of Livy's narrative comes from other authorities than Polybius. Even where Polybius seems to be the authority used divergencies from his account are found (cf. the account of events in Spain, c. 19—22, and notes). From this circumstance it has been concluded that Livy did not use Polybius directly in the 3rd decade, and that their resemblances and divergencies are to be explained on the theory that both drew from a common source. Polybius, it is thought, used Silenus directly, while Livy drew from Coelius Antipater who followed Silenus (see above). But there are some passages in which the verbal agreement between Polybius and Livy is very close. Compare the account of Hannibal's descent from the Alps, XXI. 25. 10—27, with that of Polybius III. 54. 4—55. On the theory just mentioned Livy must have copied Coelius, and Coelius Silenus exactly, while the latter must have been followed as closely by Polybius. It is more natural to suppose that Livy did use Polybius directly in the 3rd decade, though not so continuously as in the 4th; firstly because there were more authorities (notably, Fabius and Coelius Antipater) for the Second Punic War than for the wars in the East, and secondly because in dealing with events in Italy Polybius did not appear to Livy so distinctly superior to the Roman annalists, as he did when recording the affairs of Greece and Asia (cf. XXXIII. 10. 10 *Polybium secuti sumus, cum omnium Romanarum rerum, tum praecipue in Graecia gestarum*). For the same reasons even in passages where he does use Polybius, Livy does not hesitate to make alterations on minor points.

The results of this conclusion are twofold. Firstly, in passages where Polybius appears to be Livy's authority we may use him freely for interpreting Livy. Secondly, where Livy's account agrees on the whole with that of Polybius but not altogether (as in the account of Hannibal's escape from Campania, cc. 16. 5, 17. and in that of the battle of Cannae 44—49), we should not oppose Livy's view to Polybius as if it represented an independent view, instead of being based on Polybius and supplemented by other authorities.

In accordance with this conclusion those parts of Bk. 22 in which Livy appears to follow Polybius have been assigned to him. As a rule Livy prefers Polybius as an authority for events in the field, while he draws his information as to events in Rome from Roman annalists.

1—7. 6. The passage of the marshes and the battle of Trasimene from Polybius except 1. 5—20, the account of prodigies and religious measures: 5. 8, the mention of the earthquake during the battle, and 3. 11—14, of omens to Flaminius before it; the former certainly, the latter probably due to Coelius.

7, 8. Effects of the defeat in Rome, from Roman authorities.

9. 1—6. Hannibal's march. Polybius.

9. 7,—10. Religious measures and military tactics of Fabius. Roman sources.

11—15. 11. Hannibal's entry into Campania, complaints against Fabius. Roman.

15. 12,—18. Hannibal's escape from Campania, mostly from Polybius.

19—22. Events in Spain during 217 B.C. Polybius.

23—27. Discontent with Fabius, elevation of Minucius. Roman. 24. 11—14, perhaps from Fabius Pictor.

28—30. Operations in the field. Polybius. Except 29. 7, —30. 6, submission of Minucius to Fabius.

32. 1—4. Polybius.

32. 4—40. 4. Events in Rome during the winter 217—16. Roman.

INTRODUCTION. II.

On the style and grammar of Livy.

I. *Style.* Cicero was born in 106 B.C., Livy in 59 B.C., Tacitus in 54 A.D. In more than one respect Livy occupies an intermediate position between Cicero and Tacitus, partaking of the characteristics of each.

(*a*) In his oratorical works Cicero perfected the period. Livy adapted the period to historical narration. Thus in Livy we constantly find sentences in which a number of clauses expressing the circumstances of the main act are artistically grouped in subordination to a clause which expresses the main act itself. Look for instance at such a sentence as that in 11. 3. Its framework consists of an ablative absolute and a main verb + an ablative absolute (on which depends a clause introduced by *ut*), another ablative absolute (on which depends a clause introduced by *ne*), a deponent perfect participle, a clause introduced by *cum*, and lastly the main verb. See also e.g. 3. 7; 4. 4; 9. 2; 16. 5; 25. 16.

In some of Livy's sentences, so many are the subordinate clauses, the temporal adverbs *cum*, *ubi*, *postquam*, are called into requisition one after another. It may be remarked that in the Ciceronian period *cum* is used, if at all, generally at the beginning of the sentence, and if necessary is taken up again with *cumque.* In Livy the sentence very often opens with a participial clause, and the use of *cum* is deferred till later. See 9. 7; 11. 3; 22. 17. Participial clauses are used far more freely by Livy than by Cicero. Generally speaking the periods of the former are more elaborate. The reason for this is obvious. Cicero had to speak in such sentences as could be readily followed by his auditors. The relations of the several subordinate clauses to the main act, and the general result of the whole, could be studied by Livy's readers at leisure. Sometimes the elaboration of the period is carried to a fault. In his desire to make it as full as possible Livy on reaching what should be logically the main clause, sometimes makes this clause also subordinate, expressing the action by a participle or subjunctive with *cum*, or making its subject the object of the verb of the added clause. Thus two principal actions are expressed in the same sentence and the action which is expressed by the main verb is not that to which the clauses describing the circumstances are logically subordinate, though they are so grammatically.

In this book there is no good instance of such a sentence. Cf. however XXI. 33. 9 (Hannibal) *decurrit ex superiore loco et cum infesto impetu fudisset hostem suis quoque tumultum auxit.* 'Hannibal charged down from the height and'—did what? 'defeated the enemy', one would expect. No. 'Increased the confusion of his own men'. What a fiasco! Yet look again, Hannibal 'defeated the enemy' after all. *Fudit hostem* is what really corresponds to *decurrit*, but Livy anxious to include another step in the narration in the same period, inserts *cum* and throws *fudit* into a subordinate clause while expressing by the main verb an act which is really only supplementary. The meaning is 'and defeated the enemy, though at the same time he threw his men into confusion'[1].

Cf. with this 13. 3, where *moverunt* expresses the very opposite result to that which we should have expected from *cum res maior esset quam auctores.* On this clause *dubius erat* would

[1] Cf. Madvig, *Kleine Philologische Schriften,* Essay V. p. 356, where other instances are given.

have followed more appropriately, but a new clause is included in the period expressing the final result of the negotiations, and *dubius* is expressed as an accusative governed by the verb of that clause.

See also the sentence in 18. 8—10 note, and 2. 10—11.

(*b*) Livy found no imitator of his periodic style. On the other hand he may in some respects be regarded as the predecessor of Tacitus. The characteristics of Tacitus' style have been summed up in the words *brevitas, varietas, poeticus color.* *Brevitas* Livy has not. Quintilian speaks of the *lactea ubertas* of his language. But while in Cicero everything is balanced and uniform there are not wanting in Livy traces of that *varietas* which is constantly meeting us in Tacitus ; e.g. 13. 11 *ingentem fugam, terrorem latius.* 14. 14 *sedendo aut votis.* 23. 10 *simul castris praesidio et circumspectans.* 28. 1 *et perfugis indicantibus et explorantem.* Again in Livy's language we may see an approximation to poetic diction—due no doubt to the study of Vergil and Horace who now became the literary models— which becomes still more marked in the pages of the Histories and the Annals. E.g. *urgente fato* 43. 9 may be compared with Verg. *A.* 11. 653 *fatoque urgenti incumbere vellet.* *Exsors culpae* 44. 7 with *A.* VI. 428 *dulcis vitae exsortes.* *Una salutis via* 39. 17 with *A.* VI. 96; 11. 387 *via prima salutis.* Cf. also 50. 10 *haec ubi dicta dedit.* Again *aperientibus classem promuntoriis* 19. 8 is a poetical expression. These few instances drawn from the present book alone may serve to indicate Livy's relation to the two other great writers of Latin prose.

II. *Grammar.* Livy stands at the beginning of the silver age. A few points may be noticed in which he diverges from the stricter usage of the Republican writers.

The VERB. *a.* The subjunctive is used with *donec* and *priusquam* of facts in the past, where there is no idea of purpose or expectation. Cf. 8. 1; 31. 2; 38. 6; *ib.* 8.

b. The subjunctive is used with *ubi, cum, quicunque* etc. in a frequentative sense.

2. 7 *ubi procubuissent;* 38. 3 *ubi convenissent;* 12. 2 and 8.

c. Sequence of tenses. The perfect subjunctive is used with a consecutive *ut* although a secondary tense has preceded. **5.** 8 *tantus fuit ardor ut nemo senserit;* 56. 4.

d. Analogous to this are changes from secondary to primary sequence in *oratio obliqua*, made for the sake of increased vividness.

25. 14 *referret sit;* 32. 8 *duxissent...iudicaverint.*

e. With regard to the form of the verb. *forem* is used freely and becomes a mere synonym for *essem.* In Sallust and Nepos *forem* is hardly ever thus used except where there is a condition, or where the proposition refers to the future. Cicero and Caesar avoid *forem* altogether.

It is used of conditional acts, 40. 9; 41. 3; 61. 15.

In propositions referring to the future, 38. 9; 57. 5.

But to form a simple pluperfect subjunctive, not expressing a condition, in 9. 9 *quod votum foret*; 32. 6.

fui, fueram are used for *sum, eram* with participles, not only where the latter are used as adjectives and express a state, but also where participle and auxiliary together express an act.

13. 2 *dimissi fuerant;* 23. 3 *pugnatum fuerat;* 36. 8; 42. 11; 54. 7; 57. 2.   In 54. 1 on the other hand *sparsi* may express a state, cf. 24. 2.

PARTICIPLES.   These are more freely used than heretofore.

a. In agreement with a substantive, with the meaning of an abstract substantive and a genitive depending on it.

1. 8 *prodigia nuntiata;* 6. 9 *dispulsa nebula;* 26. 7; 34. 2; 37. 2; 42. 1; 47. 8; 52. 1.

b. = A conditional clause.

2. 3 *necubi consistere coactis necessaria ad usus deessent;* 6. 10 *conspectos;* 28. 8 *egressi;* 60. 9 *confertos.*

c. Absolutely, without a substantive.

4. 4 *inexplorato;* 55. 3 *palam facto.*

d. Fut. participle is used without *sum* expressing purpose.

12. 2 *commissurus.*

e. The present participle is used substantivally, especially in the genitive plural.   5. 5 *pugnantium globo...fugientium agmen;* 7. 4. 10; 7. 12; 19. 9; 42. 2; 43. 3.   The participle thus used is often best rendered by an abstract substantive, e.g. 29. 1 *clamore paventium;* 5. 4 *terrentium paventiumque clamores.*

f. Here may be classed the omission of participles, or relative clauses, so that (i) adverbs, (ii) substantives governed by a preposition are used attributively.

i. 7. 11 *postero ac deinceps aliquot diebus;* 17. 3 *quo repente discursu;* 20. 5; 23. 4; 30. 6; 39. 11.

ii. 8. 1 *ad Trasumennum pugnam;* 9. 5 *circa Arpos regionem;* 25. 7; 37. 1 *ab Hierone classis;* 38. 5; 53. 2; 58. 1; 59. 8.

The GERUNDIVE is used in the sense of a present participle 3. 10; 14. 7 *qui indignando...deos ciebamus;* 51. 9 *laniando hostem expirasset;* 55. 4.

SUBSTANTIVES. *a.* The ablative of place where is often used without a preposition.

4. 6 *campo sederat;* 15. 4 *iugis reducit;* 18. 6 *iugis ducebat;* 43. 9 *campis vehit.*

b. The same may be said of the ablative of separation.

19. 8 *procul portu.*

ADJECTIVES. *a.* Used substantivally in neut. plur. especially where *loca* is understood ; 6. 5 *omnia arta praeruptaque;* 39. 13.

b. Used substantivally in the neuter, with a genitive depending. 15. 2 *aestatis reliquum;* 45. 1 *ad multum diei.*

c. Adverbially, 4. 6 *nebula densior sederat;* 6. 4 *infesto venienti;* 7. 13; 32. 2; 45. 7.

d. The combination of prepositions with neut. adjectives and participles becomes more common ; 2. 8 *in sicco;* 3. 1; 4. 3 *in aperto;* 4. 4 *ex adverso;* 15. 5; 33. 4; 41. 1. In most cases a substantive *loco* might be supplied. Sometimes the expression has become purely adverbial. 7. 4 *auctum ex vano;* 41. 1 *ex praeparato.*

PRONOUNS. *aliis = reliquus;* 11. 9; 30. 2; 46. 1. 5; *quicunque* is used without a verb, 58. 5.

ADVERBS. *ceterum* which properly = *du reste* and is resumptive as in 53. 1, is used by Livy, as by Sallust, adversatively = *sed;* 1. 4; 5. 3; 17. 6; 18. 1 etc.

T. LIVII

AB VRBE CONDITA

LIBER XXII.

IAM ver adpetebat; *ita*que Hannibal ex hibernis movit, **1**
et nequiquam ante conatus transcendere Ap- I. Hannibal
penninum intolerandis frigoribus et cum in- leaves his winter-
genti periculo moratus ac metu. Galli, quos there are mur- **2**
5 praedae populationumque conciverat spes, post- murs against Fla-
quam pro eo, ut ipsi ex alieno agro raperent are   announced,
agerentque, suas terras sedem belli esse pre- taken to expiate
mique utriusque partis exercituum hibernis them.
videre, verterunt retro *in* Hannibalem ab Romanis odia; **3**
10 petitusque saepe principum insidiis, ipsorum inter se fraude
eadem levitate, qua consenserant, consensum indicantium
servatus erat, et mutando nunc vestem nunc tegumenta
capitis errore etiam sese ab insidiis munierat. ceterum hic **4**
quoque ei timor causa fuit maturius movendi ex hibernis.
15   Per idem tempus Cn. Servilius consul Romae idibus
Martiis magistratum iniit. ibi cum de re publica rettulisset, **5**
redintegrata in C. Flaminium invidia est: duos se consules
creasse, unum habere; quod enim illi iustum imperium,

[I.—VII. *The war in Etruria, and the battle of Trasimene.*]
6 quod auspicium esse? magistratus id a domo, publicis
privatisque penatibus, Latinis feriis actis, sacrificio in monte
7 perfecto, votis rite in Capitolio nuncupatis secum ferre; nec
privatum auspicia sequi, nec sine auspiciis profectum in
8 externo ea solo nova atque integra concipere posse. auge- 5
bant metum prodigia ex pluribus simul locis nuntiata : in
Sicilia militibus aliquot spicula, in Sardinia autem in muro
circumeunti vigilias equiti scipionem, quem manu tenuerat,
arsisse, et litora crebris ignibus fulsisse, et scuta duo san-
9 guine sudasse, et milites quosdam ictos fulminibus, et solis 10
orbem minui visum, et Praeneste ardentes lapides caelo
cecidisse, et Arpis parmas in caelo visas pugnantemque cum
10 luna solem, et Capenae duas interdiu lunas ortas, et aquas
Caeretes sanguine mixtas fluxisse fontemque ipsum Herculis
cruentis manasse *re*spersum maculis, et Antii metentibus 15
11 cruentas in corbem spicas cecidisse, et Faleriis caelum findi
velut magno hiatu visum, quaque patuerit, ingens lumen
effulsisse; sortes sua sponte adtenuatas, unamque excidisse
12 ita scriptam 'Mavors telum suum concutit'; et per idem
tempus Romae signum Martis Appia via ac simulacra 20
luporum sudasse, et Capuae speciem caeli ardentis fuisse
13 lunaeque inter imbrem cadentis. inde minoribus etiam
dictu prodigiis fides habita : capras lanatas quibusdam
factas, et gallinam in marem, gallum in feminam sese ver-
14 tisse. his, sicut erant nuntiata, expositis auctoribusque in 25
15 curiam introductis consul de religione patres consuluit. decretum, ut ea prodigia partim maioribus hostiis, partim lac-
tentibus procurarentur, et uti supplicatio per triduum ad
16 omnia pulvinaria haberetur; cetera, cum decemviri libros
inspexissent, ut ita fierent, quem ad modum cordi esse divis 30
17 *e* carminibus praefarentur. decemvirorum monitu decretum
est, Iovi primum donum fulmen aureum pondo quinqua-

[I.—VII.   *The war in Etruria, and the battle of Trasimene.*]

ginta fieret, *et* Iunoni Minervaeque ex argento dona darentur,
et Iunoni reginae in Aventino Iunonique Sospitae Lanuvii
maioribus hostiis sacrificaretur, matronaeque pecunia con- 18
lata, quantum conferre cuique commodum esset, donum
5 Iunoni reginae in Aventinum ferrent, lectisterniumque fieret,
et ut libertinae et ipsae, unde Feroniae donum daretur,
pecuniam pro facultatibus suis conferrent.   haec ubi facta, 19
decemviri Ardeae in foro maioribus hostiis sacrificarunt.
postremo Decembri iam mense ad aedem Saturni Romae
10 inmolatum est, lectisterniumque imperatum — et eum lectum senatores straverunt — et convivium publicum, ac per 20
urbem Saturnalia diem ac noctem clamata, populusque eum
diem festum habere ac servare in perpetuum iussus.

 Dum consul placandis Romae dis habendoque dilectu **2**
15 dat operam, Hannibal profectus ex hibernis,   II. Hanni-
quia iam Flaminium consulem Arretium per- bal crosses the
marshes of the
venisse fama erat, cum aliud longius, ceterum Arno, with diffi- **2**
commodius ostenderetur iter, propiorem viam culty. He loses
the sight of one
per paludes petit, qua fluvius Arnus per eos eye.
20 dies solito magis inundaverat, *H*ispanos et Afros et omne 3
veterani robur exercitus admixtis ipsorum inpedimentis,
necubi consistere coactis necessaria ad usus deessent, primos ire iussit, sequi Gallos, ut id agminis medium esset,
novissimos ire equites, Magonem inde cum expeditis Nu- 4
25 midis cogere agmen, maxime Gallos, si taedio laboris longae-
que viae, ut est mollis ad talia gens, dilaberentur aut subsisterent, cohibentem.   primi, qua modo praeirent duces, 5
per praealtas fluvii ac profundas voragines hausti paene limo
inmergentesque se tamen signa sequebantur.   Galli neque 6
30 sustinere se prolapsi neque adsurgere ex voraginibus poterant, *nec* aut corpora animis aut animos spe sustinebant,
alii fessa aegre trahentes membra, alii, ubi semel victis 7

[I.—VII. *The war in Etruria, and the battle of Trasimene.*]

taedio animis procubuissent, inter iumenta et ipsa iacentia
passim morientes ; maximeque omnium vigiliae conficiebant
8 per quadriduum iam et tres noctes toleratae. cum omnia
obtinentibus aquis nihil, ubi in sicco fessa sternerent corpora, inveniri posset, cumulatis in aqua sarcinis insuper in- 5
9 cumbebant, *aut* iumentorum itinere toto prostratorum passim
acervi tantum, quod extaret aqua, quaerentibus ad quietem
10 parvi temporis necessarium cubile dabant. ipse Hannibal,
aeger oculis ex verna primum intemperie variante calores
frigoraque, elephanto, qui unus superfuerat, quo altius ab 10
11 aqua extaret, vectus, vigiliis tamen et nocturno umore palus-
trique caelo gravante caput, et quia medendi nec locus nec
tempus erat, altero oculo capitur.

3   Multis hominibus iumentisque foede amissis cum tandem de paludibus emersisset, ubi primum in 15
sicco potuit, castra locat ; certumque per prae-
missos exploratores habuit exercitum Romanum circa Arreti moenia esse. consulis deinde
consilia atque animum et situm regionum
itineraque et copias ad commeatus expedi- 20
endos et cetera, quae cognosse in rem erat,
3 summa omnia cum cura inquirendo exequebatur. regio
erat in primis Italiae fertilis, Etrusci campi, qui Faesulas
inter Arretiumque iacent, frumenti ac pecoris et omnium
4 copia rerum opulenti ; consul ferox ab consulatu priore et 25
non modo legum aut patrum maiestatis sed ne deorum
quidem satis metuens. hanc insitam ingenio eius temeritatem fortuna prospero civilibus bellicisque rebus successu
5 aluerat. itaque satis apparebat nec deos nec homines con-
sulentem ferociter omnia ac praepropere acturum. quoque 30
pronior esset in vitia sua, agitare eum atque inritare Poenus
6 parat ; et laeva relicto hoste Faesulas petens medio Etruriae

III. Wishing to
make Flaminius
fight Hannibal
ravages the cen-
tral plain of Etru-
ria. Despite un-
favourable omens
Flaminius leaves
Arretium in pur-
suit.

[L.—VII. *The war in Etruria, and the battle of Trasimene.*]
agro praedatum profectus quantam maximam vastitatem
potest caedibus incendiisque consuli procul ostendit. Fla- 7
minius, qui ne quieto quidem hoste ipse quieturus erat, tum
vero, postquam res sociorum ante oculos prope suos ferri
5 agique vidit, suum id dedecus ratus, per mediam iam Italiam
vagari Poenum atque obsistente nullo ad ipsa Romana
moenia ire oppugnanda, ceteris omnibus in consilio salutaria 8
magis quam speciosa suadentibus, 'conlegam expectandum,
ut coniunctis exercitibus communi animo consilioque rem
10 gererent; interim equitatu auxiliisque levium armorum ab 9
effusa praedandi licentia hostem cohibendum', iratus se ex
consilio proripuit signumque simul itineri pugnaeque cum
proposuisset, 'immo Arreti ante moenia sedeamus' inquit; 10
'hic enim patria et penates sunt. Hannibal emissus e
15 manibus perpopuletur Italiam vastandoque et urendo omnia
ad Romana moenia perveniat, nec ante nos hinc moverimus
quam, sicut olim Camillum ab Veiis, C. Flaminium ab
Arretio patres acciverint'. haec simul increpans cum ocius 11
signa convelli iuberet et ipse in equum insiluisset, equus
20 repente conruit consulemque lapsum super caput effudit.
territis omnibus, qui circa erant, velut foedo omine in- 12
cipiendae rei insuper nuntiatur, signum omni vi moliente
signifero convelli nequire. conversus ad nuntium 'num 13
litteras quoque' inquit 'ab senatu adfers, quae me rem
25 gerere vetent? abi, nuntia effodiant signum, si ad convellendum manus prae metu obtorpuerint'. incedere inde 14
agmen coepit primoribus, superquam quod dissenserant ab
consilio, territis etiam duplici prodigio, milite in vulgus laeto
ferocia ducis, cum spem magis ipsam quam causam spei
30 intueretur.

Hannibal quod agri est inter Cortonam urbem Trasu- 4
mennumque lacum omni clade belli pervastat, quo magis

6 *LIVII*

[I.—VII. *The war in Etruria, and the battle of Trasimene.*]

IV. Hannibal
2 reaches lake Tra-
simene before
Flaminius, and
occupies a de-
file between the
mountains and
the lake. The Ro-
mans enter it, and
3 are attacked.

iram hosti ad vindicandas sociorum iniurias
acuat. et iam pervenerant ad loca nata
insidiis, ubi maxime montes Cortonenses
Trasumennus subit. via tantum interest perangusta, vel*ut* ad *id* ipsum de industria relicto 5
spatio; deinde paulo latior patescit campus;
inde colles insurgunt. ibi castra in aperto
locat, ubi ipse cum Afris modo Hispanisque consideret;
Baliares ceteramque levem armaturam post montis circumducit; equites ad ipsas fauces saltus, tumulis apte tegen- 10
tibus, locat, ut, ubi intrassent Romani, obiecto equitatu
clausa omnia lacu ac montibus essent.

4 Flaminius cum pridie solis occasu ad lacum pervenisset,
inexplorato postero die vixdum satis certa luce angustiis
superatis, postquam in patentiorem campum pandi agmen 15
coepit, id tantum hostium, quod ex adverso erat, conspexit;
5 ab tergo ac super caput *haud* dispectae insidiae. Poenus,
ubi, id quod petierat, clausum lacu ac montibus et circumfusum suis copiis habuit hostem, signum omnibus dat simul
6 invadendi. qui ubi, qua cuique proximum fuit, decucur- 20
rerunt, eo magis Romanis subita atque inprovisa res fuit,
quod orta ex lacu nebula campo quam montibus densior
sederat, agminaque hostium ex pluribus collibus ipsa inter
7 se satis conspecta eoque magis pariter decucurrerant. Romanus clamore prius undique orto quam satis cerneret, se 25
circumventum esse sensit, et ante in frontem lateraque pugnari coeptum est, quam satis instrueretur acies aut expediri
5 arma stringique gladii possent. consul perculsis omnibus

V. Flaminius
tries in vain to re-
store order. Each
man fights des-
perately for him-
self.

ipse satis ut in *re* trepida inpavidus turbatos
ordines, vertente se quoque ad dissonos cla- 30
mores, instruit, ut tempus locusque patitur, et,
quacumque adire audirique potest, adhortatur

[I.—VII. *The war in Etruria, and the battle of Trasimene.*]

ac stare ac pugnare iubet: nec enim inde votis aut 2
inploratione deum, sed vi ac virtute evadendum esse;
per medias acies ferro viam fieri, et quo timoris minus
sit, eo minus ferme periculi esse. ceterum prae strepitu 3
5 ac tumultu nec consilium nec imperium accipi poterat,
tantumque aberat, ut sua signa atque ordines et locum
noscerent, ut vix ad arma capienda aptandaque pugnae
conpeteret animus, opprimerenturque quidam onerati magis
iis quam tecti. et erat in tanta caligine maior usus aurium 4
10 quam oculorum. ad gemitus vulner*ato*rum ictusque corporum aut armorum et mixtos terrentium paventiumque
clamores circumferebant ora oculosque. alii fugientes pug- 5
nantium globo inlati haerebant, alios redeuntes in pugnam
avertebat fugientium agmen. deinde, ubi in omnis partis 6
15 nequiquam impetus capti, et ab lateribus montes ac lacus,
a fronte et ab tergo hostium acies claudebat, apparuitque
nullam nisi in dextera ferroque salutis spem esse, tum sibi 7
quisque dux adhortatorque factus ad rem gerendam, et nova
de integro exorta pugna est, non illa ordinata per principes
20 hastatosque ac triarios, nec ut pro signis antesignani, post
signa alia pugnaret acies, nec ut in sua legione miles aut
cohorte aut manipulo esset; fors conglo*ba*bat et animus 8
suus cuique ante aut post pugnandi ordinem dabat; tantus-
que fuit ardor animorum, adeo intentus pugnae animus, ut
25 eum motum terrae, qui multarum urbium Italiae magnas
partes prostravit avertitque cursu rapidos amnis, mare flu-
minibus invexit, montes lapsu ingenti proruit, nemo pugnantium senserit.

Tris ferme horas pugnatum est et ubique atrociter; circa 6
30 consulem tamen acrior infestiorque pugna est. VI. Flaminius
eum et robora virorum sequebantur, et ipse, is slain and the 2
quacumque in parte premi ac laborare sen- rout begins. Some
climb the cliffs,

[I.—VII.   *The war in Etruria, and the battle of Trasimene.*]

3 others take to the serat suos, inpigre ferebat opem ; insignemque
water. 6000 cut armis et hostes summa vi petebant et tuebantur
their way out but
are pursued and cives, donec Insuber eques — Ducario nomen
surrender.   erat — facie quoque noscitans consulem '*en*'
inquit 'hic est' popularibus suis, 'qui legiones nostras ce- 5
4 cidit agrosque et urbem est depopulatus. iam ego hanc
victimam manibus peremptorum foede civium dabo', sub-
ditisque calcaribus equo per confertissimam hostium turbam
impetum facit obtruncatoque prius armigero, qui se infesto
venienti obviam obiecerat, consulem lancea transfixit ; 10
5 spoliare cupientem triarii obiectis scutis arcuere. magnae
partis fuga inde primum coepit; et iam nec lacus nec
montes pavori obstabant; per omnia arta praeruptaque velut
caeci evadunt, armaque et viri super alios alii praecipitantur.
6 pars magna, ubi locus fugae deest, per prima vada paludis 15
in aquam progressi, quoad capitibus umeris*ve* extare possunt,
sese inmergunt. fuere quos inconsultus pavor nando etiam
7 capessere fugam inpulerit, quae ubi inmensa ac sine spe
erat, aut deficientibus animis hauriebantur gurgitibus aut
nequiquam fessi vada retro aegerrime repetebant, atque ibi 20
ab ingressis aquam hostium equitibus passim trucidabantur.
8 sex milia ferme primi agminis per adversos hostes eru*p*tione
inpigre facta, ignari omnium, quae post se agerentur, ex
saltu evasere et, cum in tumulo quodam constitissent, cla-
morem modo ac sonum armorum audientes, quae fortuna 25
pugnae esset, neque scire nec perspicere prae caligine
9 poterant. inclinata denique re cum incalescente sole dispulsa nebula aperuisset diem, tum liquida iam luce montes
campique perditas res stratamque ostendere foede Ro-
10 manam aciem. itaque, ne in conspectos procul inmit- 30
teretur eques, sublatis raptim signis quam citatissimo po-
11 terant agmine sese abripuerunt, postero die cum super

[I.—VII. *The war in Etruria, and the battle of Trasimene.*]

cetera extrema fames etiam instaret, fidem dante Maharbale,
qui cum omnibus equestribus copiis nocte consecutus erat,
si arma tradidissent, abire cum singulis vestimentis pas-
surum, sese dediderunt; quae Punica religione servata fides 12
⁵ ab Hannibale est, atque in vincula omnes coniecti.

Haec est nobilis ad Trasumennum pugna atque inter 7
paucas memorata populi Romani clades. quindecim milia Romanorum in acie caesa; decem
milia sparsa fuga per omnem Etruriam diver-
¹⁰ sis itineribus urbem petiere; duo milia quingenti hostium in acie, multi postea [utrimque]
ex vulneribus periere. multiplex caedes utrimque facta
traditur ab aliis; ego, praeterquam quod nihil auctum ex 4
vano velim, quo nimis inclinant ferme scribentium animi,
¹⁵ Fabium aequalem temporibus huiusce belli potissimum auctorem habui.   Hannibal captivorum, qui Latini nominis 5
essent, sine pretio dimissis, Romanis in vincula datis, segre-
gata ex hostium coacervatorum cumulis corpora suorum
cum sepeliri iussisset, Flamini quoque corpus funeris causa
²⁰ magna cum cura inquisitum non invenit.

Romae ad primum nuntium cladis eius cum ingenti ter- 6
rore ac tumultu concursus in forum populi est factus. ma- 7
tronae vagae per vias, quae repens clades adlata quaeve
fortuna exercitus esset, obvios percunctantur. et cum fre-
²⁵ quentis contionis modo turba in comitium et curiam versa
magistratus vocaret, tandem haud multo ante solis occasum 8
M. Pomponius praetor 'pugna' inquit 'magna victi sumus';
et quamquam nihil certius ex eo auditum est, tamen alius 9
ab alio inpleti rumoribus domos referunt consulem cum
³⁰ magna parte copiarum caesum, superesse paucos aut fuga
passim per Etruriam sparsos aut captos ab hoste. quot 10
casus exercitus victi fuerant, tot in curas distracti animi

VII. The fate 2
of the vanquish-
ed. Alarm and
consternation at
Rome at the news 3
of the battle.

eorum erant, quorum propinqui sub C. Flaminio consule
meruerant, ignorantium, quae cuiusque suorum fortuna
esset; nec quisquam satis certum habet, quid aut speret aut

11 timeat. postero ac deinceps aliquot diebus ad portas maior
prope mulierum quam virorum multitudo stetit aut suorum 5
aliquem aut nuntios de iis opperiens; circumfundebanturque
obviis sciscitantes neque avelli, utique ab notis, priusquam

12 ordine omnia inquisissent, poterant. inde varios vultus
digredientium ab nuntiis cerneres, ut cuique laeta aut tristia
nuntiabantur, gratulantisque aut consolantis redeuntibus 10
domos circumfusos, feminarum praecipue et gaudia insignia

13 erant et luctus. unam in ipsa porta sospiti filio repente
oblatam in conplexu eius expirasse ferunt; alteram, cui
mors filii falso nuntiata erat, maestam sedentem domi ad
primum conspectum redeuntis filii gaudio nimio exanimatam. 15

14 senatum praetores per dies aliquot ab orto usque ad occi-
dentem solem in curia retinent consultantes, quonam duce
aut quibus copiis resisti victoribus Poenis posset.

8   Priusquam satis certa consilia essent, repens alia nuntiatur clades, quattuor milia equitum cum C. 20
VIII. On the   Centenio propraetore missa ad conlegam ab
news of a further
defeat, Fabius is Servilio consule in Umbria, quo post pugnam
appointed dicta-
tor, and Minu-   ad Trasumennum auditam averterant iter, ab
2 cius master of the Hannibale circumventa. eius rei fama varie
horse.
homines adfecit: pars occupatis maiore aegri- 25
tudine animis levem ex conparatione priorum ducere recen-

3 tem equitum iacturam; pars non id, quod acciderat, per se
aestimare, sed, ut in adfecto corpore quamvis levis causa

4 magis quam *in* valido gravior sentiretur, ita tum aegrae et

[VIII.—XVIII.   *Fabius dictator.*   *The war in central Italy, and
Campania.*]

adfectae civitati quodcumque adversi incideret, non rerum
magnitudine sed viribus extenuatis, quae nihil, quod adgravaret, pati possent, aestimandum esse. itaque ad remedium 5
iam diu neque desideratum nec adhibitum, dictatorem
₅ dicendum, civitas confugit. et quia et consul aberat, a quo
uno dici posse videbatur, nec per occupatam armis Punicis 6
Italiam facile erat aut nuntium aut litteras mitti [nec dictatorem populo creare poterat], quod numquam ante eam
diem factum erat, dictatorem populus creavit Q. Fabium
₁₀ Maximum et magistrum equitum M. Minucium Rufum; his- 7
que negotium ab senatu datum, ut muros turresque urbis
firmarent et praesidia disponerent, quibus locis videretur,
pontesque rescinderent fluminum: pro urbe ac penatibus
dimicandum esse, quando Italiam tueri nequissent.
₁₅   Hannibal recto itinere per Umbriam usque ad Spole- 9
tium venit. inde cum perpopulato agro urbem   2
oppugnare adortus esset, cum magna caede   IX. Hannibal
suorum repulsus, coniectans ex unius coloniae enters Picenum.
haud nimis prospere temptatae viribus, quanta vice the Sibylline
₂₀ moles Romanae urbis esset, in agrum Picenum books are con-
avertit iter non copia solum omnis generis fru- sulted.   3
gum abundantem, sed refertum praeda, quam effuse avidi
atque egentes rapiebant. ibi per dies aliquot stativa habita, 4
refectusque miles hibernis itineribus ac palustri via proelio-
₂₅ que magis ad eventum secundo quam levi aut facili adfectus.
ubi satis quietis datum praeda ac populationibus magis 5
quam otio aut requie gaudentibus, profectus Praetutianum
Hadrianum*que* agrum, Marsos inde Marrucinosque et Paelignos devastat circaque Arpos et Luceriam proximam Apuliae
₃₀ regionem. Cn. Servilius consul levibus proeliis cum Gallis 6
factis et uno oppido ignobili expugnato, postquam de con-

legae exercitusque caede audivit, iam moenibus patriae
metuens, ne abesset in discrimine extremo, ad urbem iter
intendit.

7   Q. Fabius Maximus dictator iterum quo die magistratum
iniit vocato senatu, ab dis orsus, cum edocuisset patres plus 5
neglegentia caerimoniarum auspiciorum*que quam* temeritate
atque inscitia peccatum a C. Flaminio consule esse, quaeque piacula irae deum essent ipsos deos consulendos esse,
8 pervicit, ut, quod non ferme decernitur, nisi cum taetra prodigia nuntiata sunt, decemviri libros Sibyllinos adire iube- 10
9 rentur.   qui inspectis fatalibus libris rettulerunt patribus,
quod eius belli causa votum Marti foret, id non rite factum
10 de integro atque amplius faciundum esse, et Iovi ludos
magnos et aedes Veneri Erucinae ac Menti vovendas esse
et supplicationem lectisterniumque habendum et ver sacrum 15
vovendum, si bellatum prospere esset, resque publica in
11 eodem, quo ante bellum fuisset, statu permansisset.   senatus, quoniam Fabium belli cura occupatura esset, M. Aemilium praetorem ex conlegii pontificum sententia, omnia ea
10   X. A *ver sa-*   ut mature fiant, curare iubet.   his senatus con- 20
crum is vowed.   sultis perfectis L. Cornelius Lentulus pontifex
Other vows and   maximus consulente conlegium praetore om-
ceremonies.   nium primum populum consulendum de vere
2 sacro censet: iniussu populi voveri non posse.   rogatus in
haec verba populus: 'velitis iubeatisne haec sic fieri? si res 25
publica populi Romani Quiritium ad quinquennium proximum, sic*ut* velim eam esse salvam, servata erit hisce duellis,
quod duellum populo Romano cum Carthaginiensi est,
quaeque duella cum Gallis sunt, qui cis Alpes sunt, tum
3 donum duit populus Romanus Quiritium: quod ver adtulerit 30
ex suillo, ovillo, caprino, bovillo grege, quaeque profana

[VIII.—XVIII. *Fabius dictator. The war in central Italy, and Campania.*]

erunt, Iovi fieri, ex qua die senatus populusque iusserit.
qui faciet, quando volet quaque lege volet, facito; quo modo 4
faxit, probe factum esto. si id moritur, quod fieri oportebit, 5
profanum esto neque scelus esto; si quis rumpet occidetve
5 insciens, ne fraus esto; si quis clepsit, ne populo scelus esto,
neve cui cleptum erit; si atro die faxit insciens, probe factum 6
esto; si nocte sive luce, si servus sive liber faxit, probe factum esto; si antidea, ac senatus populusque iusserit fieri,
faxitur, eo populus solutus liber esto'. eiusdem rei causa 7
10 ludi magni voti aeris trecentis triginta tribus milibus *trecentis triginta tribus* triente, praeterea bubus Iovi trecentis,
multis aliis divis bubus albis atque ceteris hostiis. votis rite 8
nuncupatis supplicatio edicta; supplicatumque iere cum
coniugibus ac liberis non urbana multitudo tantum, sed
15 agrestium etiam, quos in aliqua sua fortuna publica quoque
contingebat cura. tum lectisternium per triduum habitum 9
decemviris sacrorum curantibus. sex pulvinaria in conspectu fuerunt: Iovi ac Iunoni unum, alterum Neptuno ac
Minervae, tertium Marti ac Veneri, quartum Apollini ac
20 Dianae, quintum Vulcano ac Vestae, sextum Mercurio et
Cereri. tum aedes votae: Veneri Erucinae aedem Q. Fabius 10
Maximus dictator vovit, quia ita ex fatalibus libris editum
erat, ut is voveret, cuius maximum imperium in civitate
esset; Menti aedem T. Otacilius praetor vovit.

25   Ita rebus divinis peractis tum de bello deque re publica 11
dictator rettulit, quibus quotve legionibus vic-   XI. Military
tori hosti obviam eundum esse patres cense-   measures. Fa-
rent. decretum, ut ab Cn. Servilio consule   bius meets Ser-
                                                 vilius and takes 2
exercitum acciperet; scriberet praeterea ex   over his army.
                                                 Servilius goes to
30 civibus sociisque quantum equitum ac peditum   Ostia to protect
videretur; cetera omnia ageret faceretque ut e   the coast with a
                                                 fleet.

[VIIL—XVIII. *Fabius dictator. The war in central Italy, and Campania.*]

3 re publica duceret. Fabius duas legiones se adiecturum ad Servilianum exercitum dixit. iis per magistrum equi-
4 tum scriptis Tibur diem ad conveniendum edixit, edicto-que proposito, ut, quibus oppida castellaque inmunita essent, uti commigrarent in loca tuta; ex agris quoque demi- 5
5 grarent omnes regionis eius, qua iturus Hannibal esset, tectis prius incensis ac frugibus corruptis, ne cuius rei copia esset, ipse via Flaminia profectus obviam consuli exercituque, cum ad Tiberim circa Ocriculum prospexisset agmen consulem-que cum equitibus ad se pro*gre*dientem, viatorem misit, qui 10 consuli nuntiaret, ut sine lictoribus ad dictatorem veniret.
6 qui cum dicto paruisset congressusque eorum ingentem spe-ciem dictaturae apud cives sociosque vetustate iam prope oblitos eius imperii fecisset, litterae ab urbe adlatae sunt, naves onerarias commeatum ab Ostia in Hispaniam ad exer- 15 citum portantes a classe Punica circa portum Cosanum
7 captas esse. itaque extemplo consul Ostiam proficisci iussus navibusque, *quae* ad urbem Romanam aut Ostiae essent, conpletis milite ac navalibus sociis, persequi hostium clas-
8 sem ac litora Italiae tutari. magna vis hominum conscripta 20 Romae erat; libertini etiam, quibus liberi essent et aetas
9 militaris, in verba iuraverant. ex hoc urbano exercitu qui minores quinque et triginta annis erant in navis inpositi, alii, ut urbi praesiderent, relicti.

12   Dictator exercitu consulis accepto a Fulvio Flacco legato 25

XII. Fabius encamps near Hannibal, but will not be drawn into a battle. His tactics. He is accused of cowardice by Minucius. per agrum Sabinum Tibur, quo diem ad con-veniendum edixerat novis milítibus, venit. inde Praeneste ac transversis limitibus in viam Latinam est egressus, unde itineribus summa cum cura exploratis ad hostem ducit, nullo 30 loco, nisi quantum necessitas cogeret, fortunae

[VIII.—XVIII. *Fabius dictator. The war in central Italy, and Campania.*]

se commissurus. quo primum die haud procul Arpis in 3
conspectu hostium posuit castra, nulla mora facta, quin
Poenus educeret in aciem copiamque pugnandi faceret.
sed ubi quieta omnia apud hostes nec castra ullo tumultu 4
5 mota videt, increpans quidem, victos tandem illos Martios
animos Romanis, debellatumque et concessum propalam de
virtute ac gloria esse, in castra rediit; ceterum tacita cura 5
animum incessit, quod cum duce haudquaquam Flamini
Semproníque simili futura sibi res esset, ac tum demum
10 edocti malis Romani parem Hannibali ducem quaesissent.
et prudentiam quidem novi dictatoris extemplo timuit; con- 6
stantiam hauddum expertus agitare ac temptare animum
movendo crebro castra populandoque in oculis eius agros
sociorum coepit; et modo citato agmine ex conspectu abibat, 7
15 modo repente in aliquo flexu viae, si excipere degressum in
aequom posset, occultus subsistebat. Fabius per loca alta 8
agmen ducebat modico ab hoste intervallo, ut neque omitteret eum neque congrederetur. castris, nisi quantum usus
necessarii cogerent, tenebatur miles; pabulum et ligna nec
20 pauci petebant nec passim; equitum levisque armaturae 9
statio, conposita instructaque in subitos tumultus, et suo
militi tuta omnia et infesta effusis hostium populatoribus
praebebat; neque universo periculo summa rerum commit- 10
tebatur, et parva momenta levium certaminum ex tuto
25 coeptorum finitimo receptu adsuefaciebant territum pristinis
cladibus militem minus iam tandem aut virtutis aut fortunae
paenitere suae. sed non Hannibalem magis infestum tam 11
sanis consiliis habebat quam magistrum equitum, qui nihil
aliud, quam quod inpar erat imperio, morae ad rem publi-
30 cam praecipitandam habebat. ferox rapidusque consiliis ac 12
lingua inmodicus primo inter paucos, dein propalam in

vulgus pro cunctatore segnem, pro cauto timidum, adfingens
vicina virtutibus vitia, conpellabat, premendoque superiorem,
quae pessima ars nimis prosperis multorum successibus
crevit, sese extollebat.

13 Hannibal ex Hirpinis in Samnium transit, Beneventanum ₅
depopulatur agrum, Telesiam urbem capit; in-
ritat etiam de industria ducem *Romanum*, si
forte accensum tot indignitatibus *ac* cladibus
sociorum detrahere ad aequum certamen possit.
2 inter multitudinem sociorum Italici generis, ₁₀
qui ad Trasumennum capti ab Hannibale di-
missique fuerant, tres Campani equites erant,
multis iam tum inlecti donis promissisque
Hannibalis ad conciliandos popularium ani-
3 mos. hi nuntiantes, si in Campaniam exercitum admovis- ₁₅
set, Capuae potiendae copiam fore, cum res maior quam
auctores esset, dubium Hannibalem alternisque fidentem ac
diffidentem, tamen, ut Campanos ex Samnio peteret, move-
4 runt. monitos, ut etiam atque etiam promissa rebus adfir-
marent, iussosque cum pluribus et aliquibus principum redire ₂₀
5 ad se dimisit. ipse imperat duci, ut se in agrum Casinatem
ducat, edoctus a peritis regionum, si eum saltum occupasset,
exitum Romano ad opem ferendam sociis interclusurum.
6 sed Punicum abhorrens ab Latinorum nominum *pronun-
tiatione os, Casilinum* pro Casino dux ut acciperet, fecit; ₂₅
aversusque ab suo itinere per Callifanum Allifanumque et
7 Calenum agrum in campum Stellatem descendit. ubi cum
montibus fluminibusque clausam regionem circumspexisset,
8 vocatum ducem percunctatur, ubi terrarum esset. cum is
Casilini eo die mansurum eum dixisset, tum demum cogni- ₃₀
9 tus est error, et Casinum longe inde alia regione esse; vir-

Marginal note: XIII. Hannibal enters Samnium. He is induced by some Campanian prisoners to cross into Campania. His guide brings him by mistake to Casilinum instead of Casinum.

[VIII.—XVIII. *Fabius dictator. The war in central Italy, and*
Campania.]

gisque caeso duce et ad reliquorum terrorem in crucem
sublato, castris communitis Maharbalem cum equitibus in
agrum Falernum praedatum dimisit. usque ad aquas Si- 10
nuessanas populatio ea pervenit. ingentem cladem, fugam 11
5 tamen terroremque latius Numidae fecerunt; nec tamen is
terror, cum omnia bello flagrarent, fide socios dimovit, videlicet quia iusto et moderato regebantur imperio nec abnue-
bant, quod unum vinculum fidei est, melioribus parere.

Ut vero, *post*quam ad Volturnum flumen castra sunt 14
10 posita, exurebatur amoenissimus Italiae ager
villaeque passim incendiis fumabant, per iuga   XIV. The Ro-
Massici montis Fabio ducente, tum prope de the Massic mount
integro seditio accensa; quieverant enim per plain being ra- **2**
paucos dies, quia, cum celerius solito ductum vaged. Minucius
15 agmen esset, festinari ad prohibendam popula- reproaching Fa-
tionibus Campaniam crediderant. ut vero in action.   **3**
extrema iuga Massici montis ventum, et hostes
sub oculis erant Falerni agri colonorumque Sinuessae tecta
urentes, nec ulla erat mentio pugnae, 'spectatum huc' inquit 4
20 Minucius '*ut* ad rem fruendam oculis, sociorum caedes et
incendia, venimus? nec, si nullius alterius nos, ne civium
quidem horum pudet, quos Sinuessam colonos patres nostri
miserunt, ut ab Samnite hoste tuta haec ora esset, quam 5
nunc non vicinus Samnis urit, sed Poenus advena, ab extre-
25 mis orbis terrarum terminis nostra cunctatione et socordia
iam huc progressus? tantum pro degeneramus a patribus 6
nostris, ut praeter quam *nu*per oram illi Punicas vagari classes dedecus esse imperii sui duxerint, eam nunc plenam
hostium, Numidarumque ac Maurorum iam factam videa-
30 mus? qui modo Saguntum oppugnari indignando non homi- 7
nes tantum sed foedera et deos ciebamus, scandentem moe-

[VIII.—XVIII. *Fabius dictator. The war in central Italy, and Campania.*]

8 nia Romanae coloniae Hannibalem lenti spectamus. fumus
ex incendiis villarum agrorumque in oculos atque ora venit;
strepunt aures clamoribus plorantium sociorum, saepius nos
quam deorum invocantium opem; nos hic pecorum modo per
aestivos saltus deviasque callis exercitum ducimus conditi 5
9 nubibus silvisque. si hoc modo peragrando cacumina sal-
tusque M. Furius recipere a Gallis urbem voluisset, quo hic
novus Camillus, nobis dictator unicus in rebus adfectis quaesitus, Italiam ab Hannibale recuperare parat, Gallorum
10 Roma esset, quam vereor ne sic cunctantibus nobis Hanni- 10
11 bali ac Poenis totiens servaverint maiores nostri. sed vir ac
vere Romanus, quo die dictatorem eum ex auctoritate patrum iussuque populi dictum Veios allatum est, cum esset
satis altum Ianiculum, ubi sedens prospectaret hostem, descendit in aecum atque illo ipso die media in urbe, qua nunc 15
busta Gallica sunt, et postero die citra Gabios cecidit Gal-
12 lorum legiones. quid? post multos annos cum ad Furculas
Caudinas ab Samnite hoste sub iugum missi sumus, utrum
tandem L. Papirius Cursor iuga Samnii perlustrando an
Luceriam premendo obsidendoque et lacessendo victorem 20
hostem depulsum ab Romanis cervicibus iugum superbo
13 Samniti inposuit? modo C. Lutatio quae alia res quam cele-
ritas victoriam dedit, quod postero die, quam hostem vidit,
classem gravem commeatibus, inpeditam suomet ipsam
14 instrumento atque adparatu, oppressit? stultitia est sedendo 25
aut votis debellari credere posse; arma capias oportet et
descendas in aecum et vir cum viro congrediaris. audendo
atque agendo res Romana crevit, non his segnibus consiliis,
15 quae timidi cauta vocant'. haec velut contionanti Minucio
circumfundebatur tribunorum equitumque Romanorum mul- 30
titudo, et ad aures quoque militum dicta ferocia evolveban-

tur; ac, si militaris suffragii res esset, haud dubie ferebant
Minucium Fabio ducem praelaturos.

Fabius, pariter in suos haud minus quam in hostis inten- 15
tus, prius ab illis invictum animum praestat.
quamquam probe scit non in castris modo suis
sed iam etiam Romae infamem suam cuncta-
tionem esse, obstinatus tamen tenore eodem
consiliorum aestatis reliquom extraxit, ut Han- 2
nibal destitutus ab spe summa ope petiti certaminis iam hibernis locum circumspectaret,
quia ea regio praesentis erat copiae, non perpetuae, arbusta vineaeque et consita omnia magis amoenis
quam necessariis fructibus. haec per exploratores relata
Fabio. cum satis sciret per easdem angustias, quibus intra- 3
verat Falernum agrum, rediturum, Calliculam montem et
Casilinum occupat modicis praesidiis, quae urbs Volturno
flumine dirempta Falernum a Campano agro dividit; ipse 4
iugis iisdem exercitum reducit misso exploratum cum quad-
ringentis equitibus sociorum L. Hostilio Mancino. qui, ex 5
turba iuvenum audientium saepe ferociter contionantem magistrum equitum, progressus primo exploratoris modo, ut ex
tuto specularetur hostem, ubi vagos passim per vicos Numidas *prospexit ac* per occasionem etiam paucos occidit, ex- 6
templo occupatus certamine est animus, exciderunt que prae-
cepta dictatoris, qui, quan*tum* tuto posset, progressum prius
recipere sese iusserat, quam in conspectum hostium veniret.
Numidae alii atque alii occursantes refugientesque ad castra 7
prope ips*a* *e*um cum fatigatione equorum atque hominum
pertraxere. inde Carthalo, penes quem summa equestris 8
imperii erat, concitatis equis invectus, cum prius, quam ad
coniectum teli veniret, avertisset hostis, quinque ferme milia

XV. Fabius remains firm. He prepares to prevent Hannibal leaving Campania. Mancinus whom he had sent to reconnoitre, advances too far and is routed.

[VIII.—XVIII. *Fabius dictator. The war in central Italy, and Campania.*]

9 continenti cursu secutus est fugientis. Mancinus, postquam
nec hostem desistere sequi nec spem vidit effugiendi esse,
cohortatus suos in proelium rediit omni parte virium inpar.
10 itaque ipse et delecti equitum circumventi occiduntur ; ceteri
etfuso [rursus] cursu Cales primum, inde prope inviis callibus 5
ad dictatorem perfugerunt.
11 Eo forte die Minucius se coniunxerat Fabio, missus ad
firmandum praesidio saltum, qui super Tarracinam in artas
coactus fauces inminet mari, ne ab Sinuessa Poenus Appiae
12 limite pervenire in agrum Romanum posset. coniunctis 10
exercit*ib*us dictator ac magister equitum castra in viam deferunt, qua Hannibal ducturus erat. duo inde milia hostes
16 aberant. postero die Poeni quod viae inter bina castra erat
2 agmine conplevere. cum Romani sub ipso
XVI. The Carthaginians at-
tack the Romans without success.
It appears that they are shut in.
To escape Han-
3 nibal devises a stratagem.
constitissent vallo haud dubie aequiore loco, 15
successit tamen Poenus cum expeditis equiti-
busque ad lacessendum hostem. carptim Poeni
et procursando recipiendoque sese pugnavere ;
restitit suo loco Romana acies; lenta pugna
et ex dictatoris magis quam Hannibalis fuit 20
voluntate. ducenti ab Romanis, octingenti hostium cecidere.
4 inclusus inde videri Hannibal via ad Casilinum obsessa, cum
Capua et Samnium et tantum ab tergo divitum sociorum
Romanis commeatus subveheret, Poenus inter Formiana
saxa ac Literni arenas stagnaque et per horridas silvas hiber- 25
5 naturus esset. nec Hannibalem fefellit suis se artibus peti.
itaque cum per Casilinum evadere non posset, petendique
montes et iugum Calliculae superandum esset, necubi Ro-
6 manus inclusum vallibus agmen adgrederetur, ludibrium
oculorum specie terribile ad frustrandum hostem commen- 30
tus, principio noctis furtim succedere ad montes statuit.

[VIII.—XVIII.   *Fabius dictator.   The war in central Italy, and Campania.*]

fallacis consilii talis apparatus fuit: faces undique ex agris 7
conlectae fascesque virgarum atque aridi sarmenti praeli-
gantur cornibus boum, quos domitos indomitosque multos
inter ceteram agrestem praedam agebat. ad duo milia ferme 8
5 boum effecta, Hasdrubalique negotium datum, ut nocte id
armentum accensis cornibus ad montis ageret, maxime, si
posset, super saltus ab hoste insessos.

Primis tenebris silentio mota castra; boves aliquanto 17
ante signa acti. ubi ad radices montium vias-
10 que angustas ventum est, signum extemplo
datur, ut accensis cornibus armenta in adversos
concitentur montis. et metus ipse relucentis
flammae a capite calorque iam ad vivom ad
imaque cornua veniens velut stimulatos furore
15 agebat boves. quo repente discursu haud
secus quam silvis montibusque accensis omnia

XVII.   Oxen 2
with lighted fag-
gots on their
horns are driven
up the mountain
Callicula.   The
Romans who
hold the pass re-
tire.   Hannibal
crosses and 3
reaches Allifae.

circa virgulta ardere; capitumque *ir*rita quassatio excitans
flammam hominum passim discurrentium speciem praebebat.
qui ad transitum saltus insidendum locati erant, ubi in summis 4
20 montibus ac super se quosdam ignis conspexere, circumven-
tos se esse rati praesidio excessere; qua minime densae
micabant flammae, velut tutissimum iter petentes summa
montium iuga, tamen in quosdam boves palatos a suis gre-
gibus inciderunt. et primo, cum procul cernerent, veluti 5
25 flammas spirantium miraculo adtoniti constiterunt; deinde, 6
ut humana apparuit fraus, tum vero insidias rati esse, cum
maiore *tu*multu concitant se in fugam. levi quoque armaturae hostium incurrere; ceterum nox aequato timore neutros
pugnam incipientis ad lucem tenuit. interea toto agmine 7
30 Hannibal transducto per saltum et quibusdam in ipso saltu
hostium oppressis in agro Allifano posuit castra.

[VIII.—XVIII. *Fabius dictator. The war in central Italy, and Campania.*]

18   Hunc tumultum sensit Fabius; ceterum et insidias esse ratus et ab nocturno utique abhorrens certa-

XVIII. Hannibal recrosses Italy and occupies Gereonium. Fabius departs for Rome, cautioning Minucius against giving battle.

2 mine suos munimentis tenuit. luce prima sub iugo montis proelium fuit, quo interclusam ab suis levem armaturam facile — etenim numero aliquantum praestabant — Romani superas-**3** sent, nisi Hispanorum cohors ad id ipsum remissa ab Hannibale *su*pervenisset. ea adsuetior montibus et ad concursandum inter saxa rupesque aptior ac levior cum velocitate corporum tum armorum habitu campestrem hostem, gravem armis statariumque, **4** pugnae genere facile elusit. ita haudquaquam pari certamine digressi, Hispani fere omnes incolumes, Romani aliquot suis amissis in castra contenderunt.

5   Fabius quoque movit castra transgressusque saltum **6** super Allifas loco alto ac munito consedit. tum per Samnium Romam se petere simulans Hannibal usque in Paelignos populabundus rediit; Fabius medius inter hostium agmen urbemque Romam iugis ducebat nec absistens nec **7** congrediens. ex Paelignis Poenus flexit iter retroque Apuliam repetens Gereonium pervenit, urbem metu, quia conlapsa ruinis pars moenium erat, ab suis desertam; dictator in **8** Larinate agro castra communiit. inde sacrorum causa Romam revocatus, non imperio modo sed consilio etiam ac prope precibus agens cum magistro equitum, ut plus consilio **9** quam fortunae confidat et se potius ducem quam Sempronium Flaminiumque imitetur; ne nihil actum censeret extracta prope aestate per ludificationem hostis; medicos quoque plus interdum quiete quam movendo atque agendo **10** proficere; haud parvam rem esse ab totiens victore hoste vinci desisse ac respirasse ab continuis cladibus — haec

[VIII.—XVIII. *Fabius dictator. The war in central Italy, and Campania.*]

nequiquam praemonito magistro equitum Romam est profectus.

[XIX.—XXII. *Events in Spain during* 217 B.C.]

Principio aestatis, qua haec gerebantur, in Hispania 19
quoque terra marique coeptum bellum est.

5 Hasdrubal ad eum navium numerum, quem a
fratre instructum paratumque acceperat, decem
adiectis quadraginta navium classem Himilconi
tradit atque ita Carthagine profectus naves
prope terram, exercitum in litore ducebat
10 paratus confligere, quacumque parte copiarum hostis occur-
risset. Cn. Scipio, postquam movisse ex hibernis hostem 4
audivit, primo idem consilii fuit; deinde minus terra propter
ingentem famam novorum auxiliorum concurrere ausus,
delecto milite ad naves inposito quinque et triginta navium
15 classe ire obviam hosti pergit. altero ab Tarracone die *ad* 5
stationem decem milia passuum distantem ab ostio Hiberi
amnis pervenit. inde duae Massiliensium speculatoriae
praemissae rettulere classem Punicam stare in ostio fluminis
castraque in ripa posita. itaque ut inprovidos incautosque 6
20 universo simul effuso terrore opprimeret, sublatis ancoris ad
hostem vadit. multas et locis altis positas turris Hispania
habet, quibus et speculis et propugnaculis adversus latrones
utuntur. inde primo conspectis hostium navibus datum 7
signum Hasdrubali est, tumultusque prius in terra et castris
25 quam ad mare et ad naves est ortus, nondum aut pulsu
remorum strepituque alio nautico exaudito aut aperientibus
classem promunturiis, cum repente eques alius super alium 8
ab Hasdrubale missus vagos in litore quietosque in tentoriis
suis, nihil minus quam hostem aut proelium eo die expec-
30 tantis, conscendere naves propere atque arma capere iubet:

XIX. A Car-
thaginian army 2
and fleet advance
from New Car- 3
thage. Cn. Sci-
pio surprises the
fleet at the mouth
of the Ebro.

[XIX.—XXII. *Events in Spain during* 217 B.C.]

9 classem Romanam iam haud procul portu esse. haec equites dimissi passim imperabant; mox Hasdrubal ipse cum
omni exercitu aderat, varioque omnia tumultu strepunt
ruentibus in naves simul remigibus militibusque fugientium
10 magis e terra quam in pugnam euntium modo. vixdum 5
omnes conscenderant, cum alii resolutis oris in ancoras
evehuntur, alii, ne quid teneat, ancoralia incidunt, raptimque
omnia *ac* praepropere agendo militum apparatu nautica ministeria inpediuntur, trepidatione nautarum capere et aptare
11 arma miles prohibetur. et iam Romanus non adpropinqua- 10
bat modo, sed derexerat etiam in pugnam naves. itaque
non ab hoste et proelio magis Poeni quam suomet ipsi
tumultu turbati, temptata verius pugna quam inita in fugam
12 averterunt classem. et cum adversi amnis os lato agmini et
tam multis simul venientibus haud sane intrabile esset, in 15
litus passim naves egerunt atque alii vadis, alii sicco litore
excepti partim armati partim inermes ad instructam per litus
aciem suorum perfugere; duae tamen primo concursu captae
20 erant Punicae naves, quattuor suppressae. Romani, quam-

quam terra hostium erat, armatamque aciem 20
toto praetentam in litore cernebant, haud
cunctanter insecuti trepidam hostium classem,
navis omnis, quae non aut perfregerant proras
litori inlisas aut carinas fixerant vadis, religatas
puppibus in altum extraxere, ad quinque et 25
viginti naves e quadraginta cepere. neque id
pulcherrimum eius victoriae fuit, sed quod una
levi pugna toto eius orae mari potiti erant.
itaque ad Onusam classe provecti; escensio ab 30
navibus in terram facta. cum urbem vi cepissent captam-
5 que diripuissent, Carthaginem inde petunt atque omnem
agrum circa depopulati postremo tecta quoque iniuncta

muro portisque incenderunt. inde iam praeda gravis ad 6
Longunticam pervenit classis, ubi vis magna sparti *erat*, ad
rem nauticam congesta ab Hasdrubale. quod satis in usum
fuit sublato, ceterum omne incensum est. nec continentis 7
5 modo praelecta est ora, sed in Ebusum insulam transmis-
sum. ibi urbe, quae caput insulae est, biduum nequiquam 8
summo labore oppugnata, ubi in spem inritam frustra teri
tempus animadversum est, ad populationem agri versi, di- 9
reptis aliquot incensisque vicis, maiore quam ex continenti
10 praeda parta cum in naves se recepissent, ex Baliaribus
insulis legati pacem petentes ad Scipionem venerunt. inde 10
flexa retro classis reditumque in citeriora provinciae, quo
omnium populorum, qui *cis* Hiberum incolunt, multorum et
ultimae Hispaniae legati concurrerunt; sed qui vere dicionis 11
15 imperiique Romani facti sint obsidibus datis populi, amplius
fuere centum viginti. igitur terrestribus quoque copiis satis 12
fidens Romanus usque ad saltum Castulonensem est progressus. Hasdrubal in Lusitaniam ac propius Oceanum concessit.

Quietum inde fore videbatur reliquom aestatis tempus 21
20 fuissetque per Poenum hostem; sed praeter-   2
quam quod ipsorum Hispanorum inquieta avi-   XXI. Man-
daque in novas res sunt ingenia, Mandonius   donius and Indibilis come to
Indibilisque, qui antea Ilergetum regulus fue-   ravage the terri- 3
rat, postquam Romani ab saltu recessere ad   tory of Roman
allies, but are
25 maritimam oram, concitis popularibus in agrum   routed. Hasdru-
pacatum sociorum Romanorum ad populan-   bal when about
to assist them
dum venerunt. adversus eos tribuni militum   is attacked and
twice defeated by
cum expeditis auxiliis a Scipione missi levi cer-   the Celtiberi.   4
tamine ut tumultuarium manum fudere mille hominibus
30 occisis, quibusdam captis magnaque parte armis exuta. hic 5
tamen tumultus cedentem ad Oceanum Hasdrubalem cis
Hiberum ad socios tutandos retraxit. castra Punica in agro 6

Ilergavonensium, castra Romana ad Novam classem erant,

7 cum fama repens alio avertit bellum. Celtiberi, qui principes regionis suae *miserant* legatos obsidesque dederant Romanis, nuntio misso a Scipione exciti arma capiunt provin-

8 ciamque Carthaginiensium valido exercitu invadunt. tria 5
oppida vi expugnant; inde cum ipso Hasdrubale duobus
proeliis egregie pugnant; ad quindecim milia hostium occi-
derunt, quattuor milia cum multis militaribus signis capiunt.

22 Hoc statu rerum in Hispania P. Scipio in provinciam
venit, prorogato post consulatum imperio ab 10

XXII. Cn.
Scipio joined by
Publius marches
to Saguntum
2 where hostages
from the whole
of Spain are con-
3 fined. By the
treachery of one
Abelux they
come into the
possession of the
4 Romans who re-
store them to the
Spaniards.

senatu missus, cum triginta longis navibus et
octo milibus militum magnoque commeatu advecto. ea classis ingens agmine onerariarum
procul visa cum magna laetitia civium sociorumque portum Tarraconis ex alto tenuit. ibi 15
milite exposito profectus Scipio fratri se con-
iungit, ac deinde communi animo consilioque
gerebant bellum. occupatis igitur Carthaginiensibus Celtiberico bello, haud cunctanter Hiberum transgrediuntur, nec ullo viso hoste Sa- 20
guntum pergunt ire, quod ibi obsides totius Hispaniae traditos
ab Hannibale fama erat modico in arce custodiri praesidio.

5 id unum pignus inclinatos ad Romanam societatem omnium
Hispaniae populorum animos morabatur, ne sanguine libe-

6 rum suorum culpa defectionis lueretur. eo vinculo Hispa- 25
niam vir unus sollerti magis quam fideli consilio exsolvit.
Abelux erat Sagunti nobilis Hispanus, fidus ante Poenis,
tum, qualia plerumque sunt barbarorum ingenia, cum for-

7 tuna mutaverat fidem. ceterum transfugam sine magnae
rei proditione venientem ad hostis nihil aliud quam unum 30
vile atque infame corpus esse ratus id agebat, ut quam

8 maxumum emolumentum novis sociis esset. circumspectis

[XIX.—XXII. *Events in Spain during* 217 B.C.]

igitur omnibus, quae fortuna potestatis eius poterat facere,
obsidibus potissimum tradendis animum adiecit, eam unam
rem maxime ratus conciliaturam Romanis principum Hispaniae amicitiam.   sed cum iniussu Bostaris praefecti satis 9
5 sciret nihil obsidum custodes facturos esse, Bostarem ipsum
arte adgreditur.   castra extra urbem in ipso litore habebat 10
Bostar, ut aditum ea parte intercluderet Romanis.   ibi eum
in secretum abductum velut ignorantem monet, quo statu sit
res: metum continuisse ad eam diem Hispanorum animos, quia 11
10 procul Romani abessent; nunc cis Hiberum castra Romana
esse, arcem tutam perfugiumque novas volentibus res; itaque,
quos metus non teneat, beneficio et gratia devinciendos esse.
miranti Bostari percunctantique, quodnam id subitum tantae 12
rei donum posset esse, 'obsides' inquit 'in civitates remitte.
15 id et privatim parentibus, quorum maxumum nomen in 13
civitatibus est suis, et publice populis gratum erit.   volt 14
sibi quisque credi, et habita fides ipsam plerumque obligat
fidem.   ministerium restituendorum domos obsidum mihi-
met deposco ipse, ut opera quoque inpensa consilium adiu-
20 vem meum, et rei suapte natura gratae quantam insuper
gratiam possim adiciam'.   homini non ad cetera Punica 15
ingenia callido ut persuasit, nocte clam progressus ad hostium stationes, conventis quibusdam auxiliaribus Hispanis
et ab his ad Scipionem perductus, quid adferret, expromit, 16
25 et fide accepta dataque ac loco et tempore constituto ad
obsides tradendos Saguntum redit.   diem insequentem ab-
sumpsit cum Bostare mandatis ad rem agendam accipiendis.
dimissus cum se nocte iturum, ut custodias hostium falleret, 17
constituisset, ad conpositam cum iis horam excitatis cus-
30 todibus puerorum profectus, veluti ignarus in praeparatas
sua fraude insidias ducit.   in castra Romana perducti; 18
cetera omnia de reddendis obsidibus, sicut cum Bostare

[XIX.—XXII. *Events in Spain during* 217 B.C.]

constitutum erat, acta per eundem ordinem, quo si Carthagi-
19 niensium nomine sic ageretur. maior aliquanto Romanorum
gratia fuit in re pari, quam quanta futura Carthaginiensium
fuerat. illos enim gravis superbos*que* in rebus secundis ex-
20 pertos fortuna et timor mitigasse videri poterat; Romanus ₅
primo adventu incognitus ante ab re clementi liberalique
initium fecerat; et Abelux, vir prudens, haud frustra videba-
21 tur socios mutasse. itaque ingenti consensu defectionem
omnes spectare; armaque extemplo mota forent, ni hiems,
quae Romanos quoque et Carthaginienses concedere in ₁₀
tecta coegit, intervenisset.

[XXIII.—XXX. *The war in Apulia. Fabius impugned and justified.*]

23   Haec in Hispania [quoque] secunda aestate Punici belli
gesta, cum in Italia paulum intervalli cladibus
Romanis sollers cunctatio Fabi fecisset; quae
ut Hannibalem non mediocri sollicitum cura ₁₅
habebat, tandem eum militiae magistrum dele-
gisse Romanos cernentem, qui bellum ratione
non fortuna gereret, ita contempta erat inter
civis armatos pariter togatosque, utique postquam absente eo temeritate magistri equitum ₂₀
laeto verius dixerim quam prospero eventu
pugnatum fuerat. accesserant duae res ad
augendam invidiam dictatoris, una fraude ac
dolo Hannibalis, quod, cum a perfugis ei monstratus ager
dictatoris esset, omnibus circa solo aequatis ab uno eo fer- ₂₅
rum ignemque et vim omnem hostilem abstineri iussit, ut
5 occulti alicuius pacti ea merces videri posset, altera ipsius
facto, primo forsitan dubio, quia non expectata in eo senatus auctoritas est, ad extremum haud ambigue in maximam

XXIII. Fabius
2 is unpopular at
Rome for his
caution, also be-
cause (1) Hanni-
bal leaves his
property unin-
3 jured, (2) he
agrees to ran-
som some cap-
tives without
consulting the
senate. He raises
the money by the
4 sale of his estate.

[XXIII.—XXX. *The war in Apulia. Fabius impugned and justified.*]

laudem verso. in permutandis captivis, quod sic primo 6
Punico bello factum erat, convenerat inter duces Romanum
Poenumque, ut quae pars plus reciperet quam daret, argenti
pondo bina et selibras in militem praestaret. ducentis 7
5 quadraginta septem cum plures Romanus quam Poenus
recepisset, argentumque pro eis debitum saepe iactata in
senatu re, quoniam non consuluisset patres, tardius
erogaretur, inviolatum ab hoste agrum misso Romam Quinto 8
filio vendidit fidemque publicam inpendio privato exsolvit.

10 Hannibal pro Gereoni moenibus, cuius urbis captae 9
atque incensae ab se in usum horreorum pauca reliquerat
tecta, in stativis erat. inde frumentatum duas exercitus 10
partes mittebat; cum tertia ipse expedita in statione erat
simul castris praesidio et circumspectans, necunde impetus
15 *in* frumentatores fieret. Romanus tunc exercitus in agro Larinati erat. praeerat Minucius
magister equitum profecto, sicut ante dictum
est, ad urbem dictatore. ceterum castra, quae
in monte alto ac tuto loco posita fuerant, iam
20 in planum deferuntur; agitabanturque pro ingenio ducis consilia calidiora, ut impetus aut
in frumentatores palatos aut in castra relicta
cum levi praesidio fieret. nec Hannibalem
fefellit cum duce mutatam esse belli rationem,
25 et ferocius quam consultius rem hostes gesturos. ipse au- 4
tem—quod minime quis crederet—, cum hostis propius esset,
tertiam partem militum frumentatum duabus in castris re-
tentis dimisit; dein castra ipsa propius hostem movit duo 5
ferme a Gereonio milia in tumulum hosti conspectum, ut
30 intentum *se* sciret esse ad frumentatores, si qua vis fieret,
tutandos. propior inde ei atque ipsis inminens Romanorum 6
castris tumulus apparuit; ad quem capiendum si luce palam

XXIV. Han- **24**
nibal first ad-
vances near the
Roman camp,
and then retreats.
Minucius gives **2**
battle, and is on
the point of being
defeated, but is
saved by the in-
tervention of De-
cimius sent by
Fabius. He an-
nounces a vic- **3**
tory.

[XXIII.—XXX. *The war in Apulia. Fabius impugned and justified.*]

iretur, quia haud dubie hostis breviore via praeventurus erat,
7 nocte clam missi Numidae ceperunt. quos tenentis locum
contempta paucitate Romani postero die cum deiecissent,
8 ipsi eo transferunt castra. tum utique exiguum spatii vallum
a vallo aberat, et id ipsum totum prope conpleverat Romana 5
acies. simul et per aversa a castris Hannibalis equitatus
cum levi armatura emissus in frumentatores late caedem
9 fugamque hostium palatorum fecit. nec acie certare Hannibal ausus, quia tanta paucitate vix castra, si oppugnarentur,
10 tutari poterat; iamque artibus Fabi [pars exercitus aberat 10
iam fame], sedendo et cunctando, bellum gerebat, receperat-
que suos in priora castra, quae pro Gereoni moenibus erant.
11 iusta quoque acie et conlatis signis dimicatum quidam auctores sunt: primo concursu Poenum usque ad castra fusum,
inde eruptione facta repente versum terrorem in Romanos, 15
Num. Decimi Samnitis deinde *inter*ventu proelium restitu-
12 tum. hunc principem genere ac divitiis non Boviani modo,
unde erat, sed toto Samnio iussu dictatoris octo milia peditum et equites quingentos ducentem in castra, ab tergo cum
apparuisset Hannibali, speciem parti utrique praebuisse novi 20
13 praesidii cum Q. Fabio ab Roma venientis. Hannibalem
insidiarum quoque aliquid timentem recepisse suos, Romanum insecutum adiuvante Samnite duo castella eo die ex-
14 pugnasse. sex milia hostium caesa, quinque admodum
Romanorum; tamen in tam pari prope clade *vanam* famam 25
egregiae victoriae cum vanioribus litteris magistri equitum
Romam perlatam.

25 De his rebus persaepe et in senatu et in contione actum
2 est. cum laeta civitate dictator unus nihil nec
famae nec litteris crederet *et*, ut vera omnia 30
essent, secunda se magis quam adversa timere
diceret, tum M. Metilius tribunus plebis id

XXV. All are elated at the news except Fabius. The tribune Metilius

[XXIII.—XXX. *The war in Apulia. Fabius impugned and justified.*]

enim *vero* ferendum esse negat; non praesentem   speaks against 4 him, saying that
solum dictatorem obstitisse rei bene gerendae   he will move that
sed absentem etiam gestae obstare et in ducen-   his power be equalized with
do bello sedulo tempus terere, quo diutius in   that of Minucius. A second consul
5 magistratu sit solusque et Romae et in exer-   should be appointed. Fabius 5
citu imperium habeat; quippe consulum alte-   replies in the
rum in acie cecidisse, alterum specie classis   senate, appoints
Punicae persequendae procul ab Italia ablega-   Regulus consul, and leaves Rome.
tum; duos praetores Sicilia atque Sardinia   Varro alone 6 speaks for the
10 occupatos, quarum neutra hoc tempore   motion.
praetore egeat; M. Minucium magistrum
equitum, ne hostem videret, ne quid rei bellicae gereret,
prope in custodia habitum. itaque hercule non Samnium 7
modo, quo iam tamquam trans Hiberum agro Poenis con-
15 cessum sit, sed Campanum Calenumque et Falernum agrum
pervas*ta*tos esse, sedente Casilini dictatore et legionibus
populi Romani agrum suum tutante. exercitum cupientem 8
pugnare et magistrum equitum clausos prope intra vallum
retentos, tamquam hostibus captivis arma adempta. tandem, 9
20 ut abscesserit inde dictator, ut obsidione liberatos extra
vallum egressos fudisse ac fugasse hostis. quas ob res, si 10
antiquus animus plebei Romanae esset, audaciter se latu-
rum fuisse de abrogando Q. Fabi imperio; nunc modicam
rogationem promulgaturum de aequando magistri equitum
25 et dictatoris iure. nec tamen ne ita quidem prius mitten- 11
dum ad exercitum Q. Fabium, quam consulem in locum C.
Flamini suffecisset. dictator contionibus se abstinuit in 12
actione minime popularis. ne in senatu quidem satis aequis
auribus audiebatur, cum hostem verbis extolleret bienniique
30 clades per temeritatem atque inscitiam ducum acceptas
referret *et* magistro equitum, quod contra dictum suum pug- 13
nasset, rationem diceret reddendam esse. si penes se summa 14

[XXIII.—XXX. *The war in Apulia. Fabius impugned and justified.*]

imperii consiliique sit, prope diem effecturum, ut sciant
homines bono imperatore haud magni fortunam momenti
15 esse, mentem rationemque dominari, et in tempore et sine
ignominia servasse exercitum quam multa milia hostium
16 occidisse maiorem gloriam esse.   huius generis orationibus 5
frustra habitis et consule creato M. Atilio Regulo, ne praesens de iure imperii dimicaret, pridie quam rogationis feren-
17 dae dies adesset, nocte ad exercitum abiit.   luce orta cum
plebis concilium esset, magis tacita invidia dictatoris favorque
magistri equitum animos versabat, quam satis audebant 10
homines ad suadendum quod vulgo placebat prodire, et
18 favore superante auctoritas tamen rogationi deerat.   unus
inventus est suasor legis C. Terentius Varro, qui priore anno
praetor fuerat, loco non humili solum sed etiam sordido
19 ortus.   patrem lanium fuisse ferunt, ipsum institorem mercis, 15
26 filioque hoc ipso in servilia eius artis ministeria usum.   is

XXVI. Ante- iuvenis, ut primum ex eo genere quaestus pe-
cedents of Varro. cunia a patre relicta animos ad spem libera-
Fabius receives
2 with dignity the lioris fortunae fecit, togaque et forum placuere,
news of the equa-
lization of his proclamando pro sordidis hominibus causisque 20
power with that adversus rem et famam bonorum primum in
of Minucius.
3 notitiam populi, deinde ad honores pervenit,
quaesturaque et duabus aedilitatibus, plebeia et curuli, postremo et praetura perfunctus iam ad consulatus spem cum
4 adtolleret animos, haud parum callide auram favoris popu- 25
laris ex dictatoria invidia petiit scitique plebis unus gratiam
5 tulit.   omnes eam rogationem, quique Romae quique in
exercitu erant, aequi atque iniqui, praeter ipsum dictatorem
6 in contumeliam eius latam acceperunt; ipse, qua gravitate
animi criminantes se ad multitudinem inimicos tulerat, 30
7 eadem et populi in se saevientis iniuriam tulit; acceptisque
in ipso itinere litteris senatus*que* consulto de aequato impe-

[XXIII.—XXX. *The war in Apulia. Fabius impugned and justified.*]

rio, satis fidens haudquaquam cum imperii iure artem impe-
randi aequatam, cum invicto a civibus hostibusque animo
ad exercitum rediit.

    Minucius vero, cum iam ante vix tolerabilis fuisset rebus **27**
5 secundis ac favore volgi, tum utique inmodice   **2**
inmodesteque non Hannibale magis victo ab   XXVII. Mi-
                                       nucius boasts
se quam Q. Fabio gloriari: illum in rebus over Fabius. He **3**
                                        proposes that each
asperis unicum ducem ac parem quaesitum shall command
Hannibali, maiore*m* minori, dictatore*m* magistro the whole army
                                        on alternate days.
10 equitum, quod nulla memoria habeat annalium, It is decided that
iussu populi aequatum in eadem civitate, in they shall divide
                                        their forces.
qua magistri equitum virgas ac secures dicta-
toris tremere atque horrere soliti sint; tantum suam felicita- **4**
tem virtutemque enituisse. ergo secuturum se fortunam
15 suam, si dictator in cunctatione ac segnitie deorum homi-
numque iudicio damnata perstaret. itaque quo die primum **5**
congressus est cum Q. Fabio, statuendum omnium primum
ait esse, quem ad modum imperio aequato utantur; se optu- **6**
mum ducere aut diebus alternis, aut, si maiora intervalla
20 placerent, partitis temporibus alterius summum ius impe-
riumque esse, ut par hosti non solum consilio sed viribus **7**
etiam esset, si quam occasionem rei gerendae habuisset.
Q. Fabio haudquaquam id placere: omnia eam fortunam **8**
habitura, quamcumque temeritas conlegae habuisset; sibi
25 communicatum cum alio, non ademptum imperium esse;
itaque se numquam volentem parte, qua posset, rerum con- **9**
silio gerendarum cessurum nec se tempora aut dies imperii
cum eo, exercitum divisurum, suisque consiliis, quoniam
omnia non liceret, quae posset servaturum. ita obtinuit, ut **10**
30 legiones, sicut consulibus mos esset, inter *se* dividerent.
prima et quarta Minucio, secunda et tertia Fabio evenerunt.
item equites pari numero sociumque et Latini nominis **11**

[XXIII.—XXX. *The war in Apulia. Fabius impugned and justified.*]

auxilia diviserunt.   castris quoque se separari magister
equitum voluit.

28   Duplex inde Hannibali gaudium fuit—neque enim quicquam eorum, quae apud hostes agerentur, eum
fallebat et perfugis multa indicantibus et per 5
suos explorantem—; nam et liberam Minuci
temeritatem se suo modo captaturum et soller-
tiae Fabi dimidium virium decessisse. tumu-
lus erat inter castra Minuci et Poenorum, quem qui occupas-
4 set, haud dubie iniquiorem erat hosti locum facturus. eum 10
non tam capere sine certamine volebat Hannibal, quamquam id operae pretium erat, quam causam certaminis cum
Minucio, quem procursurum ad obsistendum satis sciebat,
5 contrahere. ager omnis medius erat prima specie inutilis
insidiatori, quia non modo silvestre quicquam sed ne vepri- 15
6 bus quidem vestitum habebat, re ipsa natus tegendis insidiis
eo magis, quod in nuda valle nulla talis fraus timeri poterat;
et erant in anfractibus cavae rupes, ut quaedam earum
7 ducenos armatos possent capere. in has latebras, quot
quemque locum apte insidere poterant, quinque milia con- 20
8 duntur peditum equitumque. necubi tamen aut motus alicuius temere egressi aut fulgor armorum fraudem in valle
tam aperta detegeret, missis paucis prima luce ad capiendum, quem ante diximus, tumulum avertit oculos hostium.
9 primo statim conspectu contempta paucitas, ac sibi quisque 25
deposcere pellendos inde hostis ac locum capiendum; dux
ipse inter stolidissimos ferocissimosque ad arma vocat et
10 vanis minis increpat hostem. principio levem armaturam
dimittit; deinde conferto agmine mittit equites; postremo,
cum hostibus quoque subsidia mitti videret, instructis legio- 30
11 nibus procedit. et Hannibal laborantibus suis alia atque
alia increscente certamine mittens auxilia peditum equitum-

XXVIII. Mi-
nucius   gives
battle, but is sur-
2 prised by an am-
bush, and sur-
rounded.
3

[XXIII.—XXX. *The war in Apulia. Fabius impugned and justified.*]

que iam iustam expleverat aciem, ac totis utrimque viribus
certatur. prima levis armatura Romanorum, praeoccupatum 12
ex inferiore loco succedens tumulum, pulsa detrusaque terrorem in succedentem intulit equitem et ad signa legionum
5 refugit. peditum acies inter perculsos inpavida sola erat 13
videbaturque, si iusta ac [si] recta pugna esset, haudquaquam inpar futura; tantum animorum fecerat prospere ante
paucos dies res gesta; sed exorti repente insidiatores eum 14
tumultum terroremque in latera utrimque ab tergoque incur-
10 santes fecerunt, ut neque animus ad pugnam neque ad
fugam spes cuiquam superesset. tum Fabius   29
primo clamore paventium audito, dein con-   XXIX. Fa-
specta procul turbata acie 'ita est' inquit, 'non   bius comes to the
                                                    rescue. Minucius
celerius, quam timui, deprendit fortuna teme-   proposes to his
                                                    troops to go and
15 ritatem. Fabio aequatus imperio Hannibalem   thank Fabius and 2
et virtute et fortuna superiorem videt. sed   his army.
aliud iurgandi succensendique tempus erit; nunc signa extra
vallum proferte; victoriam hosti extorqueamus, confessionem
erroris civibus'. iam magna ex parte caesis aliis, aliis circum- 3
20 spectantibus fugam, Fabiana se acies repente velut caelo
demissa ad auxilium ostendit. itaque, priusquam ad con- 4
iectum teli veniret aut manum consereret, et suos a fuga
effusa et ab nimis feroci pugna hostes continuit. qui solutis
ordinibus vage dissipati erant, undique confugerunt ad inte-
25 gram aciem; qui plures simul terga dederant, conversi in 5
hostem volventesque orbem nunc sensim referre pedem,
nunc conglobati restare. ac iam prope una acies facta erat
victi atque integri exercitus, inferebantque signa in hostem,
cum Poenus receptui cecinit, palam ferente Hannibale ab 6
30 se Minucium, se ab Fabio victum.

Ita per variam fortunam diei maiore parte exacta cum in 7
castra reditum esset, Minucius convocatis militibus 'saepe ego' 8

[XXIII.—XXX. *The war in Apulia. Fabius impugned and justified.*]

inquit 'audivi, milites, eum primum esse virum, qui ipse consulat, quid in rem sit, secundum eum, qui bene monenti oboediat; qui nec ipse consulere nec alteri parere sciat, eum

9 extremi ingenii esse. nobis quoniam prima animi ingeniique negata sors est, secundam ac mediam teneamus et, 5 dum imperare discimus, parere prudenti in animum induca-

10 mus. castra cum Fabio iungamus; ad praetorium eius signa cum tulerimus, ubi ego eum parentem appellavero, quod beneficio eius erga nos ac maiestate eius dignum est, vos,

11 milites, eos, quorum vos modo arma *ac* dexterae texerunt, 10 patronos salutabitis, et, si nihil aliud, gratorum certe nobis

30 animorum gloriam dies hic dederit'. signo

XXX. Minucius thanks Fabius and resigns his joint command, becoming

2 again master of the horse. Fabius' merit is acknowledged both at Rome and in the Carthaginian camp.

dato conclamatur inde, ut colligantur vasa. profecti et agmine incedentes *ad* dictatoris castra in admirationem et ipsum et omnes, qui 15 circa erant, converterunt. ut constituta sunt ante tribunal signa, progressus ante alios magister equitum, cum patrem Fabium appellasset circumfusosque militum eius totum agmen

3 patronos consalutasset, 'parentibus' inquit 20 'meis, dictator, quibus te modo nomine, quod fando possum, aequavi, vitam tantum debeo, tibi cum meam salutem tum

4 omnium horum. itaque plebeiscitum, quo oneratus *sum* magis quam honoratus, primus antiquo abrogoque et, quod tibi mihique [quod] exercit*ib*usque his tuis, servato ac con- 25 servatori, sit felix, sub imperium auspiciumque tuum redeo

5 et signa haec legionesque restituo. tu, quaeso, placatus me magisterium equitum, hos ordines suos quemque tenere

6 iubeas'. tum dextrae interiunctae militesque contione dimissa ab notis ignotisque benigne atque hospitaliter invi- 30 tati, laetusque dies ex admodum tristi paulo ante ac prope

7 execrabili factus. Romae, ut est perlata fama rei gestae,

[XXIII.—XXX. *The war in Apulia. Fabius impugned and justified.*]
dein litteris non magis ipsorum imperatorum quam volgo
militum ex utroque exercitu adfirmata, pro se quisque Maximum laudibus ad caelum ferre. pari gloria apud Hanniba- 8
lem hostisque Poenos erat; ac tum demum *hi* sentire cum
5 Romanis atque in Italia bellum esse; nam biennio ante adeo 9
et duces Romanos et milites spreverant, ut vix cum eadem
gente bellum esse crederent, cuius terribilem famam a patribus accepissent. Hannibalem quoque ex acie redeuntem 10
dixisse ferunt, tandem eam nubem, quae sedere in iugis
10 montium solita sit, cum procella imbrem dedisse.

[XXXI.—XL. 4. *Rome during the winter* 217—6.]

Dum haec geruntur in Italia, Cn. Servilius Geminus 31
consul cum classe *centum viginti* navium cir-
cumvectus Sardiniae et Corsicae oram et obsi-   XXXI. The
dibus utrimque acceptis in Africam transmisit   consul Servilius
  lands in Africa
15 et, priusquam in continentem escensiones face-   but meets with
ret, Menige insula vastata et ab incolentibus   ill-success. He 2
  returns to Rome
Cercinam, ne et ipsorum ureretur diriperetur-   with his col-
que ager, decem talentis argenti acceptis ad   league Regulus.
  (A digression.
litora Africae accessit copiasque exposuit.   Fabius was cor-
20 inde ad populandum agrum ducti milites na-   rectly speaking
  not dictator but
valesque socii iuxta effusi, ac si *in* insulis cul-   prodictator.) 3
torum egentibus praedarentur. itaque in insidias temere 4
inlati, cum a frequentibus palantes et ignari ab locorum
gnaris circumvenirentur, cum multa caede ac foeda fuga
25 retro ad naves conpulsi sunt. ad mille hominum cum [iis] 5
Sempronio Blaeso quaestore amissum. classis ab litoribus
hostium plenis trepide soluta in Siciliam cursum tenuit,
traditaque Lilybaei T. Otacilio praetori, ut ab legato eius 6
P. Cincio Romam reduceretur; ipse per Siciliam pedibus 7
30 profectus freto in Italiam traiecit, litteris Q. Fabi accitus et

[XXXI.—XL. 4. *Rome during the winter* 217—6.]

ipse et conlega eius M. Atilius, ut exercitus ab se exacto
iam prope semenstri imperio acciperent.

8   Omnium prope annales Fabium dictatorem adversus
Hannibalem rem gessisse tradunt; Coelius etiam eum pri-
9 mum a populo creatum dictatorem scribit. sed et Coelium 5
et ceteros fugit uni consuli Cn. Servilio, qui tum procul in
10 Gallia provincia aberat, ius fuisse dicendi dictatoris; quam
moram quia expectare territa *tertia* iam clade civitas non
poterat, eo decursum esse, ut a populo crearetur, qui pro
11 dictatore esset; res inde gestas gloriamque insignem ducis 10
et augentis titulum imaginis posteros, ut, qui pro dictatore
creatus esset, fuisse dictator crederetur, facile obtinuisse.

32   Consules Atilius Fabiano, Geminus Servilius Minuciano

XXXII. The consuls carry on the tactics of Fabius with success.

2 The Neapolitans offer the Romans a present for war expenses.

exercitu accepto hibernaculis mature communitis *quod reli*quom autumni erat Fabi artibus 15
cum summa inter se concordia bellum gesserunt.
frumentatum exeunti Hannibali diversis locis
opportuni aderant carpentes agmen palatosque
excipientes; in casum universae dimicationis,
3 quam omnibus artibus petebat hostis, non veniebant; adeo- 20
que inopia est coactus Hannibal, ut, nisi cum fugae specie
abeundum *ei fuisset*, Galliam repetiturus fuerit nulla relicta
spe alendi exercitus in eis locis, si insequentes consules
eisdem artibus bellum gererent.

4   Cum ad Gereonium iam hieme inpediente constitisset 25
bellum, Neapolitani legati Romam venere. ab iis quadraginta paterae aureae magni ponderis in curiam inlatae atque
5 ita verba facta, ut dicerent: scire sese populi *Romani* aerarium bello exhauriri et, cum iuxta pro urbibus agrisque
sociorum ac pro capite atque arce Italiae, urbe Romana, 30
6 atque imperio geratur, aequom censuisse Neapolitanos, quod
auri sibi cum ad templorum ornatum tum ad subsidium for-

tunae a maioribus relictum foret, eo iuvare populum Romanum. si quam opem in sese crederent, eodem studio fuisse 7
oblaturos. gratum sibi patres Romanos populumque facturum, si omnes res Neapolitanorum suas duxissent dignosque 8
5 iudicaverint, ab quibus donum animo ac voluntate eorum,
qui libentes darent, quam re maius ampliusque acciperent.
legatis gratiae actae pro munificentia curaque; patera, quae 9
ponderis minimi fuit, accepta.

Per eosdem dies speculator Carthaginiensis, qui per **33**
10 biennium fefellerat, Romae deprensus praeci-   XXXIII. Va- ²
sisque manibus dimissus, et servi quinque et   rious minor mat-
viginti in crucem acti, quod in campo Martio   ters are transac-
                                               ted at Rome. A
coniurassent. indici data libertas et aeris gra-   dictator is appoin-
                                               ted to preside
vis viginti *milia*. legati et ad Philippum, Ma-   at the elections, 3
15 cedonum regem, missi ad deposcendum De-   but his appoint-
                                               ment is cancelled.
metrium Pharium, qui bello victus ad eum   An interregnum
fugisset, et alii *in* Ligures ad expostulandum,   follows.
                                                               4
quod Poenum opibus auxiliisque suis iuvissent, simul ad
visendum ex propinquo, quae in Bois atque Insubribus
20 gererentur. ad Pineum quoque regem in Illyrios legati 5
missi ad stipendium, cuius dies exierat, poscendum aut, si
diem proferri vellet, obsides accipiendos. adeo, etsi bellum 6
ingens in cervicibus erat, nullius *us*quam terrarum rei cura
Romanos, ne longinquae quidem, effugiebat. in religionem 7
25 etiam venit aedem Concordiae, quam per seditionem militarem biennio ante L. Manlius praetor in Gallia vovisset,
locatam ad id tempus non esse. itaque duumviri ad eam 8
rem creati a M. Aemilio praetore urbano C. Pupius et K.
Quinctius Flamininus aedem in arce faciendam locaverunt.

30   Ab eodem praetore ex senatus consulto litterae ad con- 9
sules missae, ut, si iis videretur, alter eorum ad consules
creandos Romam veniret: se in eam diem, quam iussissent,

[XXXI.—XL. 4. *Rome during the winter* 217—6.]

10 comitia edicturum. ad haec *a* consulibus rescriptum, sine
detrimento rei publicae abscedi non posse ab hoste; itaque
per interregem comitia habenda esse potius, quam consul
11 alter a bello avocaretur. patribus rectius visum est dictatorem a consule dici comitiorum habendorum causa. dictus , 5
L. Veturius Philo M. Pomponium Mathonem magistrum
12 equitum dixit. iis vitio creatis iussisque die quarto decimo
34 se magistratu abdicare, *res* ad interregnum rediit. consuli-

XXXIV. The
consular election
for 216 B.C. Can-
didature of Varro.
Speech of his sup-
porter the tri-
2 bune Herennius.
The Aristocracy
is prolonging the
war. If the peo-
ple want it finish-
ed they must
elect a novus
homo.

bus prorogatum in annum imperium. interreges proditi sunt a patribus C. Claudius Appi 10
filius Cento, inde P. Cornelius Asina. in eius
interregno comitia habita magno certamine
patrum ac plebis. C. Terentio Varroni, quem
sui generis hominem, plebi insectatione principum popularibusque artibus conciliatum, ab 15
Q. Fabi opibus et dictatorio imperio concusso
aliena invidia splendentem, volgus [et] extra-

here ad consulatum nitebatur, patres summa
ope obstabant, ne se insectando sibi aequari adsuescerent
3 homines. Q. Baebius Herennius tribunus plebis, cognatus C. 20
Terenti, criminando non senatum modo sed etiam augures,
quod dictatorem prohibuissent comitia perficere, per invi-
4 diam eorum favorem candidato suo conciliabat: ab hominibus nobilibus per multos annos bellum quaerentibus Hannibalem in Italiam adductum; ab iisdem, cum debellari 25
5 possit, fraude bellum trahi. cum quattuor legionibus universis pugnari *prospere* posse apparuisset eo, quod M. Minu-
6 cius absente Fabio prospere pugnasset, duas legiones hosti
ad caedem obiectas, deinde ex ipsa caede ereptas, ut pater
patronusque appellaretur, qui prius vincere prohibuisset 30
7 Romanos quam vinci. consules deinde Fabianis artibus,
cum debellare possent, bellum traxisse id foedus inter

[XXXI.—XL. 4. *Rome during the winter* 217—6.]

omnes nobilis ictum, nec finem ante belli habituros, quam
consulem vere plebeium, id est hominem novum, fecissent;
nam plebeios nobiles iam eisdem initiatos esse sacris et 8
contemnere plebem, ex quo contemni *a* patribus desierint,
5 coepisse. cui non [id] apparere, id actum et quaesitum 9
esse, ut interregnum iniretur, ut in patrum potestate comitia
essent? id consules ambos ad exercitum morando quaesisse; 10
id postea, quia invitis iis dictator esset dictus comitiorum
causa, expugnatum esse, ut vitiosus dictator per augures
10 fieret. habere igitur *inter*regnum eos; consulatum unum 11
certe plebis Romanae esse, et populum liberum habiturum
ac daturum ei, qui mature vincere quam diu imperare malit.

Cum his orationibus accensa plebs esset, tribus patriciis 35
petentibus, P. Cornelio Merenda, L. Manlio
15 Volsone, M. Aemilio Lepido, duobus nobilium   XXXV.   Of 2
iam familiarum plebeiis, C. Atilio Serrano et   several candi-
                                                 dates only Varro
Q. Aelio Paeto, quorum alter pontifex alter   is elected consul.
                                                 Aemilius Paulus
augur erat, C. Terentius consul unus creatur,   is induced to
                                                 stand. The Prae-
ut in manu eius essent comitia rogando con-   tors are elected.
20 legae. tum experta nobilitas parum fuisse   3
virium in conpetitoribus eius L. Aemilium Paulum, qui cum
M. Livio consul fuerat, ex damnatione conlegae, ex qua
prope ambustus evaserat, infestum plebi, diu ac multum
recusantem ad petitionem conpellit. is proximo comitiali 4
25 die concedentibus omnibus, qui cum Varrone certaverant,
par magis in adversandum quam conlega datur consuli.
inde praetorum comitia habita: creati M. Pomponius 5
Matho et P. Furius *Philus*. Philo Romae iuri dicundo
urbana sors, Pomponio inter civis Romanos et peregrinos
30 evenit. additi duo praetores, M. Claudius Marcellus in 6
Siciliam, L. Postumius Albinus in Galliam. omnes absentes 7
creati sunt, nec cuiquam eorum praeter Terentium consulem

[XXXI.—XL. 4. *Rome during the winter* 217—6.]

mandatus honos, quem non iam antea gessisset, praeteritis
aliquot fortibus ac strenuis viris, quia in tali tempore nulli
novus magistratus videbatur mandandus.

36   Exercitus quoque multiplicati sunt; quantae autem
copiae peditum equitumque additae sint, adeo 5
et numero et genere copiarum variant auctores,
ut vix quicquam satis certum adfirmare ausus
sim.   decem milia novorum militum alii
scripta in supplementum, alii novas quattuor
3 legiones, ut octo legionibus rem gererent; numero quo- 10
que peditum equitumque legiones auctas milibus peditum
et centenis equitibus in singulas adiectis, ut quina milia
peditum treceni equites essent, socii duplicem numerum
4 equitum darent, peditis aequarent [septem et octoginta
milia armatorum et ducentos in castris Romanis, cum pugna- 15
5 tum ad Cannas est], quidam auctores sunt.   illud haudquaquam discrepat, maiore conatu atque impetu rem actam
quam prioribus annis, quia spem posse vinci hostem dictator
6 praebuerat.   ceterum priusquam signa ab urbe novae legiones moverent, decemviri libros adire atque inspicere iussi 20
7 propter territos vulgo homines novis prodigiis; nam et
Romae in Aventino et Ariciae nuntiatum erat sub idem
tempus lapidibus pluvisse, et multo cruore signa in Sabinis,
8 Caere aquas *in* fonte calido manasse; id quidem etiam, quod
saepius acciderat, magis terrebat; et in via fornicata, quae 25
ad campum erat, aliquot homines de caelo tacti exanimati-
9 que fuerant.   ea prodigia ex libris procurata.   legati a
Paesto pateras aureas Romam adtulerunt.   iis sicut Neapo-
litanis gratiae actae, aurum non acceptum.

37   Per eosdem dies ab Hierone classis Ostia cum magno 30
2 commeatu accessit.   legati in senatum intro-
ducti nuntiarunt caedem C. Flamini consulis

XXXVI. The
forces are in-
creased. Omens
are announced,
and measures ta-
ken accordingly.

XXXVII.
Hiero offers the

exercitusque adlatam adeo aegre tulisse regem
Hieronem, ut nulla sua propria regnique sui
clade moveri magis potuerit. itaque, quamquam probe sciat magnitudinem populi Roma-
5 ni admirabiliorem prope adversis rebus quam
secundis esse, *ta*men se omnia, quibus a bonis fidelibusque 4
sociis bella iuvari soleant, misisse; quae ne accipere abnuant,
magno opere se patres conscriptos orare. iam omnium 5
primum ominis causa Victoriam auream pondo ducentum ac
10 viginti adferre sese; acciperent eam tenerentque et haberent
propriam et perpetuam. advexisse etiam trecenta milia 6
modium tritici, ducenta hordei, ne commeatus deessent, et
quantum praeterea opus esset, quo iussissent, subvecturos.
milite atque equite scire nisi Romano Latinique nominis non 7
15 uti populum Romanum; levium armorum auxilia etiam ex-
terna vidisse in castris Romanis; itaque misisse mille sagit- 8
tariorum ac funditorum, aptam manum adversus Baliares ac
Mauros pugnacesque alias missili telo gentes. ad ea dona 9
consilium quoque addebant, ut praetor, cui provincia Sicilia
20 evenisset, classem in Africam traiceret, ut et hostes in terra
sua bellum haberent, minusque laxamenti daretur iis ad
auxilia Hannibali submittenda. ab senatu ita responsum 10
regis *legatis* est, virum bonum egregiumque socium Hieronem esse atque uno tenore, ex quo in amicitiam populi
25 Romani venerit, fidem coluisse ac rem Romanam omni
tempore ac loco munifice adiuvisse. id perinde ac deberet
gratum populo Romano esse. aurum et a civitati- 11
bus quibusdam adlatum gratia rei accepta non accepisse
populum Romanum; Victoriam omenque accipere sedem- 12
30 que ei se divae dare dicare Capitolium, templum Iovis
optimi maximi. in ea arce urbis Romanae sacratam volentem
propitiamque, firmam ac stabilem fore populo Romano.

[XXXI.—XL. 4. *Rome during the winter* 217—6.]

13 funditores sagittariique et frumentum traditum consulibus. quinqueremes ad * * navium classem, quae cum T. Otacilio propraetore in Sicilia erat, quinque et viginti additae, permissumque est, ut, si e re publica censeret esse, in Africam traiceret. 5

38 Dilectu perfecto consules paucos morati dies, dum ab
2 XXXVIII. sociis ac nomine Latino venirent milites. tum,

For the first time quod numquam antea factum erat, iure iurando
an oath of allegi-
3 ance is adminis- ab tribunis militum adacti milites; nam ad
tered to the army eam diem nihil praeter sacramentum fuerat, 10
by the tribunes.
Speeches of Var- iussu consulis conventuros neque iniussu abi-
ro and Aemilius
Paulus. turos, et ubi ad decuriatum aut centuriatum
convenissent, sua voluntate ipsi inter sese decu-
4 riati equites, centuriati pedites coniurabant sese fugae atque
formidinis ergo non abituros neque ex ordine recessuros nisi 15
teli sumendi aut *re*petendi [et] aut hostis feriendi aut civis
5 servandi causa. id ex voluntario inter ipsos foedere ad
tribunos ac legitimam iuris iurandi adactionem translatum.
6 Contiones, priusquam ab urbe signa moverentur, consulis Varronis multae ac feroces fuere denuntiantis bellum 20
arcessitum in Italiam ab nobilibus mansurumque in visceri-
7 bus rei publicae, si plures Fabios imperatores haberet, se,
8 quo die hostem vidisset, perfecturum. conlegae eius Pauli una, pridie quam urbe proficisceretur, contio fuit, verior quam gratior populo, qua nihil inclementer in Varronem 25
9 dictum nisi id modo, mirari se, [quodne] qui dux, priusquam aut suum aut hostium exercitum, locorum situm, naturam regionis nosset, iam nunc togatus in urbe sciret, quae sibi
10 agenda armato forent, et diem quoque praedicere posset,
11 qua cum hoste signis conlatis esset dimicaturus. se, quae 30
consilia magis res dent hominibus quam homines rebus, ea ante tempus inmatura non praecepturum. optare, ut, quae

[XXXI.—XL. 4. *Rome during the winter* 217—6.]

caute ac consulte gesta essent, satis prospere evenirent;
temeritatem, praeterquam quod stulta sit, infelicem etiam 12
ad id locorum fuisse. et sua sponte apparebat, tuta cele- 13
ribus consiliis praepositurum; et, quo id constantius per-
5 severaret, Q. Fabius Maximus sic eum proficiscentem
adlocutus fertur:

'Si aut conlegam, id quod mallem, tui similem, L. **39**
Aemili, haberes, aut tu conlegae tui esses similis, supervacanea esset oratio mea; nam et duo   XXXIX. Ad- 2
10 boni consules etiam me indicente omnia e re dress of Fabius
publica fide*que* vestra faceretis, et mali nec mea us. He will find
verba auribus vestris nec consilia animis acci- than Hannibal. If
 Varro fights he
peretis. nunc et conlegam tuum et te talem will meet with 3
virum intuenti mihi tecum omnis oratio est, disaster. The
 only policy is to
15 quem video nequiquam et virum bonum et wait. Paulus'
civem fore, si altera parte claudente re publica difficult but he
malis consiliis idem ac bonis iuris et potestatis must hold his
 own.
erit. erras enim, L. Paule, si tibi minus cer-   4
taminis cum C. Terentio quam cum Hannibale futurum
20 censes; nescio an infestior hic adversarius quam ille hostis
maneat te, *cum tu* cum illo in acie tantum, cum hoc omnibus 5
locis ac temporibus sis certaturus, et adversus Hannibalem
legionesque eius tuis equitibus ac peditibus pugnandum tibi
sit, Varro dux tuis militibus te sit oppugnaturus. ominis 6
25 etiam tibi causa absit C. Flamini memoria. tamen ille consul demum et in provincia et ad exercitum coepit furere;
hic, priusquam peteret consulatum, deinde in petendo consulatu, nunc quoque consul, priusquam castra videat aut hostem, insanit. et qui tantas iam nunc procellas proelia atque 7
30 acies iactando inter togatos ciet, quid inter armatam iuven-
tutem censes facturum et ubi extemplo res verba sequitur?
atqui si *hic*, quod facturum se denuntiat, extemplo pugna- 8

[XXXI.—XL. 4. *Rome during the winter* 217—6.]

verit, aut ego rem militarem, belli hoc genus, hostem hunc
ignoro, aut nobilior alius Trasumenno locus nostris cladibus
9 erit. nec gloriandi tempus adversus unum est, et ego con-
temnendo potius quam adpetendo gloriam modum excesserim; sed ita res se habet: una ratio belli gerendi adversus 5
10 Hannibalem est, qua ego gessi. nec eventus modo hoc
docet—stultorum iste magister est—sed eadem ratio, quae
fuit futuraque, donec res eaedem manebunt, inmutabilis est.
11 in Italia bellum gerimus, in *se*de ac solo nostro; omnia circa
plena civium ac sociorum sunt; armis, viris, equis, commeati- 10
12 bus iuvant iuvabuntque; id iam fidei documentum in adversis
rebus nostris dederunt; meliores, prudentiores, constantiores
13 nos tempus diesque facit; Hannibal contra in aliena, in
hostili est terra, inter omnia inimica infestaque, procul ab
domo, ab patria; neque illi terra neque mari est pax; nullae 15
eum urbes accipiunt, nulla moenia; nihil usquam sui videt;
14 in diem rapto vivit; partem vix tertiam exercitus eius habet,
quem Hiberum amnem traiecit; plures fame quam ferro ab-
15 sumpti, nec his paucis iam victus suppeditat. dubitas ergo,
quin sedendo superaturi simus eum, qui senescat in dies, 20
non commeatus, non supplementum, non pecuniam habeat?
16 quam diu pro Gereonii, castelli Apuliae inopis, tamquam
pro Carthaginis moenibus *sedet/* sed ne adversus te qui*dem*
17 de me gloriabor; Servilius atque Atilius, proximi consules,
vide quem ad modum eum ludificati sint. haec una salutis 25
est via, L. Paule, quam difficilem infestamque cives tibi
18 magis quam hostes facient; idem enim tui, quod hostium
milites volent; idem Varro consul Romanus, quod Hannibal
Poenus imperator cupiet. duobus ducibus unus resistas
oportet. resistes autem, *si* adversus famam rumoresque 30
hominum satis firmus steteris, si te neque conlegae vana
19 gloria neque tua falsa infamia moverit. veritatem laborare

[XXXI.—XL. 4. *Rome during the winter* 217—6.]

nimis saepe aiunt, extingui numquam; gloriam qui spreverit,
veram habebit. sine, timidum pro cauto, tardum pro con- 20
siderato, inbellem pro perito belli vocent. malo, te sapiens
hostis metuat, quam stulti cives laudent. omnia audentem
5 contemnet Hannibal, nihil temere agentem metuet. nec 21
ego, ut nihil agatur, *suadeo*, sed ut agentem te ratio ducat,
non fortuna; tuae potestatis semper tu tuaque omnia sint;
armatus intentusque sis; neque occasioni tuae desis neque
suam occasionem hosti des. omnia non properanti clara 22
10 certaque erunt; festinatio inprovida est et caeca'.

Adversus ea oratio consulis haud sane laeta fuit magis 40
fatentis ea, quae diceret, vera quam facilia
factu esse. dictatori magistrum equitum into- XL. Paulus
replies, and the 2
lerabilem fuisse; quid consuli adversus conle- two consuls start
from Rome.
15 gam seditiosum ac temerarium virium atque
auctoritatis fore? se populare incendium priore consulatu
semustum effugisse; optare, ut omnia prospere evenirent; 3
sed si quid adversi caderet, hostium se telis potius quam
suffragiis iratorum civium caput obiecturum. ab hoc ser- 4
20 mone profectum Paulum tradunt prosequentibus primoribus
patrum; plebeium consulem sua plebes prosecuta, turba
conspectior, cum dignitates deessent.

[XL. 5—L. *The battle of Cannae.*]

Ut in castra venerunt, permixto novo exercitu ac vetere, 5
castris bifariam factis, ut nova minora essent
25 propius Hannibalem, in veteribus maior pars At Gereonium
the two consuls
et omne robur virium esset, consulum anni occupy one 6
camp; Servilius
prioris M. Atilium aetatem excusantem Ro- another smaller
mam miserunt, Geminum Servilium in mino- one near Hannibal.
ribus castris legioni Romanae et socium pe-
30 ditum equitumque duobus milibus praeficiunt. Hannibal, 7

[XL. 5.—L.   *The battle of Cannae.*]

quamquam parte dimidia auctas hostium copias cernebat,
8 tamen adventu consulum mire gaudere. non solum enim
nihil ex raptis in diem commeatibus superabat, sed ne unde
raperet quidem quicquam reliqui erat omni undique fru-
9 mento, postquam ager parum tutus erat, in urbes munitas 5
convecto, ut vix decem dierum, quod conpertum postea est,
frumentum superesset, Hispanorumque ob inopiam transitio
parata fuerit, si maturitas temporum expectata foret.

41   Ceterum temeritati consulis ac *prae*propero ingenio materiam etiam fortuna dedit, quod in prohiben- 10
XLI.   The   dis praedatoribus tumultuario proelio ac pro-
Romans are vic- cursu magis militum quam ex praeparato aut
torious in a skir-
mish, but Paulus iussu imperatorum orto haudquaquam par
stops the pursuit,
Hannibal leaves   Poenis dimicatio fuit. ad mille et septingenti
2 his camp with
fires burning and caesi, non plus centum Romanorum sociorum- 15
retires.   que occisis. ceterum victoribus effuse sequen-
3 tibus metu insidiarum obstitit Paulus consul, cuius eo die—
nam alternis imperitabant—imperium erat, Varrone indig-
nante ac vociferante emissum hostem e manibus, debellari-
4 que, ni cessatum foret, potuisse. Hannibal id damnum 20
haud aegerrime pati; quin potius credere velut inescatam temeritatem ferocioris consulis ac novorum maxime
5 militum esse. et omnia ei hostium haud secus quam sua
nota erant: dissimiles discordesque imperitare, duas prope
6 partes tironum militum in exercitu esse. itaque locum et 25
tempus insidiis aptum se habere ratus nocte proxima nihil
praeter arma ferenti secum milite castra plena omnis for-
7 tunae publicae privataeque relinquit, transque proximos
montis laeva pedites instructos condit, dextra equites, inpe-
8 dimenta per convallem mediam traducit, ut diripiendis 30
velut desertis fuga dominorum castris occupatum inpedi
9 tumque hostem opprimeret. crebri relicti in castris ignes,

[XL. 5.—L. *The battle of Cannae.*]

ut fides fieret, dum ipse longius spatium fuga praeciperet,
falsa imagine castrorum, sicut Fabium priore anno frustratus
esset, tenere in locis consules voluisse. ubi
inluxit, subductae primo stationes, deinde pro-
5 pius adeuntibus insolitum silentium admirationem fecit. tum satis conperta solitudine in
castris concursus fit ad praetoria consulum
nuntiantium fugam hostium adeo trepidam, ut
tabernaculis stantibus castra reliquerint, quoque
10 fuga obscurior esset, crebros etiam relictos ignes.
clamor inde ortus, ut signa proferri iuberent
ducerentque ad persequendos hostis ac protinus
castra diripienda. et consul alter velut unus
turbae militaris erat; Paulus etiam atque etiam dicere provi-
15 dendum praecavendumque esse; postremo, cum aliter neque
seditionem neque ducem seditionis sustinere posset, Marium
Statilium praefectum cum turma Lucana exploratum mittit.
qui ubi adequitavit portis, subsistere extra munimenta ceteris 5
iussis ipse cum duobus equitibus vallum intravit speculatus-
20 que omnia cum cura renuntiat insidias profecto esse; ignes 6
in parte castrorum, quae vergat in hostem, relictos, taberna-
cula aperta et omnia cara in promptu relicta; argentum quibusdam locis temere per vias velut obiectum ad praedam
vidisse. quae ad deterrendos a cupiditate animos nuntiata 7
25 erant, ea accenderunt, et clamore orto a militibus, ni signum
detur, sine ducibus ituros, haudquaquam dux defuit; nam
extemplo Varro signum dedit proficiscendi. Paulus, cum 8
ei sua sponte cunctanti pulli quoque auspicio non addixissent, nuntiari iam efferenti porta signa conlegae iussit.
30 quod quam*quam* Varro aegre est passus, Flamini tamen 9
recens casus Claudique consulis primo Punico bello memorata navalis clades religionem animo incussit. di prope ipsi 10

Marginal notes (right column):

42 XLII. The soldiers and Varro are clamorous that it should be plundered.

2 Statilius sent to reconnoitre notices some suspicious circumstances. Varro is only kept back by evil omens,

3 and the information of two fugitives from the Carthaginian camp.

4

[XL. 5.—L. *The battle of Cannae.*]

eo die magis distulere quam prohibuere inminentem pestem
Romanis; nam forte ita evenit, ut, cum referri signa in castra
11 iubenti consuli milites non parerent, servi duo, Formiani
unus, alter Sidicini equitis, qui Servilio atque Atilio consulibus inter pabulatores excepti a Numidis fuerant, profugerent 5
eo die ad dominos. deductique ad consules nuntiant omnem exercitum Hannibalis trans proximos montes sedere
12 in insidiis. horum opportunus adventus consules imperii
potentes fecit, cum ambitio alterius suam primum apud eos
prava indulgentia maiestatem solvisset.   10

43   Hannibal, postquam motos magis inconsulte Romanos
      XLIII. Han- quam ad ultimum temere evectos vidit, nequi-
2 nibal returns to quam detecta fraude in castra rediit. ibi
his camp, but is
soon compelled plures dies propter inopiam frumenti manere
by hunger to nequit, novaque consilia in dies non apud 15
move again. He
encamps   near milites solum mixtos ex conluvione omnium
Cannae.   gentium, sed etiam apud ducem ipsum orie-
3 bantur. nam cum initio fremitus, deinde aperta vociferatio
fuisset exposcentium stipendium debitum querentiumque
annonam primo, postremo famem, et mercennarios milites, 20
maxime Hispani generis, de transitione cepisse consilium
4 fama esset, ipse etiam interdum Hannibal de fuga in Galliam dicitur agitasse ita, ut relicto peditatu omni cum equi-
5 tibus se proriperet. cum haec consilia atque hic habitus
animorum esset in castris, movere inde statuit in calidiora 25
atque eo maturiora messibus Apuliae loca, simul *ut*, quo
longius ab hoste recessisset, transfugia inpeditiora levibus
6 ingeniis essent. profectus est nocte ignibus similiter factis
tabernaculisque paucis in speciem relictis, ut insidiarum par
7 priori metus contineret Romanos. sed per eundem Luca- 30
num Statilium omnibus ultra castra transque montis exploratis cum relatum esset visum procul hostium agmen, tum

[XL. 5.—L. *The battle of Cannae.*]

de insequendo eo consilia agitari coepta. cum utriusque 8
consulis eadem, quae ante semper, fuisset sententia, ceterum
Varroni fere omnes, Paulo nemo praeter Servilium, prioris
anni consulem, adsentiretur, *ex* maioris partis sententia ad 9
5 nobilitandas clade Romana Cannas urgente fato profecti
sunt. prope eum vicum Hannibal castra posuerat aversa a 10
Volturno vento, qui campis torridis siccitate nubes pulveris
vehit. id cum ipsis castris percommodum fuit, tum salutare 11
praecipue futurum erat, cum aciem derigerent, ipsi aversi,
10 terga tantum adflante vento, in occaecatum pulvere offuso
hostem pugnaturi.

Consules satis exploratis itineribus sequentes Poenum, 44
ut ventum ad Cannas est, et in conspectu Poenum habebant, bina castra communiunt eodem
15 ferme intervallo, quo ad Gereonium, sicut ante
copiis divisis. Aufidius amnis utrisque castris
adfluens aditum aquatoribus ex sua cuiusque
opportunitate haud sine certamine dabat; ex
minoribus tamen castris, quae posita trans Au-
20 fidium erant, liberius aquabantur Romani, quia
ripa ulterior nullum habebat hostium praesidium. Hanni- 4
bal spem nanctus locis natis ad equestrem pugnam, qua
parte virium invictus erat, facturos copiam pugnandi consules, derigit aciem lacessitque Numidarum procursatione
25 hostis. inde rursus sollicitari seditione militari ac discordia 5
consulum Romana castra, cum Paulus Semproniaque et Flamini temeritatem Varroni, Varro *Paulo* speciosum timidis
ac segnibus ducibus exemplum Fabium obiceret, testare- 6
turque deos hominesque hic: nullam penes se culpam
30 esse, quod Hannibal iam vel*ut* usu cepisset Italiam; se
constrictum a conlega teneri; ferrum atque arma iratis et
pugnare cupienti*bus* adimi militibus; ille: si quid proiectis 7

XLIV. The
consuls follow.
Again they make
two camps, a
larger on the same
bank of the Aufi-
dus as Hannibal,
a smaller on the
further bank. H.
tries to provoke
battle.

[XL. 5.—L.   *The battle of Cannae.*]

ac proditis ad *in*consultam atque inprovidam pugnam legionibus accideret, se omnis culpae exsortem, omnis eventus participem fore diceret; videret, ut, quibus lingua prompta ac temeraria, aeque in pugna vigerent manus.

45   Dum altercationibus magis quam consiliis tempus teritur, *5*

XLV. H. sends some cavalry across, and routs *2* a watering party from the smaller camp. Next day *3* Varro, followed by Paulus, crosses the river and draws up the army for battle. *4*

Hannibal ex acie, quam ad multum diei tenuerat instructam, cum in castra ceteras reciperet copias, Numidas ad invadendos ex minoribus castris Romanorum aquatores trans flumen mittit. quam inconditam turbam cum vixdum in *10* ripam egressi clamore ac tumultu fugassent, *in* stationem quoque pro vallo locatam atque ipsas prope portas evecti sunt.   id vero *adeo* indignum visum, ab tumultuario auxilio iam etiam castra Romana terreri, ut ea modo una causa, ne extemplo transirent flumen *15* derigerentque aciem, tenuerit Romanos, quod summa im

5 perii eo die penes Paulum fuerit.   itaque postero die Varro, cui*us* sors eius diei imperii erat, nihil consulto conlega signum proposuit instructasque copias flumen traduxit sequente Paulo, quia magis non probare quam non adiuvare *20*

6 consilium poterat.   transgressi flumen eas quoque, quas in castris minoribus habuerant, copias suis adiungunt atque ita instruunt aciem : in dextro cornu—id erat flumini propius—

7 Romanos equites locant, deinde pedites; laevom cornu extremi equites sociorum, intra pedites, ad medium iuncti *25* legionibus Romanis, tenuerunt; iaculatores cum ceteris

8 levium armorum auxiliis prima acies facta.   consules cornua tenuere, Terentius laevom, Aemilius dextrum; Gemino Servilio media pugna tuenda data.

46   Hannibal luce prima Baliaribus levique alia armatura *30*

XLVI. Han *2* nibal also crosses.

praemissa transgressus flumen, ut quosque traduxerat, ita in acie locabat, Gallos Hispanos-

[XL. 5.—L. *The battle of Cannae.*]

que equites prope ripam laevo in cornu adversus Romanum equitatum, dextrum cornu Numidis equitibus datum, media acie peditibus
firmata, ita ut Afrorum utraque cornua essent,
5 interponerentur his medii Galli atque Hispani.
Afros Romanam [magna ex parte] crederes
aciem; ita armati erant armis et ad Trebiam, ceterum magna
ex parte ad Trasumennum captis.   Gallis Hispanisque
scuta eiusdem formae fere erant, dispares ac dissimiles gladii,
10 Gallis praelongi ac sine mucronibus, Hispano, punctim
magis quam caesim adsueto petere hostem, brevitate habiles
et cum mucronibus. ante alios habitus gentium harum
cum magnitudine corporum tum specie terribilis erat. Galli
super umbilicum erant nudi; Hispani linteis praetextis pur-
15 pura tunicis, candore miro fulgentibus, constiterant. numerus omnium peditum, qui tum stetere in acie, milium fuit
quadraginta, decem equitum.   duces cornibus praeerant,
sinistro Hasdrubal, dextro Maharbal; mediam aciem Hannibal ipse cum fratre Magone tenuit.   sol, seu de industria
20 ita locatis, seu quod forte ita stetere, peropportune utrique
parti obliquus erat, Romanis in meridiem Poenis in sep-
temtrionem versis; ventus—Volturnum regionis incolae vocant—adversus Romanis coortus multo pulvere in ipsa ora
volvendo prospectum ademit.

25   Clamore sublato procursum *ab* auxiliis et pugna levibus 47
primum armis commissa; deinde equitum Gal-
lorum Hispanorum*que* laevom cornu cum dextro Romano concurrit, minime equestris more
pugnae; frontibus enim adversis concurrendum
30 erat, quia nullo circa ad evagandum relicto
spatio hinc amnis hinc peditum acies claudebant. in derectum utrimque nitentes stantibus

[XL. 5.—L. *The battle of Cannae.*]

ac confertis postremo turba equis vir virum amplexus
detrahebat equo. pedestre magna iam ex parte certamen factum erat; acrius tamen quam diutius pugnatum
4 est, pulsique Romani equites terga vertunt. sub equestris
finem certaminis coorta est peditum pugna, primo et viribus 5
et animis par, dum constabant ordines Gallis Hispanisque;
5 tandem Romani, diu ac saepe conisi, *ob*liqua fronte acieque
densa inpulere hostium cuneum nimis tenuem eoque parum
6 validum, a cetera prominentem acie. inpulsis deinde ac
trepide referentibus pedem institere ac tenore uno per prae- 10
ceps pavore fugientium agmen in mediam primum aciem
inlati, postremo nullo resistente ad subsidia Afrorum perve-
7 nerunt, qui utrimque reductis alis constiterant media, qua
Galli Hispanique steterant, aliquantum prominente acie.
8 qui cuneus ut pulsus aequavit frontem primum, dein ceden- 15
do etiam sinum in medio dedit, Afri circa iam cornua fecerant inruentibusque incaute in medium Romanis circumdedere alas; mox cornua extendendo clausere et ab tergo
9 hostis. hinc Romani, defuncti nequiquam proelio uno,
omissis Gallis Hispanisque, quorum terga ceciderant, [et] 20
10 adversus Afros integram pugnam ineunt non tantum eo
iniquam, quod inclusi adversus circumfusos, sed etiam quod

XLVIII. The
fessi cum recentibus ac vegetis pugnabant.
48 Roman allied
horse on the left
iam et sinistro cornu Romano, ubi sociorum
engage with the
Numidians. De-
equites adversus Numidas steterant, consertum 25
spite a stratagem
proelium erat, segne primo et a Punica coep-
of the Numidians
2 the fight is equal.
tum fraude. quingenti ferme Numidae, prae-
Hasdrubal ac-
cordingly inter-
ter *sol*ita arma telaque gladios occultos sub
changes the posi-
loricis habentes, specie transfugarum cum ab
tion of some of
the Numidian
suis parmas post terga habentes adequitassent, 30
3 and Gallo-Span-
ish horse.
repente ex equis desiliunt parmisque et iaculis
ante pedes hostium proiectis in mediam aciem

accepti ductique ad ultimos considere ab tergo iubentur.
ac dum proelium ab omni parte conseritur, quieti man-
serunt; postquam omnium animos oculosque occupaverat 4
certamen, tum arreptis scutis, quae passim inter acervos
5 caesorum corporum strata erant, aversam adoriuntur Romanam aciem tergaque ferientes ac poplites caedentes
stragem ingentem ac maiorem aliquanto pavorem ac tumultum fecerunt. cum alibi terror ac fuga, alibi pertinax in 5
mala iam spe proelium esset, Hasdrubal, qui ea parte prae-
10 erat, subductos ex media acie Numidas, quia segnis eorum
cum adversis pugna erat, ad persequendos passim fugientis
mittit, Hispanos et Gallos equites Afris prope iam fessis 6
caede magis quam pugna adiungit.

    Parte altera pugnae Paulus, quamquam primo statim **49**
15 proelio funda graviter ictus fuerat, tamen et   **2**
occurrit saepe cum confertis Hannibali et ali-
quot locis proelium restituit, protegentibus
eum equitibus Romanis, omissis postremo
equis, quia consulem et ad regendum equom
20 vires deficiebant. tum denuntianti cuidam,
iussisse consulem ad pedes descendere equites,
dixisse Hannibalem ferunt: 'quam mallem,
vinctos mihi traderet'! equitum pedestre proelium, quale iam haud dubia hostium victoria,
25 fuit, cum victi mori in vestigio mallent quam
fugere, victores morantibus victoriam irati trucidarent, quos
pellere non poterant. pepulerunt tamen iam paucos supe- 5
rantis et labore ac vulneribus fessos. inde dissipati omnes
sunt equosque ad fugam qui poterant repetebant. Cn. Len- 6
30 tulus tribunus militum cum praetervehens equo sedentem
in saxo cruore oppletum consulem vidisset, 'L. Aemili' 7
inquit, 'quem unum insontem culpae cladis hodiernae dei

XLIX. In the centre again Paulus and his bodyguard hold out on foot. At length they are broken. Paulus refuses to fly and **3** is borne down in the rout. Some escape to the large, some to the small camp, Var- **4** ro and 50 horse-men to Venusia.

respicere debent, cape hunc equum, dum et tibi virium
aliquid superest, *et* comes ego te tollere possum ac protegere.
8 ne funestam hanc pugnam morte consulis feceris; etiam si*ne*
9 hoc lacrimarum satis luctusque est'. ad ea consul: 'tu
quidem, Cn. Corneli, macte virtute esto; sed cave, frustra 5
mi*s*erando exiguum tempus e manibus hostium evadendi
10 absumas. abi, nuntia publice patribus, urbem Romanam
muniant ac, priusquam victor hostis advenit, praesidiis fir-
ment; privatim Q. Fabio Aemilium praeceptorum eius me-
11 morem et vixisse adhuc et mori. memet in hac strage 10
militum meorum patere expirare, ne aut reus iterum e consulatu sim aut accusator conlegae existam, ut alieno crimine
12 innocentiam meam protegam'. haec eos agentis prius turba
fugientium civium, deinde hostes oppressere; consulem igno-
rantes, quis esset, obruere telis, Lentulum in*ter* tumultum 15
13 abripuit equus. tum undi*que* effuse fugiunt. septem milia
hominum in minora castra, decem in maiora, duo ferme in
vicum ipsum Cannas perfugerunt; qui extemplo a Carthalone
atque equitibus nullo munimento tegente vicum circumventi
14 sunt. consul alter seu forte seu consilio nulli fugientium 20
insertus agmini, cum quinquaginta fere equitibus Venusiam
15 perfugit. quadraginta quinque milia quingenti pedites, duo
milia septingenti equites, *et* tanta*dem* prope civium sociorum-
16 que pars, caesi dicuntur; in his ambo consulum quaestores, L.
Atilius et L. Furius Bibaculus, et undetriginta tribuni mili- 25
tum, consulares quidam praetoriique et aedilicii—inter eos
Cn. Servilium Geminum et M. Minucium numerant, qui
magister equitum priore anno, aliquot annis ante *consul*
17 fuerat—, octoginta praeterea aut senatores aut qui eos magistratus gessissent, unde in senatum legi deberent, cum sua 30
18 voluntate milites in legionibus facti essent. capta eo proelio
tria milia peditum et equites mille et quingenti dicuntur.

[XL. 5.—L.   *The battle of Cannae.*]

    Haec est pugna *Cannensis*, Aliensi cladi nobilitate par, **50**
ceterum ut illis, quae post pugnam accidere,
levior, quia ab hoste est cessatum, sic strage
exercitus gravior foediorque.   fuga namque ad
5 Aliam sicut urbem prodidit, ita exercitum ser-
vavit; ad Cannas fugientem consulem vix quinquaginta secuti sunt, alterius morientis prope
totus exercitus fuit.
    Binis in castris cum multitudo semiermis
10 sine ducibus esset, nuntium qui in maioribus
erant mittunt, dum proelio, deinde ex laetitia
epulis fatigatos quies nocturna hostes premeret, ut ad se
transirent; uno agmine Canusium abituros esse.   eam sententiam alii totam aspernari: cur enim illos, qui se arcessant, 5
15 ipsos non venire, cum aeque coniungi possent?   quia videlicet plena hostium omnia in medio essent, et aliorum quam
sua corpora tanto periculo mallent obicere.   aliis non tam 6
sententia displicere quam animus deesse.   P. Sempronius
Tuditanus tribunus militum 'capi ergo mavultis' inquit 'ab
20 avarissimo et crudelissimo hoste, aestimarique capita vestra
et exquiri pretia ab interrogantibus, Romanus civis sis an
Latinus socius, ut ex tua contumelia et miseria alteri honos
quaeratur?   non tu, si quidem L. Aemili consulis, qui se 7
bene mori quam turpiter vivere maluit, et tot fortissimorum
25 virorum, qui circa eum cumulati iacent, cives estis.   sed 8
antequam opprimit lux, maioraque hostium agmina obsae-
piunt iter, per hos, qui inordinati atque inconpositi obstre-
punt portis, erumpamus.   ferro atque audacia *via* fit quam- 9
vis per confertos hostis.   cuneo quidem hoc laxum atque
30 solutum agmen, ut si nihil obstet, disicias.   itaque ite me-
cum, qui et vosmet ipsos et rem publicam salvam vultis'.
haec ubi dicta dedit, stringit gladium cuneoque facto per 10

Side notes:

2 L. The troops
in the large camp
urge those in the 3
smaller to join
them. The latter
refuse. But en-
couraged by a
military tribune
600 cut their way
out to the troops
in the larger 4
camp, and march
with them to Ca-
nusium.

LIVII

58

[XL. 5.—L. *The battle of Cannae.*]

11 medios vadit hostis; et cum in latus dextrum, quod patebat,
Numidae iacularentur, translatis in dextrum scutis in maiora
castra ad sescentos evaserunt atque inde protinus alio magno
12 agmine adiuncto Canusium incolumes perveniunt. haec
apud victos magis impetu animorum, quos ingenium suum 5
cuique aut fors dabat, quam ex consilio ipsorum aut imperio
cuiusquam agebantur.

[LI.—LXI. *After the battle.*]

51   Hannibali victori cum ceteri circumfusi gratularentur

               suaderentque, ut tanto perfunctus bello diei
LI. Hannibal
refuses to push quod relicum esset noctisque insequentis quie- 10
on to Rome. The
Carthaginians in- tem et ipse sibi sumeret et fessis daret militi-
2 spect the field of bus, Maharbal praefectus equitum, minime
battle.
               cessandum ratus, 'immo ut, quid hac pugna sit
actum, scias, die quinto' inquit 'victor in Capitolio epula-
beris. sequere; cum equite, ut prius venisse quam venturum 15
3 sciant, praecedam'. Hannibali nimis laeta res est visa
maiorque, quam ut eam statim capere animo posset. itaque
voluntatem se laudare *Ma*harbalis ait; ad consilium pensan-
4 dum temporis opus esse. tum Maharbal: 'non omnia nimi-
rum eidem *di* dedere; vincere scis, Hannibal, victoria uti 20
nescis'. mora eius diei satis creditur saluti fuisse urbi atque
imperio.

5   Postero die, ubi primum inluxit, ad spolia legenda foe-
6 damque etiam hostibus spectandam stragem insistunt. iace-
bant tot Romanorum milia, pedites passim equitesque, ut 25
quem cuique fors aut pugna iunxerat aut fuga. adsurgentes
quidam ex strage media cruenti, quos stricta matutino frigore
7 excitaverant vulnera, ab hoste oppressi sunt; quosdam et
iacentis vivos succisis feminibus poplitibusque invenerunt,
nudantis cervicem iugulumque et relicum sanguinem iuben- 30

[LI.—LXI. *After the battle.*]

tes haurire; inventi quidam sunt mersis in effossam terram 8
capitibus, quos sibi ipsos fecisse foveas obruentisque
ora superiecta humo interclusisse spiritum apparebat.
praecipue convertit omnes subtractus Numida mortuo super- 9
5 incubanti Romano vivus naso auribusque laceratis, cum *ille*,
manibus ad capiendum telum inutilibus, in rabiem ira versa
laniando dentibus hostem expirasset.

Spoliis ad multum diei lectis Hannibal ad minora ducit 52
castra oppugnanda et omnium primum brachio
10 obiecto flumine eos excludit, ceterum ab om-   LII. First the 2
nibus labore, vigiliis, vulneribus etiam fessis smaller and then the larger camp
maturior ipsius spe deditio est facta. pacti, surrenders. Busa, an Apulian wo- 3
ut arma atque equos traderent in capita Ro- man, assists the fugitives at Ca-
mana trecenis nummis quadrigatis, in socios nusium.
15 ducenis, in servos centenis, et ut eo pretio
persoluto cum singulis abirent vestimentis, in castra hostis
acceperunt traditique in custodiam omnes sunt, seorsum
cives sociique. dum ibi tempus teritur, interea, cum ex 4
maioribus castris, quibus satis virium et animi fuit, ad quat-
20 tuor milia hominum et ducenti equites, alii agmine, alii
palati, passim per agros, quod haud minus tutum erat, Canusium perfugissent, castra ipsa ab sauciis timidisque eadem
condicione, qua altera, tradita hosti. praeda ingens parta 5
est, et praeter equos virosque et si quid argenti—quod plu-
25 rimum in phaleris equorum erat; nam ad vescendum facto
perexiguo, utique militantes, utebantur—omnis cetera praeda
diripienda data est. tum sepeliendi causa conferri in unum 6
corpora suorum iussit. ad octo milia fuisse dicuntur fortissimorum virorum. consulem quoque Romanum conquisitum
30 sepultumque quidam auctores sunt.

Eos, qui Canusium perfugerant, mulier Apula nomine 7
Busa, genere clara ac divitiis, moenibus tantum tectisque a

[LI.—LXI. *After the battle.*]

Canusinis acceptos frumento, veste, viatico etiam iuvit, pro
qua ei munificentia postea, bello perfecto, ab senatu honores
53   habiti sunt. ceterum cum ibi tribuni militum

2 LIII. At Canusium Publius quattuor essent, Fabius Maximus de legione
Scipio and Appius Claudius prima, cuius pater priore anno dictator fuerat, 5
command. Some et de legione secunda L. Publicius Bibulus et
noble youths talk P. Cornelius Scipio et de legione tertia Ap.
of leaving Italy.
Scipio, sword in Claudius Pulcher, qui proxime aedilis fuerat,
hand, compels
3 them to swear omnium consensu ad P. Scipionem admodum
fidelity to the *adulescentem et ad* Ap. Claudium summa imperii 10
Republic.
4   delata est. quibus consultantibus inter paucos
de summa rerum nuntiat P. Furius Philus, consularis viri filius,
nequiquam eos perditam spem fovere; desperatam conplo-
5 ratamque rem esse publicam; nobiles iuvenes quosdam,
quorum principem M. Caecilium Metellum, mare ac naves 15
spectare, ut deserta Italia ad regum aliquem transfugiant.
6 quod malum, praeterquam atrox, super tot clades etiam
novum, cum stupore ac miraculo torpidos defixisset qui
aderant, et consilium advocandum de eo censerent, negat
consilii rem esse Scipio iuvenis, fatalis dux huiusce belli. 20
7 audendum atque agendum, non consultandum ait in tanto
malo esse; irent secum extemplo armati, qui rem publicam
8 salvam vellent; nulla verius, quam ubi ea cogitentur,
9 hostium castra esse. pergit ire sequentibus paucis in hospitium Metelli et, cum concilium ibi iuvenum, de quibus ad- 25
latum erat, invenisset, stricto super capita consultantium
10 gladio 'ex mei animi sententia' inquit, 'ut ego rem publicam
populi Romani non deseram, neque alium civem Romanum
11 deserere patiar; si sciens fallo, tum me Iuppiter optimus maxi-
12 mus domum, familiam remque meam pessimo leto adficiat. in 30
haec verba, M. Caecili, iures postulo ceterique, qui adestis;
qui non iuraverit, in se hunc gladium strictum esse sciat'.

[LI.—LXI. *After the battle.*]

haud secus pavidi, quam si victorem Hannibalem cernerent, 13
iurant omnes custodiendosque semet ipsos Scipioni tradunt.

Eo tempore, quo haec Canusii agebantur, Venusiam 54
ad consulem ad quattuor milia et quingenti
5 pedites equitesque, qui sparsi fuga per agros
fuerant, pervenere. eos omnes Venusini per
familias benigne accipiendos curandosque cum
divisissent, in singulos equites togas et tunicas
et quadrigatos nummos quinos vicenos et pe-
10 diti denos et arma, quibus deerant, dederunt,

LIV. At Ve-
nusia the fugi-
tives are gene- 2
rously treated.
Varro joins Sci-
pio at Canusium.
At Rome the dis-
may is indescri-
bable.

ceteraque publice ac privatim hospitaliter facta, certatumque, 3
ne a muliere Canusina populus Venusinus officiis vinceretur.
sed gravius onus Busae multitudo faciebat, et iam ad decem 4
milia hominum erant, Appiusque et Scipio, postquam inco- 5
15 lumem esse alterum consulem acceperunt, nuntium extemplo mittunt, quantae secum peditum equitumque copiae
essent, sciscitatumque simul, utrum Venusiam adduci exercitum an manere iuberet Canusii. Varro ipse Canusium 6
copias traduxit; et iam aliqua species consularis exercitus
20 erat, moenibusque se certe, etsi non armis, ab hoste vide-
bantur defensuri.

Romam ne has quidem reliquias superesse civium socio- 7
rumque, sed occidione occisum cum duobus *consulibus*
exercitum deletasque omnes copias adlatum fuerat. num- 8
25 quam salva urbe tantum pavoris tumultusque intra moenia
Romana fuit. itaque, *ne* succumbam oneri, neque adgrediar
narrare, quae edissertando minora vero faciam. consule 9
exercituque ad Trasumennum priore anno amisso non
vulnus super vulnus, sed multiplex clades, cum duobus
30 consulibus *duo* consulares exercitus amissi nuntiabantur, nec
ulla iam castra Romana nec ducem nec militem esse; Han- 10
nibalis Apuliam, Samnium ac iam prope totam Italiam

factam. nulla profecto alia gens tanta mole cladis non
11 obruta esset. conpares aut cladem ad Aegatis insulas Carthaginiensium proelio navali acceptam, qua fracti Sicilia ac
Sardinia cessere et vectigalis ac stipendiarios fieri se passi
sunt, aut pugnam adversam in Africa, cui postea hic ipse 5
Hannibal succubuit: nulla ex parte conparandae sunt, nisi

55 quod minore animo latae sunt. P. Furius

LV. The Se-
nate is summon-
ed, and on the
advice of Fabius
2 sends horsemen
to gather infor-
mation, and takes
measures for qui-
eting the confu-
3 sion in the city.

Philus et M. Pomponius praetores senatum
in curiam Hostiliam vocaverunt, ut de urbis
custodia consulerent; neque enim dubitabant 10
deletis exercitibus hostem ad oppugnandam
Romam, quod unum opus belli restaret, venturum. cum in malis sicuti ingentibus ita
ignotis ne consilium quidem satis expedirent,
obstreperetque clamor lamentantium mulierum, et nondum 15
palam facto vivi mortuique [et] per omnes paene domos
4 promiscue conplorarentur, tum Q. Fabius Maximus censuit
equites expeditos et Appia et Latina via mittendos, qui
obvios percunctando—aliquos profecto ex fuga passim dissi-
patos fore—referant, quae fortuna consulum atque exercituum 20
5 sit, et, si quid di immortales, miseriti imperii, relicum Romani nominis fecerint, ubi eae copiae sint; quo se Hannibal
post proelium contulerit, quid paret, quid agat acturusque
6 sit. haec exploranda noscendaque per inpigros iuvenes
esse; illud per patres ipsos agendum, quoniam magistratuum 25
parum sit, ut tumultum ac trepidationem in urbe tollant,
matronas publico arceant continerique intra suum quamque
7 limen cogant, conploratus familiarum coerceant, silentium
per urbem faciant, nuntios rerum omnium ad praetores
deducendos curent, suae quisque fortunae domi auctorem 30
8 expectet, custodesque praeterea ad portas ponant, qui pro-
hibeant quemquam egredi urbe, cogantque homines nullam

[LI.—LXI. *After the battle.*]

nisi urbe ac moenibus salvis salutem sperare. ubi conticuerit
[recte] tumultus, tum in curiam patres revocandos consulen-
dumque de urbis custodia esse.

Cum in hanc sententiam pedibus omnes issent, submo- **56**
5 taque foro *per* magistratus turba patres diversi
ad sedandos tumultus discessissent, tum demum litterae a C. Terentio consule adlatae
sunt: L. Aemilium consulem exercitumque
caesum; sese Canusii esse reliquias tantae
10 cladis velut ex naufragio colligentem; ad
decem milia militum ferme esse inconposito-
rum inordinatorumque; Poenum sedere ad Cannas in capti- 3
vorum pretiis praedaque alia nec victoris animo nec magni
ducis more nundinantem. tum privatae quoque per domos 4
15 clades vulgatae sunt, adeoque totam urbem opplevit luctus,
ut sacrum anniversarium Cereris intermissum sit, quia nec
lugentibus id facere est fas, nec ulla in illa tempestate
matrona expers luctus fuerat. itaque ne ob eandem causam 5
alia quoque sacra publica aut privata desererentur, senatus
20 consulto diebus triginta luctus est finitus. ceterum cum 6
sedato urbis tumultu revocati in curiam patres essent, aliae
insuper ex Sicilia litterae adlatae sunt ab T. Otacilio propraetore: regnum Hieronis classe Punica vastari; cui cum 7
opem inploranti ferre vellet, nuntiatum sibi esse aliam
25 classem ad Aegatis insulas stare paratam instructamque, ut, 8
ubi se versum ad tuendam Syracusanam oram Poeni sensis-
sent, Lilybaeum extemplo provinciamque aliam Romanam
adgrederentur; itaque classe opus esse, si regem socium
Siciliamque tueri vellent.

30 Litteris consulis praetorisque *lectis censuerunt praetorem* **57**
M. Claudium, qui classi ad Ostiam stanti
praeesset, Canusium ad exercitum mittendum

LVI. A de-
spatch arrives
from Varro with
news of the bat-
tle, and another 2
from the praetor
in Spain, asking
for reinforce-
ments.

LVII. M.
Claudius Mar-

[LI.—LXI. *After the battle.*]

cellus is sent to take over the army. On account of prodigies and outrages the

2 Sibylline books are consulted, and two men and two women buried alive. Disposition of troops. Four legions are raised from youths over

3 17, and 8000 slaves are enrolled.

scribendumque consuli, ut, cum praetori exercitum tradidisset, primo quoque tempore,
quantum per commodum rei publicae fieri
posset, Romam veniret. territi etiam super
tantas clades cum ceteris prodigiis, tum quod 5
duae Vestales eo anno, Opimia atque Floronia, stupri conpertae, et altera sub terra, uti
mos est, ad portam Collinam necata fuerat,
altera sibimet ipsa mortem consciverat; L.
Cantilius, scriba pontificius, quos nunc mino- 10
res pontifices adpellant, qui cum Floronia stuprum fecerat, a pontifice maximo eo usque virgis in comitio
4 caesus erat, ut inter verbera expiraret. hoc nefas cum inter
5 tot, ut fit, clades in prodigium versum esset, decemviri
libros adire iussi sunt, et Q. Fabius Pictor Delphos ad 15
oraculum missus est sciscitatum, quibus precibus suppliciis-
que deos possent placare, et quaenam futura finis tantis
6 cladibus foret. interim ex fatalibus libris sacrificia aliquot
extraordinaria facta; inter quae Gallus et Galla, Graecus et
Graeca in foro bovario sub terram vivi demissi sunt in locum 20
saxo consaeptum, iam ante hostiis humanis, minime Romano
7 sacro, inbutum. placatis satis, ut rebantur, deis M. Claudius Marcellus ab Ostia mille et quingentos milites, quos in
classem scriptos habebat, Romam, ut urbi praesidio essent,
8 mittit; ipse, legione classica—ea legio tertia erat—cum tri- 25
bunis militum Teanum Sidicinum praemissa, classe tradita
P. Furio Philo conlegae paucos post dies Canusium magnis
9 itineribus contendit. inde dictator ex auctoritate patrum
dictus M. Iunius et Ti. Sempronius magister equitum
dilectu edicto iuniores ab annis septemdecim et quosdam 30
10 praetextatos scribunt. quattuor ex his legiones et mille
equites effecti. item ad socios Latinumque nomen ad

milites ex formula accipiendos mittunt. arma, tela, alia
parari iubent et vetera spolia hostium detrahunt templis
porticibusque. et formam novi dilectus inopia liberorum 11
capitum ac necessitas dedit ; octo milia iuvenum validorum
5 ex servitiis prius sciscitantes singulos, vellentne militare,
empta publice armaverunt. hic miles magis placuit, cum 12
pretio minore redimendi captivos copia fieret. namque 58
Hannibal secundum tam prosperam ad Cannas
pugnam victoris magis quam bellum gerentis
10 intentus curis, cum captivis productis segrega-
tisque socios, sicut ante ad Trebiam Trasumennumque lacum, benigne adlocutus sine
pretio dimisisset, Romanos quoque vocatos,

LVIII. Han-
nibal offers to
accept a ransom
for the prisoners. 2
Ten of them are
sent to lay the
matter before the
Senate.

quod numquam alias antea, satis miti sermone adloquitur :
15 non internecivum sibi esse cum Romanis bellum ; de dignitate atque imperio certare. et patres virtuti Romanae 3
cessisse, et se id adniti, ut suae in vicem simul felicitati et
virtuti cedatur. itaque redimendi se captivis copiam facere ; 4
pretium fore in capita equiti quingenos quadrigatos nummos,
20 trecenos pediti, servo centenos. quamquam aliquantum 5
adiciebatur equitibus ad id pretium, quo pepigerant deden-
tes se, laeti tamen quamcumque condicionem paciscendi
acceperunt. placuit suffragio ipsorum decem deligi, qui 6
Romam ad senatum irent, nec pignus aliud fidei, quam ut
25 iurarent se redituros, acceptum. missus cum his Carthalo, 7
nobilis Carthaginiensis, qui, si forte ad pacem inclinaret
animus, condiciones ferret. cum egressi castris essent, unus 8
ex iis, minime Romani ingenii homo, veluti aliquid oblitus,
iuris iurandi solvendi causa cum in castra redisset, ante
30 noctem comites adsequitur. ubi Romam venire eos nuntia- 9
tum est, Carthaloni obviam lictor missus, qui dictatoris
verbis nuntiaret, ut ante noctem excederet finibus Romanis.

[LI.—LXI. *After the battle.*]

59

LIX. Speech of their leader. They deserved to be ransomed if any one ever did. It will be profitable for Rome to retain their services. The Senate should pity them because of the fate they will undergo if not ransomed.

legatis captivorum senatus ab dictatore datus est. quorum princeps 'M. Iuni vosque, patres conscripti' inquit, 'nemo nostrum ignorat nulli umquam civitati viliores fuisse captivos quam nostrae; ceterum, nisi nobis plus iusto nostra 5 placet causa, non alii umquam minus negligendi vobis quam nos in hostium potestatem venerunt. non enim in acie per timorem arma tradidimus, sed, cum prope ad noctem superstantes cumulis caesorum corporum proelium 10 extraxissemus, in castra recepimus nos; diei relicum ac noctem insequentem fessi labore ac vulneribus vallum sumus tutati; postero die, cum circumsessi ab exercitu victore aqua arceremur, nec ulla iam per confertos hostis erumpendi spes esset, nec esse nefas duceremus quinquaginta milibus homi- 15 num ex acie nostra trucidatis aliquem ex Cannensi pugna Romanum militem restare, tunc demum pacti sumus pretium, quo redempti dimitteremur, arma, in quibus nihil iam auxilii erat, hosti tradidimus. maiores quoque acceperamus se a Gallis auro redemisse, et patres vestros, asperrimos illos ad 20 condiciones pacis, legatos tamen captivorum redimendorum gratia Tarentum misisse. atqui et *ad* Aliam cum Gallis et ad Heracleam cum Pyrrho utraque non tam clade infamis quam pavore et fuga pugna fuit. Cannensis campos acervi Romanorum corporum tegunt, nec supersumus pugnae, nisi 25 in quibus trucidandis et ferrum et vires hostem defecerunt. sunt etiam de nostris quidam, qui ne in acie quidem fuere, sed praesidio castris relicti, cum castra traderentur, in potestatem hostium venerunt. haud equidem ullius civis et commilitonis fortunae aut condicioni invideo nec premendo 30 alium me extulisse velim—; ne illi quidem, nisi pernicitatis pedum et cursus aliquod praemium est, qui plerique inermes

[LI.—LXI. *After the battle.*]

ex acie fugientes non prius quam Venusiae aut Canusi constiterunt, se nobis merito praetulerint gloriatique sint in se
plus quam in nobis praesidii rei publicae esse. sed et illis 11
bonis ac fortibus militibus utemini et nobis etiam promp-
5 tioribus pro patria, quod beneficio vestro redempti atque in
patriam restituti fuerimus. dilectum ex omni aetate et 12
fortuna habetis; octo milia servorum audio armari. non
minor numerus noster est, nec maiore pretio redimi possu-
mus, quam ii emuntur—; nam si conferam nos cum illis,
10 iniuriam nomini Romano faciam. illud etiam in tali con- 13
silio animadvertendum vobis censeam, patres conscripti,
si iam duriores esse velitis, quod nullo nostro merito faciatis,
cui nos hosti relicturi sitis: Pyrrho videlicet, qui [vos] hospi- 14
tum numero captivos habuit, an barbaro ac Poeno, qui
15 utrum avarior an crudelior sit, vix existimari potest. si 15
videatis catenas, squalorem, deformitatem civium vestrorum,
non minus profecto vos ea species moveat, quam si ex
altera parte cernatis stratas Cannensibus campis legiones
vestras. intueri potestis sollicitudinem et lacrimas in vesti- 16
20 bulo curiae stantium cognatorum nostrorum expectantium-
que responsum vestrum. cum ii pro nobis proque iis, qui
absunt, ita suspensi ac solliciti sint, quem censetis animum
ipsorum esse, quorum in discrimine vita libertasque est?
sed si, me dius fidius, ipse in nos mitis Hannibal contra 17
25 naturam suam esse velit, nihil tamen nobis vita opus esse
censeamus, cum indigni ut redimeremur [a] vobis visi simus.
rediere Romam qu*ond*am remissi a Pyrrho sine pretio capti, 18
sed rediere cum legatis, primoribus civitatis, ad redimendos
sese missis; redeam ego in patriam trecentis nummis non
30 aestimatus civis? suum quisque *habet* animum, patres con- 19
scripti. scio in discrimine esse vitam corpusque meum;
magis me famae periculum movet, ne a vobis damnati ac

5—*2*

[LI.—LXI. *After the battle.*]

repulsi abeamus; neque enim vos pretio pepercisse homines credent'.

60 Ubi is finem fecit, extemplo ab ea turba, quae in comitio erat, clamor flebilis est sublatus, manusque ad curiam tendebant orantes, ut sibi liberos, fra- 5 tres, cognatos redderent. feminas quoque metus ac necessitas in foro turbae virorum inmiscuerat. senatus submotis arbitris consuli coeptus. ibi cum sententiis variaretur, et alii redimendos de publico, alii nullam publice 10 inpensam faciendam nec prohibendos ex privato redimi, si quibus argentum in praesentia deesset, dandam ex aerario pecuniam mutuam praedibusque ac praediis cavendum populo censerent, tum T. Manlius Torquatus, priscae ac nimis 15 durae, ut plerisque videbatur, severitatis, interrogatus sententiam ita locutus fertur: 'si tantummodo postulassent legati pro iis, qui in hostium potestate sunt, ut redimerentur, sine ullius insectatione eorum brevi sententiam peregissem; quid enim aliud quam admonendi essetis, ut morem traditum 20 a patribus necessario ad rem militarem exemplo servaretis? nunc autem, cum prope gloriati sint, quod se hostibus dediderint praeferrique non captis modo in acie ab hostibus sed etiam iis, qui Venusiam Canusiumque pervenerunt, atque ipsi C. Terentio consuli aecum censuerint, nihil vos eorum, 25 patres conscripti, quae illic acta sunt, ignorare patiar. atque utinam haec, quae apud vos acturus sum, Canusii apud ipsum exercitum agerem, optimum testem ignaviae cuiusque et virtutis, aut unus hic saltem adesset P. Sempronius, quem si isti ducem secuti essent, milites hodie in 30 castris Romanis, non captivi in hostium potestate essent. sed cum, fessis pugnando hostibus tum victoria laetis et

Marginal notes:

LX. Answer of Torquatus.

2 They might have sallied from the camp and found safety. They should have done

3 so even to meet destruction. They tried to prevent Sempronius from leaving the camp.

4 Having remained they did not even try to defend it.

5 ... 6 ... 7 ... 8 ... 9 ...

[LI.—LXI. *After the battle.*]

ipsis plerisque regressis in castra sua, noctem ad erumpendum liberam habuissent, et septem *milia* armatorum hominum erumpere etiam *per* confertos hostes possent, neque
per se ipsi id facere conati sunt, neque alium sequi volue-
5 runt.   nocte prope tota P. Sempronius Tuditanus non de- 10
stitit monere, adhortari eos, dum paucitas hostium circa
castra, dum quies ac silentium esset, dum nox inceptum
tegere posset, se ducem sequerentur: ante lucem pervenire
in tuta loca, in sociorum urbes posse.   si ut avorum memo- 11
10 ria P. Decius tribunus militum in Samnio, si ut nobis adu-
lescentibus priore Punico bello Calpurnius Flamma trecentis
voluntariis, cum ad tumulum eos capiendum situm inter
medios duceret hostis, dixit "moriamur, milites, et morte
nostra eripiamus ex obsidione circumventas legiones", si hoc 12
15 P. Sempronius diceret, nec viros *e*quidem nec Romanos vos
ducerem, si nemo tantae virtutis extitisset comes.   viam 13
non ad gloriam magis quam ad salutem ferentem demonstrat; reduces in patriam ad parentes, ad coniuges ac liberos
facit. ut servemini, deest vobis animus; quid, si moriendum 14
20 pro patria esset, faceretis?   quinquaginta milia civium
sociorumque circa vos eo ipso die caesa iacent. si tot
exempla virtutis non movent, nihil umquam movebit; si
tanta clades vilem vitam non fecit, nulla faciet. liberi atque 15
incolumes desiderate patriam; immo desiderate, dum patria
25 est, dum cives eius estis. sero nunc desideratis, deminuti
capite, abalienati iure civium, servi Carthaginiensium facti.
pretio redituri estis eo, unde ignavia ac nequitia abistis? 16
P. Sempronium, civem vestrum, non audistis arma capere
ac sequi se iubentem; Hannibalem post paulo audistis castra
30 prodi et arma tradi iubentem.   quam*quam quid* ego igna- 17
viam istorum accuso, cum scelus possim accusare?   non
modo enim sequi recusarunt bene monentem, sed obsistere

ac retinere conati sunt, ni strictis gladiis viri fortissimi iner-
18 tes submovissent.   prius, inquam, P. Sempronio per civium
agmen quam per hostium fuit erumpendum.   hos cives
patria desideret?   quorum si ceteri similes fuissent, neminem
19 hodie ex iis, qui ad Cannas pugnaverunt, civem haberet.   ex ₅
milibus septem armatorum sescenti extiterunt, qui erumpere
auderent, qui in patriam liberi atque armati redirent, neque
20 his sescentis hostes obstitere; quam tutum iter duarum prope
legionum agmini futurum censetis fuisse?   haberetis hodie
viginti milia armatorum Canusii fortia fidelia, patres con- ₁₀
scripti.   nunc autem quem ad modum hi boni fidelesque—
nam fortes ne ipsi quidem dixerint—cives esse possunt?
21 nisi quis credere potest aut favisse erumpentibus, qui, ne
erumperent, obsistere conati sunt, aut non invidere eos cum
incolumitati tum gloriae illorum per virtutem partae, cum ₁₅
sibi timorem ignaviamque servitutis ignominiosae causam
22 esse sciant.   maluerunt in tentoriis latentes simul lucem
atque hostem expectare, cum silentio noctis erumpendi
occasio esset.   *at* ad erumpendum e castris defuit animus
23 ad tutanda fortiter castra animum habuerunt; dies noctesque ₂₀
aliquot obsessi vallum armis, se ipsi tutati vallo sunt; tandem ultima ausi passique, cum omnia subsidia vitae deessent adfectisque fame viribus arma iam sustinere nequirent,
24 necessitatibus magis humanis quam armis victi sunt.   orto
sole hostis ad vallum accessit; ante secundam horam, nullam ₂₅
fortunam certaminis experti, tradiderunt arma ac se ipsos.
25 haec vobis istorum per biduum militia fuit.   cum *in* acie
stare ac pugnare decuerat, [cum] in castra refugerunt; cum
pro vallo pugnandum erat, castra tradiderunt neque in acie
26 neque in castris utiles.   et vos redimam*us*?   cum erumpere ₃₀
e castris oportet, cunctamini ac manetis; cum manere, castra tutari armis necesse est, et castra et arma et vos ipsos

[LI.—LXI. *After the battle.*]

traditis hosti. ego non magis istos redimendos, patres con- 27
scripti, censeo, quam illos dedendos Hannibali, qui per
medios hostis e castris eruperunt ac per summam virtutem
se patriae restituerunt'.

5 Postquam Manlius dixit, quamquam patrum quoque 61
plerosque captivi cognatione attingebant, praeter exemplum civitatis minime in captivos iam

LXI. The
Senate refuses to
inde antiquitus indulgentis, pecuniae quoque
ransom the pri- 2
soners. The en-
summa homines movit, quia nec aerarium ex-
voys return ex-
10 hauriri, magna iam summa erogata in servos
cept one who is
arrested and sent
ad militiam emendos armandosque, nec Han-
to Hannibal. An-
nibalem maxime huiusce rei, ut fama erat,
other version.
Some allies de-
egentem locupletari volebant. cum triste re-
sert. The Ro- 3
mans do not de-
sponsum, non redimi captivos, redditum esset
spair. They even
return thanks to
15 novusque super veterem luctus tot iactura
Varro.
civium adiectus esset, cum magnis fletibus
questibus*que* legatos ad portam prosecuti sunt. unus ex iis 4
domum abiit, quod fallaci reditu in castra iure iurando se
exsolvisset. quod ubi innotuit relatumque ad senatum est,
20 omnes censuerunt conprehendendum et custodibus publice
datis deducendum ad Hannibalem esse.

Est et alia de captivis fama : decem primo venisse ; de 5
eis cum dubitatum in senatu esset, admitterentur in urbem
necne, ita admissos esse, ne tamen iis senatus daretur ; mo- 6
25 rantibus deinde longius omnium spe alios tris insuper legatos venisse, L. Scribonium et C. Calpurnium et L. Man-
lium ; tum demum ab cognato Scriboni tribuno plebis de 7
redimendis captivis relatum esse, nec censuisse redimendos
senatum ; et novos legatos tris ad Hannibalem revertisse,
30 decem veteres remansisse, quod per causam recognoscendi 8
nomina captivorum ad Hannibalem ex itinere regressi reli-
*gi*one sese exsolvissent ; de iis dedendis magna contentione

[LI.—LXI. *After the battle.*]

actum in senatu esse, victosque paucis sententiis, qui deden-
9 dos censuerint; ceterum proxumis censoribus adeo omnibus
notis ignominiisque confectos esse, ut quidam eorum mortem sibi ipsi extemplo consciverint, ceteri non foro solum
10 omni deinde vita, sed prope luce ac publico caruerint. mi- 5
rari magis adeo discrepare inter auctores, quam, quid veri
sit, discernere queas.

Quanto autem maior ea clades superioribus cladibus
fuerit, vel ea res indicio *est, quod fides socio*rum, quae ad eam
diem firma steterat, tum labare coepit, nulla profecto alia de 10
11 re, quam quod desperaverant de imperio. defecere autem ad
Poenos hi populi: Atellani, Calatini, Hirpini, Apulorum
12 pars, Samnites praeter Pentros, Bruttii omnes, Lucani,
praeter hos Uzentini et Graecorum omnis ferme ora, Tarentini, Metapontini, Crotonienses Locrique, et Cisalpini omnes 15
13 Galli. nec tamen eae clades defectionesque sociorum moverunt, ut pacis usquam mentio apud Romanos fieret, neque
ante consulis Romam adventum, nec postquam is rediit
14 renovavitque memoriam acceptae cladis; quo in tempore
ipso adeo magno animo civitas fuit, ut consuli ex tanta 20
clade, cuius ipse causa maxima fuisset, redeunti et obviam
itum frequenter ab omnibus ordinibus sit et gratiae actae,
15 quod de re publica non desperasset; qui *si* Carthaginiensium
ductor fuisset, nihil recusandum supplicii foret.

NOTES.

As in a few cases reference has been made to variations of reading, it may be stated that the following abbreviations are used to denote the three principal MSS. containing the 22nd book of Livy.

P=Puteanus, so called after its possessor, in the Paris library. It is the oldest MS. for it is assigned to the 8th (by Müller to the 6th) century, and the best, though containing many errors. The other two are descended from it.

C=Colbertinus, also in the Paris library, end of the 10th or beginning of the 11th century.

M=Mediceus, in the library at Florence, 11th century.

CHAPTER I.

p. 1. 1 § 1. *itaque*] P *adpetebatque*, for which Weissenborn read *adpetebat atque*. *itaque* is better suited to the context, which is explained in the note on *et...et.*

hibernis] near Placentia XXI. 59. 1, whither he had probably returned from Liguria ib. § 10, if indeed he went to Liguria at all. See on *ante conatus* in this section.

movit] sc. *castra*. In the case of verbs which are constantly used with the same object, the object is not unfrequently omitted. There are several such verbs among those describing military operations. Cf. *ducit* 12. 2.

2 *et...et...metu*] The two participles explain why Hannibal was anxious to start as soon as the season allowed. His original intention had been to do so earlier, but he had been thwarted in it: his enforced delay had been attended with danger.

ante conatus transcendere Appenninum] The attempt here referred to is described in XXI. 58. We may doubt whether it was actually made. Polybius does not mention it, and there can hardly have been time for it and the subsequent movements described in Livy XXI. 59 between the date indicated by *prima ac dubia signa veris* ib. 58. 2 and the 'approach of spring' (*iam ver adpetebat*). More probably Hannibal passed the winter in inactivity near Placentia.

3   *intolerandis frigoribus*] abl. absol. explaining *nequiquam.*

4   § **2.** *Galli*] The sentence which follows explains *periculo et metu.*

6   *pro eo, ut...raperent*] 'instead of themselves plundering'. This would have been expressed more shortly in Greek by ἀντὶ τοῦ αὐτοὶ φέρειν καὶ ἄγειν.

   raperent agerentque] The second word refers more particularly to cattle, the first to other kinds of booty. The usual phrase is *ferre agere.*

8   *utriusque partis*] The remains of the Roman armies were in Placentia and Cremona.

9   § **3.** *verterunt retro*] 'transferred'. *retro* does not imply that they had hated Hannibal before and now renewed their hate.

10   *petitusque*] *Hannibal* is the subject, as in the opening sentence.

   que]= 'and so'.

   inter se] 'to each other'.

   fraude] This is further explained by the words *eadem...indicantium.*

12   *tegumenta capitis*] This refers to false hair, as appears from Polybius III. 78 E κατεσκευάσατο περιθετὰς τρίχας. He adds ὁμοίως δὲ καὶ τὰς ἐσθῆτας μετελάμβανε τὰς καθηκούσας ἀεὶ ταῖς περιθεταῖς. 'In like fashion he wore the clothes which matched the wig he had on at the time'; words more precise than those of Livy. Polybius calls this a 'Punic wile', ἐχρήσατο Φοινικικῷ στρατηγήματι.

13   *errore*] 'by the confusion thus caused'.

   etiam] with *errore*, 'in this way', as well as by the protection afforded him by the mutual treachery of the conspirators.

   § **4.** *ceterum*] according to its etymology = 'moreover' (cf. Fr. *du reste*). Livy and later writers use it in an adversative sense—'however'.

14   *movendi*] see on § 1 *movit.*

15   *per idem tempus*] 'about the same time', referring to § 1 *iam ver adpetebat.*

   Romae] As contrasted with his colleague Flaminius, who had ordered the legions which had wintered at Placentia to proceed to Ariminum, XXI. 63. 1, 2, and 13, and now entered on his office there.

   Such is Livy's account; but it is doubtful whether it is true. Soon after this (c. **2. 1**) we find Flaminius at Arretium in Etruria, while Servilius was posted at Ariminum (Pol. III. 86. 1). This being so, it was hardly likely that Flaminius went first to Ariminum, took over the army of the Po there, and proceeded with it across the Appennines to Arretium.

   It is m)re probable that Flaminius proceeded from Rome to Arretium

with the new levies, while Servilius went to Ariminum and there received the army which had fought at Trebia in 218 B.C. Zonaras says
this was what Servilius did (VIII. 412 C). Polybius III. 75 says the two
consuls raised troops for 217 B.C. together, and made arrangements for
markets being held 'partly at Ariminum, partly in Etruria, as they intended to march out to these places'. If the consuls raised levies
together Flaminius could not have entered office at Arretium. Polybius
does not mention his doing so, and he probably means—what from other
circumstances seems most likely—that Flaminius proceeded straight from
Rome to Arretium, as Servilius did to Ariminum.

Flaminius seems to have been treated unfairly by the historians of
the war, who were mostly men of the senatorial party. The story that
he entered office at Ariminum may have been invented after his defeat
to enhance the seeming justice of the retribution which overtook the
popular general.

idibus Martiis] The date is not consistent with the words which
precede it, for at this time the Roman Calendar was about two months
in advance of the natural year, and the Ides of March would have fallen
in the middle of January. Livy writes as if the Calendar were correct.

16   § **5.** *de re publica rettulisset*] 'moved to discuss the situation', 11. 1.

17   *redintegrata*] The previous occasion referred to was when Flaminius
was consul elect, XXI. 63. He had still earlier than this incurred the
hostility of the aristocracy as tribune in 232 B.C. and as consul in
223 B.C., XXI. 63. 2.

18   *creasse*] depending on some word of feeling or saying suggested by
invidia. se, sc. *populum.*

iustum] 'legal', because he had left the city without the *lex curiata
de imperio* having been passed.

p. 2.   1   *auspicium*] 'religious sanction for his election'. The auspices
were usually taken by the consul on his formal departure from his
province. Flaminius had left Rome *inauspicato.*

§ **6.** *id*] 'this', i.e. legal authority, sanctioned by religion, the idea
expressed by *iustum imperium...auspicium.*

publicis privatisque penatibus] 'the hearth of the family and the
state'. The whole Roman people had its *penates* as well as each family.
They had it seems a temple on the Velia. Here however the temples
of the gods of Rome on the Capitol are referred to.

The words which follow indicate the ceremonies observed by a consul
on assuming the consulship and during the opening days of his tenure of
office. They are enumerated more exactly in XXI. 63. 7—9.

The consul having assumed the *praetexta* (or robe of state) in his house proceeded to the temple of Jupiter on the Capitol (cf. *publicis privatisque penatibus*) where he offered the sacrifices vowed by his predecessor, and undertook that similar sacrifices should be offered next year. This was called *votorum nuncupatio* (recital of vows). He then held a meeting on the Capitol where matters of ceremonial were discussed, and in particular the day for the Latin festival fixed.

2 *Latinis feriis*] The next duty of the consul was to preside at the Latin festival. This was a ceremony dating from the time of the old Latin League, when the thirty cities which composed it met yearly on the Alban mount.

monte] sc. *Albano*.

3 *nuncupatis*] From its position in the list of ceremonies it is probable that this refers not to the *votorum nuncupatio* made by the consul on his entry into office (see note on *publicis privatisque penatibus*), but to special vows made by him for the success of his campaign on his formal departure for his province.

4 § 7. *auspicia*] the subject to *sequi*, which = 'to attend'. Properly qualified persons were said *habere auspicia*, 'to possess the auspices', i.e. the right of taking them. *auspicia* is thus used in a more literal sense than *auspicium* in § 5.

5 *nova atque integra*] *atque* explanatory. There is a redundancy of expression. 'For the first time and when he had never taken them before'. C. and B. give the whole passage a different sense: 'and acquire the sanction of heaven afresh in its fulness'; I think wrongly.

concipere] = first, 'to comprise in words', hence 'to formulate'. *iusiurandum c.* = 'to take an oath'. *verbis conceptis* = 'in a set form of words'. v. 17. 2 *consules vitio creatos sacrum in Albano monte non rite concepisse*, 'to announce formally'. Cf. *feriae conceptivae*, 'festivals which were announced, instead of taking place at fixed seasons'. *bellum concipere*, 'to declare war'. Here *concipere* = rather 'to take' than 'to declare' the auspices, though it properly indicates the form of words (cf. I. 18. 7) with which the ceremony was accompanied.

7 § 8. *militibus*] an ethical dative, which in meaning is practically equivalent to a genitive. Cf. I. 39. 1 *puero caput arsisse ferunt. aliquot* with *militibus*. For the prodigy cf. XLIII. 13. 6 *hasta...interdiu plus duas horas arsisse ita ut nihil eius ambureret ignis dicebat*. These flames were doubtless electrical.

8 *tenuerat*] *tenuerit* has been suggested, but Livy not unfrequently uses indic. for subj. in or. obliqua. In such cases there is in fact a change

back from the oratio obliqua, to give an impression of greater vividness
and to indicate a livelier interest in the act; e.g. III. 71. 6 *ibi infit
annum se tertium et octogensimum agere, et in eo agro de quo agitur mili·
tasse.* For much the same reason Livy often changes from secondary
back to primary sequences in oratio obliqua.

9   *sanguine sudasse*] Valerius Maximus I. 6. 5 uses the same words,
except that he has *sanguinem* for *sanguine.*

11   § **9.** *orbem minui*] a partial eclipse seems to be referred to.

Praeneste] Palestrina, in Latium, some 14 miles S.E. of Rome, and
an allied town. *Praeneste* is locative: so *Caere* XXI. 62. 8.

lapides] meteoric stones.

12   *Arpis*] in Apulia. Cf. 9. 5, 12. 3.

13   § **10.** *Capenae*] a Tuscan town founded by the Veientes, now
S. Martino.

aquas Caeretes] Caere was famous for its warm baths.

14   *ipsum*] evidently the most important of the springs there. It was
probably a warm sulphureous spring, as fountains of this kind are always
associated with Hercules.

15   *Antii*] Porto d' Anzo on the Latian coast. There was there a
famous temple of Fortuna, Hor. *C.* I. 35.

metentibus] dat. incommodi. Cf. § 8.

16   *cruentas*] probably a predicate, 'had fallen into the basket all bloody'.

§ **11.** *Faleriis*] in Etruria near the *via Flaminia*.

17   *qua patuerit*] 'from the opening'.

18   *sortes*] We do not know of any oracle at Falerii; but the
sortes were probably like those used at Antium, Praeneste and other
places where the goddess Fortuna had temples. They were slips of
wood on which proverbial phrases were written in ancient characters.
To consult the oracle the priest sacrificed to the goddess, then a boy
mixed the lots and drew one forth. See Cic. *de Div.* 11. 86, cf. XXI.
62. 5.

sua sponte] 'spontaneously', without being touched.

adtenuatas] 'shrunk', a bad sign; their swelling would have been
a good one.

excidisse] probably from the place where they were kept, not
from the urn on the consultation of the oracle. Specimens of *sortes*
have been found pierced with holes, so that they could be suspended on
a string or from pegs on the temple wall.

19   *ita scriptam*] 'with this inscription'. *scriptam = inscriptam* is
poetical.

telum]= *hastam.*

11 § **12.** *luporum*] not the wolf on the Capitol suckling Romulus and Remus: probably figures of wolves placed outside the temple of Mars as being connected with his worship. *Martiales...lupos,* Hor. *C.* **I. 17. 9.**

speciem] a predicate, 'there had been the appearance'.

22 *inter imbrem*] apparently a shower of rain is meant.

cadentis] perhaps a meteor may have afforded some ground for the story. Pliny, *N. H.* II. 35. 100, speaks of a spark (*scintillam de stella*) which fell from the sky and became larger as it approached the earth, till it had attained the size of the moon.

23 § **13.** *dictu*] with *minoribus.*

lanatas] i.e. their hair had turned into wool.

quibusdam] cf. *metentibus* § 10.

25 § **14.** *sicut erant nuntiata*] i.e. in the terms used by the narrators. *expositis* by the consuls.

27 § **15.** *maioribus...lactentibus*] the regular expressions for 'full-grown' and 'young' victims or 'sucklings', in sacrificial language.

28 *procurarentur*] *procurare prodigia*=to take measures to avert the disasters portended by omens. No single word will give this meaning except perhaps 'expiate'.

supplicatio] a solemn service either of thanksgiving, as e.g. for a victory, or, as here, of prayer, in which the temples were visited by the citizens in procession. It was usually accompanied by a *lectisternium.*

29 § **16.** *decemviri*] the keepers of the books.

libros] sc. *Sibyllinos.* They were only consulted on the occasion of extraordinary calamities for which the pontifices could prescribe no remedies. Tradition says that they had been brought to Rome in the time of the Tarquins. They were written in Greek, and were deciphered by two Greek interpreters attached to the decemviri for the purpose. Connected with the worship of the Greek Apollo, by whom the Sibyls were supposed to be inspired, their consultation is usually associated with the gradual engrafting of Greek forms of worship on the old Latin religion.

30 *cordi esse*] 'to be pleasing'. L. and S. render *cordi est* 'it lies at one's heart' as if *cordi* were a locative case. But *cordi* is a predicative dative, and *cordi esse*=to be a dear object. Cf. *corculum* used as a term of endearment, and *hoc iuvat et melli est* Hor. *S.* II. 6. 32.

31   *e carminibus*] 'in accordance with the prophecies'. The Sibylline books were written in verse. Cf. Verg. *B.* IV. 4 *Ultima Cumaei venit iam carminis aetas.*

   praefarentur] 'declared': properly the verb means to repeat a formula. Cf. *praeire verba.* The subject is *decemviri.*

32   § **17.** *pondo*] in full *fulmen pondo librarum* (or *libras*) *quinquaginta. pondo* is an ablative = 'in weight'. It is used either with the name of the weight expressed, as *unciam pondo* Plaut. *Rudens* IV. 2. 8; *ut exercitus coronam auream dictatori libram pondo decreverit* Livy III. 29. 3; or not expressed, when some case of *libra* is understood.

p. 3.   1 *fieret*] *ut* is omitted.

5   § **18.** *lectisternium*] At this ceremony images or busts of the gods were laid on couches, and a banquet, provided under the direction of the *epulones,* placed before them. Hor. *C.* I. 37. 2 *nunc saliaribus ornare pulvinar deorum tempus erat dapibus sodales.* The first *lectisternium* was celebrated in 399 B.C., being prescribed by the Sibylline books.

6   *et ipsae*] = *quoque,* 'as well as the Roman matrons'.

   Feroniae] An ancient Etruscan deity worshipped by Latins, Etruscans, and Sabines. According to Varro she was the goddess of Freedom. Slaves were emancipated in her temple at Tarracina.

8   § **19.** *Ardeae*] Capital of the Rutuli in Latium. No portents have been mentioned as occurring at Ardea, but it possessed a temple of Aphrodite, and probably the Sibylline books had directed that sacrifice should be offered to Aphrodite.

9   *aedem Saturni*] in the forum at the foot of the Mons Capitolinus. It was used as the state treasury.

10   *eum lectum*] i.e. the couch on that occasion. *lectus,* the couch or *pulvinar* referred to in the note on *lectisternium* § 18.

11   *convivium publicum*] A feast at which the whole people were entertained, also called *epulum.* Hor. *S.* II. 3. 86.

12   § **20.** *Saturnalia clamata*] sc. *sunt,* '*Saturnalia* was cried'. The cry was *io Saturnalia.* Cf. XXI. 62. 2 *infantem in foro olitorio triumphum clamasse,* i.e. cried *io triumphe.* The festival of Saturn, during which this cry was raised in the streets, was instituted in 497 B.C. It originally lasted only one day, Dec. 19th. L. II. 21. 2 *Saturnalia institutus festus dies.* Catullus XIV. 15 *Saturnalibus optimo dierum.* Julius Caesar lengthened it to 3 days, and in the time of Caligula it extended to 5 days. It was a time of merry-making, in some ways resembling our Christmas festivities, e. g. presents were exchanged. Mart. V. 18.

eum diem] i.e. the day of the Saturnalia, indicated in the preceding words.

CHAPTER II.

14   § **1**.   *dilectu*]=*dilectui*, an old form.   Cf. **11**. **5** *exercitu.*

15   *profectus ex hibernis*]   Hannibal's winter-quarters were in the plain S. of Placentia and Cremona.   Thence he crossed the Appennines probably by the road from Mutina over the Monte Cimone to Pescia. The passage of the Appennines is not expressly mentioned.   Probably, unlike the attempted passage alluded to in c. **1**. **1** and described XXI. 58, it was effected without difficulty.   See Appendix I.

16   *quia iam* etc.] the words explain why Hannibal preferred speed to convenience.

Arretium] commanding the route which passed up the Arno valley, and due South past Clusium to Rome.   The operations of **217** B.C. shew that this route was already available for armies.   But it was not till **171** B.C. that a military road was made from Rome to Arretium, and from Arretium to Bononia under the name of *via Cassia*.   Mommsen, *R. H.* **1**. 387 note.

17   § **2**.   *aliud longius, ceterum commodius*]   probably the road from Pescia to Faesulae, by Pistoria and Prato.   As it skirted the hills which bounded the marsh-land to the N. it would have lain over firmer ground, but was certainly longer.   Polybius III. 78. 6 adds another reason why Hannibal avoided this route, τὰς μὲν ἄλλας ἐμβολὰς τὰς εἰς τὴν πολεμίαν μακρὰς εὕρισκε καὶ προδήλους τοῖς πολεμίοις.   He found the other routes into the enemy's country too long and too patent to the foe.   At Faesulae he would have been too near Flaminius.

18   *propiorem viam per paludes*] *paludes*, the marshes along the course of the Arno from Faesulae to Pisa, and extending N. as far as the spurs of the Appennines from which Hannibal descended. Hannibal probably struck across them S. from Pescia to Empoli.   See Appendix I.

20   § **3**.   *et omne...robur*] 'in fact the whole flower'.   Thus *robur* includes *Hispanos et Afros*, and refers to them especially.   *robur*, lit. the strongest part.

21   *veterani*] the original army as opposed to the Gauls who had joined Hannibal in Italy.   Besides *Afri et Hispani* it contained *Ligures* and *Baliares* XXI. 22. 2.

22   *necubi*]=*ne alicubi*, not found in Cicero.
       coactis]=*si coacti essent.*

usus] 'needs'.

23 *id*]=*ii.* The Gauls are referred to, but the pronoun is attracted into agreement with *agmen.*

24 § **4.** *Magonem*] brother of Hannibal. He had been in charge of an ambuscade at the battle of Trebia XXI. 55, and later on we shall find him commanding part of the Carthaginian centre at Cannae 47. 7.

25 *cogere agmen*] Livy seems to make four divisions: Polybius makes only three, for according to him Mago commands the cavalry in the rear (οὐραγίᾳ, corresponding to *novissimos...equites* here); not a force of light-armed.

26 *ut est mollis...gens*] 'with the incapacity for enduring hardship which distinguishes their race'. *ut* with some part of *esse* is often used to cite a well-known fact in confirmation of something that has preceded. Cf. Roby § 1707 E. *Permulta alia colligit Chrysippus ut est in omni historia curiosus,* Cic. *N. D.* I. 45.

27 § **5.** *primi...sequebantur*] Polybius explains why. οἱ μὲν οὖν Ἴβηρες καὶ Λίβυες δι' ἀκεραίων τῶν ἑλῶν ποιούμενοι τὴν πορείαν μετρίως κακοπαθοῦντες ἤνυον. The Spaniards and Africans got on without being much distressed, as the marshes over which they marched were not yet trampled down.

qua modo praeirent duces] 'wherever, that is, the guides led them', the subjunctive owing to the restrictive meaning of *qua modo,* Roby § 1693, though Livy would use *qua* with the subjunctive even if the meaning of *qua* were merely indefinite and not also restrictive. See on *ubi procubuissent,* § 7.

28 *ac profundas*] 'and indeed almost bottomless'. *ac* is often used to subjoin an expression more emphatic than that which has preceded.

29 *inmergentesque se*] 'plunging into the water'. Cf. 6. 6.

tamen] correcting *hausti,* which=*quamvis hausti.* Cf. § 11 and 13. 3 *dubium Hannibalem...tamen moverunt.*

30 § **6.** *sustinere se*] to 'hold up', 'recover themselves'.

31 *corpora...sustinebant*] C. and B. 'without spirit to eke out their strength, without hope to eke out their spirit'. With these words, which express the calling of one faculty to the aid of another, cf. *animum auribus praetendere,* Plin. *Ep.* VII. 27. 8, 'using his mind to stop his ears': of one who fixed his attention on a book that he might not hear a ghost.

Polybius III. 79. 7 adds that they were only kept from retreating by the cavalry which had been charged to look after them.

32 § **7.** *ubi...procubuissent*] Livy and later writers use *ubi, qua, cum,* *utcunque, quicunque,* or the relative with the subjunctive, when the time or place of action is indefinite. The subjunctive is thus often used of repeated action. Cf. 38. 3 *ubi decuriatum convenissent coniurabant*

p. 4.   1 *et ipsa*] sc. 'like themselves'.   1. 18.

4   § 8. *obtinentibus*] 'covering'.

in sicco]   The combination of a preposition and the neuter singular of an adjective used substantivally, generally with some case of *locus* understood, is frequent in Livy. Cf. *in sicco* again in 3. 1: *ex adverso* 4. 4: *ex tuto* 12. 10.

5   *incumbebant*] Pol. III. 79. 10 καθεζόμενοι ἐπ' αὐτῶν (τῶν ὑποζυγίων) καὶ τῶν σκευῶν σωρηδὸν ὑπὲρ τὸ ὑγρὸν ὑπερεῖχον, 'sitting on the bodies of the baggage animals and on piles of baggage they kept above water'.

7   § 9. *acervi*] *iumentorum.*

tantum quod extaret aqua]   The rhythm seems to shew that these words are governed by *quaerentibus* rather than *dabant.*

ad quietem] with *necessarium.*

9   § 10. *aeger oculis*] Pol. l.c. ὑπεραλγὴς ὢν διὰ τὴν βαρύτητα τῆς ἐπενεχθείσης ὀφθαλμίας αὐτῷ, 'being in great pain from the acuteness of the ophthalmia with which he had been attacked'.

primum] can hardly be rendered, unless by 'already', which does not give the meaning quite accurately ; for *primum* really = ' in the first place', and should have been answered by *deinde,* when the sentence would have run thus: *H. aeger oculis primum ex verna intemperie... deinde vigiliis...capitur.* But the clause *elephanto...vectus* is introduced, expressing a step taken to obviate his indisposition, but, as the sequel shews, taken in vain, and therefore the clause which succeeds must be introduced by *tamen,* and *deinde* remains unexpressed.

intemperie] firstly = 'intemperateness'. Thus *intemperies caeli, aquarum* = 'a storm'. Thence it is used alone here for 'bad weather'.

10   *unus*] out of 37, XXI. 58. 11.

12   § 11. *caelo*] 'climate'.

gravante] 'affecting'.

13   *altero oculo*] Pol. ἐστερήθη τῆς μιᾶς ὄψεως. Nepos on the other hand says that only the sight of one eye was weakened. *Hann.* 4.

Cf. Juvenal X. 157:

> *o qualis facies et quali digna tabella*
> *cum Gaetula ducem portaret belua luscum.*

CHAPTER III.

14 § **1.** *foede*] 'ingloriously', as not on the field of battle; or, as is more likely, 'amid horrible misery', C. and B. *foedus* often = 'dreadful' in Livy. Cf. XXI. 36. 7 *taetra ibi luctatio fuit.*

15 *in sicco*] 2. 8.

16 *certum habuit*] = *certior factus est.*

18 *circa*] not necessarily 'all round': we should say 'under'.

20 § **2.** *copias ad commeatus expediendos*] 'the resources which the country offered for obtaining supplies', D.

21 *in rem erat*] 29. 8, 'it was to his purpose': lit. 'it tended towards'. Thus different from *ob rem, ex re esse,* which have a similar meaning.

22 *inquirendo exequebatur*] 'carefully investigated'. This verb is frequently used with abl. of the gerund. VI. 14. 13 *quaerendo.* IX. 3. 11 *percunctando* (D.).

23 § **3.** *Italiae*] depending on *primis,* 'among the most fertile in Italy'. It was less so than the plain of Campania.

Faesulas Arretiumque] The preceding words are not very applicable to the country between Faesulae (Fiesole) and Arretium, which lay along the valley of the Arno. Either Livy has made a mistake in mentioning Faesulae, or he means another place of the same name further south. Cf. on *Faesulas* § 6.

24 *frumenti...pecoris*] These words probably depend on *copia,* like *rerum;* though *opulentus* is also found with a genitive. Hor. *C.* I. 17. 14 *copia ruris honorum opulenta.*

25 § **4.** *consul*] This sentence refers back to *animum* in § 2, as the preceding sentence does to *situm regionum* and *copias.*

ferox] 'bold': the usual meaning of *ferox.*

ab] 'in consequence of'. XXI. 54. 6 *a destinato iam ante consilio avidus certaminis.*

consulatu priore] in 223 B.C. when he had vanquished the Insubres on the Oglio (Mommsen II. 82).

26 *non modo*] = *non modo non;* for if both clauses have a common predicate to which the negative belongs, and the predicate stands in the second clause, the negative which lies in *ne...quidem* may be referred to the whole. Madvig *L. G.* § 461. Cic. *Laelius* 24 *assentatio non moao amico sed ne libero quidem digna est.* In such cases *non modo* is best rendered by 'I do not say', or 'much less'. Cf. 28. 5.

legum] i.e. 'the resolutions of the comitia'. *patrum,* i.e. 'the decrees of the senate'.

maiestatis...deorum...metuens] Weissenborn gives two references to doubtful speeches of Cicero: *Cum senatui* 4, *De Domo* 70. Except for this, *metuens* with a genitive is a poetical constr. Hor. *S.* II. 2. 110 *contentus parvo metuensque futuri.* Juv. VII. 210 *metuens virgae.*

non...satis metuens] 'not much afraid', *satis* having a strong sense when a negative precedes. But the expression is ironical, meaning 'caring very little for'.

28   *prospero successu*] *successus* = 'a happy issue', without the addition of an epithet, which is rare.

civilibus bellicisque rebus] *civilibus* referring to the law which he carried as tribune in 232 B.C. for allotting the territory of the Boii in Picenum to settlers, also to the making of the *via Flaminia* and the *circus Flaminius; bellicis* referring to his victory over the Insubres in his consulship in 223 B.C.

29   *aluerat*] Cf. Tac. *Ann.* XIII. 26 *coalitam libertate irreverentiam,* 'fostered by freedom'.

30   § **5.** *quoque...vitia sua*] 'that he might yield the sooner to his special failings'.

32   § **6.** *Faesulas petens*] If Livy means the place usually known as Faesulae, i.e. the modern Fiesole, he must be mistaken here. Fiesole lies a little way north of Florence, and therefore far north of Arezzo, where Flaminius was; while Livy says that Hannibal passed to the central plain of Etruria, and therefore to the south of Flaminius.

But it is possible that he means another place further to the south. Difficulties arise in other passages over the name Faesulae. Polybius II. 25 says that in 225 B.C. the invading Gauls reached Clusium, and then marched in the direction of Faesulae (ὡς ἐπὶ πόλιν Φαίσολαν) or due N. from Clusium. Yet they are next found at Telamon, the scene of their defeat, which lies S.W. of Clusium. It is possible then that there was another Faesulae in Etruria, further to the S., and that it is to this place that Livy here refers.

Polybius' account is indeed intelligible, without supposing the existence of another Faesulae. He says that it was *from* the neighbourhood of Faesulae that Hannibal started. 'Ως γὰρ θᾶττον ποιησάμενος ἀναζυγὴν ἀπὸ τῶν κατὰ τὴν Φαισόλαν τόπων καὶ μικρὸν ὑπεράρας τὴν τῶν 'Ρωμαίων στρατοπεδείαν ἐνέβαλεν εἰς τὴν προκειμένην χώραν εὐθέως μετέωρος ἦν ὁ Φλαμίνιος κ.τ.λ., 'as soon as he had started from the neighbourhood of Faesulae, and passing a little beyond the Roman army, entered the country which lay before him, Flaminius was straightway seized with perplexity' etc. III. 82. 1.

But if intelligible it is not probable, unless he used the words τῶν κατὰ τὴν Φαισόλαν τόπων very loosely indeed (and it should be observed that this is Polybius' practice when indicating places). It is not probable that Hannibal ascended the Arno valley from the marshes, as he must have done had he gone to Faesulae, because he could hardly have eluded the notice of Flaminius (see on 2. 2 and Appendix I.).

For this reason there is little inducement to adopt D.'s conjecture *praeteriens*. More probably he ascended the Elsa from Empoli and reached the plain where Siena stands, or the Greve further to the E. than the Elsa, and joined the road leading from Florence by San Casciano and the valley of the Clanis (Chiana) and Clusium (Chiusi). In either case he leaves the enemy on his left (*laeva relicto hoste*) and reaches the central plain of Etruria (*medio Etruriae campo*), which he would not have done had he followed the valley of the Arno.

p. 5. 3 § 7. *tum*] like *nunc* and the Greek νῦν δὲ opposes an actual to a supposed state of things.

4 *ferri agique*] cf. 1. 2.

5 *suum...dedecus*] 'a personal disgrace'.

6 *atque*] intensive, 2. 5 note.
Romana] more emphatic than *Romae*.

7 § 8. *omnibus*] an exaggeration. Pol. III. 82. 4 τινῶν οἰομένων.

8 *conlegam*] Servilius, who had been posted at Ariminum.

10 § 9. *interim...cohibendum*] adversative asyndeton.

11 *effusa*] 'unchecked'. Cf. *effuse rapiebant* 9. 3.

12 *itineri pugnaeque*] The command was probably that the army should march *agmine quadrato*, in fighting order.

13 § 10. *immo...sedeamus*] Flaminius ironically affects to adopt and improve upon the cautious suggestions of his advisers. *sedere*=to remain inactive.

15 *vastando...urendo*] The ablative of the gerund is often used by Livy and Tacitus with a meaning more nearly approaching that of a present participle than of an ablative of manner or means: e.g. Tac. *A.* XIV. 31 *exturbabant agris, captivos servos appellando*.

17 *Camillum*] In 390 B.C., when Rome was besieged by the Gauls. According to Livy IX. 4. 67 it was from Ardea to Veii that Camillus was summoned, from Veii he marched to the relief of Rome. But the statement is repeated 14. 11.

19 § 11. *equus...conruit*] These ominous incidents are not mentioned by Polybius, and are probably due to Coelius Antipater. Polybius merely says τέλος δὲ ταῦτ' εἰπών, ἀναζεύξας πρόηγε μετὰ τῆς δυνάμεως.

10 *super caput*] 'over its (the horse's) head'. Plut. *Fab.* 3 renders it wrongly: κατενεχθεὶς ἐπὶ κεφαλήν.

21 **§ 12.** *velut*] indicates that what follows was the opinion of the parties concerned, not that of the writer: 'considering it'.

incipiendae rei] gen. loosely governed by *omen*, 'an ill omen for the beginning of a campaign'. XXI. 29. 4 *omen belli.*

22 *moliente*] sc. *signum*, 'striving to move it', so *ancoras moliri* XXVIII. 17, to hoist up the anchors.

24 **§ 13.** *litteras*] Flaminius alludes to the despatches from the senate recalling him to Rome, which he received just before his victory over the Insubres in 223 B.C. He did not read them till after the battle, XXI. 63. 12.

25 *ad convellendum obtorpuerint*] 'if their hands are too numb with terror to pull it up'. Just so we should render *pauci ad oppugnandum hostem* 'too few to attack the enemy'.

27 **§ 14.** *primoribus*] the officers.

superquam quod]=*praeterquam quod*, 7. 4. Cf. 6. 11 *super cetera=praeter cetera.*

28 *consilio*] Flaminius' design of attacking the enemy.

milite in vulgus] 'the soldiers generally'. 30. 7 *non magis imperatorum quam vulgo militum. in vulgus* 12. 12 has a more literal meaning.

CHAPTER IV.

31 **§ 1.** *Cortonam*] an important town. *A Perusia et Cortona et Arretio quae ferme capita Etruriae populorum ea tempestate erant*, IX. 37 fin. It lay S. of Arretium on the road to Perusia and some 8 miles N. of lake Trasimene.

Trasumennum] Lago di Perugia. ' It is a noble lake in point of size (it is 10 miles from N. to S., 8 from E. to W.), and some of the hills round it are well wooded. Its sides however are reedy, and the air on its banks is unwholesome'. Arnold, *Unpub. Journal*, Second Punic War, ed. W. J. Arnold, p. 385.

With the termination *-ennus*, cf. Sisenna, Porsenna and other Etrurian proper names.

p. 6. 1 *hosti*] cf. *militibus* 1. 8.

3 **§ 2.** *maxime subit*] 'comes close up under . *maxime=proxime. montes Cortonenses*] in particular the Monte Gualandro.

4 *via perangusta*] The defile between Mte Gualandro and the lake, on its N.W. shore, near the village of Borghetto. The road now comes down over the spurs of Gualandro. It appears from this passage that it used to run along the edge of the lake.

5   *id ipsum*] 'that very purpose'. The expression is vague, it means 'the formation of a road'.

6   *paulo latior campus*] E. of the defile just mentioned the hills recede from the lake and there is a plain varying from ½ to 1½ miles in width and about 4 miles in length. About half-way along a wooded hill, on which the village of Tuoro (Torre) now stands, advances into the plain dividing it into two basins of nearly equal size. The line of the hills to the N. of the plain thus resembles the shape of an ancient bow.

7   *inde colles insurgunt*] Vulg. *assurgunt*, P *ad insurgunt. insurgunt* implies a steep, *assurgunt* a gradual ascent. The words may refer to the elevation on which Tuoro stands (see preceding note); but more probably to the point 4 miles E. of the first defile where the hills again approach the lake and form the defile at Passignano, by which the Romans intended to leave the plain. See Appendix II. init.

   § **3.** *ibi*] not *in collibus*, but on the plain at the point where the hills began to rise, at the foot of the pass.

8   *ubi*]=*ut ibi*, hence the subjunctive.

   modo]=*tantum*, 'just'. The *Hispani et Afri* constituted however the most important part of his army.

9   *post montis circumducit*] Hannibal, encamped on the plain to the E. of Tuoro, sent his light-armed W. round to the rear of the hills which bounded the plain on the N., and especially to the hill of Tuoro itself. They were probably just behind the crest of the hills so as to be invisible to the enemy. Pol. ἐπὶ πολὺ παρατείνας ὑπέστειλε, 'placed them under cover'. Cf. § 4 *insidiae.*

10   *ipsas fauces saltus*] at the entrance of the defile (*via perangusta* § 2), near Borghetto, but probably at the E. end of the defile where it opened on to the plain.

14   § **4.** *inexplorato*] this use of the participle, either alone as in *nondum palam facto* 55. 3, *inauspicato* XXI. 63. 7, or with a clause dependent upon it, as in X. 36. 7 *edicto...ut hostem haberent*, is common in Livy and prose-writers of the Imperial times. In Cicero it is of rarer occurrence. In Caesar there are only a few instances (*bipartito, tripartito, consulto*, Draeger) and these without a dependent clause. The word expresses the whole blame attaching to Flaminius, and it is great. That he acted wrongly in pursuing Hannibal does not appear.

satis] 'quite', 3. 4 note.

15 *pandi...coepit*] not *coeptum est*, for *pandi = se pandere*, 'to deploy'.

16 *ex adverso*] the infantry under Hannibal, drawn up *in aperto* and fronting the line of march.

17 *ab tergo*] the cavalry, § 3.

super caput] the light-armed, especially those on the hill of Tuoro, immediately beneath which the Romans were passing.

haud dispectae] P *deceptae* which Madvig retains. Weissenborn *decepere insidiae;* but *decepere = ἔλαθον*, like *fefellere*, is most unusual. It can only be paralleled by Hor. *S.* 1. 3. 39 where the verb is helped out by an adjective, *amatorem quod amicae turpia decipiunt caecum vitia.*

18 § 5. *clausum habuit*] 'had got the enemy shut in'. This combination implies a more lasting effect of the action than *clausit.*

circumfusum copiis] not inconsistent with *clausum lacu ac montibus* just above, which refers to the fact that the Romans had the mountains on one flank, and the lake on the other. *circumfusum* is a picturesque expression, and further *circum, circa* are constantly used by Livy not meaning 'all round', e.g. XXI. 25. 2 *circa Padum.* Polybius however has συνεπιχείρει πανταχόθεν ἅμα τοῖς πολεμίοις. See Appendix II.

9 *simul*] with *invadendi.*

20 § 6. *qua cuique proximum fuit*] 'each man by the nearest way'. Pol. κατὰ πολλοὺς τόπους.

22 *campo...montibus*] Livy is more free than his predecessors in the use of the ablative of place without *in*, 43. 10, 59. 15.

densior] used adverbially.

23 *sederat*] 'had settled'. Parts of *sedeo* are used for the perfects and pluperfects of *sido, sidi* not being used.

inter se] denotes reciprocity. 1. 3 *ipsorum inter se fraude.*

24 *conspecta*] not *erant*, the verb is *decucurrerant,* 'the enemy's troops had a good view of each other before they charged down, and consequently did so better together'. *conspecta* may, but need not necessarily, = *conspicabilia,* cf. 7. 1 *memorata.*

25 § 7. *cerneret*] either absolute 'before he could clearly distinguish anything': cf. Ter. *Ad.* 439 *estne hic Hegio? si satis cerno, is est;* or with *se circumventum esse,* which must then be repeated with *sensit.* In this case the antithesis between *cerneret* and *sensit,* 'seeing' and 'hearing,' becomes more marked.

26 *latera*] The Romans were only being attacked on one flank (the left), for their right flank was covered by the lake, see 5. 6. The

use of the plural is rhetorical, cf. *circumfusum* § 5. Polybius on the other hand says distinctly that the Romans were completely surrounded. III. 84. 3 ἅμα γὰρ κατὰ πρόσωπον, οἱ δ' ἀπ' οὐρᾶς, οἱ δ' ἐκ τῶν πλαγίων αὐτοῖς προσέπιπτον. See App. II.

27 *expediri*] before they could get them clear, or get them ready. On the march the shield was often suspended from the left shoulder, and the helmet by strap from the right.

CHAPTER V.

29 § **1.** *ut in re trepida*] 'considering the confusion of the moment'. For this qualifying use of *ut* cf. Cic. *Fin.* IV. I. 1 *Ne tu ista exposuisti ut tam multa memoriter, ut tam obscura dilucide*, 'considering their number accurately'. *ut* is also used = *ut par erat*, 'as was natural'.

30 *vertente se quoque*] this explains *turbatos*.

ad] 'in the direction of'. They could not see their assailants.

p. **7.** 1 § **2.** *inde*] with *evadendum*, 'they must get out of this'.

2 *deum*] objective gen.

4 *ferme*] 'generally speaking'.

5 § **3.** *consilium...imperium*] referring to *adhortatur...iubet* respectively.

7 *capienda aptandaque pugnae*] 'To seize and put on for the battle'. *pugnae* dat. purpose.

8 *onerati*] Polybius III. 84. 4 διὸ καὶ συνέβη τοὺς πλείστους ἐν αὐτῷ τῷ τῆς πορείας σχήματι κατακοπῆναι. Whence it happened that most of them were cut down just in their marching equipment. See on *expediri* 4. 7.

10 § **4.** *ad*] as in § 1, or merely = 'at'. Juv. XIII. 223 *hi sunt qui trepidant et ad omnia fulgura pallent*.

corporum aut armorum] objective genitives, 'blows falling on body or armour'.

11 *terrentium paventiumque*] lit. of those who were causing or feeling fear: 'the mingled shouts of triumph or panic', C. and B., gives the meaning fairly well. This use of the gen. plur. of the participle when we should put an abstract substantive is common in Livy.

13 § **5.** *haerebant*] 'were brought to a halt'.

15 § **6.** *impetus capti*] sc. *sunt*, not unfrequent in Livy e. g. VIII. 30. 6 *aliquotiens impetu capto. impetum facere* is more common, 6. 4.

16 *a fronte*] The infantry under Hannibal, the same as *id hostium quod ex adverso erat* 4. 4, and 6. 8 *adversos hostes*.

ab tergo] the cavalry and the Gauls, 4. 4.

claudebat] the object is not expressed. Cf. XXI. 43. 3 *dextra laevaque duo maria claudunt.*

18 § **7.** *factus*]=*factus est.*

19 *illa*] properly 'the well known'. 'As usual' would give the meaning.

per] expresses the manner.

principes...triarios] only loosely enumerated, for the *hastati* really formed the first rank, the *principes* the second, in the manipular legion, 340—105 B.C. Or Livy may have made a mistake in speaking of a formation which was no longer in use in his day. Cf. *cohorte* in this section.

20 *ut pugnaret*] this may be called the definitive use of *ut.* It is really an *ut* of consequence, and is often preceded by *ita.* It might be rendered, 'with the advanced guard...fighting'. Cf. 43. 4.

antesignani] 'front rank men', so called because in a battle the standards of the first line which was engaged with the enemy were placed behind the maniples which composed it. Thus *antesignani* generally=the *hastati.* Cf. L. VIII. 11. 7 *caesos hastatos principesque, stragem et ante signa et post signa factam, triarios postremo rem restituisse.* But if necessary the *principes* could take the place of the *hastati* and then they would be *antesignani.* Livy IX. 39. 7 *cadunt antesignani et ne nudentur propugnatoribus signa fit ex secunda prima acies.* Before the time of Marius *signa* always properly means the standards of the maniples. After his time it may=either the *signa cohortium* or the eagles of the legion. Marquardt, *Staats-Verwaltung*, II. 342.

21 *alia*]=*cetera.* This use of *alius*=ὁ ἄλλος occurs not unfrequently in Livy. To give one instance, *Jovem deosque alios* XXVI. 8. 5. An incorrect and colloquial way of speaking, it is avoided by Cicero, but occurs several times in the comedians.

22 *cohorte*] the use of the word in writing of the Second Punic war is an anachronism. Before the time of Marius, 105 B.C., the legion was divided into 30 maniples, after him into 10 cohorts.

§ **8.** *animus*] 'impulse', C. and B., rather 'courage'.

23 *ante aut post*] used adverbially, 'in front or rear'.

pugnandi] with *ordinem*, sc. the post where he was to fight.

24 *animorum...animus*] The occurrence of the same word thrice is probably due rather to carelessness than design. W. refers to VI. 61. 8 where the word *arx* occurs thrice in the same sentence. One MS. gives *armorum* for *animorum.*

25   *motum terrae*] probably from Coelius Antipater, as Cicero refers to him as his authority for the same incident. *Div.* 1. 78.

28   *senserit*] the ordinary sequence would have been *sentiret*. Livy however like Nepos often uses the perf. subj. with a consecutive *ut* after a secondary tense. It is done to give greater liveliness to the narrative, and is analogous to the change from a past tense to the historic present in or. recta.

CHAPTER VI.

30   § 1. *infestior*] 'more savage'.

31   § 2. *eum*] placed first for emphasis, though it is governed by the verb of one clause only. Perhaps originally the sentence was intended to have run thus: *eum et...sequebantur...et...petebant:* but a clause was inserted describing Flaminius' own action, and the clause which should have corresponded to *et sequebantur* is added supplementarily.

    robora virorum] 'the bravest soldiers'. The general had no regular body-guard, *cohors praetoria*, till the time of Scipio Africanus minor.

p. 8. 3 § 3. *Insuber*] Polybius does not give the name of the Gaul or his words. III. 84. 6 ἐν ᾧ καιρῷ καὶ τὸν Φλαμίνιον αὐτὸν...προσπεσόντες τινὲς τῶν Κελτῶν ἀπέκτειναν.

4   *facie quoque*] as well as by his armour, which rendered him conspicuous.

5   *legiones*] Livy constantly applies Roman military terms to foreign armies.

    cecidit...depopulatus] The order of the events is inverted. In 232 B.C. Flaminius, then tribune, passed an agrarian law for placing settlers on the territory of the Senones. As consul in 223 B.C. he defeated the Insubrians N. of the Po, probably on the Oglio, a tributary of that river. XXI. 63. 2. Mommsen, *Hist. Rom.* II. 81. On each of these occasions he had roused the hostility of the *nobiles;* on the first because he deprived them of lands which they had occupied for grazing purposes; on the second because he disregarded a despatch from the senate recalling him to Rome. Dr Arnold says, 'In these last words we probably read the unquenchable hatred of the Roman aristocracy rather than the genuine language of the Gaul'.

6   *urbem*] what city is referred to is uncertain. Mediolanum was taken by Marcellus in 222 B.C.

7   § 4. *peremptorum foede*] Early in his campaign with the Insubres Flaminius was in a dangerous position, with the Po in his rear, from which he only escaped by making a capitulation to secure a free retreat.

He then retired to the territory of the Cenomani, and in conjunction with them returned and gained the victory just alluded to. This the Insubres probably regarded as a breach of the treaty.

9 *infesto venienti*] We should say 'his charge'. For this adverbial use of an adjective cf. 4. 6 *densior sederat.* 7. 13 *maestam sedentem.* It is commoner in poetry. Hor. *S.* 1. 6. 128 *domesticus otior.*

11 *triarii*] the veterans, the third line in the Roman order of battle at this time. Cf. 5, 7 *antesignani*, note.

§ 5. *magnae partis*] as opposed to *sex milia* § 8.

13 *omnia arta praeruptaque*] sc. *loca*, 'by every defile and up every cliff'. Livy often uses neut. plur. adjectives substantivally, especially when they indicate locality.

14 *evadunt*] the present is used here of attempted action.

15 § 6. *pars magna*] Polybius III. 84. 8 describes a similar scene, but this part of his narrative refers only to such of the troops as had not yet emerged from the defile. See Appendix II. οἱ δὲ κατὰ πορείαν μεταξὺ τῆς λίμνης καὶ τῆς παρωρείας ἐν τοῖς στενοῖς συγκλεισθέντες αἰσχρῶς ἔτι δὲ μᾶλλον ταλαιπώρως διεφθείροντο. 'Those who while on the march were shut in in the defile between the lake and the mountain perished disgracefully and still more miserably'.

prima] 'at the edge of the lake'.

16 *quoad...possunt*] i.e. 'till they could *only* keep head and shoulders above water'. Pol. l. c. τὸ δὲ πολὺ πλῆθος μέχρι μὲν τοῦ δυνατοῦ προβαῖνον εἰς τὴν λίμνην ἔμενε τὰς κεφαλὰς αὐτὰς ὑπὲρ τὸ ὑγρὸν ὑπερίσχον, 'with just their heads above water'.

17 *sese inmergunt*] that this = 'immersed', not 'drowned' themselves (C. and B.), appears from Polybius, quoted in the preceding note.

inconsultus pavor] 'wild panic'.

19 § 7. *gurgitibus*] 'the depths'.

21 *trucidabantur*] Polybius adds what Livy suppresses: δεόμενοι ζωγρεῖν καὶ πᾶσαν ἀφιέμενοι φωνὴν τὸ τελευταῖον οἱ μὲν ὑπὸ τῶν πολεμίων τινὲς δὲ παρακαλέσαντες αὐτοὺς διεφθάρησαν, 'Lifting up their hands and begging for quarter and crying aloud in every variety of tone, they were destroyed, some by the enemy, some by their own hands'.

22 § 8. *primi agminis*] 'the vanguard'. Pol. τῶν κατὰ τὸν αὐλῶνα, those engaged in the valley as distinguished from those shut in between the mountains and the lake. But according to Livy the whole army was between the mountains and the lake. See Appendix II.

adversos hostes] the infantry under Hannibal = *id hostium quod ex adverso erat* 4. 4.

23   *ignari*] agreeing with *milia, κατὰ σύνεσιν.* XXI. 21. 13 *quattuor milia...praesidium eosdem et obsides.*

    ignari omnium] Polybius says they pushed on, expecting to meet an enemy to attack till they found themselves to their surprise on the heights above. III. 84. 12.

24   *saltu*] probably, the second defile, at Passignano, as *saltus* 4. 3, = the first defile, at Borghetto.

    tumulo] this might be the hill on which Magione now stands. Pol. *ἐπὶ τῶν ἄκρων.*

27   § **9.** *inclinata re*] 'when the battle was decided'. The metaphor is from the turning of the scales.

    dispulsa nebula] 'the dispersion of the mist'.

28   *aperuisset diem*] 'had allowed daylight to become visible' Cf. 19. 7 *nondum aperientibus classem promuntoriis.*

    liquida iam] opposed to *vixdum certa luce* 4. 4.

30   § **10.** *conspectos*] = *si conspecti essent.*

32   § **11.** *super cetera*] = *praeter cetera.* Cf. 3. 14 *superquam.*

p. 9.   1 *extrema*] with *fames.*

    Maharbale] Polybius states that the 6000 retreated to a village of Etruria (Magione?) which was invested by Maharbal.

4   § **12.** *Punica religione*] XXI. 4. 9 *fides plusquam Punica* of Hannibal.

    fides] Polybius III. 85. 1 adds that all the prisoners, 15,000 in number, were brought before Hannibal, who made them a speech declaring that Maharbal had acted without his sanction in promising to release those who had surrendered, and inveighing ('with the vehemence', says Dr Arnold, 'often displayed by Napoleon under similar circumstances') against the Roman people. He ended by giving the Roman prisoners into the custody of the several divisions of his army. Then he turned to the Italian allies. He had not, he said, come to fight against them, but against the Romans, that they might be free. To prove the truth of his words he dismissed them without a ransom.

5   *atque...coniecti*] The conjunction in one sentence of two coordinate clauses with different nominatives is unusual in Livy, and rather inelegant; but emphatic, and Livy means to be emphatic here.

CHAPTER VII.

6   § **1.** *nobilis*] 'famous', the original meaning of the word, 39. 8.

    inter paucas memorata...clades] *inter paucas memorata* should be taken together. *inter paucas*, an idiomatic expression first used by Livy. Cf. *imprimis.*

7   *memorata*]=*memorabilis.* So *contemptus, invictus,* etc.= 'contemptible', 'invincible'. *clades,* nom. with *populi Romani.*

8   § **2.** *decem milia...petiere*] Polybius says nothing of these. From his account it appears that the whole army, with the exception of the prisoners, was destroyed.

10   § **3.** *duo milia quingenti*] Polybius says only 1500, of whom the majority were Gauls. III. 85. 5.

11   *multi...ex vulneribus*] a statement added, as Ihne suggests (*Hist.* II. 209, note), to soothe the soreness of Italian patriotism.

12   *multiplex*] 'many times as great as this'.

13   *aliis*] probably Valerius Antias, for Livy says (XXXIII. 10. 8), *si Valerio quis credat omnium rerum immodice numerum augenti.*

      § **4.** *auctum ex vano*] 'idly exaggerated'. XXI. 32. 10 *ex aperto atque interdiu,* 'openly'. MSS. *haustum ex vano,* 'drawn from an untrustworthy source'.

14   *quo*] 'to which', i.e. exaggeration.

      scribentium] 'writers'. Cf. Greek οἱ λέγοντες, 'speakers'.

15   *Fabium*] Fabius was, as Livy says, a contemporary of the Second Punic war. He wrote a history of Rome in Greek from the earliest times down to his own. Polybius blames him for partiality to his own countrymen (I. 14), and it seems likely that certain accounts unduly exalting his kinsman the dictator are due to him. Cf. the variations just noticed between his account and that of Polybius. See Introd.

      temporibus] dat. governed by *aequalem,* and governing *huiusce belli. aequalis* is however also used with a genitive.

16   § **5.** *captivorum*] partitive genitive depending on *iis,* the unexpressed antecedent to *qui.* Hannibal addressed them. See on 6. 12.

      qui...essent] the subjunctive because the persons are indefinite; 'whoever were of the Latin name'.

19   *sepeliri*] only the most illustrious. Polybius III. 85. 5 τοὺς ἐπιφανεστάτους ἔθαψεν, ὄντας εἰς τριάκοντα τὸν ἀριθμόν.

      Flamini corpus] 'So he acted afterwards to L. Aemilius and to Marcellus; and these humanities are worthy of notice, as if he wished to shew that, though his vow bound him to unrelenting enmity towards the Romans while living, it was a pleasure to him to feel that he might honour them when dead'. Arnold III. Such conduct is hardly consistent with the estimate of Hannibal's character given by Livy (XXI. 4. 9), who enumerates among his qualities *inhumana crudelitas.*

21   § **6.** *ad*] 'at'. XXI. 61. 4 *ad famam novorum hostium.* Cf. § 13.

22   *populi*] depends on *concursus.*

23 § **7.** *repens*] an adjective (= *repentina*), used adverbially. Cf. 8. 1;
21, 6.

24 *frequentis contionis modo*] describing *turba*, 'a crowd as thick as a
thronged assembly', C. and B. *modo* indicates that this was not a
formally summoned assembly. Polybius however says οἱ προεστῶτες τοῦ
πολιτεύματος συναθροίσαντες τὸν δῆμον εἰς ἐκκλησίαν.

25 *comitium*] the part of the Forum nearest to the Capitol and the
Curia; so called because it was the meeting-place of the *comitia centu-
riata*.

27 § **8.** *praetor*] *peregrinus* : M. Aemilius was *praetor urbanus*, 33. 8;
he was also in the city, § 14.

pugna magna] Plutarch, *Fabius*, 3 νενικήμεθα μεγάλῃ μάχῃ καὶ διέ-
φθαρται τὸ στρατόπεδον καὶ Φλαμίνιος ὕπατος ἀπόλωλεν.

30 § **9.** *caesum*] sc. *caesum esse*, governed by *referunt* which = *nuntiant*.

31 § **10.** *quot...tot*] for instance, a mother not knowing whether her
son had been slain or captured, or whether he was flying for his life
through Etruria, would imagine him now in one of these situations, now
in another.

32 *in curas distracti*] we should say 'distracted *by* anxieties'.

p. **10.** 3 *satis*] 'nor was anyone quite certain'. *satis* generally has this
strong meaning when preceded by an actual or virtual negative.

4 § **11.** *postero*] sc. *die.*

deinceps aliquot diebus] 'on several successive days'. The adverb
is used here instead of an adjective or relative clause.

7 *utique ab notis*] 'at least from such of the arrivals as they knew'.
utique = *saltem*. The addition of *que* gives indefiniteness to the meaning
of *uti* (cf. *quicunque* etc.), and the compound = 'anyhow'. (1) Without
a negative it = 'at least'. Cic. *Att.* XIII. 48. 2 *velim Varronis et Lollii
mittas laudationem, Lollii utique*, 'anyhow' i.e. 'at least' that of Lollius.
(2) With a negative it = 'certainly not'. L. II. 59. 4 *concurrunt ad eum
legati monentes ne utique experiri vellet imperium*, 'that anyhow he
should not aspire to supreme power', i.e. certainly not.

8 § **12.** *inde*] of time, of place 5. 2.

9 *cerneres*] 'you might have seen'. Gk. ἦν ἰδεῖν. **46.** 4 *crederes.*

10 *gratulantis...consolantis*] governed like *vultus* by *cerneres*. Polybius'
account is not so graphic, nor does he give the anecdotes which
follow. He only says, 'the Romans long unused to defeat shewed
neither moderation nor dignity under their reverse of fortune'. οὐ μετρίως οὐδὲ κατὰ σχῆμα τὴν περιπέτειαν ἔφερον, III. 85. 9.

11   *gaudia*] 'manifestations of joy'. So *luctus*.
14   § **13**. *maestam*] used adverbially. Cf. 4. 6.
      ad] § 6, *ad primum nuntium* note.
16   § **14**. *praetores*] since 227 B.C. four in number. In 217 B.C. they
were Aemilius and Pomponius, *pr. urbanus* and *peregrinus* (see on § 8
praetor), and two more, Otacilius and Mammula, afterwards employed
in Sicily and Sardinia.

CHAPTER VIII.

19   § **1**. *satis certa*] 'quite settled', see on *satis* 7. 10. *priusquam* is a
virtual negative, for the meaning is the same as would be conveyed by
cum nondum certa essent.
      priusquam...essent] Livy and Tacitus use the subjunctive with
antequam, *priusquam*, *donec*, of events in the past. Tac. *H.* IV. 35 *pugnatum donec proelium nox dirimeret*.
      repens] see on 7. 7.
21   *propraetore*] He was not one of the praetors of 218 B.C., but probably a legate of Servilius with this title.
      missa ad conlegam ab Servilio] Servilius had been originally posted
at Ariminum (Pol. III. 77. 2, 86. 1) to guard the Flaminian road
and prevent the advance of Hannibal down the eastern coast of Italy.
When it appeared that Hannibal was advancing through Etruria, Servilius resolved to effect a junction with his colleague. Polybius says III.
86. 3 πᾶσι μὲν ἐπεβάλετο τοῖς στρατοπέδοις αὐτὸς συνάπτειν. The plan of
the consuls may have been that Servilius should march rapidly along the
Flaminian road from Umbria and throw himself between Hannibal and
Rome.   The Carthaginians would thus have found themselves between
the army of Servilius in front and that of Flaminius in the rear.   (Ihne,
II. 204.)
22   *in Umbria...circumventa*] from the words *quo...iter* it appears that
they had already reached Etruria when the news of the battle reached
them.   They had followed the Flaminian road (Nissen, *Rhein. Museum*,
XX. 228), and had probably left it at Mevania to turn to the right
towards Perusia.
      Neither Polybius nor Livy mention the exact spot where the disaster
took place. Appian put it at a lake called Pleistine, otherwise unknown. Nissen thinks that the lake Pleistine, like several lakes that
existed formerly in central Italy, is now dried up, and that its bed is
to be recognized in the valley of Pistia on the road from Foligno to

Camarino. This theory is consistent with the view expressed in the
preceding note.

24   *circumventa*] Pol. adds that it was Maharbal with the light-armed
and some cavalry that was sent against them, that half the Romans were
slain at the first onset, and that the remainder were pursued to a hill
where they surrendered the next day. III. 86. 4.

26   § **2.** *ex conparatione*] 'by comparison', *ex* properly = ' in consequence
of'. *priorum* an ordinary objective gen. and not what Roby calls a genitive of the remoter object, for it represents an accusative governed by
comparare (on comparing the former disaster with it), Roby § 1312, not
an ablative with *cum* (on comparing it with the former disaster). Roby
§ 1318.

27   § **3.** *per*] expresses the standard of comparison.

28   *adfecto*] 'weakened'. *adficere* is more often used with an adverb as
in the preceding section.

p. 11. 1 § **4.** *incideret*] Madvig's alteration for P *inciderit*, perhaps
unnecessary, for the change from secondary to primary sequence is not
uncommon in Livy.

2   *magnitudine...viribus*] the ablatives express the standard of comparison.

extenuatis] stronger than *attenuatis*. It is used to express the shrink-
ing of the sacred lots, XXI. 62. 5.

quod adgravaret] the object is *vires*, 'nothing which placed any
additional strain on their strength'. *adgravare* is not used intransitively.

3   *aestimandum esse*] governed by some verb of saying suggested by
aestimare, or else by *ducere.*

4   § **5.** *iam diu...adhibitum*] the last *dictator rei gerendae causa* A.
Atilius Calatinus had been appointed 32 years before, in 249 B.C. during
the first Punic war, after the defeat of P. Claudius Pulcher and Junius
Pullus at Drepana. Dictators had however been appointed for merely
ceremonial purposes.

5   *et...nec*] notice the method of linking a positive and a negative statement.

7   § **6.** *nec dictatorem...poterat*] These words should probably be
omitted. Weissenborn and Wölfflin however retain them, reading
praetor for *populo*. The letters *pr.* (*praetor*) are often confused with *p. r.*
(*populus Romanus*). That the praetor could not choose a dictator is
certain, though he may have presided at the election when a dictator
was elected by the people.

dictatorem] Vulg. *prodictatorem.* Cf. 31. 11. But Livy is here probably following the writers whom he criticizes there. For he uses *dictator* again 9. 7. Further, it appears from *C. I. L.* I. 228. 435 that Fabius' title actually was Dictator.

10 *Maximum*] Livy IX. 46. 13 says Fabius' grandfather received this cognomen for his services, Pol. III. 83. 6 that Fabius acquired it himself.

13 § **7.** *pontes*] probably the bridges over the Nar, Tiber, and Anio.

14 *dimicandum esse*] governed by a verb of saying suggested by *negotium datum.*

  quando]=*quandoquidem,* frequent in Livy.

CHAPTER IX.

15 § **1.** *Umbriam*] Hannibal must have passed Perusia and crossed the Tiber, the boundary between Etruria and Umbria. To reach Spoletium he would follow the course of the Clitumnus, which flows into the Tiber from the S.W.

  Spoletium] (*Spoleto*) a Latin colony.

18 § **2.** *repulsus*] This unsuccessful attack is not mentioned by Polybius ; probably the inhabitants did no more than close their gates. Arnold III. 94. In the guildhall of Spoleto however is a mutilated inscription : *Populus signa vovit...tribusque dedicavit...quum Annibal L. Carsulio... C.*

19 *haud nimis prospere*] The readings of P, C, M, *minue, minu', minus,* seem to point to *minus. nimis* is given in later MSS. Madvig objects to the litotes 'none too prosperously' as pointless, and reads *haud maximae minime prospere temptatae.*

20 *moles*] in its metaphorical sense, 'difficulty', i. e. of besieging. XXI. 27. 5 *Hispani sine ulla mole...tranavere,* cf. XXI. 41. 3. W. quotes *tantae molis erat Romanam condere gentem.*

  § **3.** *agrum Picenum*] the adj. is generally *Picens, Picenum* being used as a substantive. Hannibal thus struck right across Italy to the E.

22 *praeda*] cf. Silius, *Pun.* VI. 647 *tum Palladios se fundit in agros, Picenum dives praedae.*

  effuse] 'without restraint' cf. 3. 9.

23 *rapiebant*] Polybius says Hannibal commanded his troops to kill all males of serviceable age whom they met on the march (φονεύειν τοὺς ὑποπίπτοντας τῶν ἐν ταῖς ἡλικίαις III. 86. 1). This is improbable, as it would have deterred the Italians from joining Hannibal, cf. 7, 5 note. Perhaps however the statement refers only to the Roman owners of

domain land, and settlers, of which latter there would have been many in consequence of the law of Flaminius passed in 232 B.C.

§ **4.** *ibi*] near the coast. Pol. III. 88. 1 ἐνδιέτριβε τῇ παρὰ τὸν Ἀδρίαν χώρᾳ. Hence he sent messengers by sea to Carthage with news of his achievement, which was received with exultation, ibid. 87. **4.**

stativa] *castra*, 'a fixed camp'. Pol. further mentions that Hannibal now armed the African infantry with the short swords and large shields of the Roman legionaries (III. 87. 3), many of which had been taken from the enemy.

25   *ad*] the force of the preposition is exactly given by 'as regards'.

adfectus] 'exhausted', 8. 3 *in adfecto corpore*, note. Both horses and men suffered from a kind of skin disease (called by Pol. λιμόψωρος) perhaps scurvy, to cure which Hannibal had the former washed in the old wines of the country (ib. 88. 1).

26   § **5.** *praeda...gaudentibus*] governed by *datum*. The words imply that a short rest was sufficient.

27   *Praetutianum Hadrianumque agrum*] both in the S. of Picenum. Praetutia was on the Balinus N. W. of Hadria. Hadria was a Roman burgess colony, founded 289 B.C., and situated, as before the Second Punic war the Roman burgess colonies always were, on the sea.

28   *Marsos Marrucinos Paelignos*] These were all Sabellian peoples; but while the Marrucini lived near the sea on the lower Aternus, the Marsi and Paeligni dwelt farther inland, the Marsi round the lake Fucinus, the Paeligni about Sulmo and Corfinium. It is more likely that Hannibal followed the coast road, and Polybius is probably right in mentioning the Frentani (III. 88. 4) instead of the Marsi and Marrucini. The Frentani inhabited the coast between Picenum and Apulia.

29   *devastat*] the word applies of course to the territories of the peoples mentioned.

circa]=*quae erant circa.* **7.** 11 *deinceps diebus.*

Arpos] in the N. of Apulia. Polybius III. 88. 6 says the place where he was actually encamped was Vibinum, which was some way to the S.W.

Luceriam] due W. of Arpi. It was made into a Latin colony 314 B.C. during the second Samnite war.

Apuliae] governed by *regionem.*

30   § **6.** *Servilius*] see on 8. 1, 3. 8. Polybius does not mention these engagements.

31   *ignobilis*] 'inconsiderable', cf. **7.** 1 *nobilis.*

p. 12. 1 *moenibus metuens*] 'fearing for the walls'. Verg. *G.* I. 86 *inopi metuens formica senectae*. Contrast with this the meaning of *metuens* with gen. 3. 4.

4 § **7.** *Fabius*] Polybius, a philosopher and freethinker, alludes to these ceremonies briefly. Φάβιος μετὰ τὴν κατάστασιν θύσας τοῖς θεοῖς.

iterum] he had been *dictator comitiorum habendorum causa* before, in 221 B.C., as had others, though there had been no *dictator rei gerendae causa* for 32 years, see on 8. 5.

7 *inscitia*] ignorance of tactics, 'bad generalship'.

9 § **8.** *non ferme*] 'hardly ever'.

taetra] 'dreadful'. Cf. *foede* 3. 1.

10 *libros Sibyllinos*] see on 1. 16.

12 § **9.** *foret*] used by Livy as a mere synonym for *esset;* in other classical writers only where it represents *ero* in or. recta, or expresses an unfulfilled condition. Cicero and Caesar avoid *forem* altogether.

13 § **10.** *ludos magnos*] also called Maximi, Circenses, and Romani. Instituted by Tarquinius Priscus; they were celebrated in honour of the *di magni,* Jupiter, Juno and Minerva. The games consisted of athletic contests and chariot races. They lasted originally for one day but eventually for six.

14 *Veneri Erucinae*] so called from her famous temple on Mt Eryx in Sicily. The adjective is used as a name of the goddess, Hor. *Carm.* I. 2. 33 *sive tu mavis Erycina ridens*.

Menti] Ov. *Fasti*, VI. 241 *Menti delubra videmus vota metu belli perfide Poene tui*.

15 *supplicationem lectisterniumque*] see on 1. 15 and 18.

ver sacrum] What this was is explained in 10. 3 sqq. It was an old Sabellian custom. In early times the children born during the appointed time were also dedicated to the gods. Originally they were sacrificed. Later they forfeited their citizenship, and were obliged to leave their native place on reaching manhood. It was in this fashion that the Sabellian race spread over the centre of the peninsula.

19 § **11.** *pontifices*] these, since the *Lex Ogulnia*, 300 B.C., eight in number, had the control of religious affairs in general at Rome.

CHAPTER X.

24 § **2.** *in haec verba*] 'after', or as we should say, 'in this form'; cf. *in hunc modum*.

25 *velitis iubeatis*] 'Is it your will and pleasure?' XXI. 17. 4 *latum inde ad populum vellent iuberent...bellum indici*. An asyndeton of this

kind is archaic. Hence it often occurs in legal and religious language, e. g. *sarta tecta, Jupiter optimus maximus.*

26 *Quiritium*] a genitive of that in which the thing consists, Roby § 1302. The whole expression means the Roman nation, as opposed to other nations, consisting of the burgesses, as opposed to other classes of the community. *Quirites* has been derived from Cures a Sabine town, L. I. 13. 5; and it has been thought that *Quirites, Quirinalis* etc. are words indicative of a Sabine element in the nation. A more probable derivation is *quiris* a spear. Cf. the connexion between Sabini (Safini) and Σαύνιον, a javelin.

27 *duellis*] an old form of *bellum* surviving in *perduellis.*

29 *tum*] commences the apodosis.

30 *duit*]=*det,* archaic. Cf. *creduis, perduint,* common in Plautus.

31 § **3.** *quaeque profana erunt*] the clause contains a reservation = 'provided they be not already consecrated'. One would have expected *quodque profanum erit,* as the clause corresponds to *quod ver adtulerit;* but as it occurs after the enumeration of the different kinds of victims the plural is substituted.

p. **13.** 1 *Iovi fieri*]=*sacrificari.* Cic. *Att.* I. 13. 3 *cum pro populo fieret.* Cf. *faciet* in the next section. The infinitive is added to explain *donum duit,* the meaning being *ut sacrificentur.* Livy would not use such a construction himself. He is quoting from the *Annales pontificum.*

ex qua die...iusserit] 'on and after the day appointed'. The vow was not always carried out immediately; in this case not till the year 195 B.C. (C.).

2 § **4.** *faciet*] *facere:* to sacrifice. Cf. Gk. ῥέζειν. Verg. *E.* III. 77 *cum faciam vitulo pro frugibus.*

lege] = *modo.*

quo] = *quocunque.*

3 *faxit*] fut. perf. *facio,* an old future formed by adding *so* to the stem. I. 18. 9 *adclarassis,* ib. 24. 8 *defexit,* cf. *clepsit* below.

probe] 'duly'.

4 § **5.** *profanum esto*] 'it is to be regarded as never having been consecrated'.

rumpet] 'injure'. *rumpere* was frequently used in early Latin = *corrumpere.* C.

5 *fraus*]=*damnum,* 'let him not suffer for it'. *Si plus minusve secuerunt se (sine) fraude esto,* XII. Tabb.

clepsit...cleptum erit] fut. perf. act. and pass. of the archaistic *clepere,* which belongs to the same root as κλέπτειν.

scelus] 'guilt'.

6   *cui*] dat. incommodi.

§ **6.** *atro die*] 'an evil day'. A day on which no sacrifices could be offered. Such were the days after the Kalends, Nones and Ides and the anniversaries of great national disasters, such as the defeat on the Allia (VI. 1. 12).

8   *antidea*] archaistic for *antea* as *antidhac* for *antehac.* Other prepositions have lost a final *d*, which sometimes survives in composition. Cf. *re, se* (in *semovere, secernere*) with *red- itio, sed- itio.*
    ac] = *quam.*

9   *faxitur*] fut. pass. = *factum erit.* Cf. *iussitur,* Cic. *Leg. Agr.* V. 71: *turbassitur, de leg.* III. 4, both in citations from laws.

    eo] governed by *solutus,* 'therefrom': i. e. the sacrifice, or rather the obligation to offer it.

10   § **7.** *ludi magni*] see on 9. 10.

    aeris] i.e. *assium.* The *as,* which before 269 B.C. weighed nominally 12 oz. (really 10) and was worth 2½*d.*, was now, in 217 B.C., depreciated to $\frac{1}{24}$ of its original weight and value. Plin. *N. H.* XXXIII. 45 *Q. Fabio Maximo dictatore asses unciales facti;* but for religious purposes the old system was long adhered to. *Aeris* here then means *libral asses* (*aes grave*). As they were no longer struck they were represented by an equivalent in the silver coinage, the sestertius (= 2½*d.*).

11   *Iovi*] *fieri votum est* must be understood.

    trecentis] Odd numbers in general were supposed to be pleasing to the gods (*numero deus inpare gaudet*), and three in particular was a sacred number.

13   § **8.** *supplicatio*] see on 1. 15.

15   *quos in aliqua...cura*] 'who as they were pretty well off themselves, took some thought for the country as well'. People, that is, who had 'a stake in the country'. *publica* = *reipublicae.*

17   § **9.** *decemviris sacrorum*] the same as the custodians of the Sibylline books, 9. 8.

    pulvinaria] cushioned couches, on which the images of the gods were placed, on the occasion of a *lectisternium.*

21   § **10.** *aedes*] the temples mentioned in 9. 10.

CHAPTER XI.

25   § **1.** *deque re publica rettulit*] cf. 1. 5.

29   § **2.** *scriberet*] = *conscriberet.*

p. 14. 1 § 3. *duas legiones*] Polybius III. 88. 7 says Fabius 'started from the city with the *four* legions that had been enrolled'. But Fabius had only four legions in Apulia (27. 10) after he had received two from Servilius. Probably two of the newly enrolled legions were left at Rome. These legions were used to man the fleet sent out under Servilius, and replaced by extraordinary levies. §§ 7—9.

3 *Tibur...edixit*] *edixit* governs *diem ad conveniendum* directly. Tibur, the name of the place where they were to meet, is added, governed by *conveniendum*.

4 § 4. *ut quibus...uti*] The repetition of *ut* occurs several times in Livy, generally in statements of a formal character; in a proclamation, as here; a prayer (V. 21. 5); or a decree of the senate (XXXVII. 50. 6). [These and other reff. are given by W.]

castella] places smaller than *oppida*, like the *fora* and *conciliabula* often mentioned, 'stations'. *castellum* comes from the same root as *castrum* and *casa*, the meaning of which is, 'to cover'.

inmunita] adj. = *non munita. inmunire,* Tac. *A.* XI. 19 = 'to fortify'.

6 *regionis*] with *omnes*, 'all belonging to that region'.

8 § 5. *via Flaminia*] Servilius was advancing from the North along the same road. Made by Flaminius in his censorship in 220 B.C. the *via Flaminia* was the main connection between Rome and the N.E. of Italy. It ran through Etruria to Ocriculum, thence through Umbria to Ariminum.

exercitu] dat. 2. 1 *dilectu.*

9 *Ocriculum*] the most southern town in Umbria, on the Tiber a few miles below its junction with the Nar at Interamna. Consistently with this Polybius says III. 88. 8 συμμίξας ταῖς ἀπ' Ἀριμίνου βοηθούσαις δυνάμεσι περὶ τὴν Ναρνίαν (an almost certain emendation, adopted in the Teubner text, for the MSS. Δαυνίαν).

prospexisset] 'saw in the distance'.

10 *viatorem*] 'an apparitor'. In later times the civil magistrates only (those with *potestas*) had *viatores*, the military magistrates (those with *imperium*) *lictores.* But Livy mentions the *viatores* of the consuls VI. 15.

12 § 6. *ingentem*] part of the predicate, 'impressive'.

13 *vetustate*] ablative of cause. For the fact see on 8. 5.

15 *Ostia*] generally declined as a neut. plur. of the 2nd declension.

16 *portum Cosanum*] Cosa, a harbour on the Etrurian coast, where the Mons Argentarius forms a bay, since closed up. The fleet had

probably intended to coast along by Cosa, Pisa, and Massilia to
Emporiae, which, along with Tarraco, the Romans used as their
harbour in Spain.

19   § **7.** *milite*] what soldiers? see on § 3.

navalibus sociis] seamen, as opposed to *classici* (here *miles*) the
marines. They were so called because, originally, the fleet being
of small account, only allies were employed in this capacity.

21   § **8.** *libertini*] This was quite exceptional. Not till the time
of Marius, during the social war, 89 B.C., when military service had
ceased to be regarded as a privilege, were emancipated slaves and their
children employed in this capacity.

quibus...essent] 'such of them as had children'. A subjunctive
of indefiniteness. Here the person is indefinite. The *libertini* with
children took precedence of the others by virtue of their children,
because the latter were *ingenui,* sons of free men.

aetas militaris] between 17 and 46.

23   § **9.** *alii*]=*ceteri.* This incorrect use of *alius*=ὁ ἄλλος is rare in
writers of the best period, but occurs not unfrequently in Livy and the
writers who succeed him.

CHAPTER XII.

26   § **1.** *Tibur*] he went along the *Via Valeria*, which runs in an
easterly direction from Rome.

quo] *conveniendum* governs *quo* as it does *Tibur* in 11. 3. *edixerat*
governs *diem.*

28   § **2.** *Praeneste*] i.e. to the S.E. of Tibur. It was on a hill 18 miles
from Rome, at the extremity of the *via Praenestina*, which lay between
the *via Valeria* and the *via Latina.*

transversis limitibus] 'cross-paths'. *limes* (which = *lic-mes* and belongs
to the same root as *limen, limus, obliquus*) means properly a line drawn
across; a line, whether it be a boundary line (*partiri limite campum*
Verg. *G.* I. 126), a line of fortifications (*limite acto promotisque praesidiis*
Tac. *Germ.* 29), or the line of a road or path, as here. Cf. 15. 11 *Appiae
limite.*

30   *exploratis*] a contrast to Flaminius. Cf. *inexplorato* 4. 4.

ducit] sc. *exercitum*, 'marches'. Cf. *movit* 1. 2, and note.

nullo...commissurus] 'not intending to trust himself'.

31   *cogeret*] the subjunctive, because the occasion is indefinite. See on
essent 11. 8, 'Except in so far as he was compelled at any time by
necessity'.

p. 15. 1 § 3. *quo primum die*] 'on the very first day'.

haud procul Arpis] Hannibal was already in the neighbourhood, 9. 5. Polybius III. 88. 9 says Fabius encamped near Aecae, περὶ τὰς Αἴκας καλουμένας, which lay S.W. of Arpi, while Hannibal was at Vibinum, due S. of Aecae. See on 9. 5.

2 *nulla mora facta, quin educeret*] we should say 'Hannibal lost no time...in marching out'. For *mora quin* cf. XXI. 50. 11 *nihil cunctandum visum quin...peteret.*

3 *Poenus*] the Carthaginian general.

5 § 4. *quidem*] concessive. Although he taunted them he still returned.

illos] Haupt's correction for *quos* P, for which *suos* has been read. Cf. *sua vitia* 3. 5.

Martios] in allusion to Mars being their national god. XXXVIII. 17. 18 *vobis...Martiis viris*, 'sons of Mars'.

6 *concessum de virtute*] 'they had yielded in the contest of valour'. Cic. *Att.* XII. 47. 2 *de cupiditate nemini concedam.*

7 § 5. *tacita cura*] Livy imputes such a feeling to Hannibal in order to glorify Fabius. So in Silius Italicus he complains to his brother, on a later occasion, *Fabius me noctibus aegris, in curas Fabius nos excitat. Pun.* VII. 305. Polybius says simply χρόνον δέ τινα μείνας, οὐδενὸς ἐπεξιόντος αὖθις ἀνεχώρησεν εἰς τὴν ἑαυτοῦ παρεμβολὴν (camp), III. 89. 1.

8 *Flamini Semproniqué*] P *Flaminio Sempro{nio}que. similis* with the dat. implies similarity of appearance, with the gen. similarity of nature.

12 § 6. *hauddum*]=*nondum*, a combination found in Livy alone.

13 *in oculis*] 'before his eyes'.

agros sociorum] with Flaminius the same tactics had been but too successful, 3. 7. Livy, doubtless following Fabius Pictor, is careful to point the contrast between the aristocratic and the popular general.

15 § 7. *si*]=εἰ πως, 'in hopes that'.

16 *occultus*] cf. 7. 13 *maestam sedentem.*

17 § 8. *ut neque omitteret*] 'neither losing touch of him nor' etc. For the use of *ut* cf. 5. 7 note.

19 *cogerent*] cf. *cogeret* § 2 note.

pabulum petebant] Polybius says more than this: οὐδέποτε τοὺς στρατιώτας ἤφιει προνομεύειν, οὐδὲ χωρίζεσθαι καθάπαξ ἐκ τοῦ χάρακος, 'he never allowed his soldiers to forage, nor to leave the entrenchments at all'. III. 90. 2.

21 § 9. *statio*] 'a picket'.

22   *infesta*] 'dangerous'. The word is often used in a passive sense. It is in form a passive participle (*in-fendo*).

effusis] 'scattered'. More literal than in 3. 9 and 9. 3.

24   § **10**. *parva momenta levium certaminum*] lit. 'small results of petty conflicts'. *momentum* (*movimentum*) = the impulse which turns the scale. Greek ῥοπή. Cf. Lucan's *momentumque fuit mutatus Curio rerum*. XXI. 4. 2, 43. 11. We should say 'small and unimportant conflicts'.

ex tuto] 'safely'. 15. 5.

26   *minus paenitere*] i.e. 'and have more confidence in'. Lit. 'and be less dissatisfied with', a meaning often borne by *paenitere*. Cic. *off.* I. 1. 2 *tam diu velle debebis* (*discere*) *quoad te quantum proficias non paeniteat*, 'as long as you are not dissatisfied with your progress'.

27   *paenitere*] is not used personally by the best writers, though the gerund is sometimes found. Madvig, *Lat. Gr.*, 218. 3.

§ **11**. *non magis quam*] 'not more...than': here = 'not so much... as'. So οὐ μᾶλλον ἤ is often used in Greek.

29   *imperio*] ablative of respect. As master of the horse he was of course Fabius' subordinate.

morae] i.e. *morae esse*. *morae* is a predicative dative. The construction and the use of *morae ad* are both the same as in XXI. 45. 9 *id morae, quod nondum pugnarent, ad potienda sperata rati, proelium uno animo et voce una poscunt*.

31   § **12**. *in vulgus*] 'with a view to', i.e. for the benefit of, 'the common soldiers', 3. 14 note.

p. **16**.   1   *adfingens*] 'fastening on him'.

2   *premendo*] = *deprimendo*, 'depreciating him'. Pol. III. 90. 6 τὸν Φάβιον κατελάλει πρὸς πάντας, 'he talked against Fabius to everybody'.

CHAPTER XIII.

5   § **1**. *ex Hirpinis in Samnium*] Livy does not mention Hannibal's entry into the territory of the Hirpini. We heard of him last as being in the neighbourhood of Arpi 12. 3, and according to Polybius (see note on 12. 3) encamped at Vibinum. These places are in Apulia.

The Hirpini were properly Samnites like the Caraceni, Pentri and Caudini; but the Romans, in pursuance of their policy of *divide et impera*, had separated the Ager Hirpinus from the rest of Samnium. The part of Samnium entered was the territory of the Caudini, in which Beneventum and Telesia were situated.

Beneventanum agrum] Beneventum was situated on the Calor, and on the Appian way, which now extended from Rome to Venusia. It was a Roman Colony, founded 268 B.C., and fortified; hence Hannibal did not attempt to take it.

6   *Telesiam*] the birthplace of Pontius the hero of the Second Samnite war. It was now unfortified, but full of all sorts of stores. Pol. III. 90. 9. Its position was a little N. of Beneventum, in the valley of the Calor.

7   *si forte*] εἴ πως. Cf. *si* 12. 7.

9   *aequum*] 'in the plain '. *Fabius per loca alta agmen ducebat* 12. 8.

11   § **2.** *dimissi*] cf. 7. 5.

12   *Campani equites*] The *equites* were the aristocracy of Campania, to whom the Romans had given special privileges because they did not join in the Latin war. They had the *civitas* and were allowed to exact 450 denarii a year each (they were 1600 in number when this privilege was given them, 339 B.C.) from the rest of the Campanian people. Livy VIII. 11. 5.

13   *iam tum*] at the time of their release.

16   § **3.** *Capuae potiendae*] *potior* with acc. is mostly ante- and post-classical. Not in Cicero. XXI. 45. 9 *ad potienda sperata*.

    maior quam auctores] lit. 'greater than its authors'. The meaning is 'too important to be undertaken on their authority alone'.

17   *dubium*] the causal clause *cum res maior esset* explains *dubium* and not *moverunt*. See Introd. II.

    alternis] adverbial, 'alternately'.

18   *moverunt*] Polybius says nothing of the Campanian knights. He describes Hannibal's motives thus: 'He was persuaded that he would either compel the enemy to fight, or make it clear to all that he was master of the situation, and so the allies would hasten to revolt from Rome'. III. 90. 11.

19   § **4.** *etiam atque etiam*] with *promissa*, 'their repeated promises'. 42. 4 *Paulus etiam atque etiam dicere providendum.*

    Madvig thinks *etiam atque etiam* belong to *monitos*, and reads *monitos etiam atque etiam ut*. The sense is better, but the change hardly necessary. Madvig seems to think the words must belong either to *monitos* or *adfirmarent*, while there is no reason why they should not go with *promissa*. Wlf. brackets *ut*.

    rebus] 'deeds'. Often opposed to *verba* and the like: e.g. XXI. 42. 1 *Hannibal rebus prius quam verbis adhortandos milites ratus.*

20   *aliquibus*] *aliquis* is more usual.

principum] not technical, 'leading men'.

21   § **5**. *agrum Casinatem*] It is probable that Livy has made a mistake here, and that Hannibal had all along intended to go to Casilinum, not Casinum. Casinum was in Latium, whereas H. intended to march into Campania. See § 3 fin. and Pol. III. 90. 10 ὥρμησε τολμηρῶς εἰς τὰ περὶ Καπύην πέδια. Casinum was on the Latin road only, and therefore not so good a position for preventing the Romans from bringing help to their allies (see this section) as Casilinum, which was at the point where the Latin and the Appian ways meet. If Casinum was the place to which H. intended to go, and the guide's mistake consisted in thinking that Casilinum was the object of the march, the latter would never have ascended the Vulturnus from its junction with the Calor, which was well on the way to Casinum, nor reached Casilinum by so roundabout a route as that by Cales.

No; the case was probably this. Hannibal wished to go to Casilinum; but the guide thought he said Casinum. Accordingly he ascended the Vulturnus as far as Allifae. But when H. found that he was still under the mountains of Samnium his suspicions were aroused. The mistake was discovered, and the army turning S. proceeded to its original destination. See Neumann, *Pun. Krieg.* 344. The story is indeed unlikely. Ihne condemns it as a camp anecdote; but this is the only form in which it could have gained currency.

24   § **6**. *Punicum...os*] The meaning is that Hannibal, or whoever instructed the guide, could not pronounce the name of the town distinctly, and so the latter misunderstood him. Plut. *Fabius* 6 (οἱ ὁδηγοὶ) τῆς φωνῆς διὰ βαρβαρισμὸν οὐκ ἐξακούσαντες.

abhorrens] 'ill adapted to'.

26   *suo itinere*] 'his route', i.e. the route which he should have followed.

Callifanum Allifanumque et Calenum agrum] *Callifanum* is Madvig's correction for *Calatinum*. If H. came by Cales he did not come by Calatia, for the two towns are on different passes. The site of Callifae is not known, but it was probably near Allifae, as it is mentioned in conjunction with it VIII. 25. 4. It has been identified with the modern village of Calvisi, five miles E. of Allifae. *Dict. Geogr.*

Allifae in Samnium on the Vulturnus, Cales in Campania S.W. of Allifae, at the foot of the group of hills which continue the chain of the Mons Massicus to the Vulturnus. It was a Latin colony, founded 331 B.C.

According to this account H. seems to have entered Campania by

NOTES.

the depression between Teanum to the W. and Cales to the E. Polybius' account is different. Cf. Appendix III.

27 *campum Stellatem*] Pol. III. 90. 10 εἰς τὸν προσαγορευόμενον Φάλερνον τόπον. Livy is probably the more accurate; for while the ager Falernus forms the larger part of the plain N. of the Vulturnus, the ager or campus Stellatis, the eastern part of the plain, lies between Cales and Casilinum.

§ **7.** *montibus fluminibusque*] The Stellatian plain is bounded by the Vulturnus, the Piana, and the hills between Cales and the Vulturnus. The words are more applicable to the whole Campanian plain of which Polybius III. 91. 8 uses similar language. Plut. *Fabius* 6 χώρα περι- στεφὴς ὄρεσιν (W.).

28 *circumspexisset*] 'looked round upon'. *circumspicere* generally means 'to look round anxiously for'. 15. 2 *locum castris circumspectaret.* 29. 3 *fugam circumspectantibus.*

29 *ubi terrarum*] the addition of *terrarum*, a gen. of the 'divided whole' (Roby § 1296), gives a meaning of vagueness, 'where in the world'.

§ **8.** *cum...tum demum*] 'not until'. German *erst als.*

30 *mansurum*] *manere* is often used in conversational language for 'to pass the night'. Hor. *S.* I. 5. 87 *mansuri oppidulo quod versu dicere non est.* Hence *mansiones* = 'stations' or 'night quarters for travellers'.

31 *longe*] belongs both to *inde* and *alia* 'far from there in quite another quarter'.

Casinum...esse] governed by *cognitus est.*

p. **17.** 1 § **9.** *que*] 'and so', cf. 1. 3 *petitusque,* and § 6.

2 *Maharbalem*] cf. 6. 11.

3 *agrum Falernum*] i.e. into the broader part of the plain, away to the S.W. See on *campum Stellatem* § 6.

3 § **10.** *aquas Sinuessanas*] 'the baths of Sinuessa'. *aquae* is common in this sense. Cf. *Aquae Sextiae,* now pleonastically called *Aix les bains.* Sinuessa (Mondragone), in the immediate neighbourhood of the baths, was situated on the coast where the Mons Massicus slopes down to the sea, and at the boundary of Campania. It was a Roman colony founded during the 3rd Samnite war 295 B.C., cf. 14. 5.

6 § **11.** *videlicet quia*] there is no irony, 'doubtless because'.

7 *iusto et moderato imperio*] Similarly Polybius III. 90. 14 ἐξ ὧν καὶ παρασημαίναιτ' ἄν τις τὴν κατάπληξιν καὶ καταξίωσιν τοῦ 'Ρωμαίου πολιτεύματος, 'From this fact we may infer in what awe and respect the Roman commonwealth was held'.

CHAPTER XIV.

9　§ **1.** *ut vero*] does not open the sentence quite appropriately. One would have expected it to introduce a modification or intensification of the last statement; but the last statement referred to the allies at large, while the sentence which follows describes the discontent of the army.

ad Volturnum] in the campus Stellatis close to Casilinum. Hannibal's camp is meant.

10　*amoenissimus Italiae ager*] Campania was the garden of Italy. Strabo calls it πέδιον εὐδαιμονέστατον τῶν ἁπάντων. Its volcanic soil was suited to grape culture, and the finest Italian wines, the Falernian and the Massic, were here grown. The Ager Campanus was during a long period of Roman history the principal source whence Rome drew her supplies of corn. Cic. *de Leg. Agr.* I. 7 calls it *fundum pulcherrimum populi Romani, caput pecuniae...horreum legionum, solatium annonae. Dict. Geogr.*

12　*Massici montis*] the range of hills forming the limit between Latium and Campania. It was famous for its vines. Verg. *G.* II. 143 *Bacchi Massicus humor.* Hor. *C.* II. 7. 21 *oblivioso levia Massico ciboria exple.*

Fabio] he had followed on Hannibal's track one or two day's march to the rear, Pol. III. 90. 9, and now watched his movements from the N.E., keeping open his own communications with Rome by the Latin and Appian ways. Here as in Apulia (12. 8) he remained on the high ground.

ducente] = *cum tamen duceret.*

prope] with *accensa.*

de integro] the reference is to the discontent of the troops in Apulia, 12. 12.

13　§ **2.** *quieverant*] the troops, as appears from the context; though one would have expected *socii*, the last persons mentioned, to have been the nominative, see on § 1.

14　*celerius solito*] to secure the Latin and Appian ways.

16　§ **3.** *ut vero*] introducing a climax, as often.

19　§ **4.** *spectatum...venimus*] *spectatum* is best taken as governing *caedes et incendia; ut...oculis* being a parenthesis.

20　*ut*] = *tanquam si venissemus.*

ad rem fruendam...oculis] the gerundive expresses an action, 'to feast our eyes on the sight'. It may indeed be used as a mere attribute, as the gerundive sometimes is, 'an enjoyable spectacle'. Then *spectatum* would be absolute as in Hor. *A. P.* 5 *spectatum admissi risum teneatis amici*, and *caedes et incendia* would be in apposition to *rem fruendam*. But this is less likely.

21 *nec...ne quidem*] the negative is repeated in *ne; nec quidem* is not found.

civium pudet] *pudet* with gen. which = to feel shame with reference to a thing, may mean (1) to be ashamed *of* a thing (or person), *cicatricum et sceleris pudet*, Hor. *C.* 1. 35. 33. (2) to be ashamed in face of a thing, or when one thinks of it. That is the meaning here. Cf. III. 19. 7 *pudet hominum deorumque*, 'I am ashamed before gods and men'. Roby § 1328.

22 *colonos*] in 295 B.C. during the Third Samnite war. It was a Roman (not a Latin) colony, and, like all Roman colonies founded before the Second Punic war, on the coast.

24 § **5.** *extremis...terminis*] referring perhaps to Gades, the most Western city of the ancient world, whither Hannibal went, just before starting with his army from new Carthage. XXI. **22.** 5.

26 § **6.** *pro*] absolute, 'alas'. It is generally used with a vocative or accusative, as in *Pro pudor. Pro hominum deorumque fidem*.

28 *dedecus imperii*] Philinus, a Greek historian of the Second Punic war, stated that there was actually a treaty in force before the First Punic war, forbidding the Romans to land in Sicily and the Carthaginians in Italy. Polybius denies this (III. 26. 3), but the statement bears witness to the jealousy existing between the two nations.

29 *iam factam*] not with *plenam*, 'in the possession of'. XXIV. 1. 1 *Bruttios...Carthaginiensium partis factos cernebant. Numidarum* is a possessive genitive like *Gallorum* § 9.

30 § **7.** *modo*] rhetorically used of an event which had occurred two years before. So we might say 'only yesterday'.

indignando = *indignantes*. The ablative of the gerund is often used by Livy with a sense approaching more nearly to that of the present participle, than to that of an ablative of manner or means. 3. 10 *vastandoque et urendo ad moenia Romana perveniat*. Roby § 1385.

31 *ciebamus*] 'appealed to'.

p. 18. 2 § **8.** *oculos atque ora*] generally in the inverse order, 5. 4, and more correctly, as thus *atque* is explanatory, defining *ora* more closely.

3 *strepunt*] sc. 'are deafened'.

nos] 'while we', adversative asyndeton.

5 *aestivos saltus*] 'summer pastures'. In Italy the cattle are usually sent up to the high lands in summer.

devias] 'out of the way'.

7 § **9.** *M. Furius*] Camillus who defeated the Gauls in 390 B.C.

nobis] probably both, by us and for us. 'Whom we have found for ourselves'.

8 *unicus*] ironical, 'superlative'. Catullus in a poem containing an attack on Caesar says

> *Eone nomine, imperator unice,*
> *fuisti in ultima occidentis insula?* C. XXIX. 11.

in rebus adfectis] 'in our distress'. 8. 3 *ut in adfecto corpore quamvis levis causa magis quam in valido gravior sentiretur.*

10 § **10.** *quam vereor*] = *et vereor ne eam.*

Hannibali...servaverint] A compendious expression, 'have saved these many times only to fall into the hands of Hannibal'.

11 § **11.** *sed vir...Romanus*] 'but like a man and a true Roman'. Cf. Hor. *Epod.* 1. 31

> *haud paravero*
> *quod aut avarus ut Chremes terra premam*
> *discinctus aut perdam nepos.*

ac] 'and what is more', commonly subjoins something stronger or more explicit than what has preceded. It is intensive or explanatory.

14 *Ianiculum*] the highest of the hills at Rome, and that which Camillus returning from Veii would have reached first, as it was on the right bank of the Tiber.

sedens] 'sitting inactive'. Cf. *sedeamus* 3. 10.

16 *busta Gallica*] the place where the Gauls had their camp while besieging the Capitol in 390 B.C., was so called on account of the numbers who there died from pestilence. v. 48. 3.

citra Gabios] v. 49. 6 *ad octavum lapidem Gabina via.*

17 § **12.** *Furculas Caudinas*] in 321 B.C. during the 2nd Samnite war, when the Roman army under Sp. Postumius and Titus Veturius was surprised by and surrendered to C. Pontius of Telesia, IX. 9.

20 *Luceriam*] see on 9. 5. It was in the attempt to relieve Luceria which was being besieged by the Samnites, that the Romans were surprised at Caudium.

premendo obsidendoque] 'by closely besieging'. Cf. I. 51. 3 *obsidione munitionibusque coepti premi hostes.* IX. 15. 1 *consilium habitum omnibus ne copiis Luceriam premerent.* (D.)

22 § **13.** *modo*] The battle was fought 24 years before. See on *modo* § 7.

C. Lutatio] Catulus, who defeated the Carthaginian fleet off the Aegates Insulae (W. of Sicily) in 241 B.C., and so brought the First Punic war to a close.

25 § **14.** *sedendo aut votis*] such changes of construction indicate an approximation to the style of Tacitus, between whom and Cicero Livy occupies an intermediate position.

26 *votis*] has reference to the rites with which Fabius opened his campaign, 9. 7,—10.

29 *timidi*] 'only cowards'.

§ **15.** *velut contionanti*] declaiming as though he were addressing the assembled army (*contio*) instead of a group of officers. So XXI. 53. 6 *prope contionabundus* of Sempronius.

30 *tribunorum*] i.e. *militum*. They were legionary officers, six in each legion.

equitum] These, as appears from their association with *tribuni*, were persons of dignity and not mere cavalry soldiers. They belonged to the *ordo equester*, XXI. 59. 10, who rode their own horses, as opposed to the *equites equo publico*.

31 *evolvebantur*] 'found their way to', an uncommon use of the word. The preposition signifies that the words passed *out* of the smaller into a wider circle.

p. 19. 1 *haud dubie ferebant*] 'they confidently declared'. *fero* is sometimes used alone as a verb of saying as in *fertur, ferunt*, but more often with an adverb, cf. 29. 6 *palam ferente Hannibale se ab Fabio victum*, or an ablative as *laudibus, sermonibus, fama.*

CHAPTER XV.

3 § **1.** *pariter*] qualifies *intentus* as *iuxta* does in XXIII. 28. 3 *per dubios infestosque populos, iuxta intentus...pervenit* (Wlf.). *In suos haud minus quam in hostis* is added in explanation. W., I think wrongly, says *pariter = simul*, as in 4. 6.

4 *illis*] sc. *suis*.

5 *probe*] synonymous with *satis* § 3. It is a conversational word, and so common in Plautus.

7 *tenore*] 'undeviating course', for this meaning cf. Verg. *A.* x. 340 *hasta fugit, servatque inmota tenorem.*

9 § **2.** *destitutus ab spe*] lit. 'forsaken by the hope'. In this expression *ab spe* is commoner than *spe, spes* being regarded as an agent. In *spe lapsus* on the other hand *spe* is an ablative of respect.

10   *hibernis*] dat. of work contemplated.   Roby § 1156.

11   *praesentis erat copiae, non perpetuae*] gen. of description, 'furnished supplies only for the time, not all the year round'.   The fruit, it is meant, would be available only in summer.

12   *arbusta vineaeque* etc.] These nominatives are loosely in apposition to *regio.*   The meaning would have been more regularly expressed by *tota enim consita erat arbustis vineisque.*   One may translate 'a region of orchards and vineyards, planted throughout with such produce as is grown for pleasure rather than such as is necessary for man's subsistence'.

   consita omnia] Livy often uses neut. plural adjectives without a substantive, especially when the substantive left unexpressed is *loca* as here.

   magis amoenis quam necessariis] i.e. fruit-trees rather than crops. Hence *fructibus* is used in preference to *frugibus* which is generally restricted to the produce of the fields.

14   § 8.   *satis*] generally *satis* without a negative has a weak sense, 'tolerably': with a negative a strong sense 'quite', 4. 4.   But sometimes even without a negative *satis* has a strong sense, by a kind of litotes. Thus we might say, 'Fabius knew pretty well', meaning 'knew quite well'.

   easdem angustias]   So too Polybius III. 92. 10 κατανοῶν αὐτοῦ τὴν ἐπιβολὴν ὅτι προχειρίζεται ποιεῖσθαι τὴν ἐπάνοδον ᾗπερ ἐποιήσατο καὶ τὴν εἴσοδον.   But Polybius' account is consistent with his statement. He makes Hannibal enter Campania by the road along the Vulturnus, and leave it by the same road; see Appendix III.   Livy on the other hand having represented Hannibal as coming in from Allifae, through the territory of Cales, i.e. by the pass to the W. of the hills between Cales and Casilinum, in which Teanum stands (13. 6, note), now makes Fabius especially guard positions on the E. side of those hills, in order to prevent his egress.   According to him Hannibal enters Campania by Cales and leaves it by Callicula.   The fact is, Livy has translated Polybius' statement in III. 92. 10, though in his account of Hannibal's entry he has followed a wholly different account from that of Polybius.

15   *Calliculam montem*] probably at no great distance from Casilinum, as Fabius fortifies them both with the object of blockading the same route.   It has been identified (see App. III.) with the easternmost elevation of the hills between Cales and Casilinum, separated from the rest of those hills by a depression near Bellona.   The name (connected

with Callis) would seem to mean 'the mountain with the foot-path', possibly referring to the very path which Livy represents Hannibal as following in c. **17.** Livy says the Roman troops occupied the Mons Callicula itself: Polybius, more accurately, the διεκβολή, i. e. the defile between the Mons Callicula and the Vulturnus. See passage quoted on *modicis* below.

16   *Casilinum*] on the site of the modern Capua, commanding the road along the Vulturnus to Telesia, and at the point where the Appian and Latin ways meet at the bridge over the Vulturnus.

modicis] sc. 'sufficient'. Pol. III. 92. 11 ἐπ' αὐτῆς τῆς διεκβολῆς περὶ τετρακισχιλίους ἐπέστησε.

17   *dirempta*] i. e. the river flowed through the town.

Campano] here refers particularly to the plains round Capua. On the other hand the whole country N. as well as S. of the Vulturnus is called Campania.

18   § **4.** *iugis iisdem*] along the range by which he had come, and to which Callicula belonged.

reducit] probably to the hills above Cales (§ 10), for as he had garrisoned Casilinum to defend the road along the Vulturnus, and had blocked the Appian road at Tarracina (§ 11), and seems to have intended to shut up Hannibal in Campania (16. 5), he would hardly have left the valley between Cales and Teanum, the most obvious exit, undefended.

Polybius on the other hand, speaks of no such extensive operations for preventing Hannibal's egress. According to him, Fabius was en-camped at no great distance from the troops he had placed to guard the pass (στενὰ) on the road along the Vulturnus. Pol. III. 92. 11 ἐπί τινα λόφον ὑπερδέξιον πρὸ τῶν στενῶν κατεστρατοπέδευσε, and it is possible that Livy's statement (in § 11) may mean that the guard which had been placed at Tarracina was now withdrawn in consequence of Fabius' information (§ 4) as to Hannibal's movements; while *inclusus* 16. 4, should not be taken in too strict a sense. But on the whole it appears that Livy does mean that Fabius blocked all the passes out of Campania, while Polybius only mentions his blocking the particular pass by which Hannibal was expected to escape.

19   § **5.** *ex turba iuvenum*] the clause describes *qui*, and is inserted to explain Mancinus' subsequent action. W. compares the omission of *vir* in 60. 5 *Torquatus priscae severitatis.* But Cicero or Caesar would have written *qui cum esset ex turba.* Livy's expression here is parallel with *pugna ad Trasumennum* (sc. *commissa*) **7. 1,** *omnia circa vir-*

gulta 17. 3. He is almost forced to it here by the want of a pres. participle = ὤν.

20 *audientium*] = *qui audiebant. saepe* with *audientium.*

21 *ex tuto*] cf. 12. 10.

23 *per occasionem*] 'opportunity offering', *per* expressing the circumstances.

24 § **6**. *occupatus certamine est animus*] 'his mind was seized with a desire for battle'. The change of nom. (cf. 1. 3) is not to be imitated.

   exciderunt] sc. *animo* which is not expressed as *animus* has just preceded.

27 § **7**. *alii atque alii*] i.e. 'by relays'. The meaning of the passage is that the movements of advance and retreat alternated, and that these movements were made not by the whole body simultaneously, but by different sections in turn. The whole body gradually retired towards the camp.

29 § **8**. *Carthalo*] we find Carthalo at the head of some Carthaginian cavalry at Cannae 49. 13. He is sent with the Roman prisoners to the Capital to treat if occasion offers, 58. 7, where he is described as *nobilis Carthaginiensis.*

31 *avertisset*] 'put to flight'. 19. 11 *in fugam averterunt.*

p. **20**. 3 § **9**. *in proelium rediit*] 'returned and gave battle'. *in* = 'with a view to', and is not merely local, for there had been no fighting as yet between Mancinus and Carthalo.

   omni parte virium] if *omni parte* = 'in every division' the expression is inaccurate, for Mancinus had only cavalry. More probably the whole expression means no more than 'in all respects'. The Roman cavalry was neither so numerous, nor so skilful, nor so fresh (§ 7) as the Carthaginian.

4 § **10**. *delecti equitum*] gen. of divided whole, Roby § 1292. So *circumfusos militum* 30. 2.

6 *dictatorem*] probably on the hills above Cales or Teanum guarding the exit by the valley of the Savo. See on § 4.

8 § **11**. *saltum*] the defile of Lautulae on the Appian road in S. Latium, an important strategical position.

   Tarracinam] on the coast near the southern extremity of the Pomptine marshes. Its Volscian name was Anxur. Hor. *S.* 1. 5. 26 *impositum saxis late candentibus Anxur.*

9 *coactus*] 'narrowing'.

   ab Sinuessa] A writer of the best period would have omitted *ab.* Sinuessa was as yet the extreme limit of the Carthaginian ravages.

NOTES.

Fabius feared that it might be the starting-point of a further movement
North.

Appiae limite] the line of the Appian road, see on *limitibus* 12. 2.

11 § **12.** *viam*] what road? When last mentioned Fabius was on the
Mons Massicus, or the hills above Cales. See on §§ 4, 10. *Via* may
then be the road between Cales and Casilinum, to which Fabius now
descended in order to be nearer to the 4000 men who were occupying
Callicula and at the same time to prevent Hannibal from escaping by
the depression between Cales and Teanum (Voigt, *Berlin Philolog.
Wochenschrift*). But it is not certain whether Livy is still following
the authorities from whom he gets the account of the wider scheme
of operations which consisted in blocking all the passes out of N.
Campania, or Polybius, whom he certainly follows in the narrative
of the stratagem, and who refers to the blocking of one pass only,
on the road along the Vulturnus from Casilinum to Telesia.

On the whole it seems likely that he is referring to the same
movement as Polybius in III. 92. 11 ἐπί τινα λόφον ὑπερδέξιον (favourable) πρὸ τῶν στενῶν κατεστρατοπέδευσε. By στενά Polybius means the
defile on the road along the Vulturnus (Appendix III. B). Livy
probably means by *via* the road to Callicula, for he apparently knows
nothing of the river road, as appears from 16. 5. In any case Fabius
on being joined by Minucius marched some way to the E. towards
the Vulturnus.

deferunt] from the mountains, to which Fabius had hitherto clung.
14. 8, 15. 4.

12 *ducturus*] *exercitum* is omitted. Cf. *movit* 1. 1 and note.

CHAPTER XVI.

14 § **2.** *sub ipso*] 'close under'. *ad ipsa castra* 15. 7.

15 *aequiore*] 'more favourable'. Although the Romans had descended
from the mountains they were still on higher ground than the Carthaginians as appears from *successit*, and λόφον in Polybius quoted on
15. 4.

16 *expeditis*] usually with a substantive, as *milites* or *pedites*.

17 *carptim*] *carpere*, 'to pluck'. The adv. may get its meaning either
(1) from the pass. of *carpere* and so = 'in detachments'. (Cf. XXVI. 28. 2
in multas parvasque partes carpere exercitum.) So *divisis carptim agris*,
Suet. *Dom.* 9, 'in small portions'; or (2), from the act. of *carpere*.
carpentes agmen 32. 2 = 'plucking at', hence 'assailing constantly' or

'at different points', 'harassing'. Thus *carptim* here and XLIV. 41. 7 *carptim aggrediendo* may = 'repeatedly' or 'at different points'. The word may have one of these meanings, not more than one, as W. would imply, explaining *carptim aggrediendo* as indicating constant attacks in separate detachments.

20   § **3.** *ex dictatoris voluntate*] a predicate, like *lenta*.
     ab] local, 'on the side of'. Cf. the phrase *stare ab aliquo*.

22   § **4.** *inclusus*] cf. 15. 3, 4, and 11, notes. Polybius only mentions the blocking of a single pass, that on the road up the Vulturnus.
     via ad Casilinum obsessa] 'the road (to the S.) being blocked at Casilinum', i.e. by the garrison there, 15. 3. The meaning is not 'the road to Casilinum', for what would it profit Hannibal if the road to Casilinum were open, while Casilinum itself was garrisoned?

23   *tantum...sociorum*] A picturesque expression for *tot socii*. Cf. Catullus III. 2 *quantum est hominum venustiorum*, for *homines venustiores quot estis.*

24   *Poenus*] 'while the Carthaginians'. Adversative asyndeton, 14 8 *nos.*
     Formiana saxa] Formiae was on the Appian road, in Latium, but not so far North as Tarracina 15. 11. Tradition said it was founded by the Laestrygones.

25   *Literni*] on the marshy coast of Campania between the mouth of the Vulturnus and Cumae. Silius, *Pun.* VII. 275

> *hinc Laestrygoniae saxoso monte premebant*
> *a tergo rupes, undosis squalida terris*
> *hinc Literna palus.*

The mention of Liternum is not quite accurate as in consequence of the occupation of Casilinum, Hannibal would have to remain N. of the Vulturnus.
     horridas silvas] Livy is thinking of the *Gallinaria silva* near Cumae which in the time of the empire was dangerous, being infested by brigands. Wlf.

27   § **5.** *per Casilinum*] to the S. See on *via ad Casilinum obsessa.*

28   *iugum Calliculae*] further defining *montes.* It was probably the lowest part of the Mons Callicula, 15. 3, where it could be surmounted. Pol. ὑπερβολή. Voigt has identified it with the depression at Bellona some distance W. of the Vulturnus.
     necubi] = *ne alicubi*, 2. 3.
     Romanus] The troops guarding Callicula 15. 3. *necubi...adgre-*

daretur refers to Hannibal's apprehensions of being attacked while crossing the mountains, not while he remained shut up in Campania.

29   *inclusum vallibus*] 'when he should be penned in the defile'. The plural is inaccurate, Hannibal did not think of crossing Callicula at more than one point.

§ **6.** *ludibrium oculorum*] 'an optical delusion'.

p. **21.** 1 § **7.** *ex agris*] must refer to the villages; faggots (*fasces*) might have been collected in the fields, but not torches (*faces*).

3   *domitos indomitosque*] 'broken and unbroken to the plough'. The former Polybius III. 93. 4 calls ἔργαται βόες.

4   § **8.** *ad*]=*circa*, a meaning which is repeated in *ferme*.

5   *effecta*] 'a total of some 2000 was made up'. This includes only those that were actually used. Polybius says the strongest of the plough oxen were selected for the purpose 1. c. τῶν ἐργατῶν βοῶν εἰς δισχιλίους.

Hasdrubali] the chief of the commissariat department (Pol. τὸν ἐπὶ τῶν λειτουργιῶν τεταγμένον) and therefore in charge of the beeves.

6   *accensis cornibus*] i.e. with the faggots on their horns lighted. By a still more remarkable hypallage Silius Italicus says VII. 333 *accensa inmittere silvis armenta.* Wlf.

maxime super saltus] 'just above the defile'. The oxen were not to be driven straight up the pass; for it was not intended that they should be recognized as oxen, but to the heights above it, so that the enemy should imagine that their flank had been turned.

CHAPTER XVII.

8   § **1.** *primis tenebris*] Polybius says ἅμα τῷ κλῖναι τὸ τρίτον μέρος τῆς νυκτὸς, after the middle of the third watch, or about 2 A.M.

9   *ante signa*] This is a little different from Polybius' account. He says that the oxen were driven towards an elevated pass (ὑπερβολὴ) so as to present the appearance of an army marching thither, while Hannibal himself made for the defile which was actually occupied by the enemy. In Livy the oxen and the army seem to take the same direction, though the former are some way in advance. See Appendix III. B.

§ **2.** *vias angustas*] the defile. There is no special appropriateness in the plural. It is perhaps a translation of τὰ στενὰ. Pol. III. 93. 10 αὐτὸς...ἧκε πρὸς τὰ στενὰ καὶ τὰς διεκβολάς. But these words describe the line taken by Hannibal as distinguished from that followed by the oxen.

11 *accensis cornibus*] see on 16. 8.

  in adversos montis] 'up the slope of the mountains'.

13 *vivom imaque cornua*] hendiadys, 'the quick at the base of their horns'.

15 § **3.** *quo repente discursu*] *repente* adv. qualifies *discursu*, 'at this sudden rush'. The use of adverbs in place of adjectives or relative clauses does not occur in writers of the best period, and marks Livy as belonging to the beginning of the silver age. Cf. 7. 11.

17 *circa*]=*quae circa erat*, see the preceding note.

  ardere] Madvig reads *visa ardere* unnecessarily. Plutarch, *Fabius* 6, says the oxen actually set the woods on fire πολλὴν τῆς ὕλης δι' ἧς ἔφευγον ἀνάπτονται.

19 § **4.** *qui...locati erant*] the *modica praesidia* 16. 3, 4000 men. Pol. III. 92. 11.

  in...montibus ac super se] cf. *ad montis...maxime super saltus* 16. 8. *ac* is explanatory 14. 11 note.

21 *praesidio*] 'their post'. In Polybius they hurry to repel the enemy, who, they think, is attacking where the lights are seen. ἀπολιπόντες τὰς δυσχωρίας παρεβοήθουν τοῖς ἄκροις.

22 *velut tutissimum iter*] 'thinking this the safest way'. 3. 12 *velut foedo omine.*

23 *tamen*] Although they went *qua minime densae micabant flammae*. Still the story is confused, for the lights were seen *in summis montibus*, therefore it was not surprising that the oxen should be met with on the *summa montium iuga*. See Appendix III. B.

24 § **5.** *cernerent*] sc. *boves.*

25 *flammas spirantium*] The writer purposely omits to add a substantive as the soldiers did not know what it was they saw, 'fire-breathing monsters'. Cf. for an omission with a similar purpose, XXI. 62. 5 *hominum specie procul candida veste visos, nec cum ullo congressos.*

27 § **6.** *levi armaturae*] Livy has not mentioned these before. Polybius tells how Hannibal had ordered light troops (λογχοφόροι) to follow behind the oxen till they began to run wild, when they were to pass them on either flank, and engage any troops they found at the pass. III. 93. 8.

  quoque] as well as the oxen.

28 *incurrere*] only once again with dat. XXVIII. 5. 7 usu. *incurrere in aliquid.* W.

nox neutros tenuit] *neutros pugnam incipientis* is put to represent shortly *utrosque cum neutri inciperent*, but the sense is obscured by the omission of the true object of *tenuit* (*utrosque*).

CHAPTER XVIII.

p. 22. 1 § 1. *Fabius*] he was posted on a hill at no great distance from the pass. See on 15. 12.

2   *utique*] with *nocturno*, 'at any rate'. See on 7. 11 *utique ab notis*.

3   § 2. *sub iugo*] The engagement was between the Roman guard which had abandoned the pass and the Carthaginian light-armed, who had been watching each other through the night, 17. 6. It is not apparent why the conflict should have taken place 'below the pass' and not rather on the heights above the pass to which the Romans had fled, 17. 4. Polybius says much more intelligibly, ἅμα δὲ τῷ φωτὶ συνιδὼν τοὺς ἐν τοῖς ἄκροις ἀντικαθημένους τοῖς λογχοφόροις ἐπαπέστειλέ τινας τῶν Ἰβήρων, 'at dawn seeing the Romans on the heights sitting opposite the dartmen, Hannibal sent some of the Spaniards to the assistance of his men'.

4   *ab suis*] i.e. from the Carthaginians, *suis* referring not to the subject *Romani* but to *levem armaturam*. The context prevents ambiguity. Livy is often careless in the use of *suus*, § 7, 12. 10.

7   *ad id ipsum*] 4. 3.

8   *remissa*] 'sent back'. Hannibal had himself gone through the pass during the night.

9   § 3. *concursandum*] the frequentative indicates irregular attacks, 'skirmishing'.

10   *levior*] explained by *velocitate...habitu.*
    armorum habitu] 'the character of their arms'.

11   *gravem armis*] 'heavy-armed'. XXI. 21. 11 *levium armis.*
    statarium] 'accustomed to stationary tactics'. Comparing the legionary and the soldier of the phalanx Livy says *statarius uterque miles, ordines servans*, IX. 19. 5 (C.).

12   *genere*] abl. of means.

13   § 4. *aliquot amissis*] Pol. III. 94. 6 κατέβαλον τῶν Ῥωμαίων εἰς χιλίους.

16   § 5. *super Allifas*] with *consedit.*

17   § 6. *Romam se petere*] To cause this belief he must have gone up the Vulturnus as far as Venafrum, as though he intended to strike

into the Latin road. Then he must have turned due N. and marched by Aesernia and Aufidena to Sulmo and Corfinium in the territory of the Paeligni. Thence he reached the coast, and marched S.E. along the coast-road to the mouth of the Tifernus where he turned inland to Gereonium. See Kiepert's *Atlas.*

19   *iugis*] 'along the heights', 15. 4.

absistens] usually metaphorical = 'to cease', e.g. *bello* XXI. 6. 8: here literal, 'keeping at a distance'. For Fabius' policy cf. 12. 8.

20   § **7.** *flexit*] S.W.

21   *Gereonium*] in the territory of the Frentani (though some authorities call it an Apulian town, 39. 16), a short distance E. of the border of Samnium, and S.W. of Larinum.

urbem] *in urbem* would have been more in accordance with strict usage.

23   *Larinate*] Larinum like Gereonium was a Frentanian town.

§ **8.** *sacrorum*] Pol. III. 94. 9 καταναγκασθεὶς ἐπί τινας ἀπελθεῖν θυσίας εἰς τὴν Ῥωμήν.

24   *revocatus...agens*] the main verb is *profectus est*, which is rather awkwardly loaded with two participles. Again, the present participle does not go well with *profectus est*, as Fabius doubtless gave his commands before his departure. The fact is *agit* would naturally have followed *revocatus*, but Livy substitutes *agens* and continues the sentence from his wish to include the mention of Fabius' departure in the same period.

25   *agens*] properly belongs to *precibus*, with which it is often used by zeugma: however it is here used also with *imperio* and *consilio.*

26   § **9.** *confidat...imitetur*] these verbs are in a primary tense, as they depend on *precibus agens* (which = a historic pres. *agit*).

Sempronium] the consul of the preceding year who had commanded and been defeated at Trebia. XXI. 53. 1, 54. 3.

27   *Flaminium*] cf. esp. 3. 7 sqq.

censeret] depends on some verb of saying which is understood, and which would naturally be past, as the time of the whole sentence is past. (Cf. *profectus est.*)

extracta prope] = *prope extracta.* Cf. 24. 14.

28   *per ludificationem*] 'in baffling'. *per* expresses the manner, in 15. 5 the circumstances.

29   *quiete*] 'by doing nothing'. *movendo atque agendo,* 'by movement and action'.

31   § **10.** *haec...praemonito*] The sentence is taken up again to correct the confusion noted on § 8 *revocatus...agens.*

CHAPTER XIX.

p. 23. 3 § 1. *aestatis*] shews that these events took place later than Hannibal's march into Etruria, cf. *iam ver adpetebat* 1. 1.

5 § 2. *Hasdrubal*] he had been left in charge of Spain by his brother. XXI. 22. 1 *Hasdrubali fratri viro inpigro eam provinciam destinat.*

quem...acceperat] Accurately 37 in repair out of a total of 57, XXI. 22. 4, Pol. III. 33. ˙14, but here Livy seems to follow Polybius III. 95. 2, who speaks of 'the 30 ships left him', as the addition of 10 makes them up to 40, § 3.

7 § 3. *Himilconi*] Pol. l.c. προχειρισάμενος 'Αμίλκαν, which= Hamilcar.

8 *ita*] 'so', i.e. after the preparation of the fleet, and the appointment of Himilco.

Carthagine] nova.

11 § 4. *movisse*] cf. *ducebat* 18. 6, *movit* 1. 1 note.

12 *idem consilii*]=*idem consilium*. x. 34. 5 *primo ita compositus moenibus successit tanquam idem quod ad Milioniam certaminis esset.* The intention was to fight with whatever part of the enemy's force appeared first.

fuit] sc. *ei*, which it is not necessary to insert. XXI. 18. 3 *Romani postquam Carthaginem venerunt, cum senatus datus esset* (sc. *iis*)*...tum ex Carthaginiensibus unus* etc.

13 *ingentem famam auxiliorum*] hypallage for *famam ingentium auxiliorum.*

14 *delecto*] with *ad naves.* Pol. III. 95. 5 λαβών...τοὺς ἐπιτηδειοτάτους ἄνδρας πρὸς τὴν ἐπιβατικὴν χρείαν.

inposito] sc. *in naves*, 'embarked'.

15 § 5. *altero ab Tarracone*] short for *altero die postquam ab Tarra-cone profectus erat.* XXI. 38. 1 *quinto mense a Carthagine nova.*

Tarracone] on the coast some 45 miles N.E. of the mouth of the Ebro. Along with Emporiae the Romans used it as their principal base of operations.

16 *stationem*] an anchorage. Verg. *A.* II. 23 *statio male fida carinis.*

17 *Massiliensium*] the faithful allies of Rome. We find them in-forming the Romans as to the temper of the Gauls before the Second Punic war (XXI. 20), and the movements of Hannibal (ib. 25. 1), or acting as guides up the country (ib. 26. 5). Polybius testifies to their de-votion, εὐγενῶς γὰρ εἰ καί τινες ἔτεροι κεκοινωνήκασι 'Ρωμαίοις πραγμάτων καὶ Μασσαλιῶται, πολλάκις μὲν καὶ ταῦτα μάλιστα δὲ κατὰ τὸν 'Αννεβιακὸν πόλεμον.

speculatoriae] *naves*, 'spy-ships'. They were smaller than triremes and without beaks. Pol. ταχυπλοούσας.

20 § **6**. *universo simul effuso terrore*] 'amid an outbreak of general panic'. *effuso* is used as though of a storm, *procella effusa*, VIII. 6. 3.

21 *multas et*] a Graecism. One would drop the *et* in translation.

23 § **7**. *inde*] local, 'from these'. Polybius does not mention the towers. He only says σημηνάντων δὲ αὐτοῖς τῶν σκοπῶν ἐκ πολλοῦ τὸν ἐπίπλουν τῶν ὑπεναντίων.

25 *nondum...aperientibus classem promunturiis*] 'as the fleet had not come into sight from behind the promontories'. 6. 9 *cum dispulsa nebula aperuisset diem*. With this use of *aperire* = 'to allow to be seen', cf. Verg. *A*. III. 291 *Phaeacum abscondimus arces*, sc. they sink out of sight.

26 *exaudito*] 'heard in the distance'.

28 § **8**. *vagos...quietos*] the adjectives express action. 15. 5 *vagos per vicos*.

29 *nihil minus quam*] 'anything rather than'.

p. 24. 1 *procul portu*] A prose-writer of the best period would have said *procul a portu*, cf. XXI. 5. 8 *procul Tago*.

6 § **10**. *oris*] 'stern ropes', by which the sterns of vessels were moored to the shore, while from their prows, which pointed away from the shore, were let down cables with anchors (*ancoralia*). How does *ora* come to mean a stern rope? Tyrrell (on Cic. *Att*. I. 19. 1) thinks that in nautical language the 'stern rope' which was also the 'shore rope', may have been known as the 'shore' as we call the sheet rope the 'sheet'.

in ancoras evehuntur] 'drifted out to their anchors'. See preceding note.

7 *raptim...agendo*] 'in the hurry of doing everything at a moment's notice'. *agendo = dum agunt*, cf. *indignando* 14. 7.

11 § **11**. *derexerat*] 'had drawn up in line'.

13 *verius*] a common expression in Livy. XXI. 16. 4 *tumultuatum verius quam belligeratum*, 'there had really been skirmishing rather than regular fighting'.

in fugam averterunt] used of the conquerors in 15. 8.

14 § **12**. *adversi*] the meaning can only be given by a paraphrase, 'as they could not possibly enter the mouth of the river to ascend the stream'.

15 *haud sane*] = 'certainly not'.

17 *per litus*] 'along the shore'.

19   *suppressae*] 'were sunk', an exaggeration. Polybius says two were taken with their crews, four were denuded of their oars and their marines, III. 96. 4. Livy's narrative of the events in Spain seems to be a paraphrase of that of Polybius except 20. 4—21. 8 which come from another source.

CHAPTER XX.

20   § **1.** *hostium erat*] cf. 14. 9 *Gallorum Roma esset.*

24   § **2.** *religatas*] Pol. III. 96. 6 τὰ δυνάμενα κινεῖσθαι ἀναδησάμενοι.

25   *ad*]=*circiter*, 16. 8.

28   § **3.** *eius orae mari*] 'the sea belonging to that coast', i.e. the *mare Balearicum.* Pol. l. c. κρατοῦντες τῆς θαλάσσης.

29   *Onusam*] on the coast between Saguntum and the mouth of the Ebro, XXI. 22. 5.

32   § **5.** *agrum circa*] cf. 17. 3 *omnia circa virgulta*, etc.

p. 25. 1 § **6.** *ad*] used by Livy with acc. of motion towards (with names of towns), contrary to strict usage. So § 3 *ad Onusam.*

2   *Longunticam*] not elsewhere mentioned, but probably S. of New Carthage, as it was there that the Σπαρτάριον πέδιον which produced the *spartum* began. W.

    sparti] 'esparto grass' or Spanish broom. It was used especially to make ropes, but also mats, nets etc.

4   *sublato*] sc. *eo.* For the omission of the pronoun as antecedent, cf. XXI. 21. 1 *auditis quae Romae quaeque Carthagini acta decretaque forent.*

5   § **7.** *praelecta*] This is W.'s correction for P *periectas.* The word occurs in Tacitus, *A.* VI. 1 *Campaniam praelegebat. prae=praeter* in compounds is common in Livy. Livy generally uses the simple verb, XXI. 51. 7 *oram Italiae legens.*

    Ebusum] the largest of the Pityussae Insulae S.W. of the Baliares Insulae, now Yvica.

6   § **8.** *quae caput insulae est*] Cf. Caes. *B. G.* v. 11 *flumen quod appellatur Thamesis.* On the other hand if the idea which precedes is defined, the relative generally agrees with the predicate, e.g. Cic. *Phil.* v. 14 *Pompeio, quod imperii populi Romani lumen fuit.* Madvig § 316.

    nequiquam] 'without result'. *frustra*, 'with vain exertions', W.

7   *in spem inritam*] *in* with acc. may express purpose, lit. with a view

to (the attainment of) a vain hope. Sc. 'in vain hopes of success'. **xxi.**
45. 4 *praemia pronuntiabat, in quorum spem pugnarent.*

10 § **9.** *Baliaribus*] from these islands the slingers of the Carthaginian
army were drawn.

14 § **11.** *qui...sint*] 'such of them as really submitted'. A subjunctive
of indefiniteness, the person being indefinite, as in 11. 8 *libertini,
quibus liberi essent, in verba iuraverunt.*

16 § **12.** *terrestribus quoque*] after his success on land. The reference is to 19. 4 *minus terra concurrere ausus.*

17 *saltum Castulonensem*] 'the pass of Castulo'. The town after
which it is named was the capital of Oretani on the Baetis. The pass
itself lay through what is now the E. part of the Sierra Morena.
Polybius who says nothing of the movements recorded in this chapter
represents the passage of the Ebro by the Romans after the arrival
of Scipio, 22. 4, as the first occasion on which they crossed it. III. 97. 5.

CHAPTER XXI.

20 § **1.** *per Poenum*] 'as far as it depended upon the Carthaginians',
cf. *trahantur per me pedibus omnes rei*, Cic. *Fam.* VII. 32 (D.).

22 § **2.** *Mandonius Indibilisque*] Indibilis had fought under Hanno
against Cn. Scipio in 218 B.C. and had been taken prisoner by him,
Pol. III. 76, cf. Livy XXI. 61. 7. How he regained his liberty we
do not know. The two brothers, for such they were, were constant in
their attachment to Carthage except for a brief period in 209 B.C., when
they submitted to Scipio Africanus.

23 § **3.** *Ilergetum*] they lived E. of the Ebro, along the Sicoris. Their
chief town was Ilerda, now Lerida.

24 *saltu*] the *saltus Castulonensis.*

29 § **4.** *ut*] 'as they were but an undisciplined rabble'. Cf. XXIII. 14.
1 *haec ut in secundis rebus segniter otioseque gesta.* For the use of *ut*
indicating that a fact is to be allowed for, cf. 5. 1.

p. 26. 1 § **6.** *Ilergavonensium*] along the coast South of the mouth of
the Ebro and between it and Saguntum.

Novam classem] perhaps the place called *ad novas* between Ilerda
and Tarraco, mentioned in the Antonine itinerary. W.

2 § **7.** *Celtiberi*] the most powerful tribe in Spain occupying the
central plateau which divides the basin of the Ebro from that of the
rivers flowing W. But the name Celtiberi is used with a wider signifi-
cation owing to their power over the neighbouring tribes.

7 § **8.** *ad*] cf. 16. 8.

CHAPTER XXII.

9 **§ 1.** *P. Scipio*] the consul of 218 B.C. who had been wounded in the engagement on the Ticinus (XXI. 46. 7) and had wintered at Cremona (ib. 56. 9) after the battle of Trebia. It seems to have been towards the end of summer that he arrived. Cf. 21. 1.

provinciam] The Senate put Scipio in command of the province which was to have been his in 218 B.C. XXI. 17. 1 *Cornelio Hispania evenit*. Pol. III. 97. 2 ἐπιστήσαντες στρατηγὸν Πόπλιον Σκιπίωνα κατὰ τὴν ἐξ ἀρχῆς πρόθεσιν.

11 *triginta*] Polybius says 20.

12 *commeatu advecto*] abl. absolute, not governed by *cum*.

13 **§ 2.** *ingens*] 'impressive', cf. 11. 6 *ingentem speciem dictaturae*, or merely 'swelled'.

onerariarum] sc. *navium.* Cf. *speculatoriae* 19. 5.

15 *portum...tenuit*] 'made the harbour'.

19 **§ 4.** *Hiberum transgrediuntur*] for the first time, Polybius says, III. 97. 5, οὐδέποτε γὰρ πρότερον θαρρήσαντες διαβῆναι τὸν Ἴβηρα ποταμὸν ...τότε διέβησαν καὶ τότε πρῶτον ἐθάρρησαν ἀντιποιεῖσθαι τῶν πέραν πραγμάτων. But cf. 20. 12, which is drawn from another source than Polybius.

20 *nec ullo viso hoste*] *nec ullo=et nullo*, Pol. καταπληξάμενοι τοὺς περὶ τὴν διάβασιν οἰκοῦντας. This is not inconsistent with Livy.

Saguntum] The city then had not been destroyed on its capture by Hannibal in 219 B.C., XXI. 15.

21 *pergunt ire*] 'push on', cf. 19. 4.

traditos] *in custodiam*, XXIX. 21. 3 *ii omnes...traditi in custodiam Reginis* (Wlf.).

22 *ab Hannibale*] When Hannibal was starting for Italy he took from such tribes as he mistrusted the sons of their leading men as hostages, Pol. III. 98. 1. Presumably however he took them only from the *Provincia Carthaginiensis*, 21. 7, in which case *totius Hispaniae* is an exaggeration.

23 **§ 5.** *omnium*] an exaggeration, some tribes had already joined the Romans. 20. 11, 21. 7.

24 *ne...lueretur*] this clause depends on the notion of fear conveyed by *morabatur*. Tr. 'made them hesitate, for fear of their revolt being punished'.

liberum] for *liberorum.* This with *socium* (27. 11 and 40. 6) occurs not unfrequently in Livy. The contraction with certain names of

weights and measures and numbers is commoner. Madvig, *Lat. Gr.*
§ 37. 4.

27 § **6.** *Abelux erat Sagunti nobilis Hispanus*] 'There was at Saguntum a Spanish nobleman called Abelux'. For the order cf. Cic. *Verr.*
II. 111. 21 *Nympho est Centuripinus*, 'there is a man of Centuripa
called Nympho'.

28 *qualia...sunt barbarorum ingenia*] This is equivalent in meaning to
ut sunt infida (qualia getting its meaning from *mutaverat fidem)
barbarorum ingenia*, 'with the usual fickleness of barbarian minds'; cf.
2. 4 *si...ut est mollis ad talia gens dilaberentur aut subsisterent,* note.

cum fortuna] i.e. *mutata fortuna*, but the expression is not quite
accurate for it ought to = *cum mutavisset fortunam.*

29 § **7.** *magnae rei*] either an objective genitive, 'without betraying
something important', or more probably a gen. of quality = 'of great
matter', 'important'. Cf. *tantae rei* § 12.

31 *corpus*] 'an individual'. *corpus* here means a man looked upon
as a separate material being, apart from all circumstances of character,
position etc.

32 *emolumentum*] used predicatively, 'that he (Abelux) might profit
his new allies as much as possible'. This would generally be rendered
by the dative. XXIII. 15. 14 *senties eam rem tibi emolumento esse.* (D.)

§ **8.** *circumspectis*] 'having anxiously reviewed'. 13. 7 note.

p. **27.** 1 *poterat*] the indicative shews that this is a statement of the
writer and not the thought of Abelux.

2 *potissimum*] 'by preference'.

unam] strengthens *maxime.* So *iustissimus unus:* 'far the justest
man'.

4 § **9.** *praefecti*] 'governor of the city'. On the other hand Polybius
does not imply that Bostar had any special connection with Saguntum.
He says he had been sent by Hannibal to defend the passage of the
Ebro, but had retired and encamped before Saguntum, III. 98. 5.

satis] i.e. 'well-knowing', see note on 15. 3.

6 § **10.** *in ipso litore*] 'quite on the shore', for *ipso* cf. 15. 7.
Polybius says he was within the city, τῆς Σακάνθης ἐν τοῖς πρὸς θάλασσαν
μέρεσι.

8 *in secretum*] sc. 'aside'. For the use of neut. adjectives in a local
sense cf. 47. 3 *in derectum.* 12. 10 *ex tuto.* 4. 3 *in aperto.*

10 § **11.** *cis*] from the point of view of the speaker. West.

13 § **12.** *miranti*] in a pregnant sense, 'expressing his surprise'.

subitum tantae rei donum] *tantae rei* = 'of such importance'. Cf.

NOTES. 129

magnae rei § 7. *subitum* may mean either (1) suddenly suggested or given, 'unexpected', or (2) which is better, sudden in its effects, in which case the meaning would be, 'a gift which could suddenly produce such great results'.

15 § 13. *nomen*] 'distinction', the hostages were υἱεῖς τῶν ἐπιφανεστάτων ἀνδρῶν, Pol. III. 98. 1. Madvig reads *momentum* 'influence'.

17 § 14. *habita fides...fidem*] In the first place *fides* means 'trust' as in Cic. *Div.* 11. 122 *insanorum visis non est habenda fides*, in the second 'honour' as in Ter. *Andr.* 1. 5. 55 *te oro per tuam fidem*, reposing trust in others generally engages *their* honour. With *obligat* cf. 23. 8 *fidem publicam exsolvit*, and note.

ipsam] can hardly be rendered literally, it means the fidelity in question, which it is desired to secure.

18 *domos*] 'to their several homes'; the accusative from the idea of motion in *restituere*.

21 *gratiam*] Pol. III. 98. 8 τὴν δὲ χάριν αὐξήσειν ἔφη πολλαπλασίαν, αὐτὸς γενόμενος χειριστὴς τοῦ πράγματος.

§ 15. *ad*] 'compared with'. Cic. *de Or.* II. 6. 25 *Vir bonus sed nihil ad Persium.* So πρὸς is used in Grk. λῆρός ἐστι πρὸς Κινησίαν, 'he is a mere joke to Cinesias', Ar. *Lys.* 860. In both cases the meaning of comparison is developed from that of juxtaposition, which is the preliminary step to comparison.

cetera Punica ingenia] Livy credits Hannibal with *perfidia plus quam Punica*, XXI. 4. 9. Verg. *A.* 1. 661 *Tyriosque bilingues.* Polybius describes Bostar as ἄκακον ὄντα καὶ πρᾷον τῇ φύσει, a harmless mild man.

22 *nocte clam*] words of similar meaning are often placed together without a copula in Livy, e.g. *luce palam* 24. 6, *clam furtim* XXI. 63. 9.

25 § 16. *fide*] here an 'assurance' i.e. of fidelity. Livy does not mention, as Polybius does, that the Romans hailed the prospect held out to them with exceeding joy (ὑπερβολῇ προθύμως δεξαμένων τὴν ἐλπίδα) and promised him (Abelux) valuable gifts. He is not proud of the transaction § 6.

27 *ad*] with a view to carrying out the business.

29 § 17. *excitatis*] *somno.* They were not in the plot.

31 § 18. *perducti*] 'the party', Abelux and the hostages.

p. 28. 1 *per*] expresses manner as in 18. 9 *per ludificationem.* But *eodem ordine* is the regular expression, the other not being found. P has *ordine.* Hence, *per eundem eodem ordine* has been suggested.

This is not improbable, for Polybius says the Romans employed Abelux to conduct the hostages to their homes, as he had undertaken to do for Bostar, III. 99. 6. The fulness of expression is characteristic of the whole sentence, being intended to express the completeness of the success of the stratagem.

2   **§ 19.** *Romanorum*] objective genitive.

3   *in re pari*] repeats the idea of *si...ageretur*, 'though the favour was the same as that which they (the Carthaginians) had intended to confer'.

4   *expertos*] passive as in XXI. 1. 2. So *partitus* ib. 21. 2. *emensus* ib. 30. 5.

5   **§ 20.** *Romanus*] 'the Roman general'. Publius Scipio as appears from the words which follow.

6   *ab re clementi*] '*with* an act of kindness'. Cf. *ab dis orsus* 9. 7.

7   *haud frustra*] 'with good reason'.

9   **§ 21.** *forent*] see on 9. 9.

Chapter XXIII.

12   **§ 1.** *quoque*] should probably be omitted, as a repetition of *quoque* in 22. 21.

13   *intervalli*] cf. 18. 10.

     cladibus] dative.

14   *sollers*] 'adroit'. It is said to be formed from *sollus* (=*totus*) and *ars*.

     cunctatio] cf. the well-known line of Ennius (quoted in Cic. *Off.* 1. 84).

> *Unus homo nobis cunctando restituit rem,*

adopted by Vergil, *A.* VI. 846,

> *Quo fessum rapitis Fabii? Tu Maximus ille es*
> *Unus qui nobis cunctando restituis rem.*

     § 2. *quae*] *cunctatio.*

15   *sollicitum...habebat*] 'kept H. in a state of anxiety'.

16   *cum*]=*talem.*

     militiae magistrum] 'director of the war', 'commander', on the analogy of *magister equitum*, *m. morum*, and *m. populi* which was the old expression for *dictator*. Perhaps this title suggested the nickname of 'Αννίβου παιδαγωγός which was given to Fabius at this time. Plut. *Fabius* 5.

17 *ratione...fortuna*] 'on system, and not by chance'. *Fortuna* is assimilated to *ratione*, otherwise the ablative would not have been used thus alone. *Eventus* and *ratio* are contrasted 39. 10. *Fortuna* and *ratio* 39. 21.

18 § 3. *contempta*] cf. Polybius III. 94. 8 Φάβιος δὲ κακῶς μὲν ἤκουε παρὰ τοῖς πολλοῖς, ὡς ἀνάνδρως ἐκ τοιούτων τόπων προέμενος τοὺς ὑπεναντίους. Fabius was ill spoken of among the majority, who thought he had shewn cowardice in letting the enemy escape from such a position.

19 *armatos...togatosque*] 'soldiers and civilians', the *toga* being the garb and symbol of peace. Cf. Cicero's *cedant arma togae* (*in L. Pisonem* 30) and Juv. x. 8 *nocitura toga nocitura petuntur militia*, i.e. *pace et bello.*

utique] 'at any rate'. For the meaning cf. 7. 11 note.

21 *laeto...quam prospero*] 'joyful rather than successful', because it caused exultation for the moment, but did not lead to any good result. The reference is to the engagement described later. 24. 11— 14.

verius] see on 19. 11. *dixerim*, a modest assertion.

22 *pugnatum fuerat*] Livy uses *fui fueram*, and *sum eram* indifferently to form the perf. and pluperf. pass., cf. 36. 8. The prose writers who preceded him join *fui fueram* with a participle only when it is used adjectivally and expresses a state. This is the case in 24. 2, 54. 1, where Livy's use of *fuerant* is quite correct.

25 § 4. *omnibus circa*] cf. 17. 3, etc.

ferrum ignemque] we say 'fire and sword'.

27 *ea*] *id* (sc. 'this act') is attracted into agreement with the predicate, as is usual when a pronoun is put first indefinitely as subj. or obj , e.g. *hic amor hoc studium.*

§ 5. *altera*] The second circumstance was that he had omitted to consult the senate about the captives. *Quod non expectavit* would have corresponded more closely to *quod iussit* above. But Livy diverges into a mention of the consequences of the act, instead of saying in what it consisted. This is indicated in what follows.

28 *primo*] 'in the first instance'.

forsitan] rare, except with a verb, which is usually in the subjunctive.

dubio] 'questionable'.

p. 29. 1 § 6. *primo*] *priore* the negotiators would have said, knowing of no third Punic war.

3 *quae*] i.e. *utra*, for which *quis* is sometimes used, not quite

correctly, e.g. Lucan *Phars.* I. 126 *quis iustius induit arma?* sc. Pompey or Caesar.

plus] sc. *captivorum.*

4   *pondo*] abl. = 'in weight'. Occasionally the name of the weight is not inserted, when some case of *libra* is understood. I. 17 *fulmen aureum pondo quinquaginta.*

bina et selibras] 2½ pounds = 210 denarii (as from 217—30 B.C. 84 denarii went to the libra) = about £7. 7s. (the denarius being reckoned at 8½d.).

selibras] *singulas.*

in militem] 'for each soldier'. For the distributive use of *in* cf. 52. 3 *pacti ut arma atque equos traderent, in capita Romana trecenis nummis quadrigatis,* etc.

6   § **7**. *iactata*] 'discussed'.

7   *tardius*] explained by *quoniam...consuluisset.* There was some delay because the Senate was offended at not having been consulted.

8   *erogaretur*] 'was voted from the treasury'.

9   § **8**. *fidem...exsolvit*] lit. set free the honour of the state which was engaged for the fulfilment of the promise, hence 'discharged the obligation of the state'. Cf. Pliny *Epp.* v. 10. I *libera hendecasyllaborum meorum fidem qui scripta tua communibus amicis spoponderunt,* and 22. 14 *fides...obligat fidem. publicam,* because Fabius had made the promise on behalf of the state as its representative.

10   § **9**. *Gereoni*] The narrative is resumed from c. 18. 7. There however Gereonium is spoken of as having been *deserted* by its inhabitants. Here Livy follows Polybius III. 100. 4, except that the latter says Hannibal left *most* of the houses standing.

12   *stativis*] sc. *castris* 9. 4.

§ **10**. *duas partes*] 'two-thirds'. Hannibal's object in making these arrangements was according to Polybius (III. 101. 10) 'to secure as large a store of provisions as he could, in order that he should have abundance all the time that he was in winter-quarters, not only for the men but also for the baggage animals and horses. For he placed his hopes in his cavalry more than in any part of his army'.

13   *in statione*] 'on guard'.

14   *praesidio*] sc. *futurus* (or *ut esset*) *praesidio. praesidio* is thus a predicative dative, cf. 59. 9 *praesidio castris relicti.* For the variety of expression, see Introd. II.

necunde] = *ne alicunde.* Cf. *necubi* 2. 3, 16. 5.

CHAPTER XXIV.

16 § **1.** *Larinati*] 18. 7. Larinum was rather to the N.W. of Gereonium where Hannibal was.

17 *profecto...dictatore*] *sacrorum causa* 18. 8.

20 § **2.** *in planum deferuntur*] Polybius says he descended by the ridge which projects into the plain (κατὰ τὴν ἐπὶ τὰ πεδία κατατείνουσαν ῥάχιν) and encamped near a place called Calene at its extremity, III. 101. 2.

pro] 'conformably to '.

21 *calidiora*] 'rasher'.· Cf. our expression 'hot-headed'. (D.)

23 *levi*] 'slender'.

26 § **4.** *quod minime quis crederet*] ' as would hardly have been believed '. However, according to Livy himself (cf. 23. 10), Hannibal did considerably reduce the proportion of those absent from the camp, on the approach of the enemy.

cum hostis propius esset] refers to the movement indicated by *in planum deferuntur* § 2.

29 § **5.** *tumulum*] Pol. ἐπί τινος βουνοῦ κατεστρατοπέδευσε, III. 101. 4. It was 16 stades nearer the enemy than the camp before Gereonium.

hosti conspectum] 'visible to the enemy '. Cf. *invictus* = 'invincible'.

30 *sciret*] *hostis.*

31 § **6.** *propior tumulus*] nearer to the Roman camp than the hill mentioned in § 5. Pol. γεωλόφου τινὸς ὑπάρχοντος μεταξὺ τῶν στρατοπέδων.

inde ei apparuit] sc. 'thence he (Hannibal) saw'.

32 *luce palam*] so *nocte clam* immediately after. See 22. 15 note.

p. **30.** 2 *Numidae*] apparently cavalry. Pol. λογχοφόροι 'light-armed '.

4 § **8.** *tum utique*] cf. 27. 2, lit. 'then at any rate ', = *tum vero*, and like *tum vero* introduces a climax. Cf. 7. 11, note. The preceding step is indicated in § 5, *propius movit.*

5 *conpleverat acies*] i.e. after it had been led forth from the camp. Pol. ἐξῆγε τὴν δύναμιν...καὶ τὰ βαρέα τῶν ὅπλων ἐξέταξε.

6 *per aversa a castris Hannibalis*] 'by the side (of the Roman camp) furthest removed from Hannibal's camp '. This would be by the *porta decumana*, the gate in the rear of the camp. P *castra e castris*. W. thinks some words may have fallen out, and that the passage may have run thus *per aversa castra* [*ne conspici posset*] *e castris Hannibalis*. For *aversa* neut. plur. used of locality, cf. 6. 5.

7   *caedem fugamque*] Polybius says that while the cavalry routed the stragglers the Roman infantry actually advanced to the Carthaginian camp and tried to tear down the ramparts, and were only repelled by the opportune arrival of Hasdrubal with reinforcements from the camp at Gereonium.   Livy does not represent the exploits of Minucius as so important.

9   § **9.** *ausus*] sc. *est.*

10   § **10.** *pars exercitus aberat iam fame*] this is the reading of P, al. *ferme.*   The words can hardly belong to this part of the sentence. They have no clear connection with *artibus Fabi*, which they separate most awkwardly from *sedendo et cunctando.*   Wlf. inserts them as an explanatory parenthesis after *paucitate* omitting *iam fame.*   For *iam fame* D. suggests *coacta fame*, cf. Pol. III. 101. 9 ἠναγκάζετο τοὺς μὲν ἐπὶ τὴν νομὴν τῶν θρεμμάτων ἀπομερίζειν τοὺς δ᾽ ἐπὶ τὴν σιτολογίαν.

12   *priora castra*] 23. 9.

13   § **11.** *iusta acie*] 'a regular battle', 28. 13.

     quidam] not Polybius; perhaps the annalist Fabius.   Observe that Livy notices an account which represents Fabius as saving the Romans from defeat.   See on § 8 *caedem fugamque.*   (The account here referred to bears a certain resemblance to the narrative of Polybius mentioned in that note.)

     auctores sunt] treated as one word = *tradunt*, cf. XXI. 38. 4 *ita quidam auctores sunt.*   It may even govern an acc. XXIII. 16. 15 *quod quidam auctores sunt.*

14   *fusum*] 'driven in confusion'.

17   § **12.** *Boviani*] Capital of the Samnite tribe called Pentri.

18   *unde erat*] sc. 'his native place'.

21   *praesidii*] often in Livy merely = troops.

23   § **13.** *duo castella*] perhaps referring to the two positions occupied by the Carthaginians after leaving the main camp (*stativa* 23. 10) before Gereonium, that on the *tumulus hosti conspectus* § 5, and that on the *tumulus imminens castris* § 7.

24   § **14.** *admodum*] = *circiter.*

25   *pari prope*] for the position of *prope* cf. 18. 9 *extracta prope aestate.*

     vanam] not in MSS., but inserted by all the editors: 'empty', 'lying'.   Cf. Verg. *A.* II. 80 *nec si miserum Fortuna Sinonem finxit, vanum etiam mendacemque improba finget.*

CHAPTER XXV.

28 § **1.** *contione*] used generically, 'the assembly'. *contione* is assimilated to *senatu;* otherwise one would have expected *contionibus,* as the *contio* was of course not a permanent body like the senate.

30 § **2.** *ut...essent*] The subjunctive with *ut* is here used with a concessive sense, 'even if all were true'. In or. recta this would be *ut sint.* Penelope writes to Ulysses *Protinus ut venias facta videbor anus,* Ov. *Her.* I. 116. Cf. XXI. 47. 5 *nec verisimile est, ut iam Hispanos inflati transvexerint utres.*

32 § **3.** *id enim vero...negat*] 'that this was really not to be endured'. MSS. *enim. enim vero* is Madvig's correction. *enim* might indeed be defended as indicating the ellipse of a sentence, 'Metellus (said he must speak) for it was unbearable', or as an asseverative participle, cf. *Georg.* II. 509 *hunc plausus hiantem per cuneos geminatus enim...corripuit.* But *enim vero* is especially used to express indignation. *enim,* according to Madvig, is not so used. He cites Cic. *Verr.* I. 66 *hic tum alius ex alia parte; enim vero ferendum hoc non est.*

p. **31.** 3 § **4.** *obstare*] sc. 'hinder its recognition', 'set himself against'. C. and B.

4 *sedulo*] 'purposely'.

6 § **5.** *alterum in acie*] Flaminius 6. 4.

7 *alterum...ablegatum*] Servilius 2. 7. Cf. c. 31.

8 *ablegatum*] 'despatched', in a military sense; not 'banished'. This would have been *relegatum.*

9 § **6.** *duos praetores*] T. Otacilius 31. 6 and A. Cornelius Mammula XXIII. 21. 4, where, it is true, they are both mentioned as requesting to be recalled, but only because they have no money for the payment of their troops. The passage does not seem to confirm the allegation that they were not required where they were.

12 *videret...gereret*] The other verbs in this speech (e.g. *sit, habeat, egeat*) are treated as if *negat* were a primary tense. The change is merely due to a desire for variety, and is facilitated by the fact that *negat,* an historic present, may be regarded either as a primary or as a secondary tense.

On the other hand where the speech is introduced by a verb in the past, Livy often changes to a primary sequence for the sake of greater vividness, the change being analogous to that from a past tense to the historic present in or. recta.

14 § **7.** *quo*] abl. of separation. *Poenis,* dativus commodi.

tamquam trans Hiberum agro] = *tamquam esset trans Hiberum ager.*
The reference is to the treaty of **225** B.C. with Hasdrubal, making the
Iberus the boundary between the Roman and Carthaginian territory,
XXI. **2. 7.** For the attributive use of *trans Hiberum* cf. 8. **1, 9. 5, 17. 3.**

16   *Casilini*] In **14. 1** Fabius views the devastation of the Falernian
plain from the Mons Massicus. Afterwards he occupies Casilinum to
prevent Hannibal's escape.

17   *agrum suum*] cf. **23. 4.** *tutante* is however not quite consistent with
the allegation there.

18   § **8.** *clausos*] with *retentos*, secondary predicate.
prope] following the word to which it belongs, as in **24. 14.**

19   *tamquam hostibus*] See on *tamquam trans Hiberum agro*, § **7.**

20   § **9.** *ut...ut*] the first = *cum primum*, the second = *tamquam.*

23   § **10.** *de abrogando imperio*] This would have been unconstitutional.
A Roman magistrate could not be deposed. The senate might induce
him to abdicate voluntarily, by a declaration procured from the augurs
that there was a flaw in his election (i.e. that he was *vitio creatus*), or he
might do so in deference to a senatorial decree. But if he had the
courage he might disregard the decree, as Flaminius did in **223** B.C.
(cf. **3. 13** note). *abrogabatur* is used incorrectly of the attempt to make
Flaminius resign in XXI. 63. **2.** Tiberius Gracchus' deposition of
Octavius from the tribuneship by vote of the tribes in **133** B.C. was
illegal.

nunc] 'as it was', often used like Greek νῦν δὲ to contrast an actual
with an imagined state of things.

24   *aequando iure*] It appears that Minucius was actually appointed as
a second dictator. Pol. III. 103. 4 καὶ δὴ δύο δικτάτορες ἐγεγόνεσαν ἐπὶ
τὰς αὐτὰς πράξεις, ὃ πρότερον οὐδέποτε συνεβεβήκει τοῖς Ῥωμαίοις. Polybius'
statement is confirmed by *C. I. L.* I. 1503 *Hercolei sacrum Marcus
Minuci(us) C. F. dictator vovit.*

25   *iure*] 'rights', 'position', not *imperio*, for Minucius as master of the
horse did not possess it.

§ **11.** *nec...ne quidem*] for the repetition of the negative without
destroying its negative force cf. **14. 4.**

ne ita quidem] 'not even so', i.e. not even when this resolution has
been carried.

27   *suffecisset*] cf. the expression *consul suffectus.* Fabius would not
appoint a consul, but only preside at the *comitia* held for his election.

§ **12.** *in actione minime popularis*] *in actione* = *in agendo*, 'as he
was not at all popular as a speaker'. For *popularis* Madvig reads *popu-*

lari. Then *actio*, which generally='a pleading', or a speech before senate or people would have a more general meaning, 'political action', and the meaning would be 'he refrained from speaking in support of an unpopular policy'.

28 *satis*] not *quite* 'favourably'. For the strong meaning of *satis* when a negative has preceded cf. 4. 4.

29 *verbis extolleret*] *verbis* is generally added when the meaning of *extollere* is metaphorical.

30 *clades acceptas referret*] 'recalled the disasters which had been endured'. *referre acceptum*='to put down as received', e.g. Hor. *Ep.* II. 1. 234 *rettulit acceptos regale nomisma Philippos*. But this is not the meaning here, unless, as has been suggested, *temeritati...inscitiae* be read. For the dat. of the person to whose credit the entry is made cf. V. 22. 2 *quod praedae rettulere...nec duci...nec senatui, sed Liciniae familiae acceptum referebant.*

p. 32. 1 § 14. *sit*] in oratio recta *erit*, 'if I am continued in my command'. One would have expected *esset* for *sit*, as the time of the main action is past (*audiebatur, referret*). But Livy constantly reverts to primary sequences for the sake of greater vividness. See on § 6.

2 *bono imperatore*] 'if the general be a good one'.

3 § 15. *in tempore*] 'at the right moment', ἐν τῷ καιρῷ.

6 § 16. *M. Atilio Regulo*] He had been consul in 227 B.C. and was now an old man, cf. 40. 6. With the caution of age he adopted the policy of Fabius, 32. 1.

7 *iure imperii*] 'claims to power'.

rogationis] *de aequando iure* § 10.

9 § 17. *plebis concilium*] General assemblies of the whole Roman people were called *comitia*. The term *concilium* was applied to meetings which did not include the whole people. It is especially applied to the meetings of the plebs apart from the patricians, i.e. the *comitia tributa*. The latter was convoked by a tribune (as here by Metilius) or an aedile, these being the original plebeian magistrates.

magis...invidia...versabat...quam...audebant] The meaning is *tacita invidia versabat...sed non audebant.*

10 *versabat*] 'worked on their minds', XXI. 30. 1 *advocata contione varie militum versat animos castigando adhortandoque.*

satis] 'quite', for *magis...quam audebant* implies *non audebant*. See 4. 4 note.

13 *superante*]=*abundante*, 'though the motion found abundant favour'. Cic. *de Or.* II. 83 *Pecunia superabat? at egebas.*

auctoritas] 'influential support'.

14 § **18**. *sordido*] The Romans regarded all traffic on a small scale and all manual labour as mean (*quaestus illiberales et sordidi*); especially did they despise the trades which ministered to the pleasures of the table. *minime artes eae probandae sunt quae ministrae sunt voluptatum.*

cetarii, lanii, coqui, fartores, piscatores

ut ait Terentius, Cic. *de Officiis* II. 42. 150.

15 § **19**. *ipsum institorem mercis*] 'who sold his own goods retail'. An additional disgrace, for the *lanius* usually allowed others (*mercatores*) to hawk their wares. *institor* means technically a person who sells the goods of another.

CHAPTER XXVI.

17 § **1**. *ex eo genere quaestus*] depending on *pecunia*.
pecunia] is the nominative. *ei* is omitted after *fecit*, as in 19. 4.

18 *animos*] the plural is used in speaking of an individual, implying a superabundance of courage or spirit. Cf. § 3, Verg. *A.* VII. 383 of a whipping top, *dant animos plagae.*
liberalioris] opposed to *sordidus* 25. 18. Greek ἐλεύθερος. *fortunae,* 'position'.

19 § **2**. *toga*] the *toga* was the dress of the higher, the *tunica* of the lower classes. Hor. *Ep.* I. 7. 65 *vilia vendentem tunicato scruta popello.* But *toga* is mentioned here rather with reference to its being the garb worn on public occasions; and *toga et forum* together express the idea of 'a public life'.

20 *proclamando*] 'declaiming'. The word is used in a contemptuous sense=shouting not speaking. *clamare* and *dicere* are contrasted Cic. *Div. in Caec.* § 48. Cic. *de Or.* I. 46 *non enim...proclamatorem aut rabulam* (a ranter) *hoc nostro sermone conquirimus.*

21 *rem*] *familiarem.*
bonorum] 'respectable citizens'. Livy means by *boni* members of the aristocratic party, IX. 46. 12 *ex eo tempore in duas partes discessit civitas; aliud integer populus, fautor et cultor bonorum, aliud forensis factio tendebat* (W.). Cicero often uses *boni* in this sense.

There was no public prosecutor at Rome, and the most effectual way by which a young Roman could rise to distinction was by impeaching leading men. Thus Cato the elder was prosecuted no less than 44 times in his life.

22 § **3**. *honores*] specified immediately afterwards. P has *quaestura*

quoque. If this be read *honores* refers to the *minores magistratus*, membership of the boards III. *viri capitales* and *monetales*, and X. *viri litibus iudicandis.*

23   *duabus*] this was quite exceptional.

25   § **4.** *haud parum callide*] litotes, ' with no small cunning '.

26   *dictatoria*] represents an objective genitive, 'against the dictator'. XXI. 63. 1 *consularibus impedimentis.* D. compares Cic. *Cluent.* XXVIII. 77 *ex invidia senatoria crescere.*

27   § **5.** *que...que*] used by Livy only to join two relative clauses but often thus : not in Cic. or Caes.

28   *aequi atque iniqui*] 'friends and foes '.

29   *in contumeliam*] *in* expresses purpose, but we should translate ' as an insult '. 20. 8.

30   § **6.** *ad*]=*apud.*

32   § **7.** *litteris senatusque consulto*] The despatches probably contained notice of the *senatus consultum* and directions based upon it. *Litterae* and *senatus consulta* are constantly mentioned together. XLIV. 15. 1 *senatus consultum recitatum* (in the Senate)...*litteraeque extemplo ad utramque gentem ut id sciret indicatum mitti.*

CHAPTER XXVII.

p. 33.   4   § **1.** *rebus...favore*] abl. cause. Cf. 11. 6 *vetustate iam oblitos eius imperii.* 13. 4 *fraude.*

5   § **2.** *tum utique*]=*tum vero*, which would have been written had not *vero* preceded. It corresponds to *iam ante.* Cf. 24. 8.

6   *non magis quam*] 'quite as much '. Gk. οὐ μᾶλλον ἤ, 12. 11.

victo] for the construction cf. XLII. 47. 1 *ut nulla re magis gloriaretur quam decepto per indutias rege.*

7   *Fabio*] sc. *victo.*

8   § **3.** *unicum*] ironical as in 14. 9 *nobis dictator unicus in rebus adfectis quaesitus*, note.

parem] with *Hannibali*, ' as a match for H.'.

quaesitum] 'gotten' rather than 'sought'. So Hor. *S.* I. I. 37 of the ant, *illis utitur ante quaesitis sapiens.*

9   *maiorem minori*] referring to rank.

10   *memoria annalium*] 'historic record'. Strictly speaking Minucius can only refer to the Annales Pontificum, which contained a meagre official record of important events and prodigies. Fabius the first of the annalists was *aequalis temporibus huiusce belli*, 7. 4.

12   *magistri equitum*] During the second Samnite war, in 325 B.C., the

master of the horse Q. Fabius Rullianus, contrary to the orders of the dictator and L. Papirius Cursor gave battle and won a victory. But for the prayers of the people Fabius would have had him executed. As it was he deposed him from his office. Livy VIII. 30—35.

13 *tremere...horrere*] the use of these verbs with an accusative is poetical. Roby § 1123.

§ **4**. *tantum enituisse*] for this use of *tantus* adding a reason for a statement which has preceded, cf. 28. 13. So *adeo* is often used in silver Latin.

15 *deorum*] who had given victory to Minucius 24. 14.

hominum] who had passed the plebiscitum giving him equal authority with Fabius, 26. 7.

18 *quomodo utantur*] 'how they were to arrange', a deliberative subjunctive.

§ **6**. *se optumum ducere* etc.] Polybius says that Fabius gave Minucius the choice, proposing that they should either command in turn or divide the forces, and that Minucius readily chose the latter. III. 103. 7.

20 *partitis temporibus*] 'during equally divided periods' (sc. of greater length).

23 § **8**. *eam fortunam habitura*] *fortunam* is the object. M has *omnia eram*, al. *enim*.

24 *quamcumque*] Wlf. reads less well, *quaecunque:* then the meaning would be 'that fortune would sway everything that his colleague controlled'. Cf. 29. 1.

habuisset] in or. recta *habuerit*.

sibi communicatum] 'had been divided between himself and another'. *communicare* is used with the dat. only when the other party sharing is expressed by an ablative governed by *cum*.

25 *alio*] Madvig reads *illo*, remarking that *altero* would have been written for *alio* as there are only two parties concerned. But *alio* may express contempt.

26 § **9**. *qua posset*] either (1) = *qua posset non cedere*, being taken closely in connexion with *numquam cessurum*. Then *qua* is rel. agreeing with *parte* and the meaning of the sentence is 'he would never willingly surrender the share which he could still retain in guiding matters by his counsel'; or (2) = *qua posset res gerere*, being taken more closely in connexion with *gerendarum*. Then the meaning is 'he would never willingly surrender his share of guiding affairs by his counsel wherever he could'. *qua*, adv. *pars* in this case = rightful share. So 'right'

(or='duty', a post-augustan meaning of the word. Cf. Quintilian V.
13. 1 *pars defensoris tota est posita in refutatione*).

27 *tempora*] 'periods'.

28 *exercitum*] sc. '*but* the army'. An adversative asyndeton.

29 *liceret...posset*] *servare*.

31 § **10**. *evenerunt*] 'fell to', i.e. *sorte*. XXI. **17**. 1 *Iam sortiri iussi Cornelio Hispania Sempronio Africa evenit.*

32 § **11**. *socium*] for the termination see **22**. 5 *liberum.*

p. 34. 1 *castris...separari*] abl. respect, 'to have a separate camp'.
Pol. III. 103. 8 ἀπέχοντες ὡς δώδεκα σταδίους.

CHAPTER XXVIII.

4 § **1**. *quae agerentur*] the subjunctive gives a meaning of indefiniteness 'which might be done', and so is used of repeated action, 'which
were done from time to time'.

5 *perfugis indicantibus et...explorantem*] on the change of construction
see Introd. II.

per suos] Hannibal had spies even in Rome, 33. 1. Polybius III.
104 says he learnt this from his prisoners.

6 § **2**. *liberam*] sc. now freed from the control of his colleague.

9 § **3**. *occupasset*] the subjunctive because *qui occupasset* represents
the protasis of a conditional sentence, '*quem si quis occupasset*'.

10 *iniquiorem*] cf. *aequiore* 16. 2.

locum] 'his position', i.e. the position of the enemy against whom
it was seized. Pol. III. 104. 3 ὑπεροχῆς δυναμένης ἑκατέρους βλάπτειν.

12 § **4**. *operae pretium*] 'worth the trouble'.

14 § **5**. *prima specie*] lit. 'in appearance as first viewed', 'at first
sight'.

15 *non modo*]=not *non modo non*. For if both clauses have a common
predicate to which the negative belongs, and the predicate stands in the
last clause, the negation which lies in *ne...quidem* may be referred to
the whole. Madvig § 461. E. g. Cic. *Lael.* 24 *assentatio non modo
amico sed ne libero quidem homine digna est.* In such cases *non modo* is
best rendered by 'I do not say' or 'much less'.

16 § **6**. *natus*] 4. 2 *loca nata insidiis*.

18 *et*] 'and indeed' i.e. 'the fact was'.

in anfractibus] 'in the windings of the valley'. *anfractus* is an
incorrect translation of περίκλασις in Polybius who mentions no valley.
III. 104. 4 τῶν τόπων τῶν περὶ τὸν λόφον πολλὰς ἐχόντων περικλάσεις
καὶ κοιλότητας, 'broken ground and hollows'.

ut] an instance of the 'definitive' or 'descriptive' use of *ut* 'some of
them capable of containing'. This is really an *ut* of consequence,
cf. 5. 7.

19   § 7. *quot quemque locum...poterant*] This clause distributes the
quinque milia mentioned afterwards. Pol. l.c. says the troops were
posted ἀνὰ διακοσίους καὶ τριακοσίους.

21   § 8. *necubi*]=*ne alicubi*, 2. 3.

22   *egressi*]=not 'who had gone forth', but 'who should have gone
forth' *si egressus esset.*

23   *detegeret*] *eos.*

24   *avertit*] Hannibal, last mentioned in § 4.

26   § 9. *deposcere pellendos*] 'demanded the task of dislodging': for
the use of the gerundive as an oblique predicative to the direct object of
a transitive verb, cf. 54. 2 *eos...accipiendos curandosque cum divisissent.*

27   *inter stolidissimos*] 'conspicuous among the most senseless', VII. 5.
6 *stolide ferocem.*

        ad arma vocat] the accusative is left unexpressed, as with other
verbs expressing military manoeuvres, cf. 1. 1 *movit*, 15. 12 *ducturus.*

29   § 10. *dimittit*] 'sends off', i.e. from the camp. Pol. ἐξαπέστειλε.

31   § 11. *et*] 'also', 'on his part', unlike *et* in § 5.

        alia atque alia] 'more and more'. Pol. III. 105. 2 συνεχῶς
ἐπαποστέλλοντος τοῖς ἐν τῷ λόφῳ τοὺς βοηθήσοντας.

32   *increscente*] P *aut*, C *ut crescente*, 'as was natural when the
conflict waxed fiercer', but this meaning is rather weak here. Further
Wlf. points out that this use of *ut*=*ut par erat* occurs almost ex-
clusively before prepositions beginning with a vowel.

p. 35. 1 *iustam*] 'regular', hence 'complete'.

2   § 12. *prima*] used adverbially, 'first the light-armed', or ad-
jectively, 'which had been first despatched'.

6   § 13. *iusta...pugna*] a regular, i.e. regularly conducted, fight.
illa ordinata per principes hastatosque et triarios, 5. 7 opposed to
tumultuarium certamen. Cf. XXI. 8. 7 *nihil tumultuariae pugnae
simile erat, sed iustae acies velut patenti campo constiterant.*

        recta] 'straightforward', 'front to front', a fight in which there
were no attacks on flank or rear.

7   *tantum animorum fecerat*] cf. 26. 1, the plural *animorum* indicates abundant courage.

8   *res*] 24. 11—14.

NOTES. 143

CHAPTER XXIX.

11 **§ 1.** *Fabius*] Fabius' words are not given by Polybius. They are probably from Coelius Antipater following Fabius Pictor, who glorifies his kinsman.

12 *primo*] answered by *dein.*

paventium] Livy constantly uses gen. plural participles substantively. They are best rendered by an abstract substantive. 5. 4 *terrentium paventiumque.*

13 *ita est*] 'It is as I thought', or more colloquially 'there now'. In Grk. τοῦτ᾽ ἐκεῖνο.

non celerius] the words are to be explained thus, 'quickly indeed, but not more quickly than I feared', i.e. just as soon as I feared; Plutarch *Fabius* 12 has τάχιον μὲν ἢ ἐγὼ προσεδόκων βράδιον δὲ ἢ αὐτὸς ἔσπευδε Μινούκιος ἑαυτὸν ἀπολώλεκε. If this is the correct version Livy's words should run: *Non celerius quam meruit, citius quam timui.*

14 *deprendit*] usu. *deprehendit* 'has overtaken', 'caught'. Hor. *S.* I. 2. 134 *deprendi miserum est, Fabio vel i dice vincam.*

15 **§ 2.** *Fabio aequatus*] i.e. his elevation has only resulted in his humiliation.

19 *civibus*] = *concivibus*, 'our countrymen'. It includes both the troops of Minucius and those at Rome who had voted for the bill of Metellus.

§ 3. *magna ex parte*] refers to both clauses, 'when many had been slain and many were looking for the chance to fly'.

circumspectantibus] cf. 15. 2.

20 *caelo demissa*] usu. *de caelo*, but VIII. 9. 10 *sicut caelo missus.* (D.)

21 **§ 4.** *priusquam veniret*] Livy and later writers use *antequam* and *priusquam* with the subjunctive of facts in the past, cf. 4. 7.

23 *continuit*] the subject is Fabius (suggested by *Fabiana acies*) as appears from *suos.*

24 *vage*] 'hither and thither'.

25 **§ 5.** *plures simul*] 'several together' as opposed to those who were entirely isolated.

26 *volventes orbem*] the idea contained in the substantive is repeated in the verb. We should say, 'forming a circle'. The operation corresponds to some extent, but not exactly, to forming a square, as the formation was one in which all the troops faced the enemy, but was circular instead of four-sided. Cf. Sallust *Iug.* 97 *Romani*

*veteres et ob id scientes belli...orbes fecere, atque ita ab omnibus partibus
simul tecti et instructi simul vim sustentabant.*

27   *conglobati*] 'massed together', i.e. in the order which they are
described as forming in *volventes orbem.*

    restare] 'resisted'. In Cic. and Caes. the word is only used with
the meaning of 'to remain '.

28   *exercitus*] depending on *acies*, lit. a single force had been formed
consisting of the beaten and the unbroken army; gen. of contents or of
that in which the thing consists. Roby § 1302.

29   *receptui*] dat. purpose.

    § **6.** *palam ferente*] 'openly declaring'. Cf. 14. 15 *haud dubie
ferebant (se) Minucium Fabio ducem praelaturos,* and note.

31   § **7.** *per*] expresses manner, or attendant circumstances 'amid
changing fortunes': 18. 9 *extracta aestate per ludificationem hostis.*

p. **36.** 1 § **8.** *cum primum* sqq.] this gnomè occurs in Hesiod,
Works and Days, 293:

            οὗτος μὲν πανάριστος ὃς αὐτὸς πάντα νοήσῃ,
            ἐσθλὸς δ' αὖ κἀκεῖνος ὃς εὖ εἰπόντι πίθηται,
            ὃς δέ κε μήτ' αὐτὸς νοέῃ μήτ' ἄλλου ἀκούων
            ἐν θύμῳ βάλληται, ὅδ' αὖτ' ἀχρήϊος ἀνήρ.

It is quoted by Aristotle, *Eth.* 1. 4. 7 and adapted by Cic. *Pro
Cluent.* XXXI. 84 and by Livy here.

2   *consulat*] here and just below *consulere* = 'to give counsel'.

    in rem] 'to the purpose', 3. 2.

3   *consulere*] here used absolutely.

4   *extremi*] lit. 'last', 'most worthless', cf. Sall. *Or. Phil., M. Aemilius,
omnium flagitiosorum postremus.*

    § **9.** *prima sors...ingeniique*] rather 'the highest rank in the scale
of spirit and intellect' than 'the highest lot, that of spirit etc.'; for *sors*
cf. IIor. *C.* IV. 11. 22 *non tuae sortis iuvenem.*

5   *ac*] explanatory, 'that is to say'.

6   *dum discimus*] 'till we have learnt', lit. while we are learning.
The event expected is treated as if it occupied the time of waiting, cf.
Verg. *B.* IX. 23 *Tityre dum redeo, brevis est via, pasce capellas:*
Roby § 1663.

7   § **10.** *cum Fabio*] i.e. 'with that of Fabius'. For the brachylogy
cf. XXI. 4. 8 *vestitus nihil inter aequales excellens,* ib. 45. 6.

    praetorium] 'head-quarters'.

11   § **11.** *patronos*] the soldiers of Minucius are conceived of as

liberti, owing their freedom to those of Fabius, who are thus their *patroni.*

salutabitis] the future of command : less peremptory than the imperative.

gratorum animorum] 'gratitude', for which abstract idea there is no single word in good Latin.

CHAPTER XXX.

12   § **1.** *signo dato*] by the commander.

13   *conclamatur*] not by the soldiers in general, but by the proper officers 'word was given'. *conclamatur ad arma* VII. 5. 11. Cf. Caes. *B. C.* I. 66. 2 *signum dari iubet et vasa militari more conclamari*, where the expression is elliptical; though it is possible that the actual cry was *vasa.* *vasa colligere* like *signa movere* is constantly used to indicate the breaking up of a camp. *vasa=impedimenta.*

14   *agmine*] 'in order of march'.

15   *in admirationem converterunt*] *converterunt* 'attracted their attention'. Cf. XXI. 3. 4 *cum admiratione tam ancipitis sententiae in se omnes convertisset.* The expression is here altered by the substitution of *in admirationem* for *admiratione. in* expresses consequence as in XXI. 63. 14 *id in omen magni terroris acceptum* (=*ut esset omen*). Lit. 'had attracted their attention so that they were astonished', 'had attracted their wondering attention'.

17   § **2.** *tribunal*] a raised platform, usually of turf, but in stationary camps (*stativa*) sometimes of stone, whence the general might address the assembled army (*contio*): on such occasions the standards were placed before the tribunal, as here.

   alios]=*ceteros.* This use of *alios=*ὁ ἄλλος occurs not unfrequently in Livy, but not in earlier prose writers, e.g. XXVI. 8. 5 *Iovem deosque alios.*

19   *militum*] a partitive genitive, like *delecti equitum* 15. 10.

21   § **3.** *modo*] 'just now'.

   quod fando possum] *quod=nam id tantum. possum,* sc. *facere.* The words are a comment on *nomine* which is emphatic, 'in *name,* which is all I can do in words', 'which is all that words can do; hereafter my *acts* will shew that I am grateful as a son to his father'.

23 § **4.** *oneratus...honoratus*] the play on the words may be reproduced by contrasting 'onerous' and 'honourable'. The use of words of similar sound, and of rhyming words (ὁμοιοτέλευτα) were recognized artifices with Roman writers. Quintilian gives instances of each IX. 3. 71—78, e.g. *ex oratore arator Phil.* III. 9. **22**, *quantum possis in ea semper experire ut prosis.* With the present passage cf. L. XXI. **24. 4** *hospitem enim se Galliae non hostem advenisse.*

24 *antiquo*] lit. 'I leave in its ancient state' (sc. the law), is used of rejecting a bill. *Antiquare* is properly used of rejecting a new proposal, *abrogare* of repealing an existing law. The question being here of a *plebiscitum* which has already become law *antiquo* is used rather loosely, and is more nearly explained by *abrogo*. 'I reject and repeal'.

quod sit felix] 'praying that this act may be prospered'. Cic. *div.* I. 45. 105 (*Romani*) *omnibus rebus agendis 'quod bonum faustum felix fortunatumque essent' praefabantur.*

26 *auspicium*] Only a commander-in-chief could take the auspices, consequently a *legatus* or inferior officer was said to be and act under the auspices of his commander-in-chief. To this position, in relation to Fabius, Minucius by relinquishing his *imperium* returns.

28 § **5.** *ordines*] as *tribuni, centuriones, hastati, principes, triarii.*

tenere] 'retain': there is a zeugma, for *recipere* would be more appropriate of Minucius.

29 § **6.** *interiunctae*] The preposition denotes reciprocal action, 'they clasped one another's hands'.

31 *laetus*] to be taken with *factus est*, as part of the predicate.

tristi paulo ante] sc. *qui fuerat paulo ante tristis:* for Livy's use of adverbs in the place of adjectives or relative clauses cf. **23. 4** *omnibus circa*, **17. 3** note.

32 *execrabili*] a *dies ater*, IX. 6, like the anniversary of the defeat on the Allia.

§ **7.** *perlata*] sc. *eo.* Cf. the omission of *ei*, 26. 1.

p. 37. 1 *non magis*] **27. 2.**

volgo] 'in general'. *militum vulgo = gregariorum.*

3 *laudibus ferre*] Pol. III. 105. 10 λοιπὸν ἤδη Φαβίῳ προσεῖχον τὸν νοῦν.

5 § **9.** *biennio ante*] *ante = quod antierat.* 'During the last two years'. Not quite accurate, for it was now the autumn of 217 B.C. and the first defeat of the Romans on the Ticinus had only taken place in the autumn of 218 B.C.

7   *famam*] P *eam famam*, but to express *tam terribilem, illam* would probably have been used.

10   **§ 10.** *solita sit*] Note the return to primary sequence though *dixisse* is an aorist.

cum procella imbrem] cf. XL. **2.** 1 *atrox cum vento tempestas.*

dedisse]=*edidisse.* The episode, which is described from c. 23 down to this point, thus ends in the complete justification of Fabius, cf. 23. **2** *Fabi cunctatio contempta erat inter civis armatos pariter togatosque* with 30. 7 *pro se quisque Maximum laudibus ferre*, and Ennius' lines ap. Cic. *de Sen.* 4

> *unus homo nobis cunctando restituit rem,*
> *non hic ponebat rumores ante salutem.*
> *ergo postque magisque viri nunc gloria claret.*

CHAPTER XXXI.

11   **§ 1.** *Cn. Servilius Geminus*] the narrative is resumed from 11. 7.

13   *Sardiniae*] According to Polybius III. 9. 6, the Carthaginian fleet which had taken the Roman ships near Cosa (11. 6) was off Sardinia. On the approach of Servilius it retreated to Carthage. Servilius pursued, but without success.

15   **§ 2.** *escensiones*] 20. 4.

faceret] see on *priusquam veniret* 29. 4.

16   *Menige*] The island of Meninx (now Djerba) lay S. of the Syrtis Minor. This was the island of the Lotophagi, described in the *Odyssey.*

incolentibus C.] Livy constantly uses a participle governing an acc. with the meaning of a substantive with a genitive depending upon it. **22.** 11 *novas volentibus res.*

17   *Cercina*] Karkineh, N. of the Syrtis Minor. It possessed an important harbour.

et ipsorum] like that of the people of Meninx.

18   *talentis*] perhaps indicates Fabius Pictor as Livy's authority, as he wrote in Greek. Generally Livy expresses large sums by *auri pondo*, 1. 17. The talent (Euboic) was worth £243. 15*s.*

19   *Africae*] Polybius does not mention this landing in Africa.

20   **§ 3.** *navales socii*] 'seamen', see on 11. 7.

21   *iuxta ac si*] so Sall. *Jugurtha*, 45 *castra munire iuxta ac si postes adessent.* Generally Livy uses *iuxta ac*, 32. 5 *iuxta ac pro capite Italiae.* It qualifies *effusi.*

effusi] 'dispersing'. 12. 9 *effusis populatoribus. effuse* 9. 3, *effusa* 3. 9 have a different meaning.

cultorum egentibus] 'uninhabited'. *incultis* would mean 'un-cultivated'.

23 § **4.** *a frequentibus*] opp. to *palantes*, 'by compact bodies'.

palantes] = 'straying from the others'. *vagari* = 'to wander at random'.

25 § **5.** *ad mille...amissum*] *mille* is nom., *ad* being an adverb and not affecting the construction. 41. 2 *ad mille et septingenti caesi. mille* is generally an indeclinable adjective. It is sometimes used as a sub-stantive, as here, but (except very rarely) only in nom. and acc., cf. 37. 8. Even thus it is more often followed by a plural than a sin-gular verb. XXIII. 44. 7 *mille passuum erant inter urbem castraque.* Madvig, *Lat. Gr.* § 72.

28 *Lilybaei*] now Marsala, on the extreme W. of Sicily. It was the most important naval station and fortress of the Romans in the island.

T. Otacilio] 10. 10.

29 § **7.** *ipse*] Otacilius himself as opposed to the fleet.

pedibus] 'by land'. Gk. πεζῇ.

30 *freto*] sc. *Siculo*, by the straits of Messina. For the abl. XXI. 56. 9 *Pado traiectus.*

p. **38.** 1 *et conlega eius*] added as a kind of nominative absolute, as it belongs to *accitus* alone and not to *traiecit.*

M. Atilius] Regulus the *consul suffectus*, elected in place of Flaminius, 25. 16.

2 *semestri imperio*] The maximum duration of the dictatorship was six months (Mommsen, *R. H.* I. 263). Cf. IX. 34. 12 *semestri dicta-tura.* It was often much less, cf. ibid. § 14 *qui intra vicesimum diem ingentibus rebus gestis dictatura se abdicaverunt.*

3 § **8.** *omnium*] Here follows a sort of excursus like that on the duration of the siege of Saguntum, XXI. 15, or the route of Hannibal over the Alps, ibid. 38. Livy corrects his statement in 8. 6 that Fabius was appointed dictator. Possibly he came across the view here ad-vanced in some writer after he had completed the section of the work to which c. 8 belongs.

dictatorem] 'as dictator', or 'was dictator when he carried on the war'. This would be more clearly expressed in Greek by δικτάτορα ὄντα στρατεῦσαι.

4 *Coelius*] Antipater, see Introduction I.

primum etc.] 'that he was the first who was created'. Coelius' words imply that others had been appointed dictator by the people since Fabius. This is a mistake. No other dictators were appointed by the people except Sulla and Caesar, to whom Coelius, who was a contemporary of the Gracchi about 120 B.C., could not refer. The appointment by the people in the case of Fabius was quite exceptional. Mommsen, *Röm. Staatsrecht*, II. 1. 139.

7 § **9.** *Gallia*] i.e. the *Ager Gallicus* in Umbria where Ariminum was situated. Cf. 8. 1, 9. 6.

§ **10.** *quam moram*] 'the delay thus caused'. Cf. *quo metu* XXI. 5. 4.

8 *expectare*] sc. 'to tolerate', correctly ' to await its expiration'.

9 *decursum esse*] depending on *fugit*, like *obtinuisse*.

10 § **11.** *inde*] temporal.

11 *augentis*] We should say 'the exaggerations', instead of ' those exaggerating '.

titulum imaginis] *imagines* were waxen masks representing the faces of ancestors, kept in the atrium of a Roman house. Only those who had held a curule magistracy (consul, praetor, or aedile) could be thus commemorated. Thus, Sall. *Jug.* 85 *homo veteris prosapiae ac multarum imaginum* means a man of long and illustrious ancestry. *titulus* was the inscription placed beneath such masks recording the honours and exploits of the deceased. Probably *dictator bis* appeared on the *titulus* of Fabius as on his elogium or epitaph. *C. I. L.* 1. 288. Such *tituli* may have been altered from family pride, cf. VIII. 41. 2 *vitiatam memoriam funebribus laudibus reor falsisque imaginum titulis.*

12 *obtinuisse ut crederetur*] lit. 'brought it about that he was believed '.

CHAPTER XXXII.

13 § **1.** *Atilius*] Regulus 31. 7. It is strange that only his *nomen* is mentioned here, while both the *cognomen* and the *nomen* of his colleague are given.

Geminus Servilius] the cognomen is placed first as in 40. 6.

Fabiano...Minuciano] because their camps were now separate. 27. 11—12.

14 *hibernaculis*] the consuls formed separate winter-quarters.

15 *quod reliquom*] P *quom.* C, M *eum.* It was probably now October.

17 § **2.** *diversis locis*] i.e. from each other. The two consuls acted independently, though in accordance with a common plan.

18 *opportuni aderant*] cf. 6. 4 *infesto venienti.*

carpentes] 'harassing'. See note on 16. 2 *carptim.*

19 *excipientes*] 12. 7, a term borrowed from hunting.

casum universae dimicationis]=*universo periculo* 12. 10, 'the risk of a general engagement'.

20 § **3.** *adeoque...coactus*] 'he was so far constrained by hunger'. Madvig says this is not Latin, and reads *eoque inopiae est redactus.*

21 *nisi cum fugae specie...fuisset*] *cum* = *non sine.* We should say 'unless retreat would necessarily have presented the appearance of flight'.

22 *repetiturus fuerit*] not *repetivisset*, for the verb must have been in the subjunctive because of its dependence on *ut*, irrespectively of its expressing the apodosis of a conditional sentence. The perf. subj. is used in this periphrastic conjugation, even if the verb depends on a secondary tense, as here, except in interrogative sentences, where *fuissem* is used. Roby § 1521. Livy XXIV. 26 *virgines eo cursu ex sacrario se proripuerunt ut si effugium patuisset impleturae urbem tumultu fuerint.*

25 § **4.** *Gereonium*] 23. 9.

constitisset] 'had come to a stand-still'. XXI. 49. 1.

26 *Neapolitani*] The original settlement, a colony from Cumae, was called Parthenope. On the arrival of fresh settlers, a distinction arose between the new city (Neapolis) and the old (Palaeopolis), twin cities with separate walls, though politically united. A quarrel with Palaeopolis was the occasion of the first Samnite war. Palaeopolis was betrayed to the consul Publilius, and we hear of it no more. Neapolis joined the Roman alliance on favourable terms, as a *civitas foederata*, B.C. 325.

28 *ita verba facta, ut dicerent*] 'they spoke to the following effect'. *ut dicerent* is added pleonastically in order that there may be a verb for the acc. and infin. to depend upon.

29 § **5.** *iuxta ac*]=*aeque ac.* 31. 3 note.

30 *urbe...imperio*] The repetition of *atque* so soon after *ac* is strange, and the sentence unsymmetrical. Wlf. suspects the clause as a gloss, from XXI. 35. 9. W. is inclined to strike out *capite...Italiae.*

31 § **6.** *geratur*] sc. *bellum.*

p. 39. 1 *foret*] see on 9. 9 *foret.*

2 § **7.** *si crederent*] 'had it been their belief'. The imperf. sub-

junctive can be used like the pluperfect to express a hypothetical act in the past: only the latter is used of a single or completed, the former of a continued act. Cf. Hor. *S.* I. 3. 6 *si collibuisset ab ovo usque ad mala citaret Io Bacche.*

in sese] in their persons, as opposed to their gold.

4   § 8. *duxissent...iudicaverint*] Livy often changes from secondary to primary sequence in or. obliqua, to give greater vividness to some part of the speech by representing the action from the point of view of the speaker instead of that of the narrator; but the change here is more than usually abrupt, cf. 25. 14.

5   *animo...voluntate*] ablatives of cause depending on *amplius.* Hor. C. III. 5. 40 *Carthago probrosis altior Italiae ruinis.*

CHAPTER XXXIII.

9   § 1. *speculator Carthaginiensis*] not necessarily a Carthaginian; very likely a Greek slave engaged (as many were) in trade at Rome. Hannibal's intelligence department seems to have been well served. Cf. 28. 1.

10   *fefellerat*]=Gk. λανθάνειν. XXI. 57. 3 *spe fallendi. Romae* belongs to *fefellerat* as well as to *deprensus.*

§ 2. *praecisis*]=*abscisis.* Compounds of *prae* are used to express action affecting the extremity of a thing. Cf. *praetentam in litore* 20. 1, so *praeustae sudes.*

13   *coniurassent*] the subjunctive, because this was the allegation of their accusers. The mention of the place has struck some commentators as strange, for the place of meeting would not of course enhance the offence. Hence they have rendered *coniurassent* 'had taken the military oath', i.e. had fraudulently tried to enrol themselves among the legions, cf. 23. 3 *coniurabant.* But the *Capitol,* not the *Campus* was the place where levies were held, XXVI. 31. 11. And Zonaras says 9. 1 καὶ τινες δοῦλοι συνωμοσίαν ἐπὶ τῇ Ῥώμῃ πεποιηκότες προκατελήφθησαν.

aeris gravis] 'full' or libral *asses,* worth ten times as much as the *as* then current, see on 10. 7.

14   § 8. *Philippum*] Philip V. who succeeded Antigonus Doson in 220 B.C., and against whom the Romans fought the first two Macedonian wars (216—205 B.C.: 200—197 B.C.), the second of which was brought to a close by the Roman victory at Cynoscephalae.

15   *Demetrium Pharium*] of Pharos an island on the Illyrian coast.

He had been governor of Corcyra under Teuta queen of Illyria. In the first Illyrian war 229 B.C., he had conspired against his mistress and surrendered Corcyra. For this the Romans made him governor over a great part of her dominions. Taking advantage of the pre-occupation of the Romans with the Gauls in Italy, and relying on his alliance with Antigonus Doson, he soon began to plunder Roman allies; but Aemilius Paulus was despatched against him and he was driven into exile. This is called the second Illyrian war. He was not surrendered by Philip, but remained with him, and after the battle of Cannae urged him to his alliance with Hannibal.

17   *fugisset*] subj. because, like *coniurassent* § 2, it expresses the allegation made.

       § **4.** *Ligures*] XXI. 58. 2, they had caught and handed over to him some Roman officials. ibid. 59. 10.

19   *Bois...Insubribus*] there had been a rising of these tribes in 219 B.C., XXI. 25.

20   § **5.** *Pineum*] Pineus or Pinnes was the stepson of Teuta, whom the Romans had made king in her stead, with Demetrius as his guardian, at the end of the first Illyrian war, 228 B.C.

21   *stipendium*] the yearly tribute, which the Illyrians were bound to pay under the terms of the peace of 228 B.C.

       exierat] 'had expired'. The statement is Livy's, unlike *fugisset* § 3, *vovisset* § 7.

22   *proferri*] 'to be deferred'. Madvig's correction for *proferre* P, as Pineus could hardly have deferred the day at his own pleasure.

       § **6.** *adeo*] This use of *adeo* introducing a confirmation of a statement which has preceded (cf. *tantum* 27. 4) is not found in prae-augustan prose. It is common in Tacitus. Lit. 'to such an extent', 'indeed'.

23   *in cervicibus*] of an oppressive burden, the metaphor being taken from the yoke. We should say 'on hand'. It is also used to imply dangerous proximity, in which case the metaphor is probably from the axe. XLIV. 39. 7 *quanto facilius fuit abire quam cum in cervicibus sumus.*

24   *longinquae*] sc. *rei.* XXI. 21. 5 *longinqua militia.* P *longinqua,* according to which reading there is a hypallage.

       § **7.** *in religionem venit*] lit. it becomes a matter of religious scruple. D. compares the cognate phrases, *in religionem verti,* and *religiosum or religioni est* (with an infinitive depending).

25   *aedem Concordiae*] on the *arx* beside the temple of Juno Moneta.

       per] 'during' as in *per eosdem dies* § 1, though it may express cause as XXIV. 7. 10 *Puteolos per bellum coeptum frequentari emporium.*

26   *biennio*] accurately 1½ years. At the time of the rising of the Boii and Insubres. XXI. 17. 7 and 25.

vovisset]   The subjunctive indicates that this was the complaint of the people.

27   *locatam*] 'contracted for'.

§ 8.   *duumviri*]   Generally such business was done by the Censors, but occasionally by two commissioners specially appointed.

29   *in arce*] the S.W. summit of the Capitoline hill, added to distinguish this from the better known Temple of Concord on the *Clivus Capitolinus* (the N.E. summit) erected by Camillus in 367, to commemorate the reconciliation of patricians and plebeians at the close of the struggle about the Licinian rogations.

30   § 9.   *litterae*]   See 26. 7.

32   *creandos*] sc. to preside at the election.

quam iussissent] in full, *in quam iussissent comitia indici.*

p. 40.   3   § 10.   *interregem*]   Originally the *interrex* was appointed on the death of the king.   Under the republic he was appointed for holding the Comitia for the consular elections, when the consuls had been unable to do so in their year of office.   The *interrex* was appointed only by the patrician members of the Senate, and held office only for five days.   At the end of this time another was appointed if necessary.   We hear in one instance of a fourteenth *interrex*, VIII. 23. 7.

4   *avocaretur*] this would have been subj. in or. recta.   When two actions are compared by *potius quam* the verb expressing that to which the other is preferred is put in the subjunctive.   There is really an ellipse of *ut*.

§ 11.   *rectius*] 'more in order', probably because the consuls were still in office.

7   § 12.   *vitio creatis*] 'there being a flaw in their election'.   The *vitium* might arise from the elections being conducted without the auspices being consulted (*inauspicato* XXI. 63. 7) or in consequence of their being consulted improperly (*non rite*).   The question was decided by the augurs, and was sometimes not raised till some time after the election.   IV. 7. 3 *Non tamen pro firmato iam stetit magistratus eius, quia tertio mense quam inierunt augurum decreto perinde ac vitio creati honore abiere, quod C. Curtius qui comitiis eorum praefuerat parum recte tabernaculum cepisset.*   This power of the augurs was a weapon in the hands of the aristocracy.   Herennius insinuates that it was misused in this instance, 34. 9.

vitio] abl. of manner such as is found without an adj. in some phrases

of common occurrence and old expressions, e.g. *sacramento dicere*, Roby
§ 1238.

CHAPTER XXXIV.

9 § **1.** *interreges*] one at a time. The plural is used because the
Comitia were never held by the first *interrex*.

10 *proditi*] 'nominated', the regular expression for the appointment
of an *interrex*. IV. 43. 8 *prohibentibus tribunis patricios coire ad
prodendum interregem*.

patribus] only the patrician members of the Senate, as the power
of appointment dated from a time at which the plebeians had no rights
nor political functions.

11 *eius*] *Cornelii*.

13 *patrum*] sc. the senatorial party. Since the Licinian laws in 367 B.C.
the two great divisions of the state were no longer patricians and
plebeians, but the new nobility on the one hand (cf. *nobiles homines*
§ 4) and the rest of the nation, still often called plebs, on the other.
The former consisted of families a member of which had held a curule
office. A curule office gave admission to the Senate. Thus the new
nobility became closely connected with the Senate.

In this passage we trace the development of the opposition to the
senatorial government which was begun by Flaminius (ἀρχηγὸς τῆς τοῦ
δήμου εἰς χεῖρον διαστροφῆς Pol. II. 21. 8), when he carried his agrarian
law (cf. 3. 4 note) in opposition to the wishes of the Senate 232 B.C.,
and reached an acute stage in the time of the Gracchi, 133—120 B.C.

14 § **2.** *sui generis hominem*] 'a man of their own class'.

15 *ab*] 'in consequence of', XXI. 54. 6 *a destinato consilio avidus certaminis*.

16 *opibus*] supply *concussis*. The participle in agreement with a subs.
is best rendered by a subs., as often in Livy. 'The shock given to the
position of Fabius'. Cf. XXI. 1. 5 *angebant virum Sardinia Siciliaque
amissae*.

17 *invidia*] abl. of cause.

[*et*] P has *et* which = *etiam*.

extrahere] = 'to raise forcibly'. The preposition has the same force
as in *emunitus* XXI. 7. 7. *evadere, agmen erigere*.

20 § **3.** *cognatus*] implying that he acted from interested motives.

21 *augures*] who had issued the *decretum* pronouncing the Dictator's
election void. 33. 12.

22   *per*] expresses the means.

23   *suo*] whom he recommended.

  § 4. *hominibus nobilibus*] see on *patrum* § 1.

24   *quaerentibus*] alluding to the Roman interference on behalf of the revolted mercenaries of the Carthaginians in Sardinia, their fixing the Ebro as the limit of Carthaginian influence in 225 B.C. and their espousal of the cause of Saguntum in 219 B.C.

25   *debellari*] impersonal.

26   *trahi*] This allegation was absurd, for Fabius' policy was disapproved of by a large section even in the Senate, 25. 12. However, under the circumstances it was one which it was natural to make and which was likely to be believed.

  § 5. *universis*] 'if united'. The speaker insinuates that Fabius acted from calculation in dividing the forces. 27. 9.

27   *eo, quod*] 'from the fact that'.

29   **§ 6.** *pater patronusque*] The first term only had been applied to Fabius, the second to his army. XXIX. 10. 11.

31   **§ 7.** *consules*] 32. 1.

32   *possent*] 'though they might have finished and might still finish'.

  id foedus] 'this was the compact that had been made', sc. *se bellum tracturos.*

p. 41.   1 *habituros*] *eos* is the subject. In or. recta, *habebitis.*

1   *hominem novum*] generally in the inverse order. The first man of his family who has held a curule magistracy and thus admitted it into the *nobilitas.*

3   **§ 8.** *plebeios nobiles*] see on § 1, *patrum.*

  eisdem sacris] 'the same religious ceremonies', here used metaphorically = contempt for the plebs.

4   *patribus*] Livy uses the dative of the agent pretty freely, e.g. XXI. 39. 1 *Taurinis bellum motum erat.* v. 6. 14 *Auctores signa relinquendi universis exercitibus audiuntur* (D.). By prose writers of the best period it is as a rule used only with the pass. participle.

  desierint] for the change from secondary to primary sequence see on 32. 8.

6   **§ 9.** *ut...ut*] the second *ut* expresses the ulterior purpose.

  potestate] because the patricians could continue to appoint one of their body *interrex* till the most favourable moment for the election should arrive. See on 35. 2 *in manu.*

7   **§ 10.** *ambos ad exercitum morando*] 'by both of them staying with the army'. *ambos* is in apposition to the subject of the sentence, but

connected with *morando* to add a further specification about it, though grammatically the construction does not admit of this connection.

This use is characteristic of Livy's style, being found (1) with gerundives: cf. *gerendo solus censuram obtinuit,* IX. 29. 8: *aestimando ipse secum,* XXV. 23. 11. (2) with ablatives absolute : XXI. 45. 9 *velut dis auctoribus in spem suam quisque acceptis proelium poscunt :* IV. 44. 10 *causa ipse pro se dicta damnatur.*

The point of *ambos...morando* is that if either consul had consented to leave the army the election might have been held and the interregnum avoided.

9 *expugnatum*] 'had been carried by force'.
    vitiosus]=vitio creatus 33. 12.

10 *fieret*] 'should be pronounced'.
    § 11. *unum certe*] by the *Leges Liciniae* 367 B.C.

11 *liberum habiturum*] sc. *consulatum,* 'would dispose of it as subject to no restrictions', i.e. freely.

CHAPTER XXXV.

15   § 2. *nobilium iam*] 'already ennobled' because members of them had already held a curule office. See on *patrum* 34. 1.

19   *ut*] expressing consequence.
    in manu]=in potestate, 34. 9. As presiding officer he could exercise some influence. He could dissolve the Comitia at his discretion, or refuse to accept a person as a candidate.
    eius] *Terentii.*
    rogando] 'for the election', because at an election, as well as when a bill was brought before the Comitia, the question was put before them with the form *velitis iubeatis quirites.* Cf. XXI. 17. 4 and 10. 2.
    rogando is dat. of work contemplated, Roby § 1382, connected with a subs. as e.g. in III. *viri agris dandis adsignandis.*

21   § 3. *Aemilium*] As consul in 219 B.C. he had taken Pharos and brought the second Illyrian war to a close. At the beginning of 218 B.C. he had been a member of the embassy sent to Carthage to expostulate about the siege of Saguntum.

There was a law passed 342 B.C. *ne quis eundem magistratum intra decem annos caperet ;* but it had been temporarily repealed this year. XXVII. 6. 7 *latum . . ut quoad bellum in Italia esset, ex iis qui consules fuissent quos et quotiens vellet reficiendi consules populo ius esset.*

22   *Livio*] along with Aemilius he had been accused of having unfairly divided the spoil after the Illyrian campaign, and condemned by the votes of all the tribes but one. In 207 B.C. with Tiberius Claudius Nero he won the battle of the Metaurus.

   ex] 'in consequence of', cf. *ex conparatione* 8. 2. P *et.*

   ex qua] P *et sua.* But Aemilius was not condemned, and *sua* can hardly be taken with *prope.*

23   *ambustus*] 'with his reputation blasted'. The metaphor from fire is commoner in Latin than in English, e.g. Pliny *Ep.* IV. 11. 5 *flagrabat ingenti invidia*, he was assailed with a storm of obloquy; and is especially used in connection with judicial condemnation. 40. 2 *se populare incendium priore consulatu semiustum effugisse.*

24   § 4. *comitiali*] *Dies comitiales*, days on which the Assembly might be convoked, 184 in number. *Dies fasti*, days on which only legal proceedings went on.

25   *concedentibus*] 'retiring'.

26   *par*] used substantively, 'a rival'. XXVIII. 44. 9 *habebo ergo, Q. Fabi, parem quem das Hannibalem.*

   in] 'with a view to'. *in* with the gerund expressing purpose is rare.

27   § 5. *Pomponius*] the *praetor peregrinus* of the preceding year, 7. 8. Cf. § 7.

28   *Furius*] was consul in 223 B.C. with Flaminius and acted with him in the campaign against the Insubres.

   Philo] governed by *evenit.*

   iuri dicundo] dat. of purpose with *sors evenit* as if *iuri dicundo duumvir factus est* had been written.

29   *urbana*] i.e. he was *praetor urbanus*, who decided cases *inter cives.*

   sors] that which was awarded by the lot, 'function', 'jurisdiction'. XXIII. 30. 18 *Q. Fulvius Flaccus urbanam, M. Valerius Laevinus peregrinam sortem in iuris dictione habuit.*

30   *evenit*] 'fell'. Used regularly of the lot. XXI. 17. 1 *tum sortiri iussi. Cornelio Hispania, Sempronio Africa evenit.*

   § 6. *additi*] not for the first time. There had been four praetors since 227 B.C.

   Marcellus] consul in 222 B.C. when he slew Viridomarus, and finished the Insubrian war, and capturer of Carthage in 212 B.C.

   in Siciliam] 'for Sicily'.

31   *Postumius*] he had been consul twice before, 234, 229 B.C.

   Galliam] in the hope of inducing the Gauls serving under Hannibal to return for the defence of their country. Pol. III. 106.

p. 42. 3 § 7. *novus*] 'which he had not held before'. Alarmed by the election of Terentius the Senatorial party had probably made a push to get well affected persons elected on the score of experience. Pol. III. 106. 3 οἱ δὲ περὶ τὸν Αἰμίλιον βουλευσάμενοι μετὰ τῆς συγκλήτου κ.τ.λ.

CHAPTER XXXVI.

4   § 1. *multiplicati*] only 'largely increased', for at most they were not more than doubled.

  quantae] 'as to the amount etc.', the clause depends on *variant.*

6   *variant*] XXI. 28. 5 *certe variat memoria rei actae*, where MSS. *variata.* It is also used transitively.

7   *ausus sim*] Livy does not use *ausim* in consecutive sentences.

8   § 2. *alii*] *scribunt*, to be supplied from *variant.*

9   *in supplementum*] *in* = *ut esset*, we should say 'as a reinforcement'.

10 *octo*] the more probable account. So Polybius III. 107. 9.
  gererent] *consules.*

  § 3. *quoque*] introducing a further statement by those who put the force at eight legions.

11 *milibus*] the plural of *mille* is used as a distributive in place of *millena* which is not found, only however in connection with *singuli* or some other distributive numeral. *Vicenos quinos et semisses in milia aeris solverunt*, XXXIX. 7. 5.

13 *treceni*] from this we should infer that the regular number was 200. But Livy always represents it as 300 ; cf. XXI. 17. 3. *quadringenti* has therefore been suggested as c. may have dropped out from cccc. Polybius also gives the number as 300, but inconsistently with his statement that the total number of cavalry was 6000.

  duplicem] Pol. τριπλάσιον which is probably correct.

14 *peditis*] sc. *numerum.*

  § 4. *septem...est*] most likely a gloss stating the total. Madvig retains the words reading *fuisse* after *Romanis.*

16 *auctores sunt*] = *tradunt*. Cf. 24. 11.

  § 5. *illud*] referring, as often, to what follows.

17 *discrepat*] 'on this point there is no disagreement', like *convenit* 'it is agreed'. Cf. III. 31. 8 *cum de legibus convenira, de latore tantum discreparet.*

19 *praebuerat*] 29. 6. Polybius III. 107 says it was on the capture of Canusium that the Senate resolved on an engagement, as supplies were cut off and the allies wavering.

§ 6. *ceterum*] resumptive, in the proper sense of *ceterum* (cf. Fr. *du reste*), Gk. δ' οὖν. Often used by Livy when leaving a disputed point, 'be this as it may'.

20   *moverent*] the subj. implies purpose. We cannot express the con nexion in translation, 31. 2.

libros] see on 1. 16.

21   *territos*] see on *opibus*, 34. 2.

novis] with reference to those mentioned in 1. 8 and 9. 8.

22   § **7**. *Ariciae*] 16 miles from Rome on the Appian way. Hor. *S.* 1. 5. 1 *egressum magna me excepit Aricia Roma.*

23   *signa*] *manasse* must be supplied. *manare* is used of statues sweating XXIII. 31. 15.

24   *Caere*] cf. 1. 10. P, C, M *Caedes*, for which Wlf. reads *Caediciis.* A village called Caedicii is mentioned by Pliny *H. N.* XIV. 6, as near Sinuessa, itself famous for its warm baths. Madvig emends to *sudasse et*, which makes the sentence simple.

manasse] with *multo cruore*, which is the verb of this and the pre-ceding clause as appears from its position.

§ **8**. *etiam*] belongs to *magis.*

25   *via fornicata*] probably the same as that mentioned XXXV. 10. 10 *porticum...a porta Fontinali qua in Campum iter esset perduxerunt.* C.

26   *erat*] which used to lead to the Campus.

27   § **9**. *procurata*] See on 1. 15.

28   *Paesto*] Posidonia in Lucania. The Romans planted a colony there in 273 B.C. and called the place Paestum.

CHAPTER XXXVII.

30   § **1**. *Hierone*] Hiero king of Syracuse had been the ally of the Romans since the second year of the First Punic war, 263 B.C., and continued so till his death later in this year.

classis] with *ab Hierone*, cf. such expressions as *pugna ad Trasu-mennum* 7. 1.

32   § **2**. *caedem adlatam*] 'the news of the defeat'. 36. 6 *propter territos homines.*

p. 43.   2 *propria*] 'personal'. *proprius* is opposed to *communis* as *suus* to *alienus.* Heerwagen cites XXXIII. 2. 1 *orsus a maiorum suorum suisque et communibus in omnem Graeciam et propriis in Boeotorum gentem meritis.*

3 *moveri potuerit*] corresponding to *moveri potuit* in or. recta, 'he could not have been distressed'.

4 § **3**. *probe*]=*satis* 15. 1.

5 *prope*] belonging to the word which it follows, as in 18. 9.

7 § **4**. *misisse*] the ambassadors speak in the name of Hiero.

8 § **5**. *iam omnium primum*] 'first of all then', used in passing from general to particular considerations.

9 *ducentum*] sc. *librarum*. See on *pondo* 1. 17.

10 *adferre sese*] here the ambassadors speak for themselves.

11 *propriam*] 'lasting'. Hor. *S.* II. 6. 5 *nil amplius oro,*
    Maia nate, nisi ut propria haec mihi munera faxis.

12 § **6**. *modium*]=*modiorum*.

13 *quantum opus esset*] sc. *subvehi*, or *quanto* would probably have been written : though Cic. has *dux nobis et auctor opus sunt, Fam.* 2. 6.

14 § **7**. *scire*] The ambassadors again speak in the name of Hiero as in *vidisse, misisse* below.

    Latini nominis] 'Latin allies'. Those allies who had rights originally enjoyed by members of the Latin league. The most important of these were *connubium* and *commercium* with the Romans. The *Nomen Latinum* comprised old league towns like Tibur and Praeneste and Latin Colonies.

16 *vidisse*] So § 8 *misisse*, § 12 *accipere.*
    § **8**. *mille sagittariorum*] 31. 5 note.

18 *pugnaces*] 'who were wont to fight', poetical. Hor. *C.* IV. 6. 8 *tremenda cuspide pugnax.*

20 § **9**. *evenisset*] See on 35. 5.

    Africam] According to 31. 2, this had been already done ; but the incident was, as we saw, not mentioned by Polybius.

    et hostes] as well as the Romans. *et*=*etiam*, cf. § 11 and *et ipsa* 2. 7.

21 *laxamenti*] 'freedom', lit. 'respite'. IX. 41. 12 *si quid laxamenti a bello Samnitium esset. minus* implies that the Carthaginians had already sent aid to Hannibal. Cf. 11. 6.

24 § **10**. *uno tenore*] 'uniformly'. See on 15. 1.

27 § **11**. *et*]=*etiam.*
    civitatibus] 'communities'. Paestum and Neapolis, 32. 4, 36. 9.

28 *gratia rei*] 'the goodwill implied in the act '.

30 § **12**. *dare dicare*] Asyndeton is common in archaic and therefore in legal and religious language. So *optimi maximi, velitis iubeatis* 10. 2.

31   *sacratam*] 'solemnly established'. XXI. 38. 9 *ab eo quem in summo sacratum vertice* (having a temple there) *Poeninum montani appellant. volentem*]=*benevolentem*, 'gracious'.

p. 44. 1 § 18. *traditum*] If the subjects connected are of different genders the adjective or participle of the predicate is regulated in gender, provided the singular be used, by the nearest subject. Madvig, *Lat. Gr.* 214 a.

2   *navium*] the number has fallen out. This was probably the fleet of 50 ships mentioned XXI. 51. 6, for the fleet of Servilius had been recalled, 31. 6.

CHAPTER XXXVIII.

6 § 1. *dum*]='that in the meantime'. We should say 'until'.

7 *nomine Latino*] Cf. 37. 7 note.
venirent] the subjunctive as a purpose is implied.

8 § 2. *iure iurando...adacti*] The meaning is, hitherto there had been (1) a *sacramentum*, (2) a *iusiurandum* informally administered and not compulsory. Now the *iusiurandum* was prescribed by the State and administered by the officers of the legion.

9 *adacti*] 'were bound'. *ad iusiurandum adigere*, and *iusiurandum adigere* with acc. of the person are also used.

10 § 3. *sacramentum*] a form of oath in which the swearer imprecated a curse on himself (prayed that he might be *sacer*) if he broke it: it must be distinguished from *iusiurandum*.

11 *iussu...abituros*] in the MSS. placed after *milites*, but the words express the purport of the *sacramentum* (cf. *conventuros*), not of the *iusiurandum* which was taken *ubi convenissent*.
conventuros] Cf. 11. 3 *Tibur diem ad conveniendum edixit.*
iniussu] 'without his orders'. Cf. 39. 2 *indicente me*. Plautus has *inconsultu meo, Trin.* I. 2. 130.

12 *ubi convenissent*] 'whenever'. Cf. *ubi procubuissent* 2. 7.
ad decuriatum aut centuriatum] These are substantives, 'for their division into decuries or centuries'. *decuriatus*, of the cavalry. Attached to each legion were 300 cavalry (*ala*) divided into 10 *turmae* and 30 *decuriae. centuriatus*, of the infantry. The legion contained at this time (as a rule) 4000 men divided into 30 maniples and 60 centuries. The numbers in the century and maniple varied with the size of the legion.
decuriatus is ἅπ. λεγ., and *centuriatus* elsewhere=the office of centurion. Hence Madvig reads *ad decuriandum aut centuriandum* (='for

the dividing of them'. Roby LXIV). But this quasi-passive use of the gerundive is very rare in Livy (though cf. v. 26. 3); and he uses several verbal substantives of the fourth declension not elsewhere found.

14 § 4. *coniurabant*] in a good sense. Cf. 33. 2 note.

15 *ergo*] archaic = *causa*, usually in formal documents, though once in Vergil *A.* VI. 670 *illius ergo venimus.*

16 *sumendi*] 'getting from the supply in the rear'.
repetendi] ' recovering when thrown'.

17 § 5. *id*] ' the oath'.
inter ipsos] used attributively with *foedus*. Cf. 37. 1.

19 § 6. *priusquam moverentur*] subj. of a fact in past time: in 29. 4, a purpose is implied. The narrative is here resumed from 36. 6.

20 *denuntiantis*] for constr. cf. 40. 1.
bellum] governed by *perfecturum.*

21 *arcessitum*] 34. 4 *ab hominibus nobilibus Hannibalem in Italiam adductum.*

24 § 8. *pridie quam...proficisceretur*] the constr. is the same as with *priusquam* § 6.
verior quam gratior] a regular constr. when two qualities in the same subject are compared. v. 43. 7 *qui bella fortius quam felicius gessissent.* Tacitus hating uniformity has *vehementius quam caute, Agr.* IV.

26 § 9. *qui*] = 'how'. P *quodne,* perhaps the query of a copyist who thought *quod* should follow *mirari* (D.). *quinam* has been suggested.

28 *togatus*] 'in the garb of a civilian', opposed to *armato* as in 23. 3 *inter armatos pariter togatosque.*

30 *signis conlatis*] indicating a pitched battle as in 24. 11.

31 § 11. *quam homines rebus*] merely added for the sake of the antithesis, which will not bear examination, for men do not suggest a plan of action to circumstances: the meaning is ' plans which one must modify to suit circumstances, instead of trying to force circumstances to fall in with a preconceived design'.

32 *inmatura*] proleptic = *ut inmatura essent,* 'he would not spoil by forming them before the time'.

p. 45. 1 *gesta essent*] corresponding to the accusative future in or. recta.

3 § 12. *ad id locorum*] temporal. Cf. *interea loci* Ter. *Eun.* 126.

§ 13. *et*] corresponding to *et quo* etc. Cf. 1. 1. MSS. give *id,* in which case *sua sponte* must be taken with *apparebat,* 'was self-evident'. For *sua sponte* used of inanimate objects cf. 1. 11.

CHAPTER XXXIX.

9   § **2.** *et duo boni...et mali*] hypothetically, 'if ye were both good consuls...while if ye were both bad'. So *universis* 34. 5 = *si essent universi.*

10   *me indicente*] = *non dicente.* Ter. *Ad.* III. 4. 62 *non me indicente haec fiunt.* This is rare, but *in* = *non* is compounded with several participles which have an adjectival sense, e.g. *indictus, infectus, incultus, indoctus.*

13   § **3.** *nunc*] contrasting an actual to an imaginary state of affairs. 25. 10.

te talem virum] lit. you being such as you are. The meaning is 'and see what manner of man you are'.

16   *altera parte*] the consul being regarded as representing half the state.

claudente] lit. 'halting'. P *claudet.* Cicero seems to use the form *claudeo,* which is to *claudico* as *albeo* to *albico: Tusc.* v. 8 *etiamsi ex aliqua parte clauderet.* Sallust, *claudo: Hist.* III. 25 *neque enim ignorantia claudit res.*

17   *iuris et potestatis*] because Varro as consul will have equal rights with Aemilius.

20   § **4.** *nescio an*] 'I almost think'.

hic] in Varro.

21   § **5.** *adversus Hannibalem...oppugnaturus*] The emphatic words, as indicated by the order, are, *Hannibalem, tibi: Varro, te.* The force of *tuis equitibus ac peditibus* and *tuis militibus* is not so obvious. The meaning seems to be 'while *you* will have to use all your forces horse and foot against *Hannibal, Varro* will be using your own troops against *you*'.

24   *tuis*] by rousing them against their commander. Cf. 12. 12.

§ **6.** *ominis...causa*] because the mention of his name might bring bad luck. Cf. Cic. *Phil.* IX. 4. 9 *quibus Antonius (o di immortales avertite et detestamini quaeso hoc omen).* L. XXIII. 47. 14 *nolle ominari quae captae urbi casura forent,* sc. to mention, and so run the risk of bringing about.

25   *etiam*] 'if for no other reason'.

tamen] the connexion is, I would much rather not say anything about Flaminius. Still I must mention that even he was not so wild as Minucius.

26   *furere*] indicating a temporary outburst, *insanit* a continuous state of madness.

27   *peteret*] Cf. 38. 6.

28   *videat*] the subjunctive because the sense is, 'without waiting to see'.

29   § 7. *qui*] we should say 'if he'.

30   *togatos*] 'civilians', 23. 3. Cf. 38. 9.

p. 46. 1 § 8. *aut...aut*] Notice this disjunctive method of statement. We should say 'if I am not ignorant'.

2   *nobilior*] with *Trasumenno*. Cf. 7. 1 *nobilis ad Trasumennum pugna*.

    nostris cladibus] abl. cause, as in 32. 8 *donum animo ac voluntate maius*.

3   § 9. *nec...et*] Cf. *et...nec* 8. 5.

    unum] 'before you alone'. Cf. § 17.

4   *excesserim*] with *potius*, 'I should prefer to overstep the mark'.

6   § 10. *eventus...ratio*] the latter is set forth § 11—15; the former § 16, 17.

7   *stultorum*] *Iliad* XX. 198 ῥεχθὲν δέ τε νήπιος ἔγνω.

9   § 11. *omnia circa*] 17. 3 *omnia circa virgulta*.

11   § 12. *id documentum*] 'such a proof', confirming the preceding statement like *tantum*, 27. 4.

12   *meliores*] sc. *bello*.

13   *nos*] the Romans as distinguished from the allies.

14   § 13. *omnia inimica*] 6. 5 *per omnia arta praeruptaque*.

16   *sui*] partitive gen.

17   *rapto*] with *in diem* 'the plunder of the day'. Cf. 40. 8 *commeatibus in diem raptis*. An emendation for *capto* P.

    § 14. *tertiam*] XXI. 40. 7 *duabus partibus peditum equitumque in transitu Alpium amissis*.

20   § 15. *senescat*] 'grows weaker'. A metaphor from the loss of strength attending old age, of frequent occurrence in Livy. *Senescere fama ac viribus* XXIX. 3. 15 ; *pugna senescit* V. 21. 7.

    in dies] 'from day to day' denoting increase or decrease. *in diem* § 13, 'for the (present) day'.

22   § 16. *Gereonii*] It was rather in the territory of the Frentani, N. of Apulia. Hannibal had been there since he returned from Campania, 18. 6.

23   *ne adversus te quidem*] 'not even before you, though you, unlike the rest, will credit my statements'.

24   § 17. *Servilius...Atilius*] Cf. 32. 1.

25 *ludificati*] 18. 9 *extracta prope aestate per ludificationem hostis.*
26 *infestam*] 'dangerous'.
29 § **18**. *resistas*] implying successful resistance. XXI. 57. 3 *spe fallendi resistendive.*
32 *falsa*] lit. due to false statements, sc. 'unmerited'.

§ **19**. *laborare*] 'is obscured'. Verg. *G.* II. 478 *defectus solis varios lunaeque labores. laborare* is used in a different sense, 6. 2.

p. **47.** 1 *extingui*] adversative asyndeton.
2 § **20**. *timidum*] as Minucius had called Fabius. 12. 12 *pro cunctatore segnem, pro cauto timidum conpellabat.*
5 § **21**. *nec...suadeo*] 'yet I do not advise'.
7 *tuae*] 'favourable to yourself'. So *suam*. W. quotes IX. 19. 15 *nostris locis.*

Chapter XI.

11 § **1**. *adversus*] 'in answer to'.
haud sane]= 'by no means'.
magis] with *vera*.
16 § **2**. *populare incendium*] 'the fire of popular fury', with reference to a condemnation by the *Comitia Tributa*.
17 *semustum*] 'half-consumed'. Cf. *prope ambustus* 35. 3. The clause expresses his reason for preferring to fall into the hands of the enemy.
18 § **3**. *caderet*]=*accideret*, rare. XXXV. 13. 9 *etiam si quid adversi casurum foret.* (D.)
19 § **4**. *ab*]= 'immediately after'. XXVI. 13. 4 *ab hoc sermone cum digressi essent.*
sermone] 'conversation'. Fabius' discourse is called *oratio* 39. 3 on account of its artistic form.
21 *sua*] 'devoted to him'.
22 *conspectior*] 'more conspicuous'. 24. 5.
dignitates] 'men of distinction'. Madvig calls *dignitates* as applied to men *prorsus barbarum*, and reads *dignitas deesset.* But Cicero, *Sest.* LI. 109, has *omnes honestates civitatis, omnes aetates,* sc. 'all respectable persons'.
23 § **6**. *castra*] still at Larinum, the Carthaginians being at Gereonium, 18. 7, 24. 1.
novo] the four new legions, 36. 2.

24 *bifariam*] 'in two places'. He does not say *binis* as in 44. 1, as the existing camp was only enlarged.

ut] = *ita ut*, 5. 7.

26 *omne robur virium*] 'all the flower of the forces'. *robur* = the strongest part.

27 § **6.** *M. Atilium*] 32. 5. Polybius says he fell at the battle of Cannae, III. 109. 1, probably confusing his name with that of somebody else.

excusantem] alleging in excuse, 'pleading'. XXVI. 22. 5 *oculorum valetudinem excusavit.* So *defendere* XXI. 18. 2, *cum defenderent publico consilio factum* (*esse*).

30 *duobus milibus*] the number is surprisingly small and very likely wrong. At Cannae where the arrangement was the same as here (44. 1 note) one-third of the army was in the smaller camp. *parte dimidia* makes it still more likely that this was the case here.

p. 48. 1 § **7.** *parte dimidia*] 'half as large again'. Hannibal judged from the addition of the second smaller camp. In point of fact the army had been doubled.

5 § **8.** *postquam erat*] since it had begun to be, as it still was, unsafe.

8 § **9.** *fuerit*] in or. recta, *fuit.* Cf. 37. 2. *parata* has a pregnant sense: 'was ready, and would have been carried out'.

CHAPTER XLI.

9 § **1.** *ceterum*] continuing the narrative. Wlf. says that *ceterum* here, as in some other passages, indicates the transition to a new source of information. (In this case perhaps Valerius Antias. See on 43. 6.)

consulis] Varro, as appears from the context, though he has not been referred to since 40. 4, and there in conjunction with Aemilius.

materiam] 'opportunity'.

11 *tumultuario proelio*] with *orto, ac* subjoins the ablatives of cause *procursu...iussu.* Cf. 11. 6 *vetustate oblitos.*

12 *ex praeparato*] 'after preparation'. So *ex multum ante praeparato, ex necopinato, ex insperato. ex* expresses the circumstances. Cf. 7. 4 *ex vano.*

14 § **2.** *ad mille et septingenti*] *ad* is used adverbially, and does not affect the case. XXI. 22. 3 *ad mille octingenti. ad* is thus used as a rule only with numbers composed of hundreds and thousands; hence *ad sescentos evaserunt* 50. 11; but cf. *ad mille* 31. 5.

16 *ceterum*] adversative.

18 § **8.** *alternis*] sc. *diebus*, supplied from *die*.

19 *debellari*] impersonal, 34. 4.

20 *ni cessatum foret*] 'if they had not hung back'. For *foret* see on 9. 9.

21 § **4.** *haud aegerrime*] 'with no great grief'. *haud* with the superlative is very rare. Cf. *haud nimis prospere* 9. 2.
inescatam] 'lured as by a bait' (*esca*).

23 § **5.** *omnia hostium*] 'everything about (lit. of) the enemy'. 11. 4 *omnes regionis eius*.

24 *duas partes*] i.e. the four new legions, and the forces added to the old ones, 36. 2.

25 *tironum...esse*] 'consisted of recruits'. Cf. 29. 5. XXIII. 35. 6 *tirones—ea* (=*eorum*) *maxima pars volonum erant*. *Tiro*, a substantive used adjectivally, XXI. 39. 3 *exercitu accepto tirone*.

27 § **6.** *omnis fortunae*] 'every kind of property'. For *fortuna* in this sense cf. Hor. *Ep.* I. 5. 12 *quo mihi fortunam si non conceditur uti?*

29 § **7.** *inpedimenta*] that which was necessary for the march, as distinguished from that which was left in the camp. The clause which follows expresses the object of Hannibal's dispositions generally, and not of this measure alone.

30 *mediam*] i.e. which lay between the hills on either hand. P, C *medium amnem*, M *agmen*. *medium agmen* would have to be taken as in apposition to *inpedimenta*.

31 § **8.** *velut desertis*] with *fuga dominorum*, 'in the belief that they were deserted'. 17. 4 *velut tutissimum iter petentes summa iuga*.

p. **49.** 1 § **9.** *fides fieret*] governing (*eum*) *voluisse*.

2 *sicut Fabium*] This has reference only to *falsa imagine*, as, except for the fact that there was a deception practised (cf. *ludibrium oculorum* 16. 6), the circumstances in the case of Fabius were different.

3 *in locis*] 'where they were'. Cf. 49. 4 *in vestigio*.

CHAPTER XLII.

4 § **1.** *subductae stationes*] 'the fact that the outposts had been withdrawn', 34. 2, 36. 6.

6 § **2.** *in castris*] with *conperta*.

7 *praetoria*] Each of the consuls had a separate *praetorium* (general's tent) even when their armies were combined.

8 *nuntiantium*] depending on *concursus*, the participle is used substantively. XXI. 2. 6 *ridentis speciem*, 43. 3.

9 *quoque*]=*et quo*.

11 § **3.** *signa proferri*] implying an advance of the whole army. Cf. *conlatis signis* 24. 11.

iuberent] *consules*.

12 *protinus*] as they went forward, 'on the way', 50. 11.

13 § **4.** *unus*] 'any common soldier'. *unus* implies an individual not regarded as in any way distinguished from others. Catullus XXII. 10 *unus caprimulgus aut fossor* 'any bumpkin'. Cf. 22. 7.

16 *sustinere*] 'to hold his own against'.

Marium] himself a Lucanian, 43. 7.

17 *praefectum*] used for the commander of the bodies of 30 (*turmae*) into which the cavalry was divided, probably the first of the three *decuriones* in the *turma*, 38. 3.   It is used with reference to the Roman as well as the allied cavalry.   It should be distinguished from *praefectus socium*, one of the three officers who commanded each allied legion. These, unlike the officers of the allied cavalry, were Romans.

18 § **5.** *portis*] a poetic construction. XXI. 54. 4 *obequitare portis*.

20 *cum cura*] with *speculatus*.

§ **6.** *ignes*] the grounds for his belief are expressed in this clause.

21 *vergat in*] 'which lay towards'. *vergere ad* is usual. P *adinhostem*.

22 *cara*] 'valuables'. XXI. 60. 9 *omnibus fere caris rebus*.

24 *vidisse* etc.] the omission of *se* is a Graecism, 34. 7.

28 § **8.** *pulli*] the sacred chickens.   These were kept in the camp under the charge of the *pullarius* when the army was on a campaign, that omens might be taken from their feeding.   If they refused to eat it was considered an unfavourable sign, and the engagement was deferred; if on the contrary they ate greedily so that some of the food fell from their beaks and struck the ground (*tripudium solistimum*) victory might be anticipated.   Cicero ridicules the practice. *de Div.* II. 35. 73 *inclusa in cavea et enecta fame si in offam pultis invadit et si aliquid ex eius ore cecidit hoc tu auspicium...putas?*

quoque] implying that the refusal of the chickens to eat confirmed his misgivings.

auspicio] abl. instrument, 'by the auspices'.   It is possible however that *auspicio* may mean 'at the taking of the auspices'. Cf. II. 36. 8 *ludis*; VIII. 13. 10 *comitiis*; XXXII. 9. 1 *Latinis*.

addixissent]=*annuissent*, 'had given their assent'. I. 55. 3 *cum sacellorum exaugurationes* (desecration) *admitterent aves, in Termini fano non addixere.* In a negative sense, *cum aves abdixissent,* Cic. *de Nat. Deorum,* I. 17. 31.

30 § **9.** *Flamini*] he had neglected the auspices on leaving Rome XXI. 63. 7, but it is not mentioned that he did so before the battle of Trasimene. Cf. however Cic. *Div.* II. 33 *Flaminius non paruit auspiciis, itaque periit cum exercitu.*

31 *Claudi*] P. Claudius Pulcher, defeated at Drepana during the First Punic war, 249 B.C. Cic. *de Nat.. Deorum,* II. 2. 7 *cum cavea liberati pulli non pascerentur mergi eos in aquam iussit, ut biberent, quoniam esse nollent.*

Punico bello] with *clades,* not *memorata.*

memorata] 'famous', 7. 1.

32 § **10.** *prope ipsi...prohibuere*] The sentence has two points, an instance of Livy's fondness for welding two clauses into one. Cf. 17. 6. 'It may almost be said, the gods themselves interfered, but it was to defer, not to prevent the disaster which was hanging over the Romans'.

p. 50. 2 *forte*] does not contradict *di prope ipsi.* It only means that the deserters had not come on purpose to warn the Romans.

3 § **11.** *Formiani*] 16. 4.

4 *Sidicini*] of Teanum Sidicinum in Campania.

8 § **12.** *imperii potentes* etc.] 'enabled them to recover their authority'.

9 *ambitio*] 'desire for popularity'.

suam primum] 'first his own' implying, and then that of his colleague. *suam* refers per synesim to *consul* suggested by *ambitio.*

CHAPTER XLIII.

11 § **1.** *motos*] from their position.

12 *evectos*] 'carried away'. Unlike 19. 10.

nequiquam] with *rediit.*

15 § **2.** *in dies*] generally only when there is an idea of increase or decrease. This is contained to some extent in *novas,* as in the inceptive verb in *qui senescat in dies,* 39. 15.

16 *mixtos ex conluvione*] 'composed of a medley'.

19 § **3.** *exposcentium*] 42. 2 *concursus nuntiantium;* 19. 9 *fugientium magis quam euntium modo.*

20 *annonam*] 'the price of provisions', often with the meaning of 'a high price'. Plaut. *Trin.* II. 4. 3 *Cena hac annona est sine sacris hereditas.*

primo...postremo] the intermediate stages are omitted.

21   *transitione*] 40. 9.

23   § **4.** *ita ut*] defining *fuga*, we should say 'and hurrying away'. *ita* is often omitted, 5. 6, 40. 5.

25   § **5.** *movere*] cf. I. I note. According to Polybius Hannibal had moved to the neighbourhood of Cannae, followed it seems by the Roman army, while Atilius and Regulus were still consuls, and it was in consequence of his seizure of the stores there that the Senate resolved to put eight legions at the disposal of the new consuls and risk a battle, III. 107.

     in calidiora...Apuliae loca] Cannae was both on lower ground and further S. than Gereonium. Correctly speaking, at Gereonium Hannibal had been in the territory of the Frentani, not in Apulia.

26   *maturiora messibus*] 'riper for harvest'. I. 3. I *nondum maturus imperio Ascenius erat.*

     simul ut] The other objects which he had in view are indicated in *calidiora...maturiora.*

27   *transfugia*] ἀποστάσεις, used for the first time in Livy; *eo* must be supplied before *transfugia*, corresponding to *quo.*

28   § **6.** *similiter*] 'as before', 41. 9. Weissenborn thinks this recurrence of the same statement is due to Livy's having incorporated two accounts of the same incident in his narrative, a longer and more elaborate from Valerius Antias (40. 7,—42) and a shorter and simpler from Coelius Antipater, 43.

31   § **7.** *Statilium*] 42. 4.

p. 51.   2 § **8.** *eadem*] sc. Paulus for waiting, Varro for fighting.

4   § **9.** *ex sententia*] The MSS. have *sententia* alone which can hardly stand. For *ex* cf. 9. 11 *ex conlegii pontificum sententia. de* is also used, especially in the phrase *de amicorum sententia.*

5   *nobilitandas*] 'to make it famous'. Cf. 7. 1; 39. 8.

     Cannas] on the right bank of the Aufidus at no great distance from the sea. Polybius calls it a town, Κάνναν πόλιν: Livy, a village, § 10.

6   § **10.** *aversa*] 'with its back to'.

7   *Volturno*] so called because it blew across Apulia from over Mt Vultur in Apulia (see map). Now known as Scirocco, an E.S.E. wind. Consequently Hannibal's camp faced W.N.W.

     campis] 'along' or 'over the plains'. Cf. 15. 4 *iugis.*

9   § **11.** *cum derigerent*] 'when they drew up in line', 19. 11. *aversi*] with *pugnaturi.*

10   *offuso*] 'blown in their faces'. P *effuso p.* which='clouds of dust'.

CHAPTER XLIV.

12 **§ 1.** *Poenum...Poenum*] the first, Hannibal: the second, the Carthaginians.

13 *ad Cannas*] 'in the neighbourhood of Cannae'. Not to Cannae, for it was in the possession of Hannibal (see on 43. 5 *movere*). The main body of the Romans remained on the northernmost or left bank of the Aufidus. See Appendix IV.

14 *bina*] a larger on the left bank of the Aufidus, and a smaller on the right (*trans Aufidium* § 3).

eodem intervallo] the distance is not mentioned in 40. 5. It is only stated that the small camp was the nearer to Hannibal, as was the case here. Polybius III. 110. 9 says 10 stades (=rather more than 1¼ miles).

15 *sicut ante divisis*] i.e. unevenly. *divisis* is not to be taken with *intervallo*. Polybius says two-thirds of the army were in the larger camp, and one-third in the smaller.

16 **§ 2.** *Aufidius*] generally Aufidus, now Ofanto. Although the most considerable stream in Apulia it is shallow and easily fordable in summer. In winter it is a rushing torrent. Hor. *C.* III. 30. 10 *dicar qua violens obstrepit Aufidus;* ib. IV. 9. 2 *longe sonantem Aufidum*. Polybius says it is the only river in Italy which cuts through the line of the Apennines, but it does not do so in fact.

utrisque castris] the two camps of the Romans.

17 *adfluens*] 'flowing near'.

aditum dabat] 'could be approached'.

ex sua cuiusque opportunitate] lit. 'according as it was convenient for each person', 'more or less conveniently in each case'. The words can hardly be taken with *haud sine certamine*, 'not without a conflict at the most convenient spots' as W. suggests.

19 **§ 3.** *trans Aufidium*] Pol. III. 110. 10 πέραν...ἀπὸ διαβάσεως πρὸς τὰς ἀνατολάς, 'on the further bank E. of the ford'. Polybius conceives the Aufidus as flowing from S. to N. In point of fact its general direction is N.E. so this must mean on the right (southernmost) bank.

21 *nullum praesidium*] This is inconsistent with 43. 10, where it is stated that Hannibal was encamped near Cannae. Livy has omitted to mention, as Polybius (III. 111. 11) does, that on the arrival of the Roman armies, Hannibal encamped on the same side on which the larger Roman camp was. See Appendix IV.

22 **§ 4.** *natis*] cf. 4. 2, 28. 5, the perfectly level plain on the left bank of the Aufidus is meant.

qua parte] sc. *equitatu.* Paulus was aware of this, and refused to fight on the N. bank. οὐκ ἔφη δεῖν συμβάλλειν ἱπποκρατούντων τῶν πολεμίων δυσαρεστούμενος τοῖς τόποις, III. 110. 2.

24 *derigit*] 43. 11.

procursatione]=*procursu* 41. 1, 'a sally'.

25 § **5.** *rursus*] referring to 41. 2, 42. 4.

28 *exemplum Fabium obiceret*] *Fabium* is in apposition to *exemplum*, 'taunted him with copying the example of Fabius'.

29 § **6.** *hic*] Varro.

penes se] 'rested with him'. *penes* is used especially with the idea of praise or blame. XXI. 46. 8 *penes quem perfecti huiusce belli laus est.*

30 *usu cepisset*] 'had gained a prescriptive right to', cf. Lucr. III. 971 *vitaque mancipio* (fee simple) *nulli datur omnibus usu.* According to the XII. tables, undisturbed possession of land for two years gave a title.

32 § **7.** *ille*] Paulus.

proiectis] 'sacrificed', especially in the sense of 'to throw away as worthless'. Hor. *S.* II. 3. 100 *qui servos proicere aurum in media iussit Libya.*

p. **52.** 1 *inconsultam*] 'ill-advised'.

2 *exsortem*] a poetic word. Verg. *A.* VI. 428 *dulcis vitae exsortes.* For gen. cf. 49. 7.

3 *videret*] Varro.

4 *manus*] *eorum.* For the omission of the relative cf. Verg. *A.* XI. 172

> *magna tropaea ferens quos dat tua dextera leto.*

CHAPTER XLV.

5 § **1.** *altercationibus*] Pol. III. 110. 3 ἦν ἀμφισβήτησις καὶ δυσχρηστία περὶ τοὺς ἡγέμονας.

6 *ad multum diei*] 'till late in the day'. Cicero would say, *ad multam noctem.*

7 *cum ceteras reciperet*] while recalling the rest', as opposed to the Numidians.

8 § **2.** *ex minoribus castris*] with *aquatoribus* cf. 44. 3. Polybius τοῖς ὑδρευομένοις ἀπὸ τῆς ἐλάττονος παρεμβολῆς.

9 *trans flumen*] i.e. to the right bank. See on 44. 3.

13 § **8.** *evecti*] 'rode on'. The force of *e* is 'beyond the limit to which they might have been expected to keep'.

14 § **4.** *auxilio*] 'body of allies', rare in singular with this sense.

16 *tenuerit*] = *retinuerit*.

quod...fuerit] explaining *causa*, 'the only reason that checked them...was the fact that'.

18 § **5.** *cuius sors erat*] *sors* with *imperii*, 'the duty of commanding', 'the office of commander'. For the meaning of *sors* cf. 35. 5. *eius diei* depends on and describes *imperii*. P, C *cui*. The words seem hardly necessary as *penes Paulum* etc. have just preceded. They are added to emphasize the fact that it was Varro not Paulus who was responsible for that day's disaster.

nihil] stronger than *non*, 'without consulting him in anything'. C. compares IV. 33. 5 *ea species nihil terruit equos*, 'not a whit'.

19 *proposuit*] 'exposed to view', 'hoisted', for the signal of battle was a red flag.

traduxit] to the right or S. bank of the river.

20 *quia magis...poterat*] 'as while he could not approve he could not abstain from helping'.

21 § **6.** *transgressi*] *consules*.

23 *id erat flumini propius*] Pol. τοὺς μὲν οὖν τῶν Ῥωμαίων ἱππεῖς παρ' αὐτὸν τὸν ποταμὸν ἐπὶ τοῦ δεξιοῦ κέρατος κατέστησε.

24 *equites*] a little over 6000, Pol. III. 113. 6. As there were 8 legions each with 300 horse, we should have expected 7200. 36. 3.

pedites] sc. *sociorum*.

25 § **7.** *extremi*] 'on the extreme flank'.

intra] with *tenuerunt* as if it were a substantive = τὰ εἴσω, the position further in', i.e. than the cavalry on the extreme left.

pedites] again *sociorum*. Thus each wing consisted of cavalry and a detachment of allies, while the Roman legions occupied the centre.

ad medium etc.] 'adjoining, towards the centre, the Roman legions'. The order seems to indicate that this is the meaning, rather than 'adjoining the legions who were in the centre'. However *ad medium* may mean 'in the centre'. W. compares XXXVI. 11. 3 *quique ubique, ad Boeotiam maxime* (= *in Boeotia*) *praepositi erant hibernis*. Polybius III. 113. 3 adds a statement regarding the way in which the Roman infantry generally was drawn up, πυκνοτέρας ἢ πρόσθεν τὰς σημαίας καθιστάνων καὶ ποιῶν πολλαπλάσιον τὸ βάθος ἐν ταῖς σπείραις τοῦ μετώπου, 'drawing up the maniples in closer order than usual, and making the depth in each maniple many times as great as the front'.

27 *prima acies facta*] 'formed the first line'. They stood however well in advance of the main body. Pol. III. 113. 4 πάσης δὲ τῆς δυνάμεως προέστησε τοὺς εὐζώνους ἐν ἀποστάσει (at an interval).

CHAPTER XLVI.

30 § 1. *alia*]=*reliqua*.

31 *transgressus*] Pol. l. c. κατὰ διττοὺς τόπους.

ut quosque traduxerat] 'as fast as he got them across the river', not *quemque* for the troops were brought across not individually but in detachments.

p. 53. 4 § 2. *firmata*] 'being composed of' not 'strengthened with'. There were no other troops there besides those mentioned. XXI. 46. 5 *cornua Numidis firmat*.

Afrorum essent] 'consisted of Africans', cf. 41. 5. *Afri* would include Carthaginians, Libyphoenices and African allies.

cornua] the wings, so to speak, of the infantry by itself. Polybius expresses the same thing thus. 'He placed on the left wing the Spanish and Gallic cavalry, adjoining them half the Carthaginian heavy armed (who were thus one wing of the infantry, and faced the *pedites sociorum* 45. 6), and next to them the Spanish and Gallic infantry. Beside these he placed the rest of the Carthaginians (who were thus the other wing of the infantry, and faced the *pedites sociorum* 45. 7), while upon the right he drew up the Numidian cavalry'.

5 *Galli atque Hispani*] Polybius explains the way in which these were drawn up (cf. 47. 5 note). 'Taking the middle ranks of the Spaniards and Gauls he advanced them, and following out the same principle, drew up their remaining ranks so as to unite them with the wings (ζυγοῦντα) making the formation in the form of a crescent, (μηνοειδὲς ποιῶν τὸ κύρτωμα), and making the ranks of those that composed it shallow, intending to keep the Africans as a kind of ambush in the fight and let the Spaniards and Gauls bear the brunt of the danger', III. 113. 9. μηνοειδὲς is not to be taken quite literally, as there are tactical difficulties in the way of drawing up men in the form of a crescent. Probably the formation is correctly described as a truncated wedge, which however was not solid, the ranks being shallow.

6 § 4. *Afros*] this is the subject, *esse* being omitted.

magna ex parte] probably a mere anticipation of *magna ex parte* which follows.

7   *ita*] sc. as Romans.

     ad Trebiam] sc. *captis.*

9   **§ 5.** *eiusdem formae*] i.e. the shields of the Gauls were like those of the Spaniards, not like those of the Romans.

     dispares ac dissimiles] 'different in appearance and in use'. Explained by what follows.

10   *mucronibus*] 'points'. Pol. III. 114. 3 ἡ δὲ Γαλατικὴ μάχαιρα μίαν εἶχε χρείαν τὴν ἐκ καταφορᾶς, καὶ ταύτην ἐξ ἀποστάσεως. 'The Gaulish sword was of no use except to deal a downward blow, and this from a distance'.

11   *brevitate habiles*] *brevitate,* 'handy by reason of their shortness', 'short and handy'. 11. 6 *vetustate oblitos.*

12   *ante alios*] with *terribilis.* Madvig's emendation for P *antetalius,* Vulg. *et alius.*

     habitus] 'character', 'appearance'.

14   **§ 6.** *praetextis purpura*] 'bordered with purple', Pol. περιπορφύροις.

15   *constiterant*] we should say 'which as they stood there shone' etc.

     numerus...milium...quadraginta] 'the number was 40,000'. Gen. of that in which the thing consists, Roby § 1302.

18   **§ 7.** *Hasdrubal*] the same who carried out the stratagem for eluding Fabius, 16. 8, and who was in charge of the commissariat department (ὁ ἐπὶ τῶν λειτουργιῶν τεταγμένος) Pol. III. 93. 4.

     Maharbal] 6. 11; 13. 9. Polybius III. 14. 7 and Appian say Hanno commanded the right wing. This Hanno was son of Bomilcar a Sufete, and a nephew of Hannibal. We have heard of him before at the passage of the Rhone where he crossed the river higher up than Hannibal and took the Gauls in the rear.

19   *Magone*] He had commanded an ambush at the battle of Trebia, XXI. 54. 1. Polybius describes him as ὄντα νέον μὲν ὁρμῆς δὲ πλήρη καὶ παιδομαθῆ περὶ τὰ πολεμικά.

20   **§ 8.** *locatis*] probably abl. absol. (= *iis locatis*), though it may possibly be dat. in apposition to *utrique parti* which is dat. commodi.

21   *Romanis*] So Polybius III. 113. 2 λαμβάνων πᾶσι τὴν ἐπιφάνειαν (front) τὴν πρὸς μεσημβρίαν.

22   **§ 9.** *Volturnum*] repeated from 43. 10. Appian adds that Hannibal had had the field of battle ploughed up in order that the Romans might be the more troubled with the dust.

23   *in ipsa ora*] 'right in their faces', for this use of *ipse* cf. 15. 7.

CHAPTER XLVII.

25 § **1.** *levibus armis*] 'light-armed'. 3. 9 *auxiliis levium armorum.*
They fought awhile without decisive result (τὰς μὲν ἀρχὰς ἐπ' ἴσον ἦν ὁ
κίνδυνος), but after the defeat of the Roman cavalry on the right the
heavy infantry on each side allowed them to pass through their ranks
(διαδεξάμενα) and advanced to the attack themselves. Pol. III. 115. 1.

26 *equitum...cornu*] 'the left wing consisting of Gaulish cavalry'.
Roby § 1302.

28 *equestris pugnae*] which was usually conducted by repeated attacks.
Sall. *Iug.* 59. 3 *non uti equestri proelio solet sequi deinde cedere sed
adversis frontibus concurrere.*

30 § **2.** *nullo spatio*] Polybius attributes the tactics employed to the
fact that the enemy were uncivilized, not to the nature of the ground.
ἐποίουν μάχην ἀληθινὴν καὶ βαρβαρικήν.

ad evagandum] for riding right or left so as to take the enemy in
flank, 'for evolutions'.

31 *claudebant*] the object is omitted as in 5. 6 *a fronte et ab tergo
hostium acies claudebat.*

32 § **8.** *in derectum*] 'straight on'.

stantibus...confertis postremo] 'first brought to a standstill then
jammed together'.

p. 54. 1 *turba*] abl. cause as in 46. 6.

2 *detrahebat*] After *nitentes* we should have expected *detrahebant*,
but the verb is put in the singular because *vir virum amplexus* inserted
in apposition to *nitentes* is nearer to it.

4 *terga vertunt*] Aemilius who was commanding this wing escaped.
μετασχὼν ἐπί τι τοῦ τῶν ἱππέων ἀγῶνος ὅμως ἔτι τότε διεσώζετο.

§ **4.** *sub*] here probably = 'just after'; though it may also = 'just
before', e.g. *sub noctem*. See on *levibus armis* § 1.

6 *par, dum*] Madvig's correction for *parum. Pares* used commonly to
be read, agreeing with *ordines*, a colon being placed after *pugna.*

constabant] 'remained unbroken'.

7 § **5.** *conisi, obliqua fronte*] P *consiliaequa*, vulg. *connisi aequa*, which
has been corrected by Lipsius to *c. obliqua fronte.*

W. and Wlf. both explain *obliqua fronte* as meaning that the
Romans pushed forward each extremity of their centre, so as to enclose
the projecting curve of the enemy's centre; in other words *obliqua*
implies that the Roman front was concave. But there is nothing else
in the description to suggest that the Romans tried to surround the
projecting part of the enemy's line. *inpulere* for which Polybius has

διέκοψαν suggests rather the opposite idea. Livy may have understood the passage quoted in the next note as implying that the Roman centre was more advanced than the wings, and *obliqua* may signify convex. But there is no word corresponding to it in Polybius' account which in other respects Livy here follows very closely, and the correction though generally accepted is hardly satisfactory.

acie densa] Pol. III. 115. 6 τετυκνωκότες ἀπὸ τῶν κεράτων ἐπὶ τὰ μέσα, 'having closed up from the wings towards the centre'.

8   *cuneum*] See on 46. 3 *Galli. cuneus* is not a very appropriate word as it generally means a deep formation, or a column, while the Gauls and Spaniards were drawn up but few deep. But it is used to indicate the convexity of the formation irrespective of its depth.

9   *a cetera prominentem acie*] This does not mean that the central ranks of the Gauls and Spaniards had other troops behind them, but that they were more advanced than the troops to right and left of them.

10   § 6.   *tenore uno*] 'uninterruptedly', 37. 10.

praeceps] governs *pavore* and agrees with *agmen*.

11   *mediam primum aciem...postremo subsidia*] These words might seem to imply that the Gauls and Spaniards, like the Romans, were drawn up in three lines one behind the other. This was not the case. *mediam aciem* means the central part of the infantry, that is the Gauls and Spaniards as opposed to the Africans drawn up on either side of them. It represents Polybius' οὐ γὰρ ἅμα συνέβαινε τὰ κέρατα καὶ τὰ μέσα συμπίπτειν ἀλλὰ πρῶτα τὰ μέσα, III. 115. 7. 'The wings and the centre did not give way at the same time, but the centre first', because, he continues, 'the Gauls were drawn up in a crescent with its convex side towards the enemy'. The Africans are called *subsidia* 'reserves', not as implying that they were in the rear of the Gauls and Spaniards but only because the latter were intended to engage with the Romans first. Pol. III. 113. 8 βουλόμενος ἐφεδρείας μὲν τάξιν ἐν τῇ μάχῃ τοὺς Λίβυας αὐτῶν ἔχειν, 'wishing to keep the Africans among the infantry as a reserve line'.

12   *Afrorum*] gen. of that in which the thing consists.   Roby § 1302.

13   § 7.   *reductis alis*] ablative absolute like *prominente acie*. The Africans themselves constituted the *alae*. 46. 3 *ut Afrorum cornua essent.*

15   § 8.   *cuneus*] referring to *cuneus* § 5; §§ 6 and 7 being merely explanatory.

aequavit frontem] 'made the line level'.

16   *sinum dedit*] 'formed a hollow'.

circa] 'on either side', often in this incomplete sense. XXI. 25. 2 *circa Padum*. ibid. 43. 4 *circa Padus amnis*.

cornua fecerant] i.e. instead of being not so far advanced as their centre they now formed the horns of a crescent in relation to it, while it formed the concave part of the crescent. Plut. *Fabius* 16 ἡ δὲ φάλαγξ τοῦ Ἀννίβου μεταβαλοῦσα τὸ σχῆμα μηνοειδὴς ἐγεγόνει.

17   *circumdedere alas*] 'outflanked them'. Polybius adds that the Africans on the right now faced to the left (κλίναντες ἐπ' ἀσπίδα) and those on the left to the right (ἐπὶ δόρυ). Thus they both faced the flanks of the Roman troops between them. III. 115. 10.

18   *et ab tergo*] an exaggeration. Polybius says that they were caught between two forces (μέσους ἀποληφθῆναι) and that they faced right and left and fought against those who were assailing them on either *flank* (τοὺς ἐκ τῶν πλαγίων προσπεπτωκότας), III. 115. 12.

20   § **9.** *quorum terga ceciderant*] 'in whose rear they had wrought havoc'.

21   *eo*] 'from the fact that'. Cf. 34. 5.

CHAPTER XLVIII.

24   § **1.** *sinistro cornu*] The battle on the Roman left, §§ 1—6. It was going on simultaneously with the engagement on their right. 47. 1—3.

26   *segne*] 'spiritless'. 'The Numidians neither suffered nor inflicted any serious loss but kept the Romans in check (ἀπράκτους)'. Pol. III. 116. 5.

     a...fraude] 'began with a stratagem on the part of the Carthaginians'. 9. 7 *ab diis orsus*.

27   *fraude*] This stratagem is not mentioned in Polybius; the account of it is probably taken from Coelius. It is given in Appian with some variations.

28   § **2.** *arma*] 'armour'.

30   *parmas...habentes*] as a sign that their intentions were peaceful.

32   § **3.** *in mediam aciem*] This would naturally mean that the Roman left wing opened their ranks to receive them; but Wölfflin's explanation is probably the right one. In Appian (and presumably in Coelius) the stratagem is carried out by Celtiberians, and the scene is enacted in the centre. The Celtiberi are praised by Servilius and placed in the rear of the centre. Livy substitutes Numidians for Celtiberians and so shifts the scene from the centre to the Roman left wing.

NOTES.

179

in mediam aciem is a fragment of the original account which he has
omitted to alter, and means 'into the centre'.

p. 55. 1 *ultimos*] 'the rear ranks'.

3 § **4.** *occupaverat*] 'had engrossed', 15. 6.

4 *scutis*] i.e. the large oblong shields carried by the Romans, as
opposed to the small round shields (*parmae* § 3) which they had
brought with them. They hoped thus to pass as Roman soldiers.

5 *aversam*] sc. 'in the rear'.

8 § **5.** *alibi fuga*] on the Roman right. 47. 3.

alibi...in mala spe proelium] in the Roman centre. 47. 10.

9 *Hasdrubal, qui ea parte praeerat*] *ea parte* means the Carthaginian
right opposed to the Roman left, as distinguished from the Roman right
and centre indicated by *alibi...alibi.* That this is meant is further
indicated by *segnis pugna*, cf. § 1.

But Hasdrubal had not been placed in command of the Carthaginian
right, but Maharbal, 46. 7. What was he doing here? Polybius makes
this clear, III. 116. 7. According to him Hasdrubal having cut to
pieces the Roman right (τοὺς περὶ τὸν ποταμὸν ἱππεῖς: 47. 3) came to
the aid of the Numidians fighting against the Roman left. The latter
now began to retreat. Accordingly Hasdrubal abandoning the pursuit
to the Numidians, whom he saw to be more efficacious than the
Spaniards and Gauls when once the enemy had begun to waver,
proceeded with the latter to help the Africans attacking the Roman
centre in the rear.

This passage accounts for the presence of Hasdrubal on the right
wing, and we may infer from the account of his movements on arriving
there, that he took over the command from Maharbal.

10 *subductos*] 'withdrawn'. 42. 1.

ex media acie] from the centre of the left wing. The expression
can only be understood if we suppose that Hasdrubal drew up the
Gaulish and Spanish horse to right and left of the Numidians, so that
the latter became the *media acies.* Unless indeed it means that he
withdrew only a part of the Numidians.

11 *fugientis*] Livy seems to mean that Hasdrubal withdrew the
Numidians from the conflict with the allied cavalry on the Roman left
against whose resistance they were making little way (*quia segnis...erat*)
and sent them in pursuit of the Roman right which he had routed, 47. 3.
But this account is unintelligible. When Hasdrubal turned against the
Roman centre there would have been no troops left to fight against the
Roman left. Again Polybius says that Hasdrubal had already nearly

12—2

annihilated the Roman right (ἀποκτείναντες τοὺς περὶ τὸν ποταμὸν ἱππεῖς πλὴν πάνυ ὀλίγων). Livy has misunderstood Polybius. The latter says that on the mere approach of Hasdrubal the allied horse on the left began to retreat (προιδόμενοι τὸν ἔφοδον...ἀπεχώρουν) which Livy does not mention. It was the pursuit of these that he abandoned to the Numidians (τοὺς μὲν φεύγοντας παρέδωκε τοῖς Νόμασι). III. 116. 7—8.

12 § 6. *Afris*] so Polybius προσπεσὼν τοῖς Ῥωμαϊκοῖς στρατοπέδοις κατὰ νώτου...ἐπέρρωσε τοὺς Λίβυας. III. 116. 8.

CHAPTER XLIX.

14 § 1. *parte altera*] the centre, as appears from *Hannibali* § 2, compared with 46. 7. It is called 'the other part' as it was only on the left wing that the Romans still resisted.

Paulus] Polybius says that on the defeat of the Roman right (47. 3) Paulus rode up to the centre and engaged with the enemy, III. 116. 3. This may be merely omitted in Livy's account. However, according to another narrative followed by Appian, Paulus had commanded in the centre in the first instance, attended by 1000 horse, and it is probable that Livy has combined this with that of Polybius.

15 *fuerat*] for *erat* cf. 23. 3 note.

16 § 2. *cum confertis*] 'with a compact body'—of horse. Livy is probably thinking of the 1000 horse which Appian gives Paulus (see preceding note). Polybius says the cavalry on the Roman right had been cut to pieces. Cf. note on 48. 5 *fugientis*.

18 *omissis*] 'abandoning'.

19 *et*]=*etiam*.

20 § 3. *denuntianti*]=*nuntianti*, but with the sense of an important announcement, 38. 6. Madvig *renuntianti*.

22 § 4. *quam mallem...traderet*] the subject of *traderet* is *consul*. The meaning is—well, I had rather he had handed them over to me bound hand and foot: he might have done so just as well, seeing that they have given up their only means of escape. The view that the words were spoken in earnest, and express a regret at their certain destruction, is not probable.

24 *quale*] sc. *esse debuit*, 'such as might have been expected'. C. compares *pugna fuit quale inter fidentes sibimet ambo exercitus*, III. 62. 6.

25 *in vestigio*] 'where they stood'. XXI. 44. 6 *nusquam te vestigio moveris*. Cf. *in locis* 41. 9.

27   § **8**. *superantis*] 'surviving'. *superantis* is in apposition to the object which is not expressed.

29   *repetebant*] 'recovered'.

30   § **6**. *praetervehens*] used as though *praetervehor* were not a passive but a deponent, in default of a present passive participle, 'riding by'. Elsewhere Livy expresses this by *praevehi*. Except in this passage *praetervehi* = 'to sail by'.

31   *oppletum*] = *perfusum*. Archaistic.

32   § **7**. *insontem cladis*] 44. 7 *exsors culpae.*

p. 56.   1 *respicere*] 'to look on with favour'. Verg. *E.* I. 28 *libertas quae sera tamen respexit inertem.*

5   § **9**. *macte*] root *mak*, cf. μάκαρ, probably a participle from an extinct verb *mago* = *augeo*. It is a vocative used as nom., with imperative as here, or without. Cf. Verg. *A.* IX. 641 *macte nova virtute puer.* It does not vary with the construction. II. 12. 14 *iuberem te macte virtute esse. virtute* is abl. of cause.

7   § **10**. *publice patribus*] 'To the senate as a body'. 22. 13 *et privatim parentibus...et publice populis gratum erit.*

8   *priusquam advenit*] This is quite regular, being an instance of the indic. present used to express an action about to be commenced. E.g. *nunc redeo ad inceptum.* Sall. *Iug.* 4. Roby § 1462. 50. 8.

9   *privatim*] 'personally'.

10   *et vixisse...et mori*] 'died as he had ever lived'.

    § **11**. *in strage...expirare*] cf. Hor. *C.* I. 12. 38 *animaeque magnae prodigum Poeno superante Paulum.*

11   *reus iterum*] cf. 40. 3.

    e] 'in consequence of'. *ex comparatione* 8. 2.

12   *existam*] 'come forward'.

    alieno crimine] *alium criminando.* Cf. *dictatoria invidia* 26. 4.

13   § **12**. *eos agentis*] P *exigentes.* The pronoun is generally omitted with the participle when the persons have been distinctly indicated before, but this is not the case here.

14   *oppressere*] 'came upon them'.

18   § **13**. *Cannas*] but according to 43. 9 Hannibal's camp was in the immediate neighbourhood of this place. Livy has omitted to mention that Hannibal shifted his camp to the left bank of the river some days before the battle. See App. IV.

    Carthalone] cf. 15. 8.

20   § **14**. *alter*] Varro.

21   *insertus*] 'joining', a correction for P *infestus.*

quinquaginta] Polybius says 70. Plut. *Fabius* 16 ὀλιγοστὸς ἀφίπ-
τευσεν.

Venusiam] past Canusium, and 28 miles from the scene of battle.
Venusia was on the borders of Lucania and Apulia. It was a
Roman colony, founded 291 B.C. at the close of the third Samnite
war, and was afterwards famous as the birthplace of Horace.

22   § **15.** *quadraginta quinque milia*] To these 48,200 must be added
4,500 captured in the battle, 6,400 taken in the smaller camp, 52. 2,
49. 13, 50. 11, and 6,400 in the larger, 49. 13, 52. 4. 14,500 are
mentioned as escaping, 54. 1 and 4. The total number of the army
according to 36 was 87,200. Polybius with less probability says
that 70,000 (III. 117. 4) were killed out of a total roughly given as
80,000 (III. 113. 5).

23   *tantadem*] 'equally large'. This is Madvig's conjecture for *tanta.*
tantusdem is used once in Plautus, and in the *Digest. Tantidem* (at the
same price) and *tantundem* occur in classical Latin.

24   § **16.** *L. Atilius*] not the consul of 217 whose praenomen was
Marcus. 40. 6.

25   *tribuni militum*] legionary officers, 6 to the legion.

26   *quidam*] sc. *ex tribunis militum.*

29   § **17.** *eos*] sc. the curule magistracies. By the Lex Ovinia, date
uncertain, but perhaps soon after 367 B.C.; see on 34. 1, *patrum.*

CHAPTER L.

p. 57. 1 § **1.** *Aliensi*] The defeat of the Romans by the Gauls on the
Alia 390 B.C. which was followed by the occupation of the whole of
Rome except the Capitol.

nobilitate] cf. 43. 9 *nobilitandas.*

3   § **2.** *quia...cessatum*] 'because of the enemy's inaction'.

4   § **3.** *fuga ad Aliam*] 7. 1 *ad Trasumennum pugna.*

namque] in prose of the best period always the first word in the
sentence.

6   *ad Cannas*] not, of course, with *fugientem.*

quinquaginta] 49. 14, he was joined by a larger number afterwards,
54. 1.

7   *alterius*] lit. 'belonged to the other', i.e. shared the fate of the other,
XXI. 11. 1 *totus prope senatus Hannibalis fuit,* 'was with Hannibal'.

9   § **4.** *binis*] 44. 1.

11   *mittunt*] to those in the smaller camp.

ex laetitia] attributively with *epulis*, 'feasts of triumph'.

13   *Canusium*] five miles from the battle-field to the S.W.

abituros] *se* is omitted as in 37. 7.

14   *alii*] of those in the smaller camp.

15   § 5. *venire*] in or. recta *veniunt*.

coniungi] sc. *sibi*.

18   § 6. *P. Sempronius*] adversative asyndeton. According to Appian (*Hann.* 26) he was chosen commander of the larger camp.

20   *aestimari capita et exquiri pretia*] 'to have a price set upon your heads, and your ransoms ascertained'.

22   *Latinus socius*] we should have expected *socius* alone, for the Latin allies or *nomen Latinum* were a particular class of allies (see on 7. 5), while the question here was between the Romans on one side and the allies on the other, for the former were assessed at 400 denarii, the latter at 200, 52. 3. But *Latinus* is inserted to balance *Romanus*, and thus the clause gives merely a specimen of the cases which would arise. However *nomen Latinum* is used incorrectly to indicate the allies in general, 7. 5.

23   § 7. *non tu*] sc. *males*.

se] with *nolo*, *volo* and some other verbs of wishing an acc. (of the pronoun) with infin. is sometimes used instead of the simple infinitive. Madvig, *Lat. G.* § 399, 4.

25   *cives*] = *concives*.

26   § 8. *opprimit*] sc. *nos*, 'surprises us'. The pres. indic. is not incorrect, cf. 49. 10; but of events in the future, especially when there is an idea of prevention as here, the subjunctive is more usual with *antequam*.

27   *inordinati*] 'not in their ranks'.

inconpositi] 'not in their divisions'.

28   § 9. *fit*] the sentiment is general, 'can be made'.

quamvis per confertos] = *per quamvis confertos*, 'no matter how dense they be'.

29   *quidem*] strengthens *cuneo*, 'while with a column' etc. XXI. 30. 7 *nullas profecto terras inexsuperabilis humano generi esse: Alpes quidem habitari.*

30   *ut si*] = *velut si* which is more usual.

32   § 10. *haec ubi dicta dedit*] A phrase common in Vergil. The hexameter and a half probably come from Ennius through Coelius.

p. 58. 1 § 11. *latus dextrum*] The smaller Roman camp must have been either W. of the Carthaginians on the left bank of the river, or

E. of them on the right bank, for the battle was fought on the same bank as that on which the smaller camp was situated, and in the battle the Romans rested their right on the river. Now if the small camp was E. of the Carthaginians and on the right bank troops leaving it would have exposed their left flank to the enemy in crossing to the larger camp. This looks as if Livy thought the battle was fought on the left bank contrary to the view taken in Appendix IV. q.v. But Livy's narrative is not consistent.

3   *ad sescentos*] see on 41. 2 *ad mille et septingenti.*

      inde] with *adiuncto*, when *protinus* is best rendered 'on their way' as in 42. 3; or with *pervenerunt, protinus* meaning 'straight on'.

      alio agmine] the same as *agmine* mentioned in 52. 4.

5   **§ 12.** *impetu animorum*] 'the impulse of that courage' etc.

Chapter LI.

9   **§ 1.** *bello*] used instead of *pugna* because this victory had practically brought the war to an end.

      diei...quietem] The obvious rendering is the best, 'the remainder of the day and the repose of the following night'.

12   **§ 2.** *Maharbal*] Gellius x. 24. 6 gives the same story as *Coelianum illud. Si vis mihi equitatum dare et ipse cum cetero exercitu me sequi die quinti Romae in Capitolio curabo tibi cena sit cocta.* Coelius, he adds, took it from Cato's *Origines*. Livy probably took it from Coelius.

15   *venisse*] sc. *te*, suggested by *sequere.*

16   **§ 3.** *res*] sc. 'the idea' i.e. of such a rapid termination to the war. *statim* is the emphatic word.

19   *temporis*] the gen. with *opus esse* is found once again in Livy, XXIII. 21. 5. It is a Graecism. Cf. δεῖ μοί τινος.

      § 4. *nimirum*]=*ne mirum* (*sit*), for *ni* or *nei*=*ne;* not so strong as *mirum ni* (=*nisi*). 'Of a truth'.

21   *satis creditur*] 'it is generally believed'. This was a favourite topic for rhetorical disputation. Juv. VII. 163 *an petat urbem a Cannis*. Yet it is doubtful whether Hannibal could have taken Rome, cf. 9. 2. Maharbal could certainly not have done so. Mommsen says, 'This unexampled success appeared at length to mature the great political combination for the sake of which Hannibal had come to Italy'. The news of the victory reduced the peace party at home to silence. Men and money were sent from Carthage. Philip of Macedon and Hieronymus the new king of Syracuse joined the Carthaginian alliance. Capua,

several communities in central Italy and all lower Italy passed over to the side of Hannibal, cc. 19—22. Hannibal had reason to wait.

23 § **5.** *foedam*] 'woeful', 3. 1.

24 *stragem*] concrete, 'scene of slaughter'.

insistunt] elsewhere *insistere* is used with the dative (47. 6) or the infinitive. Madvig accordingly reads *exeunt*, but without support from the MSS.

25 § **6.** *ut quem*]=*ut quemque*; *que* in *cuique* doing double duty.

27 *stricta*] 'drawn together', 'closed'. Then *excitaverant*='had revived', sc. by staunching the blood. *stricta* may however mean 'touched' and therefore 'smarting'. Then *excitaverant*='had roused from their unconsciousness'.

p. 59. 1 § **7.** *haurire*] 'to shed', a poetical use of the word. Tacitus has *iugulum hausisse*, *H.* 1. 41. But here *haurire* belongs only to *sanguinem*.

§ **8.** *mersis*] 'thrust'.

3 *interclusisse spiritum*] sc. 'had suffocated themselves'. *cum (imber) spiritum includeret* XXI. 58. 4, means only, 'rendered respiration difficult'.

4 § **9.** *convertit omnes*] sc. *in se*, 'attracted the attention of all'. XXI. 111. 4 *cum admiratione...in se omnes convertisset.*

superincubanti] the word occurs here only.

7 *laniando*] 'while he tore'. Cf. 3. 10 for the use of the abl. of the gerund = a present particle.

expirasset] *Romanus*.

CHAPTER LII.

8 § **1.** *ducit*] sc. *exercitum*. Cf. 1. 1 note.

9 *brachio*] a line of earthworks. Hirtius, *Bell. Hispan.* 5 *ut eum ab oppido excluderet brachium ad pontem ducere coepit* (C.).

10 *flumine*] the Aufidus. The object was to prevent their getting water. 59. 5 *cum aqua arceremur.*

§ **2.** *ab omnibus...fessis*] This means that all joined in making the surrender, *omnibus fessis* would only give the reason for the surrender.

12 § **3.** *pacti* (from *paciscor*) with *trecenis nummis*, lit. 'having covenanted (for their safety) at the price of' etc. Cf. XXI. 61. 11 *viginti argenti talentis pacti deduntur, ut traderent* = *ita ut traderent*, adds a condition of the agreement. Cf. 43. 4; 5. 7 note.

13 *in capita Romana*] 'for every Roman'. So *in socios*, 23. 6 *in militem*.

14　　*nummis quadrigatis*] silver denarii (8½*d*.), so called because they were stamped with a representation of Jupiter in a four-horse chariot ; 300=£10. 12*s*. 6*d*. The price per man had risen since 217 B.C. Cf. 23. 6 note.

15　　*et ut*] depending on *pacti*. XXXIV. 29. 12 *pactus ut abducere milites liceret.*

16　　*singulis*] besides what they had on, 'a single change of raiment', 6. 11.

17　　*seorsum*]=*sevorsum* 'separately'. So *prorsum*=*provorsum.*

20　　§ **4.** *hominum*]=*peditum*, as opposed to *equites*. XXI. 27. 1 *equites virique. ad* with *milia* alone. The number of cavalry is given accurately. Cf. *ad sescentos* 50. 11.

23　　*tradita*] Polybius who says nothing about the capture of the smaller camp gives a different account of the capture of the larger. Paulus left 10,000 men in his camp who were to attack that of Hannibal during the battle. They were on the point of taking it when Hannibal returned and drove them back to their own camp. There 2000 of them were slain and the remainder taken prisoners, III. 117. 11.

24　　§ **5.** *si quid*] sc. *erat.*

25　　*phaleris*] 'trappings', bosses affixed to the bridle, head-stall, etc. *ad vescendum facto*] sc. 'plate for the table', *argentum mensarium. facto*='worked'.

26　　*utique*]=*saltem*, 7. 11 ; 23. 3. *omnis cetera*] elsewhere the order is *cetera omnis.*

27　　§ **6.** *sepeliendi*] not passive, the object is not expressed. Roby, Introd. LXIV. b.

28　　*octo milia*] Polybius says 4000 Gauls, 1500 Spaniards and Africans and 200 horse. Cf. 49. 15 note.

29　　*consulem*] Cf. 7. 5 note.

32　　§ **7.** *Busa*] The name Busidius has been found on a stone at Canusium.

CHAPTER LIII.

p. **60.**　4 § **2.** *de legione prima*] *de* with abl. is often used in this connection instead of the genitive. From this and similar uses *de* (or *di*) became the sign of the genitive in the Romance languages.

10　　§ **3.** *adulescentem*] 19. In the account of the engagement at Ticinus in 218 B.C. he is described as 17, XXI. 46. 7. *summa imperii*] of course only at Canusium in the absence of Varro at Venusia, 54. 1.

11 § **4.** *inter paucos*] 'with a few others'.

12 *summa rerum*] 'the general condition of affairs'.

13 *perditam spem fovere*] a short way of expressing 'it was in vain that they cherished hope, as all hope was lost'. Cf. XXI. 12. 3 *temptata est exigua spes pacis.*

desperatam conploratamque] i.e. 'given up', as though by the physicians, and 'mourned for', as though already dead, 55. 3.

15 § **5.** *quorum principem*] sc. *esse.* The acc. with infin. is used instead of *sit* because *quorum = et eorum.* It is possible however, though not likely, that *quorum principem* (which = *et eorum principem*) has the same verb as *iuvenes.* Cf. IV. 43. 6 *aliae, inter quas et agrariae legis, seditiosae actiones existunt.*

16 *spectare*] sc. 'were thinking of taking to'.

regum] as Philip of Macedon or Ptolemy king of Egypt, to offer their services as mercenaries.

17 § **6.** *praeterquam*] for *praeterquam quod erat,* 'besides being terrible', XXVI. 13. 14 *effugere morte praeterquam honesta etiam leni possum.*

18 *stupore ac miraculo*] depending on *torpidos,* best taken as a hendiadys, 'by stupefaction at this strange proposal'. In no case does *miraculum* = 'astonishment'.

20 *consilii rem*] 'matter for a council'.

fatalis] 'predestined'. XXX. 28. 1 *velut fatalem eum...ducem horrebant.*

23 § **8.** *nulla verius...hostium castra esse*] 'no camp is more truly a camp of the enemy than that in which etc.' P has *nullo.* The true reading may possibly be *nullo in loco* which would correspond more closely with *ubi.* For *verius* cf. 19. 11.

ea] = *talia.*

24 § **9.** *pergit*] of prompt or energetic action, 19. 4, 'he went straight to' etc.

hospitium] 'lodging'.

27 § **10.** *ex mei animi sententia*] a common formula in oaths and declarations, 'to the best of my knowledge and belief'; here 'solemnly'. *quod ex tui animi sententia iuraris, id non facere periurium est,* Cic. *De off.* III. 29. 108. There is an ellipse of *iuro.*

ut] *ita me di ament,* 'so help me heaven', which corresponds to *ut...non deseram,* is omitted. C. compares the inscription *ex mei animi sententia ut ego iis inimicus ero quos C. Caesari Germanico inimicos esse cognovero.* Cf. the use of *sic* in prayers

sic tibi Cyrnaeas fugiant examina taxos,
incipe si quid habes. Verg. *E.* IX. 30.

28   *neque*] still part of the protasis. The apodosis is omitted, see preceding note.

29   § 11. *sciens*] 'wittingly', 10. 5, he has sworn 'to the best of his knowledge'.

   fallo] absolute, 'break my word'.

30   § 12. *in haec verba*] 'in this form'. Cf. 10. 2 note.

31   *iures*] for the omission of *ut* cf. 3. 13 *nuntia effodiant signum.*

p. 61.   2   *custodiendos*] 52. 3 *traditi in custodiam.*

CHAPTER LIV.

3   § 1. *Venusiam*] Varro had fled thither after the battle with some 50 horsemen, 49. 14.

4   *ad*] used adverbially. Cf. 41. 2, note.

5   *fuerant*] for *erant*. Cf. 23. 3. Introd. II.

6   § 2. *per familias*] 'among various households'.

8   *togas et tunicas*] sc. *singulas.* Cf. the use of *milia = singula milia*, 36. 3. They received an outer and an inner garment. The *toga* was the garb of the civilian, 26. 1. It was probably worn on garrison duty and in winter-quarters by officers and *equites* only. Thus in XXIX. 36. 2 only 1200 *togae* are sent to the army but 12,000 *tunicae.*

9   *quadrigatos nummos*] 52. 3 note.

11   § 3. *publice...privatim*] 'by the town'...'by individual citizens', 49. 10.

12   *muliere Canusina*] 52. 7.

13   § 4. *gravius*] i.e. than that borne by the people of Venusia, or better, 'constantly heavier'; this suits the imperfect better.

   et] introducing an explanation of *multitudo*, 'and indeed'.

   decem milia] Others then must have come besides the 600 from the smaller camp 50. 11, and the 4200 from the larger camp 52. 4.

17   § 5. *sciscitatum*] supine, corresponding in sense with *nuntium mittunt* which = *aliquem mittunt nuntiatum.*

19   § 6. *consularis exercitus*] about two legions. These were what are afterwards alluded to as the *Cannenses legiones*, which were kept on garrison duty in Sicily during the remainder of the war by way of punishment.

23   § 7. *occidione occisum*] 'utterly destroyed'. A common phrase in Livy. So XXIX. 27. 3 *auctibus augere.* Compare such Hebraisms as

'Thou hast led captivity captive', or ἐπιθυμίᾳ ἐπεθύμησα, St Luke xxii. 15.

24 *fuerat*] for *erat* as in § 1.

25 § **8**. *salva urbe*] 'while the city was still safe '. The words exclude the disaster on the Alia, 50. 1.

27 *edissertando*] 'by a detailed account '. *Edissertare* is a Plautine word. Livy generally uses *edisserere* like Cicero.

§ **9**. *consule...amisso*] These words are contrasted with *cum duobus...amissi*, 'In the preceding year one consul and his army had been lost at Trasimene, but now etc. '

28 *non vulnus super vulnus*] as would have been the case if a new disaster of no greater magnitude than that of Trasimene had been announced.

29 *multiplex*] 'far greater'. Cf. *multiplicati* 36. 1. Not 'many times as great', for it was only twice as great according to the method of reckoning adopted.

30 *exercitus amissi*] in apposition to *multiplex clades*, 'The loss of two armies'. 36. 6 *propter territos homines*.

nec...esse] depending on *nuntiabatur* supplied from *nuntiabantur*.

31 § **10**. *Hannibalis factam*] 14. 6 *Numidarum...iam factam.*

p. **62**. 1 *profecto*] 'assuredly'.

mole cladis] *moles* indicates difficulty, 9. 2, or weight. The expression is stronger than *tam gravi clade.* 'A crushing defeat'.

2 § **11**. *conpares*] The subjunctive is potential, ' one might compare with them'. P *comparesset* for which Madvig reads *compares scilicet*, against C and M.

cladem] with *Carthaginiensium.*

Aegatis insulas] The victory of C. Lutatius Catulus in 241 B.C. which brought the First Punic war to a close.

4 *Sardinia*] This is inaccurate. Sicily was ceded on the conclusion of the war, with an indemnity of 3200 talents. In 238 B.C. the Romans, taking advantage of a revolt of the Carthaginian mercenaries in Sardinia, demanded the surrender of that island with a further indemnity of 1200 talents. The Carthaginians were unable to refuse the request.

vectigalis ac stipendiarios] The former is used especially of those who paid amounts proportionate to the produce of the land, the latter of those who paid a fixed amount. The distinction is sometimes disregarded as in XXXIII. 47. 2, where the Carthaginian indemnity is called *vectigal.* If this is the case here both words express the same

idea. Otherwise *vectigalis* is historically inaccurate; for the Carthaginians paid the Romans no taxes, only the indemnity referred to in
the preceding note.

5   *pugnam...in Africa*] the battle of Zama 202 B.C. in which Hannibal
was defeated by Scipio, *fatalis dux huius belli* 53. 6.

6   *nulla*] there is an adversative asyndeton, as the words contain the
answer to *conpares*.

   conparandae] 'comparable'. In negative and quasi-negative sentences
the gerundive sometimes has the meaning of possibility rather than of
obligation. Roby § 1403. Tibullus, IV. 4. 2 *votaque pro domina vir
numeranda facit.*

CHAPTER LV.

8   § 1. *Philus...Pomponius*] 35. 5.

10   § 2. *dubitabant...venturum*] Livy often uses *dubitare* with the acc.
and infinitive.   In Caesar and Cicero it is followed by *quin*.

14   § 3. *ne consilium quidem*] They could not even form a plan, much
less take any action.

   expedirent] properly to extricate, as though from the confusion
around them.   4. 7 *arma expediri.*

15   *obstreperet*] sc. *consultantibus*, 'deafened'. Cf. 14. 8.

   nondum palam facto] sc. *qui vivi qui mortui essent*, 'as the truth
was not yet published'. Cf. *inexplorato* 4. 4 note.

18   § 4. *Appia via*] 1. 12 note.

   Latina] 12. 2 note.

19   *obvios*]=*qui obvii essent*, 7. 11.

   profecto...fore] The reading of C² for P, C *profectos...forte. profecto* here, as often, is best rendered by 'must'. D. compares XXVI.
15. 13 *cum negaret...profecto satis conpotem mentis esse*, 'when he said
that he *must* certainly be out of his mind'.

20   *referant*] after *censuit* one would have expected *referrent;* but Livy
often prefers primary to secondary sequences for the sake of vividness.

21   § 5. *relicum...fecerint*] 'have allowed to survive'.

25   § 6. *illud*] explained by *ut...tollant...arceant* etc. 'the other task,
that of calming the tumult' etc.

   ipsos] explained by *quoniam...sit.*

   magistratuum parum] 16. 4 *tantum sociorum.* The absence of the
only surviving consul is referred to.

27   *publico*] properly *loco:* sc. 'from appearing in public'.

30 § **7.** *suae...expectet*] There is a sudden change of subject. This clause refers to the people generally, not to the praetors.

fortunae...auctorem] *auctor*='informant'. Ov. *Met.* XI. 666 *non haec tibi nuntiat auctor ambiguus.* 'The bearer of tidings affecting themselves'. 24. 11 *auctores sunt.*

31 § **8.** *ponant*] the subject is *praetores* again.

p. 63. 2 *recte*] probably due to a repetition of the last part of the preceding word.

revocandos] The senators were to restore order before deliberating on the situation.

<h2 style="text-align:center">CHAPTER LVI.</h2>

4 § **1.** *in hanc sententiam...issent*] 'had voted for this motion'. Questions in the Senate were decided by a division (*discessio*). The presiding magistrate used the following form, *Qui haec sentitis in hanc partem, qui alia omnia in illam partem ite qua sentitis,* Plin. *Ep.* VIII. 14. 9.

pedibus] indicating that they voted 'without discussion'. Thus those senators who were not usually called upon to speak in the Senate (*qui non rogabantur sententiam*) were called *pedarii* (*quia pedibus in sententiam ibant*).

submota] the technical term for the removal of a crowd by the lictors. III. 48. 3 *i, lictor, submove turbam.* So *submoto* 'after room had been made', XXVIII. 37. 15.

5 *diversi*] 'in different directions', adj. for adv. as in 32. 2 *opportuni aderant.*

6 *tum demum*] cf. 13. 8 note. Dio says Varro sent neither message nor messenger immediately after the defeat.

7 *litterae*] especially of an official communication, 'a despatch', 33. 9.

9 § **2.** *reliquias cladis*] 'survivors from the disaster'. Cf. Verg. *A.* I. 30 *Troas, reliquias Danaum.*

11 *decem milia*] But there were already 10,000 men at Canusium, 54. 4, without counting the 4500 at Venusia, 54. 1, whom Varro subsequently brought there, 54. 6. D. suggests *quindecim millia.*

inconpositorum inordinatorum] not yet organised in centuries, maniples and legions. For *ordines* cf. 50. 8. In 50. 8 these words only refer to temporary disorder.

12 § **3.** *in*] in the matter of, 'about'.

14   *nundinantem*] properly 'marketing', in a contemptuous sense 'haggling'. Cf. Ennius' line *non cauponantes bellum* (making a traffic of war) *sed belligerantes.* Cic. *Off.* 1. 38. *nundinari* may govern an acc. *n. senatorium nomen* Cic. *Verr.* II. 2. 122. This is an emendation for P *nuntiantem.*

    § **4.** *per domos*] 'from house to house'.

15   *opplevit*] an archaistic compound. 49. 6.

16   *sacrum...Cereris*] not the regular Cerealia as these were celebrated in April, while the battle of Cannae was fought in June.

    intermissum sit] the perfect subjunctive though a secondary tense has preceded, as often in Livy. See on 5. 8 *senserit.*

    nec lugentibus] it was a joyful ceremony, and was performed by matrons in white garments who enacted the search for and discovery of Proserpina by Ceres.

17   *tempestate*] slightly more emphatic than *tempore.*

18   *expers fuerat*] 'had not been plunged in grief', i. e. when it was desired to celebrate the festival. 'Could be found who had escaped bereavement'.

19   § **5.** *desererentur*] 'should be neglected'.

20   *diebus triginta*] 'to thirty days', lit. by thirty days, thirty days being made the limit of the mourning. Generally mourning for parents or children lasted a year.

22   § **6.** *litterae*] as in § 1.

    Otacilio] 31. 6.

23   *Hieronis*] 37. 1 note.

25   § **7.** *stare*] 'were lying at anchor'. Verg. *A.* VI. 902 *stant litore puppes.*

26   § **8.** *se*] Otacilius, the logical subject of the whole sentence which depends on 'Otacilius wrote'.

27   *aliam*]=*reliquam.* Cf. 11. 9, note. Since the close of the First Punic war the Romans had held the Western portion of the island of which the chief town was Lilybaeum, while the Eastern and smaller portion remained in the hands of Hiero king of Syracuse.

28   *classe*] besides that which he himself already commanded.

Chapter LVII.

30   § **1.** *praetoris*] more correctly *propraetoris* as in 56. 6, for Otacilius had been praetor in the preceding year, 37. 13.

31   *M. Claudium*] *Marcellum,* 35. 6. One of the most vigorous and successful of the Roman commanders. In 222 B.C. he brought the

Insubrian War to a close and slew Viridomarus with his own hand, thus gaining the *spolia opima* for the third and last time in Roman history. In 215 B.C. he repulsed Hannibal before Nola. In 212 B.C. he took Syracuse. But in 208 B.C. he was surprised by a body of Numidians and slain.

classi] probably the fleet mentioned in 31. 5.

32   *praeesset*] the subjunctive, because it forms part of the resolution.

p. 64. 2 *primo quoque tempore*] 'at the very first opportunity'. XLII. 10. 5 *Latinis feriis in primam quamque diem indictis*.

3   *per commodum* etc.] 'in so far as the interests of the State allowed'. *per*, as in 21. 1 *fuissetque (quietum) per Poenum hostem*. This is more likely than that *per* indicates the manner as in 29. 7 etc. and that *per commodum* = 'conveniently'.

4   § 2. *super*]=*praeter*. XXI. 46. 1 *super cetera*, lit. 'on the top of'. Cf. 3. 14 *superquam quod*.

6   *Vestales*] They were at this time six in number, taken from the noblest families. Their duty was to keep alive the sacred fire in the temple of Vesta in the Forum. Their conduct was subject to strict supervision from the *pontifex maximus*. The punishment for neglecting the sacred fire was scourging, for inchastity death, in the manner here described.

7   *stupri conpertae*] an extension of the use of the genitive expressing the charge. Cf. Sall. *Cat.* 52 *manifesti rerum capitalium*.

et] what follows is merely parenthetical. Of course the Romans were terrified at the crime of the Vestals, not at its punishment.

8   *Collinam*] so called because it stood on the Quirinal, which was known as *Collis* not *mons*.

necata] i.e. buried alive.

10   § 3. *quos*] sc. *scribas*. A *constructio ad sensum*, as if *unus e pontificis scribis* had preceded. XXVII. 11. 3 *infantem quos androgynos vulgus...appellat*. C.

minores pontifices] We know no more of these than that there were three of them, forming a *collegium*. Macrobius describes them as observing the moon in order to report to the *rex sacrificulus*, in connexion with keeping the calendar.

12   *comitio*] see on 7. 7.

13   § 4. *hoc nefas*] the guilt of the Vestals.

14   § 5. *decemviri libros*] see on 1. 16.

15   *Fabius Pictor*] cf. 7. 4 and Introd. I.

Delphos ad oraculum] 54. 1 *Venusiam ad consulem*. The answer,

L. XXII.   13

mentioned in XXIII. 11. 1, was that if the Romans performed certain ceremonies which were prescribed *victoria duelli populi Romani erit.*

16   *suppliciis*]=*supplicationibus*, archaic.

18   § **6.** *fatalibus*] sc. the Sibylline books.

20   *foro bovario*] on the edge of the Velabrum, near the Circus Maximus.

21   *minime Romano*] The Sibylline books which prescribed the sacrifice were of Greek origin; still the stories of the self-devotion of Curtius and the two Decii, and the old Latin custom of the *ver sacrum* (see on 9. 10) probably indicate that human sacrifices were anciently offered in Italy.

24   § **7.** *scriptos habebat*] not=*scripserat*, 'had with him already enrolled'.

   urbi praesidio] there was already a garrison there, 11. 9.

25   § **8.** *tertia*] but the third legion belonged to the land forces and had fought at Cannae, 53. 2. Either *tertia* refers to a fresh enumeration of the forces, or Livy is using a different authority from that which he there follows.

26   *Teanum Sidicinum*] so called to distinguish it from Teanum in Apulia. It commanded the Latin road at the point where it entered Campania.

27   *Philo*] *praetor urbanus,* 35. 5.

28   § **9.** *ex auctoritate patrum*] the Senate, that is, resolved to communicate with Varro asking him to appoint a dictator.

29   *dictus*] by the consul. Apparently Varro also appointed the master of the horse. This was usually done by the dictator. Cf. 33. 11.

30   *iuniores*] those between 17 and 46.

   ab] i.e. those of 17 and upwards.

31   *praetextatos*] boys under 17, who still wore the *toga praetexta* (a robe with a purple border). At 17 the *toga virilis* was assumed.

32   § **10.** *effecti*] 16. 8.

   Latinum nomen] see on 7. 5.

p. 65. 1 *ex formula*] 'in accordance with the terms of their treaties with Rome'.

   arma, tela, alia] asyndeton enumerativum is frequent in business details. C. *arma*=defensive, *tela*=offensive weapons.

3   § **11.** *formam*] 'kind'. P has *alia formam*, for which *aliam formam* is generally read.

5   *servitiis*] abstract for concrete.

   vellentne] hence Livy speaks of the latter as *volones* volunteers, XXIII. 35. 7. Roman citizens were of course bound to serve.

CHAPTER LVIII.

8 **§ 1.** *ad Cannas pugnam*] 7. 1.

11 **§ 2.** *Trebiam Trasumennumque*] Livy did not mention that this was done after the battle of Trebia. For Trasumene cf. 7. 5.

12 *sine pretio*] in 52. 3 it is stated that the ransom for each ally had been fixed at 200 denarii.

14 *quod*] sc. *fecerat.*

15 *de dignitate*] sc. only for honour.

certare] sc. *se*, cf. 34. 7.

16 **§ 3.** *et...et*] 'as...so'. *Romanae* and *suae* are the emphatic words.

17 *id adniti ut*] perhaps on the analogy of *id agere ut. adniti* governs an accusative (of the pronoun) only in this conjunction.

19 **§ 4.** *in capita*] 'per head'. 52. 3 *in capita Romana.*

quadrigatos] Cf. 52. 3.

20 **§ 5.** *aliquantum*] 'a considerable amount' According to to 52. 3 it was arranged that all the Roman troops horse and foot alike were to pay 300 denarii.

21 *equitibus*] dat. *incommodi.*

quo] abl. of price, like *nummis* in 52. 3.

pepigerant] absolute 'had made agreement', sc. for their release. W. compares Plaut. *Bacch.* 879 *ducentis Philippis pepigi. pepigi* is generally used as the perf. of *paciscor*, instead of *pactus sum* (but cf. 59. 6) which is rare.

22 *quamcumque*] Without a verb *quicumque* has the sense of *quivis* or *quilibet.* But in Cic. Sall. Caes. it is used thus only in the ablative. *quacunque de re*, Cic. *Ep. Q. F.* 11. 8. 1. *quocunque modo*, Sall. *Iug.* 103.

25 **§ 7.** *Carthalo*] 15. 8; 49. 13.

28 **§ 8.** *minime Romani ingenii*] 'no true Roman'; *vir ac vere Romanus* 14. 11; for *minime* cf. 57. 6.

31 **§ 9.** *dictatoris verbis*] 'in the name of the dictator'.

CHAPTER LIX.

p. 66. 1 § 1. *senatus datus est*] 'an audience in the Senate was given them'.

2 *patres conscripti*] This has been explained as standing for *patres et conscripti* referring to the original patrician members of the Senate, and the plebeian members afterwards added to their number. But the meaning is simply, 'fathers on the roll of the Senate'.

13 --?

4   *viliores*] cf. 60. 7. But the statement can hardly be reconciled with
§§ 7, 18.

5   § **2.** *ceterum*] adversative, 1. 4 note.

nisi...causa] 'unless we think better of our case than we ought
to think'.

plus iusto] a compendious expression like *maturior spe* 52. 2.

6   *minus neglegendi*]=*qui minus neglegendi sunt.*

8   § **3.** *per*] expressing the cause. In 29. 7 it expresses the manner.

13   § **5.** *victore*] used adjectivally.

aqua arceremur] 52. 1.

14   *confertos*] an exaggeration, see 50. 9.

15   *quinquaginta milibus*] in round numbers. The number of those
who fell on the field is given more accurately in 49. 15.

16   *aliquem...militem*] *aliquem* is emphatic. *militem* is used collectively,
'that *some* soldiers should survive'.

19   § **7.** *acceperamus*] the pluperfect because the time of the surrender
is referred to.

a Gallis auro] After the battle of the Alia and the capture of
Rome in 390 B.C. According to the story the transaction was inter-
rupted by the appearance of Camillus.

20   *illos*] lit. 'those well known'. Cf. 5. 7. The meaning here is 'as
is well known'.

ad] 'as regards'. Ter. *Ad.* v. 3. 45 *ad omnia alia aetate sapimus
rectius.*

21   *tamen*] as if *quamvis* had preceded.

22   *misisse*] referring to the embassy, of which Fabricius was the head,
sent to Pyrrhus after the battle of Heraclea, or to exchange or ransom
prisoners. This was in 280 B.C., more than 66 years earlier, so the
senators who sent it could hardly be the fathers of those now addressed.

§ **8.** *et...et...utraque*] 'both battles, both that at the Alia and that
at Heraclea'.

24   *pavore*] an exaggeration as regards the battle of Heraclea, at which
the Romans inflicted a loss of 7000 men on the enemy. However this defeat was due in part to their fear of Pyrrhus' elephants to
which they were then opposed for the first time.

25   *nec...nisi in quibus*] 'and only those of us survive whom' etc.

27   § **9.** *fuere*] Madvig's correction for P *refugerunt* which does not
go well with *in acie.*

28   *praesidio relicti*] Livy has not mentioned this before. From 52.
2 and 4 the only occupants of the two camps seem to be the fugitives

from the battle. Polybius III. 117. 8 says that Aemilius left 10,000 men in his camp and does not mention the fugitives.

30 § **10.** *premendo*] 'depreciating'. 12. 12 *premendo superiorem.*

31 *ne illi quidem*] '*and yet* even they could not' etc.

32 *qui plerique*] 'most of whom'.

p. **67.** 1 *prius quam*] *constiterunt* must strictly speaking be supplied after *quam*, 'who did not stop till (they did so) at Venusia'.

2 *praetulerint*] the hypothetical subjunctive, 'nor could they prefer themselves to us'. Cf. IX. 24. 7 *hoc quidem adscensu vel tres armati quamlibet multitudinem arcuerint.* Roby § 1540.

4 § **11.** *utemini*] with *bonis* and *fortibus*, 'you will find them good and brave soldiers'.

promptioribus quod...fuerimus] 'the more zealous for having been restored'.

7 § **12.** *fortuna*] 'position'. For the statement cf. 57. 9—11.

9 *emuntur*] by the State from their owners.

nam] a sentence is left unexpressed. 'I compare only our cost and not our worth with those of the slaves'.

11 § **13.** *censeam*] the subjunctive expresses a modest statement, 'I venture to think'.

12 *si iam*] 'even if'. XXI. 47. 5 *ut iam Hispanos inflati transvexerint utres.*

faciatis] not quite correctly used, for *quod = duriores esse.*

13 *cui hosti*] the clause depends on *animadvertendum.*

§ **14.** *videlicet*] ironical, 'I suppose'.

hospitum numero habuit] 'treated as guests'. Caesar, *B. G.* VI. 6 *aliquem hostium numero habere.*

14 *an*] 'or rather'.

ac] 'and what is more'. 14. 11 *vir ac vere Romanus.*

15 *existimari*] 'to be decided'. Sall. *Iug.* 85. 14 *nunc vos existimate facta an dicta pluris sint.*

16 § **15.** *squalorem*] referring to their garments, *deformitatem* to their appearance generally. 11. 23. 2 *obsita squalore vestis.*

19 § **16.** *intueri*] the doors of the Senate house always remained open while the assembly was sitting.

in vestibulo] not inconsistent with 60. 1 *in comitio,* for the *vestibulum* was properly not part of a building but the space or courtyard in front of it. Becker's *Gallus* 237.

24 § **17.** *sed*] marking an abrupt change of subject.

me dius fidius] an elliptical expression for *ita me deus fidius iuvet,* 'good heavens'. *fidius* is connected with *fides*; and *deus fidius* refers to the Sabine deity *Semo Sancus*, 'the god of fidelity'. Cf. Ζεὺς πίστιος.

mitis] i.e. if he were to release us.

26   *indigni ut*] *qui* is more usual, both occur in XXIII. 42. 10 *quos ut socios haberes dignos duxisti, haud indignos iudicas quos in fidem receptos tuearis.*

27   § 18. *capti*]=*captivi.*

29   *redeam*] What Roby calls the interrogative of command, § 1610, it is common in indignant questions. Cf. Hor. *S.* II. 3. 264 *exclusit; revocat; redeam? non, si obsecret.*

nummis] *denarii*, as appears from 52. 3. Otherwise *nummus* generally = *sestertius.*

30   § 19. *suum quisque habet animum*] sc. others may think differently.

32   *ne abeamus*] depending on the meaning of fearing contained in *movet.* Cf. 22. 5 *pignus...morabatur, ne...culpa ..lueretur.*

CHAPTER LX.

p. 68. 3   § 1. *comitio*] 7. 7 note.

5   *liberos* etc.] *asyndeton enumerativum.* Not *maritos* nor *patres* for women and children were not allowed to approach the Senate house. The former however stood in the Forum.

7   § 2. *necessitas*] 'the pressure of necessity', as they depended on their husbands for support.

8   *senatus consuli coeptus*] lit. 'began to be consulted'. The Senators, at least the more prominent among them (see on *pedibus*, 56. 1), were asked their opinion in turn. 'The debate began'.

submotis] 56. 1.

arbitris] witnesses, 'strangers', i. e. the 10 envoys.

9   § 3. *variaretur*] 'there was a difference'. *vario* may be either transitive or intransitive, and it is used impersonally in the passive in the same sense as intransitively in the active. I. 43. 11 *si variaret.*

10   *de publico*] ἀπὸ κοινοῦ, 'out of the public funds'. So *ex privato* § 4.

11   *nec*]='yet not'.

prohibendos redimi] one may say *redimi prohibentur* on the same principle as *iubeor hoc facere.* This use is extended to the gerundive. III. 28. 7 *iam se ad prohibenda circumdari opera Aequi parabant.*

12   § 4. *in praesentia*] ablative, though *in praesens* is used.

13 *dandam mutuam*] 'should be lent '.

14 *praedibus...praediis*] ablatives of the means. *Praes* is a surety, one who pledges his property as a security. Festus, 222 *praes est qui populo se obligat. praedia* the properties pledged.

populo] probably *dativus commodi*, rather than dative of the agent, 'that security should be procured for the state'.

15 § 5. *Manlius*] he was an old man, for he had been censor in 231 B.C. His principal exploit was the conquest of Sardinia, 235 B.C.

priscae severitatis] The genitive of quality is sometimes (but not in Cicero) joined directly to a proper noun, without the interposition of *vir* etc. III. 27. 1 *T'arquitium, patriciae gentis.*

interrogatus] *rogatus* is more usual in this sense.

19 § 6. *eorum*] depending on *ullius*, 'without attacking any of them'.

20 § 7. *quid aliud quam*] practically = *tantum*. The expression is really elliptical and stands for *quid aliud mihi faciendum esset quam ut admonerem.* XXXIV. 46. 7 *Galli per biduum nihil aliud* (sc. *fecerunt*) *quam per biduum steterunt parati.*

21 *necessario...exemplo*] ablative of means. It was necessary now, for Hannibal's design was to diminish the desperate valour of the Romans by holding them out some hopes of escape in case of surrender. Pol. VI. 58. 9. Cf. 58. 2.

rem militarem] 'military discipline'.

22 *nunc*] Gk. *νῦν δέ.* 39. 3.

23 *praeferri*] *se* is omitted.

29 § 8. *P. Sempronius*] 50. 6 sqq.

32 § 9. *tum...laetis*] as though a *cum* corresponding to *tum* had preceded. But this is omitted, as it would have come next to *cum* = 'when'. For a similar omission cf. 50. 4.

et ipsis] 'like the Romans'. *et* = *quoque*, 2. 7.

p. 69. 1 *plerisque*] The Numidians who surrounded the camp (50. 11) are excepted.

3 *etiam per confertos*] = *etiam si conferti essent.*

4 *per se*] = *sponte.*

6 § 10. *paucitas*] 24. 9.

9 *posse*] *se.*

§ 11. *si ut...si ut*] Madvig's correction for *sicut...sicut.*

10 *P. Decius*] This was the P. Decius Mus who devoted himself to death in the Latin war at the battle of Vesuvius, 340 B.C. The occasion here referred to was in 343 B.C., during the first Samnite

war, when he saved the Roman army from being attacked in a defile
by seizing a hill commanding the enemy's camp.

11   *priore*]   The speaker of course knows of only two Punic wars.

Calpurnius Flamma]   The Roman army was surrounded in a defile
near Camarina, when Calpurnius cut his way out and saved it, 258 B.C.
Livy, *Epit.* 17.

15   § **12.** *diceret*]   The imperfect subjunctive may be used to express an
unfulfilled condition in the past if the action is continuous, 46. 4. So
duceret.   extitisset on the other hand expresses a single act.

16   § **13.** *viam*]   There is an adversative asyndeton here, 'as it is he
points you out'.

17   *non magis quam*]   'quite as much as', cf. 27. 2.

demonstrat...facit]   Sempronius.   The orator carries his hearers back
to the moment of the action, and the presents have here a future sense.
Cf. XXI. 13. 7 *corpora servat inviolata si velitis exire.*

19   § **14.** *ut servemini*]   middle, 'to save yourselves'.

24   § **15.** *incolumes*]   opposed to *deminuti capite*, 'full citizens'.

desiderate etc.]   The meaning is 'You may long for your country
(lit. 'long for it') while you are full citizens of it, or rather, I should
say, while it still is your country, and you citizens of it, but not now.
Now you are not citizens at all, but belong to the Carthaginians'.

25   *deminuti capite*]   *Caput*=the sum total of the rights of a Roman
citizen.   He possessed *familia, civitas, libertas.*   The loss of the first
(as by adoption) entailed *capitis deminutio minima*, of the second *c. d.
minor*, of all three *c. d. maxima.*   'Your status impaired' or rather, as
this was a case of *capitis deminutio maxima*, 'your rights forfeited'.   Cf.
Hor. *C.* III. 5. 42 *capitis minor* of the captive Regulus.   *abalienati*
and *servi facti* only explain *deminuti*, but in the force of the terms the
three expressions constitute a climax.

26   *abalienati*]=*privati.*   The usual meaning is 'to estrange'.

iure civium]   practically the same as *civitate*, 'their rights as citizens'.

27   § **16.** *pretio*]   'at the cost of a ransom'.   Cf. *auro repensus scilicet
acrior miles redibit*, Hor. *C.* III. 5. 25, with which ode the whole of this
speech may be compared in tone.

28   *audistis*]   'obeyed'.

29   *post paulo*]=*paulo post*, cf. *maiorem aliquanto* 48. 4.

30   *prodi*]   but *capere iubentem* above.   The voice is changed only for
variety or euphony.

32   § **17.** *obsistere*]   There is no mention of resistance in 50. 10.

p. 70.   1   *conati sunt, ni...submovissent*]   The true apodosis *et retinuissent* is left out. The irregularity, as in all mixed conditional sentences, is due to a rapid transition of thought. Cf. Verg. *B.* IX. 45 *numeros memini* (*et canerem*) *si verba tenerem.*

3 § **18.** *hos*]=*tales.*

4 *desideret*] ' is she to wish them back ?' See on 59. 18 *redeam.*

7 § **19.** *neque obstitere ; quam tutum* etc.] The coordinate statement of premise and conclusion, and also the interrogative form of the conclusion, are more emphatic than *cum non obstiterint, multo tutius fuisset.*

10 § **20.** *milia...fortia fidelia*] XXI. 55. 1 *duodeviginti milia Romana erant.*

fortia fidelia] asyndeton with words of similar meaning.

12 *nam*] The clause omitted is 'I don't say brave', 59. 12.

fortes] sc. *se esse.*

dixerint] potential subjunctive like *praetulerint,* 59. 10.

13 § **21.** *nisi quis*] ironical, ' for I don't suppose anyone believes'.

aut favisse] Madvig's correction for *fuisse ut* P, for which W. read *fuisse usui.* The correction is recommended by the correspondence of *aut favisse* and *aut non invidere.*

qui]=*eos qui.*

15 *incolumitati*] merely 'safety' here.

19 § **22.** *at*] introduces ironically a plea which might be made for the prisoners.

defuit...habuerunt] Notice the paratactic arrangement. We should say '*if* they lacked courage...they were *at any rate* bold enough' etc.

23 § **23.** *adfectis*] 'weakened', 8. 3 *in adfecto corpore.*

24 § **24.** *orto sole*] The statement of the facts begins rather abruptly. We should preface it with ' No '.

25 *ante secundam*] sc. before eight o'clock. But according to 52. 1 the camps were attacked late in the afternoon.

27 *haec vobis*] *vobis* is *dat. ethicus,* 'Such, mark you'. Cic. *Fam.* 9. 2 *At tibi repente venit ad me Caninius mane.*

§ **25.** *cum...decuerat*] P *decuerit.* But coincidence of the time of two acts is expressed by *cum* with the indicative. The pluperfect is used because the act if performed would be in the past. *Refugiunt cum pugnare decuit* but *Refugerunt cum pugnare decuerat.*

30 § **26.** *et*] strengthens the indignant question, like εἶτα in Greek. Dem. *Olynth.* 1. 24 εἶτ' οὐκ αἰσχύνεσθε;

redimamus] cf. § 18 *desideret,* 59. 18.

CHAPTER LXI.

p. 71. 5 **§ 1.** *dixit*] 'had finished speaking'.

6 *cognatione attingebant*] 'were nearly related to '.

7 *iam inde*] more commonly with an ablative: e.g. *iam inde ab initio*, 'from the very beginning'.

9 *movit*] 'weighed with them'. XXI. 38. 3 *Alimentus maxime me auctor moveret*.

§ 2. *quia*] P *quam*, for which *qua* has been read. *qua* suits *locupletari*, but *exhauriri* not so well.

10 *erogata*] 23. 8.

servos] 57. 11

12 *rei*] sc. *pecuniae*.

13 *locupletari*] There might have been some point in this argument if Rome had been the only market for Hannibal's captives. As it was during the war he got 100 talents by the sale of his prisoners in Greece, XXXIV. 50. 5.

14 **§ 3.** *redimi*] present used for future, as indicating greater certainty, 'were not to be ransomed'. Cf. 60. 13 *facit*, note.

15 *super*] 57. 2 note.

18 **§ 4.** *quod exsolvisset*] 'because, as he thought'.

22 **§ 5.** *alia*] Cicero, *de Officiis*, III. 115 gives the same story on the authority of Acilius, merely saying however that several men returned in the way described and were accordingly disgraced.

primo] P has *primos*, which agrees with Pol. VI. 58. 2 δέκα τοὺς ἐπιφανεστάτους, but leaves *deinde* without anything to correspond to it.

24 *ita...ne*] The qualification is introduced in the consecutive clause, 'on condition that they should not however'. More often it is placed in the main clause, as *ita tamen...ne daretur*. For *ita...ne* Cicero writes *ita ut ne*.

§ 6. *morantibus*] *iis*, ablative absolute.

25 *longius spe*] 52. 3 *maturior spe deditio*.

insuper] 56. 6.

26 *Scribonium* etc.] In lists of proper names either asyndeton or poly-syndeton is used.

28 **§ 7.** *relatum*] This is the first recorded occasion on which a motion was brought forward in the senate by a tribune, ordinarily this was done by a consul.

30 **§ 8.** *per causam*] 'under the pretext'. XLIV. 16. 6 *primo subtrahere se per alias atque alias causas. per* expresses the manner as in

18. 9 *extracta aestate per ludificationem hostis.* With *causam* cf. *causari* 'to allege in excuse', 'plead'.

31 *religione*] the obligation imposed by their oath.

p. 72. 2 *censuerint*] note the reversion to primary sequence.

§ **9.** *proxumis censoribus*] abl. absolute.

3 *notis*] the marks or expressions of censure affixed by the censors to the names of misdemeanants on the roll of citizens. The censors could (1) expel a man from the Senate, *eicere e senatu*; (2) deprive him of his horse, if an *eques*, *adimere equum*; (3) *movere a tribu*, which generally took the form of removing a man from a country tribe to one of the less honourable city tribes; (4) *aerarium facere*, or *referre in aerarios*, place him among the lowest class of citizens who paid a poll-tax, but had no vote.

5 *deinde vita*] *deinde* is used attributively, 'their subsequent life'.

7. 11 *deinceps diebus.*

caruerint] lit. 'did without', 'shunned'.

6 § **10.** *quid veri sit*] 40. 8 *quicquam reliqui erat.*

7 *queas*] 'one could'. An instance of the use of the 2nd person singular of the subjunctive to express a hypothetical action the subject of which is undefined, 46. 4 *crederes.*

9 *vel*] 'even this' i.e. 'this alone', to adduce no other proof. XXI. 13. 3 *vel ea fides sit.*

fides sociorum] the wasting of Campania had failed to shake it, 39. 12.

10 *profecto*] 'assuredly'.

11 § **11.** *defecere*] The effect of the following passage is to make the results of Cannae appear more crushing than they really were. Similarly Polybius says III. 118. 5 τὴν Ἰταλιωτῶν δυναστείαν παραχρῆμα διὰ τὴν ἧτταν ἀπεγνώκεισαν, 'in consequence of the defeat the Romans immediately relinquished the supremacy of Italy'. But on the one hand the defections which are here mentioned together did not occur simultaneously but were spread over several years, and on the other it should be remembered that everywhere the aristocratic party in the towns stood out against defection, which impeded Hannibal's progress, and that in the Roman and Latin Colonies the Romans held the chief strategical points of Italy. No Roman, no Latin ally had as yet joined the Carthaginians.

12 *Atellani, Calatini*] inhabitants of Campanian towns near Capua. Atella is best known in connexion with the *Fabulae Atellanae*, a species of early provincial drama. VII. 2. 11. The revolt of Capua is not mentioned, though it took place earlier than that of the two towns here referred to. Pol. III. 118. 3 Καπυανῶν τινες ἐκάλουν τὸν Ἀννίβαν.

Hirpini] a Samnite tribe, but separated politically from the rest of Samnium after its submission to Rome, 13. 1.

Apulorum pars] Polybius only mentions the people of Arpi, l.c.

13 § 12. *Pentros*] a Samnite canton, the capital of which was Bovianum.

Bruttii] except Consentia and Petelia, the latter of which made a gallant resistance.

14 *praeter*] 'besides'.

Uxentini] Uxentum (now *Ugento*) on the E. shore of the Tarentine gulf almost at the extremity of Calabria.

Graecorum...ora] *Magna Graecia.*

Tarentini] Tarentum was not captured by the Carthaginians till 212 B.C. For three years it was valuable to Hannibal as a port, but in 209 B.C. it was recovered by the veteran Fabius.

16 *Galli*] these had revolted in 218 B.C. XXI. 55. 4.

§ 13. *moverunt*] 'induced'.

17 *usquam*] i.e. either among Senate or people.

18 *Romam adventum*] In Livy an accusative of the place whither is often attached with or without a preposition to a verbal substantive expressing motion. XXXV. 49 *concursatio regis Lamiam.* XXI. 11. 13 *Hannibalis in Oretanos profectio.* Before him such a use is rather poetical, e.g. Verg. *A.* VI. 542 *hac iter Elysium nobis*, though instances are found in Cicero and Caesar. Madvig, § 233.

24 § 15. *nihil recusandum supplicii*] 'there was no punishment to which he would not have had to submit'.

foret] *foret, esset, fuisset* are sometimes used with the gerundive instead of *fuit* etc. where stress is laid on the conditional nature of the action.

APPENDIX I.

THE ROUTE OF HANNIBAL ACROSS THE APENNINES, AND THROUGH THE MARSHES OF THE ARNO.[1]

[See map in Arnold's *Second Punic War*, ed. W. J. Arnold, p. 39.]

THE words *via propior per paludes* c. 2. 2 have been generally thought to refer to some pass over the Apennines, which Livy thus distinguishes from another pass, described as *iter longius ceterum commodius*, which Hannibal thought it best not to cross. (Arnold III. 86, Mommsen II. 120, Neumann, *Punische Krieger*, 330.)

But it has been pointed out that at the time to which Livy refers the whole of the district which lies along the lower Arno between Florence and Pisa was in all probability marshland. It was so in the Middle Ages when the prosperity of Pisa declined; it must have been so at the time of the Punic Wars, before the Arno was embanked.

On this marshland *all* the routes over the Apennines from the valley of the Po into Northern Etruria debouched, while no one of them led over it. Therefore none of them could be distinguished from the others, or correctly described at all, as *via propior per paludes*.

The words then refer not to the route by which Hannibal crossed the Apennines to reach the marshland, but that which he followed when he actually reached it. Livy means the reader to take the passage over the Apennines for granted. An attempt to cross them made earlier in the year (alluded to in c. 1. 1) has been already minutely described (XXI. 58). On this occasion the difficulties met

---

[1] Cf. Arnold's *Second Punic War*, ed. W. J. Arnold, note D, p. 387, of which this appendix is a summary.

with being inconsiderable Livy may have thought it unnecessary to record the passage a second time.

At the same time it is necessary to have an idea by which pass Hannibal crossed the Apennines if we wish to know what route he followed when he reached the marshes.

I.   There are four possible passes. (1) From Parma over La Cisa, and down the valley of the Macra to Luna. (2) From Rhegium Lepidum (Reggio) by Sassalbo also to Luna. (3) From Mutina (Modena) over the Monte Cimone and down the Serchio to Lucca, or diverging eastwards to Pescia. (4) The route now followed by the railway, from Bononia (Bologna) to Pistoria (Pistoia).

(1) The first is the easiest and most obvious route, supposing Hannibal to have started from his winter quarters in the plain S. of Cremona and Placentia. But there is this objection. Pisa with its two outpost towns, Luna and Lucca, formed a defensive position on the west of the Apennines similar to that formed by Ariminum with Placentia and Cremona on the east. It is likely that all three towns were fortified and garrisoned, in which case this road would have been commanded by Luna.

(2) The Reggio route has no advantages, being difficult and circuitous, and is open to the same objection as the road from Parma.

(3) That branch of the Mutina route which debouches at Lucca would have been commanded by that town, but the branch which leads to Pescia may have been followed. On the other hand this route is difficult.

(4) The pass from Bologna to Pistoria is open to this objection, that the distance between the latter place to Faesulae is so small (only 20 miles) that Hannibal could hardly have taken four days in covering it. (Livy 2. 7; Polybius III. 79. 8.) If Hannibal came as far east as this he could hardly have eluded the notice of Flaminius, which Polybius says (III. 78. 6) he wished to do.

It is impossible to decide with certainty between these four roads. On the whole the balance of probability seems to incline in favour of the route which, starting from Mutina, crosses the Monte Cimone and diverging eastwards reaches the plain at Pescia.

II.   The starting-point thus provisionally settled, it remains to consider the goal of Hannibal's route across the marshes. Livy says it was Faesulae (c. 3. 6), whence Hannibal would naturally have followed the Arno upwards. But had Hannibal marched up the valley of the Arno he could not have passed Flaminius at Arretium without an engagement. This is not the only difficulty raised by the mention of *Faesulae* in the passage quoted (see note on c. 3. 6) and it seems probable that if Livy is not altogether mistaken he means by Faesulae some other place than Fiesole, near Florence. Polybius says expressly that Hannibal wished to follow a route which was withdrawn from the enemy's ken; at Fiesole he would have been under the eyes of Flaminius. His words are, 'He considered that most of the ways into the enemy's country were too long and too patent to the foe, but that that which led into Etruria through the marshes though difficult was short and would enable him to take Flaminius' troops by surprise'. III. 78. 6. It seems then far more likely that instead of going to Faesulae and immediately entering the valley of the Arno he struck southwards across the marshes from Pescia to Empoli. Then he ascended the Elsa, which flows into the Arno on its left bank, reached Siena and the valley of the Clanis, which he ravaged, and so reached a point south of Flaminius without passing under his eyes.

Via propior per paludes then refers to the line between Pescia to Empoli. The longer but more convenient way, *iter longius ceterum commodius*, would be the road from Pescia by Pistoia, Prato and Fiesole to Florence. Longer it certainly would be, but at the same time more convenient, for as it skirted the hills which bounded the marshland to the north it passed over comparatively firm ground. On the other hand it was, as Polybius says, πρόδηλος τοῖς πολεμίοις, for it would have brought Hannibal into the Arno valley, where he would have been directly under the notice of Flaminius, and would have found it impossible to pass him without an engagement.

APPENDIX II.

THE BATTLE OF TRASIMENE.

I. Livy's account is clear. The Romans are marching from W. to E. parallel with the N. shore of the lake. They find their way barred by a force in front; at the same time they are attacked on their left flank, while the enemy's cavalry in the rear makes retreat impossible. After three hours' fighting they are completely routed, and many of them are driven into the lake.

[There are a few minor points on which doubts have been raised. Some think that the infantry under Hannibal was not posted in the plain to bar the Roman advance, as explained in the note on 4. 3, but on the hill on which Tuoro stands (see on 4. 3). But a force on the hill of Tuoro could hardly be described as *ex adverso* (4. 3) with reference to the Romans advancing E., though it is true that the hill projects a considerable distance into the plain. Again, this division is contrasted with that which was above the Romans (*super caput*). If it had been on the Tuoro hill it would have been equally *super caput* with the other division. Most of those who think that the Tuoro hill was occupied by the infantry, place the light-armed further E. at the defile of Passignano, and refer *hostium acies...a fronte* (5. 6) to the light-armed. But the light-armed would not be so well adapted to bar the enemy's progress as to assail them with missiles in flank. Again, if this were so, the expressions *ex adverso* 4. 4, and *adversos hostes* 6. 8, refer to different forces, to the infantry in the first case, to the light-armed in the second. And what would *super caput insidiae* 4. 4 refer to on this supposition?

The other alternative is that the light-armed were W. of the infantry between Tuoro and Monte Gualandro. But this theory restricts the field of battle rather too much, and leaves the defile at Passignano unguarded. It is not necessary to say more of this, as we have seen that there are objections to supposing that Hannibal was posted on the Tuoro hill.]

II. Polybius's account varies considerably from that of Livy. He thus describes the ground which was the principal scene of the battle. III. 83. I, 'In the defile was a valley with a plain in it (αὐλὼν ἐπίπεδος) having on each of its long sides high continuous hills, and for its short sides, on that which is opposite and fronts you, a rugged and difficult steep (λόφος), and on that which is behind you, the lake, which leaves quite a narrow entrance to the valley along the foot of the mountains. Accordingly having traversed the valley parallel to the lake (the words παρὰ τὴν λίμνην are probably a gloss,—they directly contradict what Polybius has just said as to the position of the αὐλών), he occupied the hill opposite the line of march himself, and encamped upon it with the Spaniards and Africans; with the Baliares and darters he went forward (κατὰ τὴν πρωτοπορείαν), and leading them round by a detour up to the hills on the right-hand side of the valley, he placed them under cover in an extended line. In like fashion he led the cavalry and the Gauls round the hills on the left and drew them up along them in a continuous line, so that the last of them were opposite the entrance itself, which leads along the lake and the foot of the mountains into the above-mentioned place'.

In Polybius then the Romans fight with the lake in their rear, in Livy with the lake on their right flank.

Nissen, who thinks that the two accounts may be reconciled, explains this discrepancy by saying that the Romans on entering the plain turned to the left to attack Hannibal who was on the Tuoro hill (the λόφος of Polybius). They thus had the lake in their rear. Afterwards, abandoning the attempt, they continued their march E. In this way the supposed inconsistency between 4. 7 (*in frontem lateraque pugnari*) and 5. 6 (*ab lateribus montes ac lacus*) is explained. At the time referred to in 4. 6, the Romans are facing towards Tuoro, at the time indicated in 5. 6 they are pushing on towards Passignano.

But if there were really these two separate movements why is it that neither Polybius nor Livy says so? And how is this theory compatible with the statement of both authors that the Romans were surprised on the march, and that the battle began while they were yet in marching order?

And there remains a greater difficulty when we try to adapt Polybius' description to the plain between Gualandro and Passignano. Polybius' αὐλὼν ἐπίπεδος may seem to correspond to Livy's *patentior campus*. But if we understand by the hill on one of the 'short' sides of the valley the Tuoro hill, projecting from the centre of the semicircle of hills which bound the plain on the N., and by the 'long' sides (τὰς ἐς μῆκος πλευρὰς) the hills which diverge from the Tuoro height to the defile under Gualandro in one direction and that at Passignano in the other (which is in itself improbable enough), then the other 'short' side is the shore of the lake between Borghetto and Passignano, in reality the longest side of the four. The latest writers on the subject have recognized the hopelessness of adapting Polybius' description to the plain which Livy seems to indicate as the scene of battle.

III. ¹ Polybius' words clearly apply to a long narrow valley with steep heights rising on either side. After passing through the defile of Passignano the road leaves the lake at La Torricella and turning S.E. ascends the hills to Magione. Between these two points it has been maintained that Polybius' αὐλὼν ἐπίπεδος lies. The lake is in the rear, an ascent in front. There are steep heights on either side of the road.

Before the road leaves the lake the hills come close down to the water leaving a narrow passage along the shore (cf. the passage quoted from Polybius above). Hannibal occupied the high ground in front. The Baliares and light-armed were posted on the hills on the S.W. side of the valley (δεξιὸs and εὐώνυμοs in Polybius' description must be understood with reference to the general direction of Hannibal's march, i.e. towards Magione), the Gauls and cavalry on those to the N.E. of the valley, the cavalry, however, mainly on the heights commanding the road where it still runs parallel to the lake.

The situation suits Polybius' description of the battle. He distinguishes that part of the battle which took place in the valley (cf. III. 84. 11 τοὺs κατὰ τὸν αὐλῶνα) and that which was fought in the defile at the entrance of the valley. The Romans in the valley were attacked on all sides (συνεπεχείρει πανταχόθεν τοῖs πολεμίοιs III. 84. 1). Those caught in the defile (οἱ ἐν τοῖs στενοῖs συγκλεισθέντεs ibid. 8) were driven by the cavalry into the lake. Livy, it is contended, confuses these two parts of the battle in a general account. (Cf. *latera* 4. 7 with *ab lateribus montes ac lacus* 5. 6.)

It must be admitted that Livy is not incapable of selecting the most striking feature in the accounts of the battle, and representing it as the whole. But there are not wanting objections to the theory which places the scene of the battle between Torricella and Magione.

Höfler, who has visited the spot, declares roundly that the valley as described by Polybius exists only on paper. Dr Arnold, also an eyewitness, writes, 'The road turns from the lake and ascends the hills. Yet although they form something of a curve there is nothing to deserve the name of a valley'. *Hist. Rome*, III. 88.

Voigt[1], the advocate of this situation, himself admits that there could not have been room in and about the valley for the 30,000 Romans and 80,000 Carthaginians, and supposes that most of the Romans were cut off between the mountains and the lake, though Polybius (III. 84. 1) says that the majority of the troops had already entered the αὐλών when the signal for attack was given. Further, Faltin[2] points out that there could hardly have been time for Flaminius to have reached a point so far E. of his camp of the previous night at Borghetto before the day had quite broken (*vixdum satis certa luce*, 4. 4) or the morning mist was off the ground. Lastly, the defile

1 *Philologische Wochenschrift.* III. 595.
2 *Berliner Philologische Wochenschrift,* IV. 1050.

near Torricella was a most unsuitable place for the operations of cavalry.

In view of these considerations there seems no choice but to place the scene of the battle in the plain on the N. shore of the lake, and to prefer Livy's account of the battle to that of Polybius.

APPENDIX III.

HANNIBAL'S ENTRANCE INTO AND ESCAPE FROM CAMPANIA.

[See Kiepert's *Carta dell Italia Centrale*, or the section of it given in Arnold's *Second Punic War*, ed. W. J. Arnold, to face p. 55.]

A. The part of Campania into which Hannibal descended is bounded on the N.W. by the Mons Massicus, on the N.E. by a prolongation of the chain to which the Mons Massicus belongs, on the S.E. by the Vulturnus, and on the S.W. by the sea.

The regular routes by which it might be approached were as follows: (1) the Via Appia passed between the foot of the Mons Massicus and the sea at Sinuessa. (2) Higher up the slopes of the Mons Massicus was a road between Suessa and Teanum. (3) E. of the Mons Massicus is a wide depression commanded by Teanum and to a less extent by Cales, which lay further to the S.E. This is an obvious way into Campania, and is now followed by the railway from Rome to Naples. Then the ground rises again in a group of hills, nameless, as a whole, in modern as it was in ancient times, the chief summit of which is Mte Maggiore (2600 ft.). (4) Next comes the valley of the Vulturnus, and a road along it from Telesia in Samnium, guarded at its outlet by Casilinum. Lastly, (5) there is a passage from the S.E. (the line followed by the Via Appia when it leaves Campania for Samnium) from Caudium to Capua, and by a bridge over the Vulturnus to Casilinum.

Livy, 13. 3, says Hannibal came from the territory of Allifae through that of Cales into the Stellatian plain. The mention of Cales shews that Livy meant that Hannibal entered Campania by the depression between Massicus and Mte Maggiore, commanded by Teanum. He

14—2

may indeed have meant that he came over the hills called after Mte Maggiore, in a straight line between Allifae and Cales. But this is not probable, for there is nothing in his account to shew that Hannibal came otherwise than by one of the regular roads into Campania. Had Livy meant that Hannibal came over the Mte Maggiore he would surely have mentioned that he came by an 'iter impeditum', or 'transversis limitibus'. In any case if Hannibal came past Cales he did not come by the route along the Vulturnus and past Casilinum.

Polybius, III. 92. 1, says Hannibal crossed from Samnium by the pass opposite, or in the region of, the hill called Eribianus (διελθὼν ἐκ τῆς Σαυνίτιδος τὰ στενὰ κατὰ τὸν Ἐριβιανὸν καλούμενον λόφον). We do not know of any elevation called Eribianus, but it has been identified by Prof. Voigt (*Berliner Philologische Wochenschrift*, IV. 1561, sqq.) with M. Erbano in the group of mountains N. of Telesia. If this supposition be correct Polybius' statement may reasonably be understood as referring to the road from Telesia down the Vulturnus to Casilinum (4). That this is Polybius' meaning becomes more probable when one refers to an enumeration of the passes into Campania given by Polybius immediately before the passage quoted above. He says there are only three passes from central Italy into Campania, (*a*) one from Samnium, (*b*) one from Latium, (*c*) one from the country of the Hirpini (i.e. Southern Samnium) εἰσβολαὶ τρεῖς ὑπάρχουσι μόνον ἐκ τῆς μεσογαίου, στεναὶ καὶ δύσβατοι, μία μὲν ἀπὸ τῆς Σαυνίτιδος, δευτέρα δ' ἀπὸ τῆς Λατίνης, ἡ δὲ κατάλοιπος ἀπὸ τῶν κατὰ τοὺς Ἱρπίνους τόπων. Now which pass does Polybius mean by (*a*) 'the pass from Samnium', for this is evidently the same as that which he says below was actually taken by Hannibal?

The pass from Latium (*b*) must be the road by Teanum (3). It cannot be the Via Appia from the north (1), or the road from Suessa (2), for Polybius is only speaking of passes ἐκ τῆς μεσογαίου. The pass from the Hirpini (*c*) must evidently be the pass from Caudium, the Via Appia from the S. (5).

The pass from Samnium (*a*) must then be the road from Telesia down the Vulturnus to Casilinum (4).

Here then we have a discrepancy. Livy seems to say that Hannibal entered Campania on the W. side of the group of Mte Maggiore, Polybius that he entered it on the E. side. Polybius does not mention the incident of the guide's mistake (13. 6 and note), and consistently with this does not take Hannibal so far out of the direct road to Campania in a North-westerly direction.

Whom shall we follow?

I think, in this case, Polybius, for the following reasons: (1) the road down the Vulturnus is certainly a shorter and better way from Telesia to the Falernian and Stellatian plains than round by Allifae and Cales. (2) There are, as we have seen (note on 13. 5), certain difficulties in the story of the guide's mistake between Casinum and Casilinum. Even when corrected it does not appear very probable. (3) Livy having said that Hannibal entered Campania by Cales 13. 6, following some authority other than Polybius, afterwards seems to waver, for he implies, 15. 3. that Hannibal left Campania by the same route by which he entered it, and whatever be the route by which he makes Hannibal leave Campania it is certainly not the route by Cales and Teanum. In his account of Hannibal's escape he follows Polybius, though not accurately. See below.

B. It remains to consider the question, by what route did Hannibal leave Campania?

Let us take Polybius' account first, as it is clearer than that of Livy. He says that Fabius saw that Hannibal intended to escape by the same road by which he had entered Campania, that is, as we have seen, by the road along the Vulturnus. Of course this need not necessarily imply that he actually did so; but as Polybius represents Hannibal's tactics as consisting not in taking an unexpected route but in inducing the enemy to abandon the road which he had been expected to and did follow, we may conclude that, according to Polybius at any rate, Hannibal left Campania, as he had entered it, by the river-road.

To consider Polybius' narrative more closely. Fabius had placed 4000 men to guard the passage from Campania (ἐπ' αὐτῆς τῆς διεκβολῆς), probably at the point where the hills which stretch E. of Cales to the Vulturnus almost come down to the river, and where there is now a bridge called Ponte Annibale. Fabius himself was encamped on some high ground before the defile, ἐπί τινα λόφον ὑπερδέξιον πρὸ τῶν στενῶν κατεστρατοπέδευσε.

His object probably was to take the Carthaginians in the rear when engaged with the troops who were guarding the defile. The Carthaginians were encamped close under the foot of the hills (III. 93. 1 ποιησαμένων τὴν παρεμβολὴν παρ' αὐτὴν τὴν παρώρειαν). Hannibal on his side pointed out to those who had the charge of the oxen a pass lying between his own camp and the defile, i.e. probably E. of his camp, the defile being still further E. (III. 93. 5 ὑπερβολήν τινα μεταξὺ κειμένην τῆς αὐτοῦ στρατοπεδείας καὶ τῶν στενῶν). It was in the direction of this ὑπερβολή, or elevated pass, that the oxen were to be driven. This was not the place occupied by the enemy, for though the light-armed troops who followed the oxen were ordered to seize the heights and engage with any of the enemy they might happen to find (ἵνα... συμπλέκωνται τοῖς πολεμίοις ἐάν που συναντῶσι πρὸς τὰς ὑπερβολὰς) it is plain they did not expect to find the place regularly defended. Meantime Hannibal himself marched towards the defile leading out of Campania (ἧκε πρὸς τὰ στενὰ καὶ τὰς διεκβολὰς). The Romans who were guarding the defile (οἱ ἐπὶ τοῖς στενοῖς φυλάττοντες) seeing the lights going in the direction of the pass (πρὸς τὰς ὑπερβολὰς) thought that Hannibal was making his attack in that direction, and abandoning the difficult defile hurried to the heights to stop him (παρεβοήθουν τοῖς ἄκροις). There they fell in with the light-armed who had accompanied the oxen to the ὑπερβολαί, and remained drawn up over against them till day dawned. Hannibal meantime, his object gained, led his army through the defile.

From Polybius it appears then that Hannibal escaped by the river road, while the oxen were driven up to the hills to the W. of the position occupied by the Roman troops guarding the road, who were thus led to believe that their flank was turned. Throughout the whole account the clearest distinction is maintained between the passage over the hills by which the oxen were driven (ὑπερβολή) and the defile between the hills and the Vulturnus by which Hannibal's main army passed (διεκβολή or τὰ στενά).

Livy's account differs from that of Polybius in both these particulars.

(1) He says, 16. 5, *Itaque cum per Casilinum evadere non posset*, (which may mean the road along the Vulturnus, to which otherwise there would be no reference in Livy's account) *petendique montes et iugum Calliculae superandum esset, ludibrium commentus* etc. The words 'as he had to make for the mountains and surmount the ridge of Callicula' must surely mean that Hannibal was forced to go that way with his army, not merely that he had the oxen driven that way, in order that he might himself be able to go another way.

(2) For the second point. In Polybius the oxen are sent to the ὑπερβολαί, the army goes to the στενά. In Livy the oxen are sent on first to clear the way, the army follows in the same direction which they have taken. Cf. 17. 1 *primis tenebris silentio mota castra; boves aliquanto ante signa acti.* Livy does not indeed mean that the oxen were driven straight up the pass occupied by the enemy, for then the latter would immediately have seen the nature of the appearance which

terrified them. This they did not do till later, 17. 6. He means that they were driven by side-paths, but in the same direction as was afterwards followed by the army to points above the pass. In Polybius the guard on the defile sees lights moving towards the pass at a point in the hills some distance from their own position, and they hurry to stop the enemy. In Livy they see the lights immediately above them, *in montibus ac super se* 17. 4, and retreat to the highest points in the mountains.

Generally speaking there is a close resemblance between the two narratives. Livy seems to have taken his account from Polybius but not to have understood the situation. Thus *iugum* (*Calliculae*) 16. 5 and *iugum* (*montis*) 18. 2 seem to be translations of ὑπερβολή, while *saltus* in 16. 8, 17. 4 and 17. 7 seems to be a translation of διεκβολή, and *vias angustas* 17. 2 of the convertible expression τὰ στενά. But he says nothing to lead us to suppose that the course of the oxen lay over the *iugum* as distinguished from that of the army which passed over the *saltus*. On the contrary, in 16. 5 (quoted above) he implies distinctly that the army went over the *iugum Calliculae*.

Supposing that Livy's account is independent from that of Polybius and that he means that Hannibal did cross the hills, he may have reached Allifae (17. 7) either by striking into the road from Casilinum to Caiatia immediately after crossing Callicula, and following it from Caiatia to Allifae, or he may have followed the track (marked in Kiepert's map) which led to Allifae straight over the hills.

But besides being less clear than Polybius', Livy's account is less probable. It would have been a most difficult, if not impossible, task to transport a large army encumbered with baggage over a hill-path at night as Livy says was done. Everything inclines us to prefer the narrative of Polybius.

APPENDIX IV.

THE BATTLE OF CANNAE.

ON which bank of the Aufidus was the battle of Cannae fought? The question has given rise to much discussion.

I. To take the account of Polybius first. In III. 107. 2 it is stated that Hannibal seized Cannae. Presumably he remained encamped there. (Cf. Livy 43. 10.) On arriving in his neighbourhood Paulus encamped with two-thirds of his army on the Aufidus (τοῖς μὲν δυσὶ μέρεσι κατεστρατοπέδευσε παρὰ τὸν Αὔφιδον, 110. 8) and made a camp for the remaining third on the other side of the river (τῷ δὲ τρίτῳ πέραν ἀπὸ διαβάσεως πρὸς τὰς ἀνατολὰς ἐβάλετο χάρακα). Polybius conceives the river as flowing from S. to N. Its real direction is S.E. to N.E. He means then that the smaller camp was placed on the right bank. This too we should infer from the use of the word πέραν, which as the Roman army was advancing from N. to S. would naturally indicate the southernmost bank. After making a speech to his army Hannibal encamps on the same bank on which the larger camp of the Romans is placed. This means, as I think, that he crossed to the left bank and encamped there (III. 111. 11 παραχρῆμα κατεστρατοπέδευσε, ποιούμενος τὸν χάρακα παρὰ τὴν αὐτὴν πλευρὰν τῇ μείζονι στρατοπεδείᾳ τῶν ὑπεναντίων). He here offers battle. On Paulus' refusing to fight he sends the Numidians to attack the watering parties from the smaller camp (*trans flumen*, L. 45. 2). But next day Varro being in command crosses from the larger camp (ἐκ τοῦ μείζονος στρατοπέδου διαβιβάζων τὸν ποταμὸν, 113. 2) and draws up his troops for battle. Hannibal also crosses, and does the same, 113. 6, and the battle is fought on the same bank as the smaller camp, i.e. the right bank.

This conclusion is, it seems to me, a fair inference from Polybius' narrative, the statement that the smaller camp was E. of the river, and that the battle was fought on the same side as the smaller camp, leaving little doubt as to what his meaning is.

This view is confirmed by two statements which follow. (1) Varro draws up his troops facing the south (λαμβάνων πᾶσι τὴν ἐπιφάνειαν πρὸς τὴν μεσημβρίαν, 113. 2), and (2) rests his right wing on the river (τοὺς μὲν οὖν τῶν ʹΡωμαίων ἱππεῖς παρʼ αὐτὸν τὸν ποταμὸν ἐπὶ τοῦ δεξιοῦ κέρατος κατέστησε, 113. 3). These two statements taken together must imply that he was on the right bank, for the general direction of the river is N.E., or as Polybius conceives it due N.

II. Although not entirely consistent with itself the narrative of Livy does on the whole indicate the same position for the battle as that of Polybius. Hannibal is encamped at Cannae 43. 10. The Romans approach and form two camps, the smaller *trans Aufidium,* which as they were advancing from N. to S. surely means the southernmost bank. Hannibal offers battle on the bank on which the larger camp of the Romans is. That this bank is meant appears from the fact that on Paulus' refusing to fight Hannibal sends the Numidians across the river (*trans flumen,* 45. 2) to attack the watering parties from the smaller camp. Next day both armies cross the river (45. 5) in order to fight. In Livy as in Polybius the battle is fought on the same bank as that occupied by the smaller camp.

The point of difference in Livy is that he never mentions the transference of Hannibal's camp from Cannae to the left bank of the Aufidus. Apparently Hannibal remained encamped near Cannae, 43. 10, south of the Aufidus, so that the statement that he crossed the river to fight, 46. 1, would mean that he crossed to the N. or left bank.

But if this is his meaning it is incompatible with the rest of his description. According to this when Hannibal, on being refused battle, sends the Numidians across the river to attack the watering parties from the smaller camp, he sends them to the left bank, while it is natural to infer from the use of *trans* (see above) that the smaller camp was on the right bank. He goes on to state like Polybius that the Romans had their right wing on the river (45. 6), and that they looked south during the battle (46. 9). The direction of the river being what it is these two statements are absolutely incompatible, if we suppose the battle was fought on the left bank.

Livy has made a mistake in omitting to mention the transference of Hannibal's camp to the left bank of the Aufidus, whence he crossed to fight the battle on the right bank. Possibly the passage of Polybius in III. 111. 11 may have escaped him. Possibly he misunderstood it, for it contains no explicit statement that the camp was pitched on the other side of the river. It is only on comparison with the rest of Polybius' narrative that it becomes evident that this is meant. With the exception above-mentioned, and one other of small importance (referred to in note on 50. 11), the narrative of Livy like that of Polybius indicates the right bank as the scene of the battle.

Two difficulties are raised as against this view. Whether, even if they exist at all, they are sufficient to justify us in disregarding the definite statements of both historians that the Romans rested their right flank on the river and faced south, the reader must decide.

i. The places to which the Roman fugitives escaped after the battle, Canusium and Venusia, lay W. of the battle-field. It would then be natural to suppose that the Romans were drawn up W. of the Carthaginians, otherwise they must have cut their way through the Carthaginians in order to reach these places.

But surely the narrative indicates that this is precisely what was done by the small proportion of the army which escaped. The Romans were attacked in rear all along the line (L. 47. 6, 48. 4) while the thin ranks of the Spanish and Gallic infantry in their front may well have given way before their desperate efforts to break through.

ii. The ground on the N. or left bank is more favourable to the operations of cavalry than that on the right bank, and would for this reason have been selected by Hannibal, who was strong in cavalry.

But we have the assurance of one who has lately studied the question on the spot[1] that while the plain to the N. is a dead level, there is good fighting ground on the right bank also for cavalry as well as infantry. It appears that Hannibal would have *preferred* fighting on the left bank (44. 4 *spem nanctus locis natis ad equestrem pugnam facturos copiam pugnandi consules*). But the Romans did not wish to fight there. Paulus refused battle, according to Polybius[2] because he did not like the ground, and foresaw that the Carthaginians would soon be obliged to shift their camp (i.e. from the left bank to the neighbourhood of their stores at Cannae?) by want of supplies. And Varro when in command next day crossed from the left to the right bank before giving battle.

The objections then do not seem to be such as to disturb the conclusion arrived at above, that the battle was fought on the right bank of the Aufidus.

---

[1] Strachan Davidson, *Selections from Polybius*, Prolegomena, p. 39. Cf. p. 669.

[2] ὁ δὲ Λεύκιος δυσαρεστούμενος τοῖς τόποις, ὁρῶν δ᾽ ὅτι ταχέως ἀναγκασθήσονται μεταστρατοπεδεύειν οἱ Καρχηδόνιοι διὰ τὸν πορισμὸν τῶν ἐπιτηδείων εἶχε τὴν ἡσυχίαν.

VOCABULARY.

ABBREVIATIONS.

A. stands for *Aulus*

ā, ab, prep. *from, by, on the side of*

abaliēno, 1, *estrange, deprive*

abdico, 1, *resign*

abdūco (dūco), 3, *take away*

abeo (eo), 4, *depart*

abhorreo, 2, *shrink from, mis-pronounce*

ablēgo, 1, *send off*

abnuo, 3, -nui, -nuitum, *refuse*

abripio, 3, -ripui, -reptum, *take away, hurry off*

abrogo, 1, *deprive, annul*

abscēdo (cēdo), 3, *depart*

absisto, 3, -stiti, *stand off, avoid*

abstineo, 2, -tinui, -tentum, *abstain from, spare*

absum (sum), irreg. *am absent, am distant*

absūmo (sūmo), 3, *use up, destroy*

abundo, 1, *am rich in, overflow*

āc, conj. *and, also, than, as*

accēdo (cēdo), 3, *approach, am added*

accendo, 3, -cendi, -censum, *inflame, rouse*

accido, 3, -cidi, *happen, fall upon*

accio, 4, *summon*

accipio, 3, -cēpi, -ceptum, *receive, hear, meet with*

accūsātor, -ōris, m. *accuser*

accūso, 1, *charge, accuse*

ācer, ācris, ācre, adj. *eager, ardent*

acervus, -i, m. *heap*

aciēs, -ēi, f. *line, battle*

ācriter, adv. *fiercely*

actiō, -ōnis, f. *public act, speech*

acuo, 3, -ui, -ūtum, *sharpen, irritate*

ad, prep. *to, at, for*; as adv. *approximately*

adactiō, -ōnis, f. *compulsion, administering*

addīco (dīco), 3, *assent, award*

addo, 3, -didi, -ditum, *add*

addūco (dūco), 3, *bring, incite*

adeo (eo), 4, *approach, consult*

adeō, adv. *so far, moreover*

adequito, 1, *ride up to*

adfectus, adj. *weakened*

adfero (fero), 3, *bring near, allege, report*

adficio, 3, -fēci, -fectum, *affect, weaken*

adfingo, 3, -finxi, -fictum, *attribute*

adfirmo, 1, *strengthen, assert, fulfil*

adflo, 1, *blow towards*

adfluo, 3, -fluxi, -fluxum, *flow towards*

adgravo, 1, *make heavier*

adgredior, 3, -gressus, dep. *approach, attack*

adhibeo, 2, *apply, summon*

adhortātor, -ōris, m. *inspirer*

adhortor, 1, dep. *encourage*

adhūc, adv. *so far, hitherto*

ādicio, 3, -iēci, -iectum, *add, turn towards*

adigo, 3, -ēgi, -actum, *summon, bind*

adimo, 3, -ēmi, -emptum, *take away, deprive*

aditus, -ūs, m. *approach, opening*

adiungo (iungo), 3, *join to, place near*

adiuvo, 1, -iūvi, -iūtum, *help*

adloquor, 3, -locūtus, dep. *speak to*

admīrābilis, adj. *wonderful, admirable*

admīrātiō, -ōnis, f. *wonder, surprise*

admisceo (misceo), 2, *mingle with*

admitto (mitto), 3, *let in, commit, admit*

admodum, adv. *quite, at most*

admoneo, 2, *remind*

admoveo (moveo), 2, *move up*

adnītor (nītor), 3, dep. *endeavour, press on*

adorior (orior), 4, dep. *attack*

adparātus, see **apparātus**

adpello, 1, see **appello**

adpeto (peto), 3, *seek for, approach*

adpropinquo, 1, *come near*

adsentior, 4, -sensus, dep. *agree*

adsequor (sequor), 3, dep. *follow, overtake*

adsuēfacio (facio), 3, *habituate*

adsuesco, 3, -suēvi, -suētum, *become accustomed to*

adsuētus, adj. *familiar with*

adsum (sum), irreg. *am present, help*

adsurgo (surgo), 3, *rise up*

adtenuo, 1, *shrink, shorten*

adtollo, 3, defect. *elevate, praise*

adtonitus, adj. *awe-struck*

adulescens, -entis, c. *youth*

adveho (veho), 3, *bring up*

advena, -ae, c. *stranger*

advenio (venio), 4, *approach, arrive*

adventus, -us, m. *arrival*

adversārius, -i, m. *opponent*

adversor, 1, dep. *oppose*

adversus, adj. *opposite, unfavourable*

adversus, prep. *towards, against*

adverto (verto), 3, *turn towards*

advoco, 1, *summon*

aecus, see **aequus**

aedēs, -is, f. *temple*; pl. *house*

aedīlicius, adj. *of an aedile*; as noun, *one who has been an aedile*

aedīlis, -is, m. *inspector of buildings*

aedīlitās, -ātis, f. *inspectorship*

aeger, -gra, -grum, adj. *ill, infirm*

aegrē, adv. *hardly, with difficulty*

aegritūdō, -inis, f. *sickness, sorrow*

aequālis, adj. *level, contemporary*

aequē, adv. *equally, just as*

aequo, 1, *make equal, level*

aequus, adj. *level, equal, just, friendly*

aes, aeris, n. *copper, bronze, money*

aestās, -ātis, f. *summer*

aestimo, 1, *value*

aestīvus, adj. *summer*

aetās, -ātis, f. *age, life, time*

affero, see **adfero**

ager, agri, m. *land, field*

agito, 1, *move, agitate, discuss*

agmen, -inis, n. *column, army on the march, line (of ships)*

ago, 3, ēgi, actum, *move, transact, discuss*

agrestis, -is, m. *peasant*

āio, 3, defect. *say, assert*

āla, -ae, f. *wing, cavalry*

albus, adj. *white*

aliā, adv. *by another way*

aliās, adv. *elsewhere, at another time*

alibi, adv. *elsewhere*

aliēnus, adj. *belonging to another*; **aes aliēnum**, *debt*

aliō, adv. *to another place*

aliquantum, adv. *somewhat*

aliquantum, -i, n. *a good deal*

aliqui, -qua, -quod, adj. *some*

aliquis, -quid, pron. *someone*

aliquot, indecl. adj. *several*

aliter, adv. *otherwise*

alius, -ia, -iud, adj. *other, else, another*

alo, 3, alui, altum and alitum, *feed, increase*

altē, adv. *on high, deeply*

alter, -era, -erum, pron. *the one, the other, second*
altercātiō, -ōnis, f. *dispute*
alternīs, adv. *by turns*
alternus, adj. *alternate, every other*
altus, adj. *high, deep*
ambiguē, adv. *doubtfully*
ambitiō, -ōnis, f. *ambition*
ambō, -ae, -ō, adj. *both*
ambustus, adj. *scorched, slandered*
amīcitia, -ae, f. *friendship*
āmitto (mitto), 3, *lose, let slip*
amnis, -is, m. *river*
amoenus, adj. *pleasant*
amplector, 3, -plexus, dep. *embrace*
amplius, adv. *more*
amplus, adj. *large, important*
an, conj. *or, whether, or whether*
ancora, -ae, f. *anchor*
ancorāle, -is, n. *cable*
anfractus, ūs, m. *curve, circuit*
angustiae, -ārum, f. pl. *strait, pass*
angustus, adj. *narrow*
animadverto (verto), 3, *notice*
animus, -i, m. *spirit, heart, courage, purpose*
annālēs, -ium, m. pl. *records, annals*
anniversārius, adj. *annual*
annōna, -ae, f. *grain, price, scarcity*
annus, -i, m. *year, season*
ante, adv. and prep. *before*
anteā, adv. *before*
antequam, conj. *before*
antesignāni, -ōrum, m. pl. *standard-guards*
antideā, adv. old form of **anteā**
antīquitus, adv. *anciently, of old*
antīquo, 1, *reject, repeal*
antīquus, adj. *ancient*
aperio, 4, aperui, apertum, *open, reveal*
apertus, adj. *open, unguarded*
apparātus, -ūs, m. *preparation, stores*
appāreo, 2, *am evident, come forward*
appello, 1, *call, name*

appello (pello), 3, *put in (to harbour)*
aptē, adv. *suitably*
apto, 1, *adjust, get ready*
aptus, adj. *suited, fit*
apud, prep. *near, among, before*
aqua, -ae, f. *water*
aquātor, -ōris, m. *water-carrier*
aquor, 1, dep. *fetch water*
arbiter, -tri, m. *witness, judge, stranger*
arbustum, -i, n. *plantation*
arceo, 2, *keep away*
arcesso, 3, -īvi, -ītum, *summon*
ardeo, 2, arsi, arsum, *am on fire, am eager*
ardor, -ōris, m. *eagerness, heat*
arēna, -ae, f. *sand*
argentum, -i, n. *silver, money*
āridus, adj. *dry*
arma, -ōrum, n. pl. *arms, troops*
armātūra, -ae, f. *troops*
armātus, adj. *armed man*
armentum, -i, n. *herd*
armiger, -eri, m. *armour-bearer*
armo, 1, *arm*
arripio, 3, -ripui, -reptum, *seize*
ars, artis, f. *skill, trick, trade*
artūs, -uum, m. pl. *joint, limb*
artus, adj. *close, crowded*
arx, arcis, f. *citadel, height*
asper, -era, -erum, adj. *rough, harsh, perilous*
aspernor, 1, dep. *reject, despise*
ast, at, conj. *but, again*
āter, atra, atrum, *black, dismal*
atque, conj. *and, moreover, as*
atquī, conj. *but yet, nay rather*
ātrōciter, adv. *horribly, fiercely*
ātrox, -ōcis, adj. *fierce, shocking*
attingo, 3, attigi, attactum, *touch, reach, concern*
auctor, -ōris, m. *originator, authority, adviser, informant*
auctōritās, -ātis, f. *authority, importance, influence*
audācia, -ae, f. *boldness*
audāciter, adv. *boldly*
audeo, 2, ausus, semi-dep. *dare*

audio, 4, *hear, listen to*
augeo, 2, auxi, auctum, *increase, strengthen, exaggerate*
augur, -uris, c. *priest, diviner*
aura, -ae, f. *breeze*
aureus, adj. *golden*
auris, -is, f. *ear*
aurum, -i, n. *gold*
auspicium, -i, n. *omen*
aut, conj. *either, or*
autem, conj. *but, well then*
autumnus, -i, m. *autumn*
auxiliāris, adj. *auxiliary*
auxilium, -i, n. *help*; pl. *auxiliaries*
avārus, adj. *greedy, covetous*
āvello, 3, -velli, -vulsum, *pull away*
āversus, adj. *turned away, unseen*
āverto (verto), 3, *turn aside, alter*
avidus, adj. *eager, greedy*
āvius, adj. *lonely, pathless*
āvoco, 1, *call away, remove*
avus, -i, m. *grandfather*

barbarus, adj. and noun, m. *foreign, barbarian*
bellicus, adj. *military*
bello, 1, *fight*
bellum, -i, n. *war*
bene, adv. *well*
beneficium, -i, n. *benefit, kindness*
benignē, adv. *courteously, liberally*
bīduum, -i, n. *space of two days*
biennium, -i, n. *period of two years*
bifāriam, adv. *in two places*
bīni, -ae, -a, pl. numer. adj. *two each, two*
bonus, adj. *good, loyal*
bōs, bovis, c. *ox, cow*
bovārius, adj. *belonging to cattle*
bovillus, adj. *bovine*
brāchium, -i, n. *arm, line of earth-works*
brevis, adj. *short*
brevitās, -ātis, f. *brevity, shortness*
būbus, dative and ablative pl. of bōs
bustum, -i, n. *tomb*

C. stands for *Gaius*; Cn. for *Gnaeus*
cacūmen, -inis, n. *summit*

cado, 3, cecidi, cāsum, *fall, fall out*
caecus, adj. *blind, unsuspecting*
caedēs, -is, f. *slaughter*
caedo, 3, cecīdi, caesum, *kill, beat*
caelum, -i, n. *sky, heavens, climate*
caerimōnia, -ae, f. *rite, worship*
caesim, adv. *with the edge*
calcar, -āris, n. *spur*
calidus, adj. *hot*
cālīgō, -inis, f. *mist, gloom*
callidē, adv. *cunningly, skilfully*
callis, -is, m. *mountain-track*
calor, -ōris, m. *heat*
campester, -tris, -tre, adj. *level*
campus, -i, m. *plain*
candidātus, -i, m. *candidate*
candor, -ōris, m. *whiteness*
cano, 3, cecini, cantum, *sound*
capesso, 3, -īvi, -ītum, *take in hand, manage*
capio, 3, cēpi, captum, *take, begin, injure, charm*
capra, -ae, f. *she-goat*
caprīnus, adj. *goatish*
captīvus, -i, m. *prisoner*; as adj. *captured*
capto, 1, *entrap*
caput, -itis, n. *head, chief, capital, political rights*
careo, 2, *lack, lose*
carīna, -ae, f. *keel*
carmen, -inis, n. *song, verse, spell*
carpo, 3, carpsi, carptum, *pluck, worry*
carptim, adv. *piece-meal, in different places*
cārus, adj. *dear, valuable*
castellum, -i, n. *fort*
castra, -ōrum, n. pl. *camp*
cāsus, -ūs, m. *accident, chance, disaster*
catēna, -ae, f. *chain*
causa, -ae, f. *cause, reason, excuse, sake*
cautē, adv. *prudently*
cautus, adj. *careful*
caveo, 2, cāvi, cautum, *beware, give security*
cavus, adj. *hollow*

cēdo, 3, cessi, cessum, *go, yield, retire*
celer, -eris, -ere, adj. *swift*
celeritās, -ātis, f. *speed, activity*
celeriter, adv. *quickly*
censeo, 2, -ui, -um, *think, value, vote*
censor, -ōris, m. *valuer, censor*
centēni, pl. numer. adj. *hundred each*
centum, indecl. numer. adj. *hundred*
centuriātus, adj. *divided into centuries*
centuriātus, -ūs, m. *division into centuries*
centuriō, -ōnis, m. *centurion*
cerno, 3, crēvi, crētum, *perceive, decide*
certāmen, -inis, n. *contest*
certē, adv. *surely, at least*
certo, 1, *strive with, struggle*
certus, adj. *sure, certain*
cervix, -īcis, f. *shoulder, neck*
cesso, 1, *delay, am idle*
[cēter] -era, -erum, adj. *the rest, other*
cēterum, adv. *otherwise, but, in any case*
cieo, 2, cīvi, citum, *stir up, summon*
circā, adv. and prep. *around, about*
circum, adv. and prep. *all around, about*
circumdo (do), 1, *surround*
circumdūco (dūco), 3, *lead round*
circumeo (eo), 4, *march round, make the rounds*
circumfero (fero), 3, *carry round*
circumfundo (fundo), 3, *pour round, crowd round*
circumspecto, 1, *look anxiously about*
circumspicio, 3, -spexi, -spectum, *survey, consider*
circumveho (veho), 3, *convey round, sail round*
circumvenio (venio), 4, *surround, cheat*
cis, prep. *on this side of*

citātus, adj. *driven fast, galloping*
citerior, -ōris, adj. *nearer*
citrā, prep. *on this side of*
cīvīlis, adj. *civic, public, urbane*
cīvis, -is, c. *citizen*
cīvitās, -ātis, f. *citizenship, state*
clādēs, -is, f. *disaster, massacre*
clam, adv. and prep. *secretly, unknown to*
clāmo, 1, *shout, call upon, announce*
clāmor, -ōris, m. *outcry, noise*
clārus, adj. *clear, famous*
classicus, adj. *naval*
classis, -is, f. *fleet, division*
claudeo, 2, *limp, am crippled*
claudo, 3, clausi, clausum, *shut, surround, end*
clēmens, -entis, adj. *merciful*
clepo, -psi, -ptum, *steal*
coacervo, 1, *heap up*
coepi, coepisse, defect. *begin*
coerceo, 2, *restrain, punish*
cōgito, 1, *reflect, ponder, intend*
cognātiō, -ōnis, f. *relationship, kin*
cognātus, adj. and noun, *kin, kinsman*
cognosco, 3, -nōvi, -nitum, *ascertain, learn*
cōgo, 3, coēgi, coactum, *gather, compel, bring up the rear*
cohibeo, 2, *restrain, discipline*
cohors, -ortis, f. *cohort* = 3 *manipuli*
cohortor, 1, dep. *encourage, admonish*
colligo, 3, -lēgi, -lectum, *bring together*
collis, -is, m. *hill*
colo, 3, colui, cultum, *cultivate, inhabit, worship, preserve*
colōnia, -ae, f. *settlement, colony*
colōnus, -i, m. *farmer, settler*
comes, -itis, c. *companion*
comitia, -ōrum, n. pl. *election*
comitiālis, adj. *electoral*
comitium, -i, n. *voting-place*
commeātus, -ūs, m. *supply, provisions*

commīgro, 1, *remove together, transfer*

commīlitō, -ōnis, *fellow-soldier, comrade*

comminiscor, 3, -mentus, dep. *devise, invent*

committo (mitto), 3, *entrust, join battle, risk*

commodum, -i, n. *advantage, opportunity*

commodus, adj. *convenient*

commūnico, 1, *share*

commūnio, 4, *fortify strongly*

commūnis, adj. *common, shared*

cōnātus, -ūs, m. *effort*

concēdo (cēdo), *yield, retire, concede*

concieo, 2, -cīvi, -citum, *stir up, assemble*

concilio, 1, *win over, secure*

concilium, -i, n. *assembly, council*

concipio, 3, -cēpi, -ceptum, *take (auspices), understand, compose*

concitātus, adj. *rapid*

concito, 1, *rouse, cause*

conclāmo, 1, *cry out together, give an order*

concordia, -ae, f. *agreement, harmony*

concurro, 3, -curri, -cursum, *flock together, join battle*

concurso, 1, *run to and fro, am busy, fight*

concursus, -ūs, m. *assembly, charge*

concutio, 3, -cussi, -cussum, *shake violently, weaken*

condiciō, -ōnis, f. *terms, situation*

condo, 3, -didi, -ditum, *hide, put away, establish*

confero (fero), 3, *bring together, join battle, compare, devote*

confertus, adj. *close packed, crowded*

confessiō, -ōnis, f. *admission*

conficio, 3, -fēci, -fectum, *finish, ruin, wear out*

confīdo, 3, -fīsus, semi-dep. *trust, feel sure*

confīīgo, 3, -flixi, -flictum, *dash together, fight*

confugio (fugio), 3, *take refuge, have recourse to*

congero (gero), 3, *heap up, store*

conglobo, 1, *form a square, close up*

congredior, 3, -gressus, dep. *meet, contend with*

congressus, -ūs, m. *conference, contest*

cōnicio, 3, -iēci, -iectum, *hurl*

cōniecto, 1, *guess*

cōniectus, -ūs, m. *range, throwing*

conītor (nītor), 3, dep. *struggle*

cōniungo (iungo), 3, *join closely*

cōniunx, -iugis, c. *wife* or *husband*

cōniūro, 1, *conspire*

conlābor (lābor), 3, dep. *collapse*

conlēga, -ae, m. *colleague*

conlego, see colligo

conlēgium, -i, n. *association, brotherhood*

conlīgo, 1, *bind together*

conluviō, -ōnis, f. *sweepings, dregs*

cōnor, 1, *try, undertake*

conparātiō, -ōnis, f. *comparison, preparation*

conparo, 1, *collect, compare*

conpello, 1, *call to, rebuke*

conpello (pello), 3, *force together, constrain*

conperio, 4, -perui, -pertum, *prove, find out*

conpetītor, -ōris, m. *rival candidate*

conpeto (peto), 3, *am capable, agree*

conpleo, 2, -plēvi, -plētum, *fill up, man*

conplexus, -ūs, m. *embrace*

conplōrātus, -ūs, m. *lamentation*

conplōro, 1, *mourn for, give up for lost*

conpōno (pōno), 3, *put together, arrange, agree*

conprehendo, 3, -di, -sum, *seize, include, understand*

conquīro, 3, -quīsīvi, -quīsītum, *search for, collect*

conruo, see corruo

consaepio, 4, -saepsi, -saeptum, *fence round, blockade*

consalūto, 1, *hail, salute*

conscendo, 3, -di, -sum, *mount (horse), board (ship), climb*

conscisco, 3, -īvi, -ītum, *decree; commit suicide*

conscrībo (scrībo), *enrol, compose*

consensus, -ūs, m. *agreement, concord*

consentio (sentio), 4, *agree, conspire*

consequor (sequor), 3, *overtake*

consero, 3, -serui, -sertum, *connect, join battle*

conservātor, -ōris, m. *preserver*

consīderātus, adj. *cautious*

consīdo, 3, -sēdi, -sessum, *settle, encamp*

consilium, -i, n. *plan, council of war, advice, prudence*

consisto, 3, -stiti, -stitum, *halt, stand fast, stop*

consitus, adj. *overgrown, planted*

consōlor, 1, dep. *comfort*

conspectus, adj. *conspicuous*

conspectus, -ūs, m. *sight*

conspicio, 3, -spexi, -spectum, *behold, descry*

constans, -antis, adj. *steadfast, consistent*

constanter, adv. *firmly*

constantia, -ae, f. *perseverance, constancy*

constituo, 3, -ui, -ūtum, *place, determine, appoint*

consto, 1, -stiti, -stātum, *stand firm, consist of*

constringo (stringo), 3, *fetter, constrain*

consul, -ulis, m. *consul*

consulāris, noun and adj. *of consular rank, ex-consul*

consulātus, -ūs, m. *office of consul*

consulo, 3, -sului, -sultum, *consult, provide for, regard*

consultē, adv. *carefully*

consulto, 1, *deliberate*

consultum, -i, n. *decree*

contemno, 3, -tempsi, -temptum, *despise*

contendo, 3, -di, -tum, *strive, hasten*

contentiō, -ōnis, f. *strife*

conticesco, 3, -ticui, *become silent, cease*

continens, -entis, f. *district, mainland*

continens, -entis, adj. *unbroken, adjacent*

contineo, 2, -tinui, -tentum, *restrain, confine*

contingo, 3, -tigi, -tactum, *border on, happen, fall by lot*

continuus, adj. *successive, unbroken*

contiō, -ōnis, f. *public meeting, oration*

contiōnor, 1, *make a speech, harangue*

contrā, prep. *against, in reply*; as adv. *on the other hand*

contraho (traho), 3, *draw close, bring about, diminish*

contumēlia, -ae, f. *insult, disgrace*

convallis, -is, f. *deep valley, defile*

conveho (veho), 3, *convey*

convello, 3, -velli, -vulsum, *pluck up, dislodge*

convenio (venio), 4, *come together, agree, suit*

converto (verto), 3, *turn round, change, upset*

convīvium, -i, n. *feast*

convoco, 1, *call together*

co-orior (orior), 4, *arise, break out*

cōpia, -ae, f. *plenty*; pl. *troops*

cor, cordis, n. *heart*; **cordi est**, *it is pleasing*

corbis, -is, m. or f. *basket*

cornū, -ūs, n. *horn, trumpet, wing of army*

corpus, -oris, n. *body, person*

corrumpo (rumpo), 3, *destroy, spoil*

corruo (ruo), 3, *collapse*

crēber, -bra, -brum, adj. *frequent, crowded*

crēbrō, adv. *frequently*

crēdo, 3, -didi, -ditum, *believe, trust, suppose*

creo, 1, *create, elect*

cresco, 3, crēvi, crētum, *grow, increase*

crīmen, -inis, n. *accusation*

crīminor, 1, dep. *accuse, defame*

crūdēlis, adj. *cruel*

cruentus, adj. *bloodstained*

cruor, -ōris, m. *blood*

crux, crucis, f. *cross*

cubīle, -is, n. *couch, bed*

culpa, -ae, f. *blame, fault*

cultor, -ōris, m. *farmer, worshipper, supporter*

cum, prep. *with, with the help of*

cum, conj. *when, since, though, whenever*; cum...tum, *not only...but also*

cumulo, 1, *heap up, load*

cumulus, -i, m. *heap*

cunctanter, adv. *slowly*

cunctātiō, -ōnis, f. *delay, hesitation, masterly inactivity*

cunctātor, -ōris, m. *delayer*

cunctor, 1, dep. *delay*

cuneus, -i, m. *wedge, phalanx*

cupiditās, -ātis, f. *desire, covetousness*

cupio, 3, -īvi, -ītum, *desire*

cūr, interr. adv. *why?*

cūra, -ae, f. *care, trouble, anxiety, pains*

cūria, -ae, f. *senate-house*

cūro, 1, *take pains, take care of, cause*

curro, 3, cucurri, cursum, *run*

cursus, -ūs, m. *course, pace*

curūlis, adj. *official, senatorial*

custōdia, -ae, f. *guard, confinement, picket*

custōdio, 4, *guard, protect*

custōs, -ōdis, c. *guardian*

D. stands for *Decimus*

damnātiō, -ōnis, f. *condemnation*

damno, 1, *condemn*

damnum, -i, n. *loss, harm*

dē, prep. *down from, away from, concerning, made of*

dēbello, 1, *bring war to an end, subdue*

dēbeo, 2, *owe, ought*

dēcēdo (cēdo), 3, *withdraw, decrease*

decem, indecl. numer. adj. *ten*

decemviri, -ōrum, m. pl. *commission of ten*

dēcerno (cerno), 3, *decide, decree, fight*

decet, 2, impers. *it befits, it is proper*

dēcipio, 3, -cēpi, -ceptum, *deceive*

decuriātus, adj. *divided into decuriae (decades)*

decuriātus, -ūs, m. *division into decuriae*

dēcurro (curro), 3, *run down, have recourse to*

dēdecus, -oris, n. *disgrace*

dēditiō, -ōnis, f. *surrender*

dēdo, 3, -didi, -ditum, *surrender*

dēdūco (dūco), 3, *lead down, found a colony, remove*

dēfectiō, -ōnis, f. *desertion, revolt*

dēfendo, 3, -di, -sum, *defend*

dēfero (fero), 3, *bring to land, hand over, report, accuse*

dēficio, 3, -fēci, -fectum, *am lacking, revolt*

dēfīgo (fīgo), 3, *fasten down, paralyse, hold fast*

dēformitās, -ātis, f. *disorder, shame*

dēfungor, 3, -functus, dep. *perform, get rid of*

dēgenero, 1, *become degenerate*

dēgredior, 3, -gressus, dep. *descend*

dēicio, 3, -iēci, -iectum, *hurl down, dislodge, deprive*

dein, short form of **deinde**

deinceps, adv. *in turn, successively*

deinde, conj. *then, afterwards*

dēleo, 2, -ēvi, -ētum, *wipe out, annihilate*

dēligo, -lēgi, -lectum, 3, *select*

dēmīgro, 1, *depart, change abode*

dēminūtus, adj. *deprived of*

dēmitto (mitto), 3, *let down, depress, send down, bury*

dēmonstro, 1, *show clearly, point out*

dēmum, adv. *at last, indeed, forsooth, only when*

dēni, -ae, -a, pl. numer. adj. *ten each*

dēnique, adv. *finally, and then, in short*

dens, dentis, m. *tooth*

densus, adj. *thick, crowded*

dēnuntio, 1, *announce, give warning*

dēpello (pello), 3, *expel, dissuade*

dēpopulor, 1, dep. *lay waste*

dēposco (posco), 3, *demand*

dēprendo, 3, -di, -sum, *seize, surprise*

dērectus, adj. *straight, direct*

dērigo (rego), 3, *draw up, direct*

dēscendo, 3, -di, -sum, *descend*

dēsero, 3, -serui, -sertum, *abandon*

dēsīdero, 1, *need, long for*

dēsilio, 4, -silui, -sultum, *leap down, dismount*

dēsino, 3, -sii, -situm, *cease*

dēsisto, 3, -stiti, -stitum, *leave off*

dēspēro, 1, *despair of, give up*

dēstituo, 3, -ui, -ūtum, *forsake, cease, deprive*

dēsum (sum), irreg. *am missing, desert, fail*

dētego (tego), 3, *uncover, reveal*

dēterreo, 2, *deter, frighten away, discourage*

dētraho (traho), 3, *draw down, entice, disparage*

dētrīmentum, -i, n. *damage, defeat, harm*

dētrūdo, 3, -si, -sum, *thrust down, drive off*

deus, -i, m. *god*

dēvasto, 1, *lay waste*

dēvincio (vincio), 4, *bind, win over*

dēvius, adj. *off the highway, roundabout*

dexter, adj. *right-handed, right, lucky, skilful*

dextera, -ae, f. *right hand, handshake*

dextrā, adv. *on the right*

diciō, -ōnis, f. *dominion, control*

dico, 1, *dedicate*

dīco, 3, dixi, dictum, *say, deliver, decree, appoint*

dictātor, -ōris, m. *dictator*

dictātōrius, adj. *dictatorial*

dictātūra, -ae, f. *dictatorship*

dictum, -i, n. *saying, command*

diēs, diēi, m. and f. *day, time*; **in diēs**, *daily*

differo, 3, distuli, dīlātum, *postpone, differ*

difficilis, adj. *difficult, surly*

diffīdo, 3, -fīsus, semi-dep. *distrust, despair*

dignitās, -ātis, f. *merit, rank*; pl. *dignitaries*

dignus, adj. *worthy, deserving*

dīgredior, 3, -gressus, dep. *separate, depart*

dīlābor (lābor), 3, dep. *disappear, desert*

dīlectus, -ūs, m. *levy of troops*

dīmicātiō, -ōnis, f. *pitched battle*

dīmico, 1, *fight*

dīmidium, -i, n. *half*

dīmidius, adj. *half*

dīmitto (mitto), 3, *dismiss, send out*

dīmoveo (moveo), 2, *separate, dislodge*

dirimo, 3, -ēmi, -emptum, *separate, interrupt*

dīripio, 3, -ripui, -reptum, *plunder*

discerno (cerno), 3, *perceive, divide*

disco, 3, didici, *learn*

discordia, -ae, f. *quarrel*

discors, -ordis, adj. *disagreeing, opposed*

discrepo, 1, -ui, *vary, disagree*

discrīmen, -inis, n. *difference, crisis, hazard*

discurro (curro), 3, *hurry to and fro*

discursus, -ūs, m. *hurrying, confusion*

dīsicio, 3, -iēci, -iectum, *scatter, rout*

dispār, -paris, adj. *unequal, not well matched*

dispello (pello), 3, *disperse*

dispicio, 3, -spexi, -spectum, *descry, perceive*

displiceo, 2, *displease*

dispōno (pōno), 3, *arrange, distribute*

dissentio (sentio), 4, *disagree*

dissimilis, adj. *unlike*

dissipo, 1, *scatter, rout*

dissonus, adj. *discordant, confused*

disto (sto), 1, *am distant, differ*

distraho (traho), 3, *pull asunder, perplex*

diū, adv. *for a long time*

dius fīdius, see note

dīversus, adj. *opposite, scattered*

dīves, dīvitis and dītis, adj. *rich*

dīvido, 3, -vīsi, -vīsum, *divide*

dīvīnus, adj. *divine*

dīvitiae, -ārum, f. pl. *wealth*

dīvus, -i, m. *god;* as adj. *godlike*

do, 1, dedi, datum, *give, take pains*

doceo, 2, docui, doctum, *teach, inform*

documentum, -i, n. *lesson, proof, warning*

dolor, -ōris, m. *pain, grief, indignation*

dolus, -i, m. *device, trick*

dominor, 1, dep. *rule*

dominus, -i, m. *lord, owner*

domitus, adj. *tamed, subdued*

domus, -ūs, f. *house, home*

dōnec, conj. *until, so long as*

dōnum, -i, n. *gift*

dubiē, adv. *doubtfully*

dubito, 1, *doubt, hesitate*

dubius, adj. *doubtful, uncertain*

ducēni, -ae, -a, pl. numer. adj. *two hundred each*

ducenti, -ae, -a, pl. numer. adj. *two hundred*

dūco, 3, duxi, ductum, *lead, prolong, reckon*

ductor, -ōris, m. *leader, general*

duellum, old form of **bellum**

dum, conj. *while, as long as, provided that, until*

duo, -ae, -o, pl. numer. adj. *two*

dūplex, -icis, adj. *double, twofold*

dūrus, adj. *hard, hardy, stern*

duumviri, -ōrum, m. *pair of magistrates*

dux, ducis, c. *guide, general*

ē, ex, prep. *from, out of, after;* ē rēpublicā, *for the good of the state*

ēdicō (dico), 3, *publish, decree*

ēdictum, -i, n. *proclamation*

ēdisserto, 1, *explain in detail*

ēdo, 3, -didi, -ditum, *give forth, utter, cause*

ēdoceo (doceo), 2, *instruct, inform*

ēdūco (dūco), 3, *lead out*

effero, efferre, extuli, ēlātum, *carry forth, exalt, bury*

efficio, 3, -fēci, -fectum, *effect, make, cause*

effodio, 3, -fōdi, -fossum, *dig, excavate*

effugio (fugio), 3, *escape, avoid, escape the attention of*

effulgeo, 2, -fulsi, *shine forth, glitter*

effundo (fundo), 3, *pour forth, let loose*

effūsē, adv. *unrestrainedly*

effūsus, adj. *disorderly, immoderate*

egeo, 2, *need*

ego, mei, pron. *I*

ēgredior, 3, -gressus, dep. *go forth, land, leave*

ēgregiē, adv. *excellently, finely*

ēgregius, adj. *excellent, special, remarkable*

elephantus, -i, m. *elephant*

ēlūdo, 3, -lūsi, -lūsum, *baffle, deceive, escape*

ēmergo (mergo), 3, *emerge, escape*

ēmitto (mitto), 3, *send out, let slip*

emo, 3, ēmi, emptum, *buy*

ēmolumentum, -i, n. *profit, advantage*

ēn, interjection, *lo! see!*

enim, conj. *for, indeed*

enimvērō, conj. *to be sure, really*

ēnītesco, 3, -nitui, *shine forth, am conspicuous*

eo, īre, īvi, itum, *go*

eō, adv. *thither, so far, in order that, by that much*

epulae, -ārum, f. pl. *banquet, feasting*

epulor, 1, dep. *feast*

eques, -itis, m. *horse soldier, knight*

equester, -tris, -tre, adj. *mounted, knightly*

equidem, adv. *for my part, truly, of course*

equitātus, -ūs, m. *cavalry*

equus, equi, m. *horse*

ergā, prep. *towards*

ergō, adv. *therefore, then, for the sake of*

ēripio, 3, -ripui, -reptum, *snatch, rescue*

ērogo, 1, *vote, pay out*

erro, 1, *wander, mistake*

error, -ōris, m. *wandering, delusion*

ērumpo (rumpo), 3, *burst out, issue*

ēruptiō, -ōnis, f. *sortie*

ēscensiō, -ōnis, f. *landing, expedition*

esto, imperative of **sum**

et, conj. and adv. *both, and; even, also*

etenim, conj. *and in fact, moreover*

etiam, conj. *also, even; again and again*

etsī, conj. *even if, although*

ēvādo (vādo), 3, *go forth, avoid, escape*

ēvagor, 1, dep. *spread out, extend*

ēveho (veho), 3, *convey out, ride out, drift, carry away*

ēvenio (venio), 4, *happen, fall to the lot of*

ēventus, -ūs, m. *result, fate, accident*

ēvolvo (volvo), 3, *roll out, spread abroad*

ex, see **ē**

exanimātus, adj. *half-dead, exhausted*

exaudio, 4, *hear at a distance, overhead, grant*

excēdo (cēdo), 3, *go out, abandon*

excido, 3, -cidi, *fall out, am forgotten*

excīdo, 3, -cīdi, -cīsum, *destroy*

excieo, 2, -īvi, -itum, *rouse, excite*

excipio, 3, -cēpi, -ceptum, *capture, cut off, receive*

excito, 1, *stir up, increase*

exclūdo, 3, -clūsi, -clūsum, *shut off*

excūso, 1, *plead, excuse*

execrābilis, adj. *accursed, calamitous*

exemplum, -i, n. *model, precedent*

exeo (eo), 4, *go out, expire*

exequor, see **exsequor**

exercitus, -ūs, m. *army*

exhaurio (haurio), 4, *drain, exhaust*

exigo (ago), 3, *drive out, demand, spend, finish*

exiguus, adj. *slender, limited*

existimo, 1, *judge, consider, think*

existo, see **exsisto**

exitus, -ūs, m. *departure, end, passage*

exorior (orior), 4, dep. *arise, spring from*

expecto, 1, *wait, wait for, hope for*

expedio, 4, *set free, prepare*; impers. *it is profitable*

expedītus, adj. *unimpeded, light-armed, travelling light*

experior, 4, -pertus, dep. *try, test, have experience of*

expers, -ertis, adj. *not sharing in, destitute of*

expīro, 1, *breathe out, die*

expleo, 2, -ēvi, -ētum, *fill up, complete*

explōrātor, -ōris, m. *scout*

explōro, 1, *reconnoitre, learn*

expōno (pōno), 3, *set out, land, expose, explain*

exposco (posco), 3, *implore, demand*

expostulo, 1, *demand, complain*
exprōmo, 3, -prompsi,-promptum, *bring out, disclose*
expugno, 1, *take by storm, obtain*
exquīro, 3, -quīsīvi, -quīsītum, *search carefully, investigate*
exsequor (sequor), 3, dep. *follow up, search out*
exsisto, 3, -stiti, -stitum, *appear, exist*
exsolvo (solvo), 3, *unbind, pay off, release*
exsors, -ortis, adj. *not sharing in, innocent*
extemplō, adv. *immediately*
extendo (tendo), 3, *stretch out, enlarge*
extenuo, 1, *lessen, weaken*
externus, adj. *outward, foreign*
extinguo, 3, -tinxi, -tinctum, *quench, destroy*
exto, 1, *project, stand out*
extollo (tollo), 3, *exalt, praise*
extorqueo, 2, -torsi, -tortum, *wring from, extort*
extrā, prep. and adv. *outside*
extraho (traho), 3, *draw forth, prolong, raise, spend*
extrāordinārius, adj. *special*
extrēmus, adj. *outermost, utmost, last, worthless*
exuo, 3, -ui, -ūtum, *strip, despoil, lay aside*
exūro (ūro), 3, *burn up, scorch*

faciēs, -iēi, f. *appearance, face*
facile, adv. *easily*
facilis, adj. *easy*
facio, 3, fēci, factum, *make, do, cause, sacrifice, incur*
facultās, -ātis, f. *power, opportunity, stores, property*
fallax, -ācis, adj. *deceitful, treacherous*
fallo, 3, fefelli, falsum, *deceive, escape detection*
falsō, adv. *falsely, unjustly*
falsus, adj. *false, deceptive, undeserved*

fāma, -ae, f. *reputation, glory, tradition, report*
famēs, -is, f. *hunger, famine*
familia, -ae, f. *household, clan*
fās, n. indecl. *divine law, allowable*
fascis, -is, m. *faggot, bundle*
fātālis, adj. *fated, predestined*
fateor, 2, fassus, dep. *confess*
fatīgātiō, -ōnis, f. *weariness*
fatīgo, 1, *harass, tire out*
fātum, -i, n. *fate*
faucēs, -ium, f. pl. *throat, narrow pass*
faveo, 2, fāvi, fautum, *favour, protect*
fax, facis, f. *torch*
fēlīcitās, -ātis, f. *good fortune*
fēlix, -īcis, adj. *lucky*
fēmina, -ae, f. *woman, female*
femur, -oris, n. *thigh* (dative pl. often **feminibus**)
ferē, adv. *nearly, almost, usually*
fēriae, -ārum, f. pl. *holiday, festival*
ferio, 4, defect. *strike, sacrifice, slay*
fermē, adv. *nearly, about, usually*
fero, ferre, tuli, lātum, 3, *carry, plunder, endure, lead, say, propose* (*a law*)
ferōcia, -ae, f. *fury, bellicosity*
ferōciter, adv. *defiantly, recklessly*
ferox, -ōcis, adj. *reckless, warlike*
ferrum, -i, n. *iron, sword*
fertilis, adj. *fertile*
fessus, adj. *tired, disabled*
festīnātiō, -ōnis, f. *haste*
festīno, 1, *hurry*
festus, adj. *solemn, festal*
fidēlis, adj. *faithful*
fidēs, -ei, f. *faith, credit, word of honour, loyalty, trust, assurance*
fīdo, 3, fīsus, semi-dep. *trust, confide*
fīdus, adj. *loyal, trustworthy*
fīgo, 3, fixi, fixum, *fasten, stick fast*
fīlius, -i, m. *son*
findo, 3, fidi, fissum, *split open*

VOCABULARY.

finio, 4, *bound, finish, limit*
finis, -is, m. *end, limit, territory* (pl.)
finitimus, adj. *adjoining*
fio, fieri, factus, semi-dep. *become, happen, am made*
firmo, 1, *strengthen, prove, am composed of*
firmus, adj. *strong, constant*
flagro, 1, *blaze, burn*
flamma, -ae, f. *flame*
flebilis, adj. *lamentable, tearful*
flecto, 3, flexi, flexum, *bend, turn, change*
fletus, -ūs, m. *weeping*
flexus, -ūs, m. *bend, corner*
flumen, -inis, n. *river, current*
fluo, 3, fluxi, fluxum, *flow*
fluvius, -i, m. *river*
foede, adv. *foully, disgracefully*
foedus, adj. *foul, disgraceful, horrible*
foedus, -eris, n. *treaty*
fons, fontis, m. *spring, source*
[for], 1, defect. dep. *speak*
fore, foret, *from sum*
forma, -ae, f. *shape, beauty*
formido, -inis, f. *fear, dread*
formula, -ae, f. *form of words, legal formula*
fornicātus, adj. *vaulted, arched*
fors, fortis, f. *chance, luck*
forsitan, adv. *perhaps*
forte, adv. *by chance, accidentally, perchance*
fortis, adj. *strong, brave*
fortūna, -ae, f. *luck, fate*; pl. *position, property*
forum, -i, n. *market, market-place*
fovea, -ae, f. *pit*
foveo, 2, fōvi, fōtum, *cherish, assist*
frango, 3, frēgi, fractum, *break, crush, dishearten*
frāter, -tris, m. *brother*
fraus, fraudis, f. *deceit, trick, loss*
fremitus, -ūs, m. *murmuring, grumbling*
frequens, -entis, adj. *frequent, crowded*

frequenter, adv. *in great numbers, frequently*
fretum, -i, n. *strait, straits of Messina*
frīgus, -oris, n. *frost, cold*
frons, frondis, f. *leaf*
frons, frontis, f. *forehead, front of an army*
fructus, -ūs, m. *fruit, profit, effect*
frūgēs, -um, f. pl. *crops*
frūmentātor, -ōris, m. *forager*
frūmentor, 1, dep. *collect corn*
frūmentum, -i, n. *grain*
fruor, 3, fructus and fruitus, dep. *enjoy*
frustrā, adv. *in vain*
frustror, 1, dep. *trick, disappoint*
fuga, -ae, f. *flight, rout, escape*
fugio, 3, fūgi, fugitum, *flee, avoid*; impers. *it escapes the notice of*
fugo, 1, *put to flight*
fulgeo, 2, fulsi, *shine, glitter*
fulgor, -ōris, m. *gleam, glitter*
fulmen, -inis, n. *lightning, thunderbolt*
fūmo, 1, *smoke*
fūmus, -i, m. *smoke*
funda, -ae, f. *sling*
funditor, -ōris, m. *slinger*
fundo, 3, fūdi, fūsum, *pour, rout, shed*
fūnestus, adj. *disastrous, mournful*
fūnus, -eris, n. *burial, destruction*
furo, 3, defect. *am mad, rave*
furor, -ōris, m. *madness, rage*
furtim, adv. *stealthily, secretly*
futūrus, future participle of **sum**

gallīna, -ae, f. *hen*
gallus, -i, m. *cock*
gaudeo, 2, gāvīsus, semi-dep. *rejoice*
gaudium, -i, n. *joy*
gelidus, adj. *cold*
gemitus, -ūs, m. *sigh, groan*
gens, gentis, f. *clan, tribe*
genus, -eris, n. *family, race, kind, mode*

gero, 3, gessi, gestum, *wear, carry on, wage (war), behave*
gladius, -i, m. *sword*
globus, -i, m. *ball, mass*
glōria, -ae, f. *glory, boasting, fame*
glōrior, 1, dep. *boast*
gnārus, adj. *skilful, knowing*
grātia, -ae, f. *favour, influence, thanks, sake*
grātulor, 1, dep. *congratulate*
grātus, adj. *pleasing, pleasant*
gravis, adj. *heavy, unwholesome, grievous, important*
gravitās, -ātis, f. *weight, importance, dignity*
graviter, adv. *deeply, severely, with dignity*
gravo, 1, *burden, annoy, trouble*
grex, gregis, m. *flock, herd, troop*
gurges, -itis, m. *eddy, current*

habeo, 2, *have, hold, consider, deliver (speech)*
habitus, -ūs, m. *state, condition, manner*
haereo, 2, haesi, haesum, *stick fast, keep together*
hastāti, -ōrum, m. pl. *first line*
haud, adv. *by no means*
haud-dum, adv. *not yet*
haudquāquam, adv. *by no means, far from*
haurio, 4, hausi, haustum, *drain off, shed (blood), draw out*
hercule, adv. *by Hercules, assuredly*
hiātus, -ūs, m. *cleft, abyss*
hīberna, -ōrum, n. pl. *winter-quarters*
hībernāculum, -i, n. *hut, winter-residence*
hīberno, 1, *pass the winter*
hībernus, adj. *wintry*
hīc, adv. *here, hereupon*
hīc, hic-ce, haec, hŏc, pron. *this one, the latter*
hiems, -emis, f. *winter, storm*
hinc, adv. *from here, on this side, after this*
hodiē, adv. *to-day*

hodiernus, adj. *this day's*
homo, -inis, c. *human being, man, infantry*
honor (honōs), -ōris, m. *public office, fame*
honōro, 1, *honour*
hōra, -ae, f. *time, hour*
hordeum, -i, n. *barley*
horreo, 2, *shudder, tremble at, fear*
horreum, -i, n. *storehouse, granary*
horridus, adj. *bristly, wild, savage*
hospes, -itis, m. *host, guest, foreigner*
hospitāliter, adv. *hospitably*
hospitium, -i, n. *hospitality, lodging, inn*
hostia, -ae, f. *victim*
hostīlis, adj. *hostile*
hostis, -is, c. *public enemy*
hūc, adv. *hither, to this*
huius-ce, genitive of hic-ce
hūmānus, adj. *human, humane*
humilis, adj. *low, humble, slight*
humus, -i, f. *earth, ground*

iaceo, 2, *lie*
iacto, 1, *throw about, boast, discuss*
iactūra, -ae, f. *loss*
iaculātor, -ōris, m. *javelin-thrower*
iaculor, 1, dep. *throw javelins*
iaculum, -i, n. *javelin*
iam, adv. *now, already, soon;*
  iam dūdum, *now for some time*
ibi, adv. *there*
ictus, -ūs, m. *blow, thrust*
ictus, adj. *struck, wounded*
īdem, eadem, idem, pron. *same*
idūs, -uum, f. pl. *ides*
iēre, 3rd pl. perfect indicative of eo
igitur, conj. *therefore, then*
ignārus, adj. *unaware, ignorant of*
ignāvia, -ae, f. *laziness, cowardice*
ignis, -is, m. *fire, camp-fire*
ignōbilis, adj. *unknown, low born, obscure*
ignōminia, -ae, f. *dishonour*
ignōminiōsus, adj. *shameful*

ignōro, 1, *am ignorant*
ignōtus, adj. *unknown*
ille, illa, illud, pron. *he, that*
illīc, adv. *there, yonder*
illico, adv. *on the spot*
imāgō, -inis, f. *image*; pl. see notes
imber, -ris, m. *shower*
imitor, 1, dep. *imitate*
immō, adv. *rather, nay more, on the contrary, yes indeed*
immolo, 1, *sacrifice*
immortālis, adj. *immortal*
impavidus, adj. *undaunted*
imperātor, -ōris, m. *general*
imperito, 1, *hold rule, command*
imperium, -i,n. *military command, authority, empire*
impero, 1, *command*
impetus, -ūs, m. *charge, violence*
imprōvīsus, adj. *unforeseen, unexpected*
īmus, adj. *lowest, deepest*
in, prep. *in, into, against, in the case of*
inbellis, adj. *unwarlike*
inbuo, 3, -ui, -ūtum, *stain, imbue*
incalesco, 3, -ui, *grow hot*
incautē, adv. *carelessly*
incautus, adj. *careless*
incēdo (cēdo), 3, *advance, enter, assail*
incendium, -i, n. *conflagration*
incendo, 3, -di, -sum, *set on fire, burn up, inflame*
inceptum, -i, n. *attempt, beginning*
incido, 3, -cidi, -cāsum, *fall into, attack, happen*
incīdo, 3, -cīdi, -cīsum, *cut, inscribe, cut off*
incipio, 3, -cēpi, -ceptum, *begin*
inclēmenter, adv. *roughly, severely*
inclīno, 1, *incline, bend, decide*
inclūdo, 3, -si, -sum, *shut in*
incognitus, adj. *unknown*
incola, -ae, c. *inhabitant*
incolo (colo), 3, *inhabit*
incolumis, adj. *safe, unhurt*
incolumitās, -ātis, f. *safety*

incompositus, adj. *disorderly, undisciplined*
inconditus, adj. *irregular, straggling*
inconsultē, adv. *unadvisedly*
inconsultus, adj. *rash, planless*
increpo, 1, -ui, -itum, *rebuke, grumble at*
incresco (cresco), 3, *increase*
incumbo, 3, -cubui, -cubitum, *lean upon, exert*
incurro (curro), 3, *charge, attack*
incurso, 1, *make frequent attacks*
incutio, 3, -cussi, -cussum, *strike upon, impress*
inde, adv. *then, thence, ever since*
index, -icis, c. *informer*
indīcens, -entis, adj. *not speaking*
indicium, -i, n. *information, evidence, sign*
indico, 1, *point out, inform against*
indīco (dīco), 3, *declare, enjoin*
indignitās, -ātis, f. *disgrace, indignity*
indignor, 1, dep. *am indignant*
indignus, adj. *unworthy, undeserving, intolerable*
indomitus, adj. *untamed, fierce*
indūco (dūco), 3, *lead into, persuade, resolve*
indulgentia, -ae, f. *complaisance*
indulgeo, 2, -dulsi, -dultum, *yield to, show kindness*
industria, -ae, f. *work*; **dē industriā**, *on purpose*
ineo (eo), 4, *enter, enter upon, devise*
inermis, adj. *unarmed*
iners, -ertis, adj. *sluggish, spiritless*
inesco, 1, *bait, decoy*
inexplōrātō, adv. *without reconnoitring*
infāmia, -ae, f. *disgrace, infamy*
infāmis, adj. *disreputable, infamous*
infēlix, -īcis, adj. *unfortunate*
inferior, -ōris, adj. *lower, worse*
infero (fero), 3, *bring in, attack, inflict*
infestus, adj. *hostile, dangerous*

ingenium, -i, n. *disposition, ability*

ingens, -entis, adj. *huge*

ingredior, 3, -gressus, dep. *enter, begin*

inimīcus, -i, m. adj. and noun, *adversary, unfriendly*

inīquus, adj. *not level, unfair, hostile*

initio, 1, *initiate, consecrate*

initium, -i, n. *beginning*

iniungo (iungo), 3, *join, inflict, enjoin*

iniūria, -ae, f. *harm, affront*

iniussū, ablative m. sing. only, *without orders*

inlicio, 3, -lexi, -lectum, *entice, mislead*

inlīdo, 3, -si, -sum, *strike against*

inlūcesco, -luxi, *grow light, dawn*

inmātūrus, adj. *unripe*

inmensus, adj. *unlimited, endless*

inmergo (mergo), 3, *plunge in*

inmineo, 2, *overhang, threaten, impend*

inmisceo (misceo), 2, *intermingle*

inmitto (mitto), 3, *send against, let go*

inmodestē, adv. *impudently*

inmodicē, adv. *excessively*

inmodicus, adj. *extravagant*

inmūnītus, adj. *unfortified*

inmūtābilis, adj. *unalterable*

innocentia, -ae, f. *integrity*

innōtesco, 3, -tui, *become known*

inopia, -ae, f. *scarcity, lack*

inops, -opis, adj. *destitute, helpless*

inordinātus, adj. *disordered*

inpār, -aris, adj. *unequal, no match for*

inpavidus, see **impavidus**

inpedīmentum, -i, n. *hindrance, obstacle*; pl. *baggage*

inpedio, 4, *hinder, entangle, block*

inpello (pello), 3, *drive, urge on, push*

inpendium, -i, n. *expense, payment*

inpendo, 3, -di, -sum, *pay for, employ*

inpensa, -ae, f. *outlay, cost*

inpiger, -gra, -grum, adj. *energetic*

inpigrē, adv. *actively, eagerly*

inpleo, 2, -ēvi, -ētum, *fill*

inplōrātiō, -ōnis, f. *entreaty*

inplōro, 1, *entreat*

inpōno (pōno), 3, *embark, put on, impose*

inprōvidus, adj. *unawares, careless*

inquam, inquis, inquit, defect. *say I, says you, says he*

inquiētus, adj. *restless, inactive*

inquīro, 3, -quīsīvi, -quīsītum, *search for, enquire into*

inrīto, 1, *provoke, inflame*

inruo (ruo), 3, *charge, rush in*

insānio, 4, *am mad*

insciens, -entis, adj. *unaware*

inscientia, -ae, f. *inexperience*

inscītia, -ae, f. *ignorance, stupidity*

insectātiō, -ōnis, f. *accusation, attack*

insector, 1, dep. *attack, accuse*

insequor (sequor), 3, dep. *follow, follow up closely*

insero, 3, -serui, -sertum, *insert, mingle*

insideo (sedeo), 2, *lie in wait*

insidiae, -ārum, f. pl. *ambush, stratagem*

insidiātor, -ōris, m. *lier-in-wait, waylayer*

insignis, adj. *conspicuous, striking, eminent*

insilio, 4, -ui, *leap upon, mount (a horse)*

insisto, 3, -stiti, *approach, enter upon*

insitus, adj. *inborn, natural*

insolitus, adj. *unusual*

insons, -ontis, adj. *guiltless, blameless*

inspicio, 3, -spexi, -spectum, *look closely at, examine*

institor, -ōris, m. *tradesman, hawker*

insto, 1, -stiti, *am near, threaten, press on*

instrūmentum, -i, n. *apparatus, tool, means*

instruo, 3, -struxi, -structum, *arrange, provide, equip*

insula, -ae, f. *island*

insuper, adv. *above, in addition*

insurgo (surgo), 3, *rise up, rise against*

integer, -gra, -grum, adj. *whole, fresh, untouched*

intemperiēs, -ēi, f. *bad weather*

intendo (tendo), 3, *direct, stretch*

intentus, adj. *intent upon, eager*

inter, prep. *between, among, during*

interclūdo, 3, -si, -sum, *shut off*

interdiū, adv. *by day*

interdum, adv. *occasionally*

intereā, adv. *meanwhile*

interim, adv. *meanwhile*

interiungo (iungo), 3, *join with each other*

intermitto (mitto), 3, *neglect, discontinue*

internecīvus, adj. *mutually destructive*

interpōno (pōno), 3, *interpose, interfere*

interregnum, -i, n. *gap, interregnum*

interrex, -rēgis, m. *temporary magistrate*

interrogo, 1, *ask to speak, question*

intersum (sum), irreg. *lie between, am present at*

intervallum, -i, n. *space between, interval of time*

intervenio (venio), 4, *interpose*

interventus, -ūs, m. *intervention*

intolerābilis, adj. *unbearable, unrestrainable*

intolerandus, adj. *intolerable*

intrā, adv. and prep. *within*

intrābilis, adj. *able to be entered*

intro, 1, *enter, penetrate*

intrōdūco (dūco), 3, *bring in*

intueor (tueor), 2, dep. *contemplate*

inundo, 1, *flood, overflow*

inūtilis, adj. *useless*

invādo (vādo), 3, *enter, invade*

inveho (veho), 3, *import, attack*; passive, *ride, sail*

invenio (venio), 4, *find*

invictus, adj. *invincible*

invideo (video), 2, *envy, grudge*

invidia, -ae, f. *envy, unpopularity*

inviolātus, adj. *unhurt, inviolable*

invīto, 1, *invite, entertain*

invītus, adj. *unwilling*

invius, adj. *impassable, pathless*

invoco, 1, *invoke*

ipse, -a, -um, pron. *self*

īra, -ae, f. *anger*

īrascor, 3, īrātus, *am angry*

irritus, adj. *useless, random*

is, ea, id, pron. *he, she, it; that*

iste, -a, -ud, pron. *that of yours*

ita, adv. *so, thus, on condition*

itaque, conj. *therefore*

item, adv. *also, likewise*

iter, itineris, n. *road, march, journey*

iterum, adv. *again, for the second time*

iubeo, 2, iussi, iussum, *order, bid, urge*

iūdicium, -i, n. *judgment, court, decision*

iūdico, 1, *judge, condemn*

iugulum, -i, n. *throat*

iugum, -i, n. *yoke, mountain-range*

iūmentum, -i, n. *beast, baggage-animal*

iungo, 3, iunxi, iunctum, *join*

iūnior, -ōris, adj. *young*

iurgo, 1, *blame, quarrel*

iūro, 1, *take oath, swear*

iūs, iūris, n. *right, law, justice*

iūsiūrandum, iūrisiūrandi, n. *oath*

iussū, ablative m. sing. only, *by order of*

iustus, adj. *proper, ordinary, just*

iuvenis, adj. *young*; as noun, *a youth*

iuventūs, -ūtis, f. *youth, men of military age*

iuvo, 1, iūvi, ūtum, *help*

iuxtā, adv. and prep. *equally, side by side; near*

L. stands for *Lūcius*
labo, 1, *totter, fail*
labor, -ōris, m. *toil, hardship*
lābor, 3, lapsus, dep. *slip, fall*
labōro, 1, *toil, am in danger, am obscured*
lacero, 1, *rend, slander*
lacesso, 3, -īvi, -ītum, *harass, worry*
lacrima, -ae, f. *tear*
lactens, -entis, adj. *sucking, new-born*
lacus, -ūs, m. *lake*
laetitia, -ae, f. *gladness*
laetus, adj. *joyful*
laevā, adv. *on the left*
laevus, adj. *lefthand, favourable*
lāmentor, 1, dep. *wail*
lānātus, adj. *woolly*
lancea, -ae, f. *lance*
lanio, 1, *tear to pieces*
lanius, -i, m. *butcher*
lapis, -idis, m. *stone*
lapsus, -ūs, m. *slip, fall*
lātē, adv. *widely*
latebra, -ae, f. *hiding-place, pretence*
lateo, 2, *lie hid, escape notice*
lātrō, -ōnis, m. *highwayman*
lātus, adj. *broad, extensive*
latus, -eris, n. *side, flank*
laudo, 1, *praise*
laus, laudis, f. *praise, merit*
laxāmentum, -i, n. *respite*
laxus, adj. *loose, undisciplined*
lectisternium, -i, n. *feast for the gods*
lectus, -i, m. *couch, bed*
lēgātus, -i, m. *general, ambassador*
legiō, -ōnis, f. *legion, ten cohorts*
lēgitimus, adj. *lawful*
lēgo, 1, *depute, despatch*
lego, 3, lēgi, lectum, *choose, read, coast along*
lentus, adj. *tough, sluggish, indifferent*
lētum, -i, n. *death, destruction*
levis, adj. *light, trivial, fickle*
levitās, -ātis, f. *lightness, fickleness*

lex, lēgis, f. *law, terms*
libens, -entis, adj. *willing, ready*
līber, -era, -erum, adj. *free, free from*
liber, -ri, m. *book*
līberālis, adj. *noble, generous*
līberē, adv. *freely, liberally*
līberi, -ōrum, m. pl. *children (*)freeborn)*
lībero, 1, *set free, discharge*
lībertās, -ātis, f. *liberty, boldness*
lībertīna, -ae, f. *freed woman*
lībertīnus, -i, m. *freed slave*
licentia, -ae, f. *licence, lawlessness*
licet, 2, impers. *it is allowed*
lictor, -ōris, m. *consul's officer*
lignum, -i, n. *timber, firewood*
līmen, -inis, n. *threshold, door*
līmes, -itis, m. *boundary, line, path*
līmus, -i, m. *mud*
lingua, -ae, f. *tongue, language*
linteus, adj. *made of flax, linen*
liquidus, adj. *flowing, liquid, clear*
littera, -ae, f. *letter (of alphabet);* pl. *a letter, literature*
lītus, -oris, n. *shore*
loco, 1, *station, contract for, lease, hire*
locūplēto, 1, *enrich*
locus, -i, m. *place, post, scope;* pl. **loca,** *district*
longē, adv. *far, diffusely, by far*
longinquus, adj. *distant, tedious*
longus, adj. *long, tedious*
loquor, 3, locūtus, dep. *speak*
lōrīca, -ae, f. *cuirass*
lūcesco, 3, defect. *shine, dawn*
luctus, -ūs, m. *mourning*
lūdibrium, -i, n. *mockery, deception*
lūdificātiō, -ōnis, f. *derision, baffling*
lūdificor, 1, dep. *deceive, frustrate*
lūdus, -i, m. *game, sport, school*
lūgeo, 2, luxi, luctum, *mourn*
lūmen, -inis, n. *light*
lūna, -ae, f. *moon*
luo, 3, lui, *expiate, pay for*
lupus, -i, m. *wolf*
lux, lūcis, f. *light, daylight*

M. stands for *Marcus*; **M'.** for *Mānius*

macte, *well done!* see note

macula, -ae, f. *spot, stain*

maestus, adj. *sad*

magis, adv. *more, rather*

magister, -tri, m. *chief, master, ruler, steersman*

magisterium, -i, n. *mastership, office*

magistrātus, -ūs, m. *office, magistrate*

magnitūdō, -inis, f. *greatness, size*

magnus, adj. *great, important, valuable*

māiestās, -ātis, f. *majesty, dignity, sovereign power*

māior, -ōris, adj. *greater, more important*

māiōrēs, -um, m. pl. *ancestors*

mālo, 3, malle, mālui, defect. *prefer*

malum, -i, n. *misfortune, injury*

malus, adj. *evil, bad*

mandātum, -i, n. *order, task*

mando, 1, *entrust, command*

maneo, 2, mansi, mansum, *stay, remain, abide by, await*

mānēs, -ium, m. pl. *souls of the dead, the world below*

manipulus, -i, m. *company of soldiers*

māno, 1, *drip, ooze*

manus, -ūs, f. *hand, power; band, troop*

mare, -is, n. *sea*

maritimus, adj. *belonging to the sea, maritime*

Mars, Martis, m. *god of war; war*

martius, adj. *sacred to Mars; the month of March*

mas, maris, m. *male*

māter, -tris, f. *mother*

māteria, -ae, f. *timber*

mātrōna, -ae, f. *married woman*

mātūrē, adv. *early, speedily*

mātūritās, -ātis, f. *ripeness, completeness*

mātūrus, adj. *early, ripe, fit*

mātūtīnus, adj. *morning*

Māvors, see **Mars**

maximē, adv. *very greatly, especially*

maximus, adj. *very great*

medeor, 2, dep. defect. *heal, restore*

medicus, adj. *healing*; as noun, *physician*

mediŏcris, adj. *ordinary, moderate*

medius, adj. *middle, central*

melior, -ōris, adj. *better*

membrum, -i, n. *limb*

memor, -oris, adj. *mindful, remembering*

memoria, -ae, f. *memory, lifetime*

memoro, 1, *mention, make famous*

mens, mentis, f. *mind, feelings, intention*

mensis, -is, m. *month*

mentiō, -ōnis, f. *mention*

mercennārius, adj. *hired, mercenary*

mercēs, -ēdis, f. *reward, wages, bribe*

mereo, 2, *earn, deserve, serve in the army*

mergo, 3, mersi, mersum, *sink, plunge*

merīdiēs, -ēi, m. *noon, south*

meritō, adv. *deservedly*

meritum, -i, n. *desert, merit, blame*

merx, mercis, f. *merchandise*

messis, -is, f. *harvest*

-met, suffix of emphasis

meto, 3, messui, messum, *mow, reap*

metuo, 3, -ui, -ūtum, *dread*

metus, -ūs, m. *dread, apprehension*

meus, adj. *my, mine*

mico, 1, *quiver, flash*

mīles, -itis, m. *soldier*

mīlitāris, adj. *military, warlike*

mīlitia, -ae, f. *military service, warfare*

mīlito, 1, *serve as a soldier*

mille, indecl. adj. *thousand*; pl. **mīlia,** *thousands; miles*

minae, -ārum, f. pl. *threats*

minimē, adv. *least, by no means*

minimus, adj. *very small, least*

ministerium, -i, n. *task, business*

minor, -ōris, adj. *smaller, inferior*

minuo, 3, -ui, -ūtum, *diminish, eclipse*

minus, adv. and indecl. noun, *less*

mīrāculum, -i, n. *marvel*

mīrē, adv. *wonderfully*

mīror, 1, dep. *wonder, am amazed*

mīrus, adj. *wonderful*

misceo, 2, miscui, mixtum or mistum, *mix, mingle, confuse*

misereor, 2, dep. *pity*

miseria, -ae, f. *distress, misfortune*

miseror, 1, dep. *pity*

missilis, adj. *throwable, missile*

mītigo, 1, *soften, assuage*

mītis, adj. *merciful, gentle*

mitto, 3, mīsi, missum, *send, release*

moderātus, adj. *reasonable*

modicus, adj. *moderate, scanty*

modius, -i, m. *peck (of corn)*

modo, adv. *just now, only, sometimes*

modus, -i, m. *manner, measure, limit*

moenia, -ium, n. pl. *fortifications*

mōlēs, -is, f. *mass, weight, difficulty, pier*

mōlior, 4, *strive, build, move*

mollis, adj. *soft, pliant, changeable*

mōmentum, -i, n. *movement, cause, moment*

moneo, 2, *advise, warn*

monitus, -ūs, m. *reminder, warning, advice*

mons, montis, m. *mountain*

monstro, 1, *show, point out*

mora, -ae, f. *delay, obstacle*

morior, 3, mortuus, dep. *die*

moror, 1, dep. *delay, wait*

mors, mortis, f. *death*

mōs, mōris, m. *manner, custom;* pl. *character*

mōtus, -ūs, m. *movement, rebellion*

moveo, 2, mōvi, mōtum, *move, trouble, inspire, persuade*

mox, adv. *soon*

mūcrō, -ōnis, m. *point*

mulier, -eris, f. *woman*

multiplex, -icis, adj. *manifold, far greater*

multiplico, 1, *multiply, increase*

multitūdō, -inis, f. *crowd, number*

multō, adv. *by far, much*

multum, adv. *much*

multus, adj. *much, many*

mūnificē, adv. *bountifully*

mūnificentia, -ae, f. *generosity*

mūnīmentum, -i, n. *fortification*

mūnio, 4, *build, fortify, protect*

mūrus, -i, m. *wall*

mūto, 1, *change, exchange*

mūtuus, adj. *borrowed, lent*

nam, namque, conj. *for, for indeed*

nanciscor, 3, nactus or nanctus, dep. *get, obtain*

narro, 1, *tell*

nāsus, -i, m. *nose*

nātūra, -ae, f. *nature, character*

nātus, adj. *destined by nature, suited*

naufragium, -i, n. *shipwreck, ruin*

nauta, -ae, m. *sailor*

nauticus, adj. *nautical*

nāvālis, adj. *naval;* socii nāvālēs, *crew*

nāvis, -is, f. *ship*

-ne, conj. *whether, or*

nē, conj. *lest, that...not*

nē...quidem, adv. *not even*

nebula, -ae, f. *mist*

nec, conj. *neither, nor, and...not*

necessārius, adj. *needful, related*

necesse, adj. indecl. *needful, necessary*

necessitās, -ātis, f. *necessity*

necne, adv. *or not*

neco, 1, *put to death, destroy*

nēcubi, adv. *that...nowhere, lest anywhere*

nēcunde, adv. *lest from anywhere*

nefās, indecl. noun, *sin, abomination*

neglegentia, -ae, f. *carelessness, neglect*

neglego, 3, -lexi, -lectum, *neglect, despise*

nego, 1, *deny, refuse*

negōtium, -i, n. *business, operation, duty*

nēmō, defect. noun, m. and f. *no one*

neque, see **nec**

nequeo, 4, defect. *am unable*

nēquīquam, adv. *in vain*

nēquitia, -ae, f. *negligence, villainy*

nescio, 4, *not to know, am ignorant*

neu, nēve, conj. *nor, and...not*

neuter, -tra, -trum, adj. *neither*

nī, conj. *if...not, unless*

nihil, indecl. noun and adv. *nothing, in no way*

nīmīrum, adv. *without doubt, of course*

nimis, adv. *too much, too*

nimius, adj. *excessive*

nisi, conj. *if...not, unless, except*

nītor, 3, nixus and nīsus, dep. *lean upon, press on, strive*

no, 1, *swim*

nōbilis, adj. *well-born, noble, famed*

nōbilitās, -ātis, f. *high birth, nobility, excellence*

nōbilito, 1, *make famous*

nocturnus, adj. *night, nocturnal*

nōmen, -īnis, n. *name, race, reputation, reason*

nōn, adv. *not*

nōndum, adv. *not yet*

noscito, 1, *know, recognise*

nosco, 3, nōvi, nōtum, *get to know, examine*

noster, -tra, -trum, adj. *our*

nota, -ae, f. *mark, note*

nōtitia, -ae, f. *knowledge, notoriety*

nōtus, adj. *well known, acquaintance*

novissimus, adj. *last, rearguard*

novus, adj. *new, strange, revolutionary*

nox, noctis, f. *night, darkness*

nūbēs, -is, f. *cloud*

nūdo, 1, *strip, expose*

nūdus, adj. *bare, exposed*

nullus, adj. *no, none*

num, interr. adv. *whether, surely*

numero, 1, *count, reckon*

numerus, -i, m. *number*

nummus, -i, m. *coin*

numquam, adv. *never*

nunc, adv. *now, as it is*

nuncupo, 1, *name, utter a vow*

nundinor, 1, dep. *bargain, haggle*

nuntio, 1, *announce*

nuntius, -i, m. *message, messenger*

nūper, adv. *lately*

ob, prep. *on account of*

ōbicio, 3, -iēci, -iectum, *oppose, expose, reproach*

obligo, 1, *bind, pledge*

oblīquus, adj. *sidelong, across*

oblīviscor, 3, -lītus, dep. *forget*

oboedio, 4, *obey, listen to*

obruo (ruo), 3, *overwhelm, oppress*

obsaepio, 4, -saepsi, -saeptum, *fence in, close*

obscūrus, adj. *obscure, unknown, dark*

obses, -idis, c. *hostage*

obsideo (sedeo), 2, *besiege, blockade, close*

obsidiō, -ōnis, f. *siege, blockade*

obsisto, 3, -stiti, -stitum, *oppose, stand in the way*

obstinātus, adj. *resolved, stubborn*

obsto, 1, -stiti, -stitum, *obstruct, prevent*

obstrepo, 3, -ui, -itum, *clamour at*

obtineo, -tinui, -tentum, *hold, maintain, gain one's point*

obtorpesco, 3, -pui, *become numbed, paralysed*

obtrunco, 1, *behead, slaughter*

obviam, adv. *in the way, to meet*

obvius, adj. *meeting, passer-by*

occaeco, 1, *blind*

occāsiō, -ōnis, f. *opportunity*

occāsus, -ūs, m. *setting*

occidiŏ, -ŏnis, f. *destruction,
  extermination*
occīdo, 3, -cīdo, -cīsum, *kill*
occido, 3, -cidi, -cāsum, *fall, set,
  am ruined*
occultus, adj. *secret, hidden*
occupo, 1, *seize, occupy, anticipate*
occurro (curro), 3, *meet, attack*
occurso, 1, *make attacks*
ŏcius, adv. *more swiftly, rather
  rapidly*
octingenti, -ae, -a, pl. numer. adj.
  eight hundred
octo, numer. adj. indecl. *eight*
octōgintā, numer. adj. indecl.
  eighty
oculus, -i, m. *eye*
odium, -i, n. *hatred*
offero, 3, offerre, obtuli, oblātum,
  offer, show, meet
officium, -i, n. *service, kindness,
  duty*
offundo (fundo), 3, *spread over,
  assail*
ŏlim, adv. *formerly, hereafter,
  once*
ŏmen, -inis, n. *portent, warning*
omitto (mitto), 3, *let slip, neglect,
  leave*
omnis, adj. *all, every*
onerārius, adj. *merchant-, cargo-*
  (nāvēs, *ships*)
onerātus, adj. *loaded, overwhelmed*
onus, -eris, n. *burden*
opera, -ae, f. *trouble, pains*
[ops], opis, f. *help*; pl. opēs, opum,
  wealth, resources
oportet, 2, impers. *it behoves, one
  ought*
opperior, 4, -ertus, dep. *wait for,
  watch*
oppidum, -i, n. *town*
oppleo, 2, -ēvi, -ētum, *cover, fill*
opportūnitās, -ātis, f. *convenience,
  opportunity*
opportūnus, adj. *timely*
opprimo (premo), 3, *crush,
  surprise*
oppugno, 1, *attack*

optimus (optumus), adj. *best,
  excellent*
opto, 1, *wish, choose*
opulentus, adj. *rich*
opus, -eris, n. *work, fortification,
  effort*
opus, indecl. noun, *need*
ōra, -ae, f. *border, shore, cable*
ōrāculum, -i, n. *oracle*
ōrātiŏ, -ōnis, f. *speech*
orbis, -is, m. *ring, disc, circuit,
  world*
ordino, 1, *arrange, dispose*
ordior, 4, orsus, dep. *begin (a
  speech)*
ordŏ, -inis, m. *order, rank, class*
orior, 4, ortus, dep. *arise, have
  origin, am born*
ornātus, -ūs, m. *equipment*
ōro, 1, *beg, entreat*
ōs, ōris, n. *mouth, face, eyes,
  tongue*
ostendo, 3, -di, -sum, *exhibit,
  disclose*
ostium, -i, n. *door, harbour-mouth*
ōtium, -i, n. *leisure, ease, quiet*
ovillus, adj. *belonging to sheep*

P. stands for *Publius*
pābulātor, -ōris, m. *forager*
pābulum, -i, n. *fodder*
paciscor, 3, pactus, dep. *covenant,
  settle*
pāco, 1, *pacify, subdue*
pactum, -i, n. *agreement*
paene, adv. *almost*
paenitet, 2, impers. *repent, regret*
pālātor, -ōris, m. *straggler*
pālor, 1, dep. *wander, straggle*
palūs, -ūdis, f. *marsh*
paluster, -tris, -tre, adj. *swampy*
pando, 3, -di, -sum, *spread, open
  out, deploy*
pango, 3, pepigi, pactum, *fasten,
  stipulate, agree*
pār, paris, adj. *equal, proper, a
  match for*
parco, 3, peperci, parcitum *or*
  parsum, *spare* .

parens, -entis, c. *parent*
păreo, 2, *obey*
pario, 3, peperi, partum, *bring forth, obtain, win*
pariter, adv. *equally, together*
parma, -ae, f. *round shield*
paro, 1, *prepare, provide*
pars, partis, f. *side, part, duty*
particeps, -ipis, adj. *sharing, partner*
partim, adv. *partly*
partio, 4, *share, divide*
partus, adj. *won*
parum, adv. *too little, insufficiently*
parvus, adj. *small, insignificant*
passim, adv. *in all directions, promiscuously*
passus, -ūs, m. *pace, step*
patens, -entis, adj. *open, unobstructed*
pateo, 2, *lie open, extend*
pater, -tris, m. *father*; pl. **patrēs**, *the senate*
patera, -ae, f. *sacrificial bowl*
patesco, 3, -ui, *become broad*
patior, 3, passus, dep. *allow, suffer*
patria, -ae, f. *fatherland, city*
patricii, -ōrum, m. pl. *nobles*
patrōnus, -i, m. *protector, defender*
pauci, -ae, -a, pl. adj. *few*
paucitās, -ātis, f. *fewness*
paulō, adv. *by a little, slightly*
paulum, adv. *somewhat*; as a noun, *a little*
paveo, 2, pāvi, *am dismayed, dread*
pavidus, adj. *panic-stricken*
pavor, -ōris, m. *panic*
pax, pācis, f. *peace*
pecco, 1, *err, sin, make a mistake*
pecūnia, -ae, f. *money*
pecus, -oris, n. *flock, herd*
pedes, -itis, m. *footsoldier*
pedester, -tris, -tre, adj. *pedestrian, on foot*
peditātus, -ūs, m. *infantry*
pello, 3, pepuli, pulsum, *push, drive, defeat*
penātēs, -ium, m. pl. *household gods, home*

penes, prep. *in the power of, at the command of*
penso, 1, *weigh, consider*
per, prep. *through, over, across, by means of*
perago (ago), 3, *accomplish, finish*
peragro, 1, *traverse, pass through*
perangustus, adj. *very narrow*
percello, 3, -culi, -culsum, *overturn, smite, dishearten*
percommodus, adj. *very advantageous*
percunctor, 1, dep. *question closely*
perdo, 3, -didi, -ditum, *destroy, lose*
perdūco (dūco), 3, *conduct, prolong, induce*
peregrīnus, adj. *foreign*; and as noun, *foreigner*
pereo (eo), 4, *perish, am ruined*
perexiguus, adj. *very small*
perfero (fero), 3, *convey, accomplish, endure, pass (law)*
perficio, 3, -fēci, -fectum, *complete, bring about*
perfringo (frango), 3, *shatter, break through*
perfuga, -ae, m. *refugee, deserter*
perfugio (fugio), 3, *take refuge, desert*
perfugium, -i, n. *refuge, shelter*
perfungor, 3, -functus, dep. *discharge, endure*
pergo, 3, perrexi, perrectum, *go straight, hasten*
perīculum, -i, n. *danger, risk*
perimo (emo), 3, *destroy, cut off*
perinde, adv. *just as*; with **ac sī**, *just as if*
perītus, adj. *practised, knowing*
perlustro, 1, *wander about, survey*
permaneo (maneo), 2, *remain, persist*
permisceo (misceo), 2, *mix up, confuse*
permitto (mitto), 3, *commit, allow, let loose*
permūto, 1, *interchange*
pernīcitās, -ātis, f. *swiftness, agility*

peropportūnē, adv. *very conveniently*

perpetuus, adj. *long-lasting, unbroken*

perpopulātiō, -ōnis, f. *devastation*

perpopulor, 1, dep. *devastate*

persaepe, adv. *very often*

persequor (sequor), 3, dep. *pursue, prosecute*

persevēro, 1, *persevere, persist*

persolvo (solvo), 3, *pay in full, suffer*

perspicio, 3, -spexi, -spectum, *examine, explore*

persto, 1, -stiti, -stātum, *persist, endure*

persuādeo (suādeo), 2, *persuade*

pertinax, -ācis, adj. *persevering, obstinate*

pertraho (traho), *decoy, conduct, prolong*

pervasto, 1, *ravage*

pervenio (venio), 4, *arrive, attain, reach*

pervinco (vinco), 3, *defeat, prevail upon*

pēs, pedis, m. *foot*

pessimus, adj. *very bad, vile*

pestis, -is, f. *plague, destruction*

petītiō, -ōnis, f. *request, candidature*

peto, 3, -īvi, -ītum, *ask, seek, attack, make for*

phalera, -ae, f. *metal plate, ornament*

piāculum, -i, n. *sin-offering, victim*

pignus, -oris, or -eris, n. *pledge, proof*

placeo, 2, *please, decide*

plāco, 1, *appease, reconcile*

plānus, adj. *level, clear, simple*

plēbēiscītum, -i, n. *decree of the people*

plēbēius, adj. *of the plebs, popular, common*

plebs, -is and **plēbēs,** -ēi, f. *common people*

plēnus, adj. *full*

plērīque, -aeque, -aque, pl. adj. *most, very many*

plērumque, adv. *mostly, frequently*

plōro, 1, *bewail, mourn*

pluit, 3, plūvit, defect. *it rains*

plūrimus, adj. *very much, most*

plūs, plūris, n. *more*; also as adv. *more*

Poenus, adj. *Carthaginian*

pondō, adv. *by weight*; as indecl. noun, *pound*

pondus, -eris, n. *weight, importance*

pōno, 3, posui, positum, *put, place, base on, lay aside*

pons, pontis, m. *bridge*

pontifex, -icis, m. *high-priest*

pontificius, adj. *of a high-priest*

poples, -itis, m. *thigh, back of knee*

populābundus, adj. *engaged in plunder*

populāris, adj. *of the people, democratic*

populāris, -is, m. *fellow-countryman*

populātiō, -ōnis, f. *devastation*

populātor, -ōris, m. *plunderer*

populus, -i, m. *a people, the people*

porta, -ae, f. *gate, door*

porticus, -ūs, f. *porch, colonnade*

porto, 1, *carry*

portus, -ūs, m. *harbour*

posco, 3, poposci, *demand, call for*

possum, posse, potui, defect. *am able, can, am powerful*

post, adv. and prep. *after, behind*

posteā, adv. *afterwards*

posterus, adj. *following, future*

postquam, conj. *after*

postrēmō, adv. *last of all, finally*

postrēmus, adj. *last*

postulo, 1, *demand*

potens, -entis, adj. *powerful, able to control*

potestās, -ātis, f. *power*; with **facere,** *put in one's control*

potior, 4, *get possession, occupy*

VOCABULARY.

potissimum, adv. *especially, above all*

potius, adv. *rather*

prae, prep. *in front, because of, compared with*

praealtus, adj. *very high, very deep*

praebeo, 2, *provide, show, present*

praecaveo (caveo), 2, *beware*

praecēdo (cēdo), 3, *go before, excel*

praeceps, -cipitis, adj. *steep, headlong, rash*

praeceptum, -i, n. *advice, instruction*

praecīdo, 3, -cīdi, -cīsum, *cut the end off, cripple*

praecipio, 3, -cēpi, -ceptum, *instruct, forestall, order*

praecipito, 1, *throw down, hurry, overthrow*

praecipuē, adv. *principally*

praeda, -ae, f. *booty*

praedātor, -ōris, m. *plunderer*

praedico, 1, *declare*

praedīco (dīco), 3, *fix beforehand, predict*

praedium, -i, n. *land, farm*

praedor, 1, dep. *plunder*

prae-eo (eo), 4, *lead the way*

praefectus, -i, m. *chief, commander*

praefero (fero), 3, *carry before, prefer*

praeficio, 3, -fēci, -fectum, *put in command*

praefor, 1, dep. defect. *publish, predict*

praelego (lego), 3, *sail past, patrol*

praeligo, 1, *bind in front, fasten on*

praelongus, adj. *very long*

praemitto (mitto), 3, *send out, send ahead*

praemium, -i, n. *reward, profit, booty*

praemoneo, 2, *forewarn*

praeoccupo, 1, *seize beforehand*

praeparātus, adj. *prepared in advance*

praeparo, 1, *equip*

praepōno (pōno), 3, *set over, prefer*

praeproperē, adv. *very hastily*

praeproperus, adj. *rash*

praeruptus, adj. *steep, rugged*

praes, praedis, m. *surety, bondsman*

praesens, -entis,adj. *ready,present, prompt, helpful*

praesentia, -ae, f. *present time*

praesideo (sedeo), 2, *protect, manage*

praesidium, -i, n. *protection, guard, garrison*

praesto, 1, -stiti, -stitum or -stātum, *surpass, am preferable, guarantee, provide, show*

praestō, adv. *ready*

praesum (sum), *rule over, superintend*

praetendo, 3, -tendi, -tentum, *stretch before, allege, spread*

praeter, prep. *past, besides, along, except*

praeterea, adv. *moreover, besides*

praeteritus, adj. *past*

praeterquam quod, adv. *except that*

praeterveho (veho), 3, *carry past, sail along*

praetextātus, adj. *youthful, under military age*

praetextus, adj. *woven, border*

praetor, -ōris, m. *judge, chiefjustice*

praetōrium, -i, n. *general's tent, G.H.Q.*

praetōrius, adj. *praetorian, of praetorian rank*

praetūra, -ae, f. *praetorship*

praevenio (venio), 4, *outstrip, anticipate*

prāvus, adj. *perverse, criminal*

premo, 3, pressi, pressum, *crush, stop, follow close, cover, disparage*

pretium, -i, n. *price, reward;* **pretium operae,** *worth while*

prex, precis, f. *prayer, entreaty*

prīdiē, adv. *on the day before*

prīmō, adv. *at first, first*

prīmōrēs, -um, m. pl. *nobles, dignitaries*

prīmum, adv. *in the first place*;
cum prīmum, *as soon as*

prīmus, adj. *first, most eminent*

princeps, -cipis, c. *leader, chief*;
pl. 2nd line of the legiō

prīncipium, -i, n. *beginning*

prior, -ōris, m. *first (of two),
former*

prīscus, adj. *ancient, traditional*

pristinus, adj. *previous, former*

prius, adv. *before*

priusquam, conj. *before, until*

prīvātim, adv. *privately, personally*

prīvātus, adj. *private, not state-
owned*; as noun, *ordinary citizen*

prō, prep. *for, before, instead of,
according to*

prō, interjection, *alas!*

probē, adv. *rightly, for certain*

probo, 1, *test, approve, recommend*

prōcēdo (cēdo), 3, *go forward,
make progress, succeed*

procella, -ae, f. *storm*

prōclāmo, 1, *declare loudly, defend*

procul, adv. *far, far from*

prōcumbo, 3, -cubui, -cubitum,
fall down, lean over, sink

prōcūro, 1, *attend to, expiate*

prōcurro (curro), 3, *run forward*

prōcursātiō, -ōnis, f. *attack*

prōcurso, 1, *make attacks*

prōcursus, -ūs, m. *charge*

prōdeo (eo), 4, *come forward*

prōdigium, -i, n. *omen*

prōditiō, -ōnis, f. *treachery, be-
trayal*

prōdo, 3, -didi, -ditum, *nominate,
betray, publish*

prōdūco (dūco), 3, *bring forward,
prolong*

proelium, -i, n. *battle, skirmish*

profānus, adj. *not sacred, common*

profectō, adv. *assuredly*

prōfero (fero), 3, *bring out, reveal,
postpone*

prōficio, 3, -fēci, -fectum, *make
progress, succeed*

proficiscor, 3, profectus, dep. *start*

profugio (fugio), 3, *take refuge,
escape*

profundus, adj. *deep*

prōgredior, 3, -gressus, dep. *advance*

prohibeo, 2, *prevent, keep off*

prōicio, 3, -iēci, -iectum, *throw
before, abandon, give up*

prōlābor (lābor), 3, dep. *fall
forward, decay*

prōmineo, 2, *project*

prōmiscuē, adv. *generally, everywhere*

prōmissum, -i, n. *promise*

prōmitto (mitto), 3, *promise*

promptus, -ūs, m. in promptū, *in
sight, ready*

promptus, adj. *ready*

prōmulgo, 1, *publish, give notice*

prōmunturium, -i, n. *promontory,
mountain peak*

prōnuntiātiō, -ōnis, f. *pronuncia-
tion, speech*

prōnus, adj. *leaning forward,
downhill, inclined to*

prōpalam, adv. *openly, notoriously*

prope, adv. and prep. *nearly,
near*

propediem, adv. *very soon*

properē, adv. *speedily, hurriedly*

propero, 1, *hasten*

propinquus, adj. *neighbouring,
related to*

propior, -ōris, adj. *nearer, later*

propitius, adj. *favourable, kind*

prōpōno (pōno), 3, *put forth,
publish, purpose*

prōpraetor, -ōris, m. *provincial
praetor, ex-praetor*

proprius, adj. *one's own, special*

prōra, -ae, f. *prow, bows*

prōripio, 3, -ripui, -reptum, *hurl
forward, rush out*

prōrogo, 1, *prolong*

prōruo (ruo), 3, *rush out, overthrow*

prōsequor (sequor), 3, dep. *attend,
follow*

prospecto, 1, *see far off, view*

prospectus, -ūs, m. *sight, view*

prosper, -era, -erum, adj. *prosperous, favourable*

prosperē, adv. *successfully*

prōspicio, 3, -spexi, -spectum, *provide for, descry*

prōsterno (sterno), 3, *overthrow*

prōtego (tego), 3, *cover, protect*

prōtinus, adv. *straightway, on the way*

prōveho (veho), 3, *transport, exalt, sail on*

prōvideo (video), 2, *foresee, take care, provide*

prōvincia, -ae, f. *province*

proximē, adv. *just previously, next, very nearly*

proximus, adj. *next, nearest, recent*

prūdens, -entis, adj. *cautious, skilled, aware*

prūdentia, -ae, f. *wisdom, foresight*

-pte, emphasises pronouns

publicē, adv. *publicly, by authority*

publicus, adj. *belonging to the people, public*

pudet, 2, impers. *it shames*

puer, -eri, m. *boy*

pugna, -ae, f. *fight, battle*

pugnax, -ācis, adj. *fond of fighting, armed*

pugno, 1, *fight*

pulcher, -chra, -chrum, adj. *handsome, best*

pullus, -i, m. *chicken*

pulsus, -ūs, m. *stroke*

pulvīnar, -āris, n. *cushioned couch*

pulvis, -eris, m. *dust*

punctim, adv. *with the point*

Pūnicus, adj. *Carthaginian*

puppis, -is, f. *stern (of ship)*

purpura, -ae, f. *purple*

Q. stands for *Quintus*

quā, adv. *where, by what road*

quācumque, adv. *wheresoever*

quadrāgintā, indecl. numer. adj. *forty*

quadriduum, -i, n. *a space of four days*

quadrīgātus, adj. *stamped with a four-horse chariot*

quadringenti, -ae, -a, pl. numer. adj. *four hundred*

quaero, 3, quaesīvi, quaesītum, *seek, ask*

quaeso, 3, quaesīvi, defect. *beg, pray, ask*

quaestor, -ōris, m. *paymaster*

quaestūra, -ae, f. *quaestorship*

quaestus, -ūs, m. *profit*

quālis, adj. *of what sort, such as*

quam, adv. *than, as, how*

quamquam, conj. *although*

quamvīs, conj. *although*; adv. *however*

quandō, interr. adv. *when?, ever*; conj. *when, since*

quantum, adv. *as much*

quantus, adj. *how much, as much*

quartus, numer. adj. *fourth*; **quartusdecimus,** *fourteenth*

quassātiō, -ōnis, f. *shaking*

quattuor, indecl. numer. adj. *four*

-que, conj. *and, both*

queo, 4, defect. *am able*

queror, 3, questus, dep. *complain*

questus, -ūs, m. *lamentation*

quī, quae, quod, relative pron. *who, which*; indefinite, *any*

quia, conj. *because*

quīcumque, quaecumque, quodcumque, pron. *whosoever*

quīdam, quaedam, quoddam, pron. *a certain one*

quidem, adv. *indeed*; **nē...quidem,** *not even*

quiēs, -ētis, f. *repose, sleep, inactivity*

quiesco, 3, -ēvi, -ētum, *rest*

quiētus, adj. *inactive, calm*

quīn, conj. *that not, but that*; adv. *why not? moreover*

quīnam, quaenam, quodnam, interr. pron. *who? who pray?*

quindecim, indecl. numer. adj. *fifteen*

quingēni, -ae, -a, pl. numer. adj.
five hundred each

quingenti, -ae, -a, pl. numer. adj.
five hundred

quīni, -ae, -a, pl. numer. adj. *five
each*

quinquāgintā, indecl. numer. adj.
fifty

quīnque, indecl. numer. adj. *five*

quinquennium, -i, n. *space of five
years*

quīnquerēmis, -is, f. *galley with
five banks of oars, quinquereme*

quīntus, numer. adj. *fifth*

quippe, adv. *in fact, indeed*

quirītēs, -ium, m. pl. *citizens*

quis, quae, quid, interr. pron.
who? what?

quī, quae, quod, interr. adj. *what?*

quisnam, quidnam, interr. pron.
who, pray?

quisquam, quidquam, pron. *any
one*

quisque, quaeque, quodque, pron.
each, every

quō, interr. adv. *whither? for
what purpose?*

quoad, conj. *as long as, until, as
far as*

quod, conj. *because, as to the fact
that*

quondam, adv. *once, formerly*

quoniam, conj. *since, because*

quoque, adv. *also, too*

quot, interr. adj. indecl. *how
many? as many*

rabiēs, -em, -ē, f. *madness*

rādix,-īcis, f. *root, base of mountain*

rapidus, adj. *swift*

rapio, 3, rapui, raptum, *seize,
carry away*

raptim, adv. *hurriedly*

ratiō, -ōnis, f. *method, reason,
reckoning*

recēdo (cēdo), 3, *retire*

recens, -entis, adj. *fresh, recent,
vigorous*

receptus, -ūs, m. *retreat, shelter*

recipio, 3, -cēpi, -ceptum, *receive,
recover, accept*

recognosco, 3, -gnōvi, -gnitum,
recollect, recognise, review

rectus, adj. *straight, correct, just,
straightforward*

recupero, 1, *win back*

recūso, 1, *shrink from, refuse*

reddo, 3, -ddidi, -dditum, *restore,
pay up, deliver, render*

redeo (eo), 4, *go back, am reduced
to*

redimo (emo), 3, *buy back, ransom*

redintegro, 1, *renew*

reditus, -ūs, m. *return*

redūco (dūco), 3, *lead back*

redux, -ucis, adj. *returned, coming
home*

refero (fero), 3, *bring back, report,
retreat, lay before (the senate),
recall*

refertus, adj. *full, crowded*

reficio, 3, -fēci, -fectum, *repair,
refresh*

refugio (fugio), 3, *take refuge,
recoil*

rēgīna, -ae, f. *queen*

regiō, -ōnis, f. *district*

regnum, -i, n. *kingdom*

rego, 3, rexi, rectum, *rule*

regredior, 3, -gressus, dep. *retire*

rēgulus, -i, m. *prince, petty king*

relicus, see reliquus

rēligiō, -ōnis, f. *worship, scruple,
oath, awe*

religo, 1, *fasten, tow*

relinquo, 3, -līqui, -lictum, *leave
behind, abandon*

rēliquiae, -ārum, f. pl. *remains,
remnants*

reliquus, adj. *remaining, left*

relūceo, 2, -luxi, *shine*

remaneo (maneo), 2, *remain,
survive*

remedium, -i, n. *remedy, healing*

rēmex, -igis, m. *rower*

remitto (mitto), 3, *send back,
relax, give up, let off*

rēmus, -i, m. *oar*

renovo, 1, *renew, restore*

reor, 2, ratus, dep. *think*

repello (pello), 3, *thrust back, repulse*

repens, -entis, adj. *hasty, sudden*

repente, adv. *suddenly*

repeto (peto), 3, *go back to, recommence, recall, claim*

requiēs, -ētis, f. *repose*; also acc. requiem, abl. requiē

rēs, rei, f. *thing, property, business, benefit*; in rem, *useful*

rescindo, 3, -scidi, -scissum, *break down, destroy*

rescrībo (scrībo), 3, *write back, re-enlist*

resisto, 3, -stiti, -stitum, *resist, stand firm*

resolvo (solvo), 3, *release, disperse*

respergo, 3, -si, -sum, *sprinkle*

respicio, 3, -spexi, -spectum, *look back, look to, honour*

respīro, 1, *breathe, breathe again*

respondeo, 2, -di, -sum, *answer*

responsum, -i, n. *reply*

respublica, rēipublicae, f. *state, state affairs*

restituo, 3, -ui, -ūtum, *restore, rally*

resto, 1, -stiti, *remain, stand firm*

retineo, 2, -tinui, -tentum, *hold back, maintain*

retraho (traho), 3, *recall*

retrō, adv. *back*

reus, -i, m. *accused, defendant*

reverto (verto), 3, *return*

revoco, 1, *recall*

rex, rēgis, m. *king*

rīpa, -ae, f. *bank*

rīte, adv. *duly*

rōbur, -oris, n. *strength, pick (of troops)*

rogātiō, -ōnis, f. *request, proposal for a law, bill*

rogo, 1, *ask, propose a law, ask a question*

ruīna, -ae, f. *fall, ruin, disaster*

rūmor, -ōris, m. *rumour, reputation*

rumpo, 3, rūpi, ruptum, *burst, damage, destroy*

ruo, 3, rui, rutum, *fall, rush*

rūpēs, -is, f. *cliff, precipice, rock*

rursus, adv. *back, again*

sacer, -cra, -crum, adj. *sacred, accursed*

sacrāmentum, -i, n. *military oath, obligation*

sacrātus, adj. *dedicated, holy*

sacrificium, -i, n. *sacrifice*

sacrifico, 1, *sacrifice*

sacrum, -i, n. *rite; festival, sacrifice*

saepe, adv. *often*

saevio, 4, *rage against, clamour*

sagittārius, -i, m. *archer*

saltem, adv. *at least, at any rate*

saltus, -ūs, m. *mountain pass, valley*

salūs, -ūtis, f. *safety, health, greeting*

salūtāris, adj. *healthful, beneficial, safe*

salūto, 1, *greet, salute*

salvus, adj. *safe, sound*

sānē, adv. *indeed, very*

sanguis, -inis, m. *blood, race, strength*

sānus, adj. *healthy, sane, sensible*

sapiens, -entis, adj. *wise*

sarcina, -ae, f. *soldier's pack*

sarmentum, -i, n. *twigs, faggot*

satis, adv. and indecl. noun, *enough, quite*

saucius, adj. *wounded*

saxum, -i, n. *rock, boulder*

scando, 3, -di, -sum, *climb*

scelus, -eris, n. *crime*

sciens, -entis, adj. *knowing, cunning*

scīlicet, adv. *evidently, for example*

scio, 4, *know, know how*

scīpiō, -ōnis, m. *staff (of office)*

sciscitor, 1, dep. *question, investigate*

scītum, -i, n. *decree*; see plebs

scrība, -ae, m. *clerk*

scrībo, 3, scripsi, scriptum, *write, enrol, inscribe*
scūtum, -i, n. *shield*
sē, sēsē, pron. *himself, themselves*
sēcrētus, adj. *private, hidden*
secundum, prep. *down, according to, after*
secundus, adj. *following, second, favourable*
secūris, -is, f. *axe, hatchet*
secus, adv. *otherwise*
sed, conj. *but*
sedeo, 2, sēdi, sessum, *sit, loiter, blockade*
sēdēs, -is, f. *abode, home*
sēditiō, -ōnis, f. *mutiny, strife, sedition*
sēditiōsus, adj. *turbulent, seditious*
sēdo, 1, *appease, check*
sēdulō, adv. *carefully, intentionally*
sēdulus, adj. *careful*
segnis, adj. *inactive, slow*
segnitiēs, -em, -ē, f. *sluggishness*
sēgrego, 1, *set apart*
sēlībra, -ae, f. *a half-pound*
semel, numer. adv. *once, the first time*
sēmenstris, adj. *half-yearly*
sēmiermis, adj. *half-, badly armed*
semper, adv. *always*
sēmustus, adj. *half-burnt, singed*
senātor, -ōris, m. *senator*
senātus, -ūs, m. *senate*
senesco, 3, -ui, *grow old, become weak*
sensim, adv. *gradually*
sententia, -ae, f. *opinion, vote*
sentio, 4, sensi, sensum, *feel, perceive, judge*
seorsum, adv. *apart*
sēparo, 1, *divide, distinguish*
sepelio, 4, -īvi, -pultum, *bury*
septem, indecl. numer. adj. *seven*
septemdecim, indecl. numer. adj. *seventeen*
septentriō, -ōnis, m. *north*
septingenti, -ae, -a, numer. adj. *seven hundred*

sequor, 3, secūtus, dep. *follow, result*
sermō, -ōnis, m. *discourse, talk*
sērō, adv. *late, too late*
servīlis, adj. *servile*
servitium, -i, n. *slavery, slaves*
servitūs, -ūtis, f. *slavery*
servo, 1, *preserve, observe, watch*
servus, -i, m. *slave*
sescenti, -ae, -a, pl. numer. adj. *six hundred*
sēsē, see sē
seu, conj. *whether, or*
sevēritās, -ātis, f. *strictness, severity*
sex, indecl. numer. adj. *six*
sextus, numer. adj. *sixth*
sī, conj. *if, if perchance, on condition that*
sīc, adv. *thus, so*
siccitās, -ātis, f. *drought*
siccus, adj. *dry*
sīcut, sīcutī, adv. *just as, for instance*
signifer, -eri, m. *standard-bearer*
signum, -i, n. *mark, statue, standard, sign, seal, constellation*
silentium, -i, n. *silence*
silva, -ae, f. *wood, forest*
silvestris, adj. *woody, wild*
similis, adj. *like, resembling*
similiter, adv. *similarly*
simul, adv. *together, at the same moment, as soon as*
simulācrum, -i, n. *image, apparition*
simulo, 1, *pretend*
sine, prep. *without*
singuli, -ae, -a, pl. numer. adj. *one each*
sinister, -tra, -trum, adj. *lefthand, unlucky, favourable*
sino, 3, sīvi, situm, *allow, permit*
sinus, -ūs, m. *fold, bay, lap*
situs, -ūs, m. *position, lie of the land, neglect*
situs, adj. *situated, placed*
sīve, see seu

societas, -ātis, f. *alliance, community*
socius, -i, m. *ally, friend;* **socii nāvāles,** *crew*
sōcordia, -ae, f. *folly, indifference, sloth*
sōl, sōlis, m. *sun*
soleo, 2, -itus, semi-dep. *am wont*
sōlitūdō, -inis, f. *loneliness, wilderness*
solitus, adj. *usual, ordinary*
sollers, -ertis, adj. *skilful, ingenious*
sollertia, -ae, f. *cleverness, quickness*
sollicito, 1, *tempt, instigate, harass*
sollicitūdō, -inis, f. *anxiety*
sollicitus, adj. *anxious, uneasy*
solum, -i, n. *soil, ground*
sōlum, adv. *only*
sōlus, adj. *alone, desert, only*
solvo, 3, solvi, solūtum, *loosen, set sail, pay, free*
sonus, -i, m. *sound*
sordidus, adj. *filthy, base, vile*
sors, sortis, f. *lot, duty, fate*
sospes, -itis, m. *safe, fortunate*
sospita, -ae, f. *preserver*
spargo, 3, -si, -sum, *scatter, sprinkle*
spartum, -i, n. *esparto grass*
spatium, -i, n. *space, time, interval, room*
speciēs, -ēi, f. *appearance, display, pretence*
speciōsus, adj. *showy, brilliant*
specto, 1, *look, look on at, have in view*
specula, -ae, f. *watch-tower*
speculātor, -ōris, m. *watcher, spy*
speculātōrius, adj. *for spying*
speculor, 1, dep. *watch, spy*
sperno, 3, sprēvi, sprētum, *scorn, spurn*
spēro, 1, *hope, hope for*
spēs, spei, f. *hope*
spīca, -ae, f. *ear of corn*
spīculum, -i, n. *point, javelin*
spīritus, -ūs, m. *breath, pride*
spīro, 1, *breathe*

splendeo, 2, *shine*
spolio, 1, *despoil*
spolium, -i, n. *spoils*
sponte, ablative f. sing. only, *of one's own accord*
squālor, -ōris, m. *neglect, dirt*
stabilis, adj. *firm, lasting*
stagnum, -i, n. *pool, swamp*
statārius, adj. *stationary*
statim, adv. *immediately*
statiō, -ōnis, f. *moorings, post, outpost*
statīva, -ōrum, n. pl. *permanent camp*
statuo, 3, -ui, -ūtum, *set up, resolve*
status, -ūs, m. *position, condition*
sterno, 3, strāvi, strātum, *lay flat, strew, overthrow*
stimulo, 1, *goad, incite*
stīpendiārius, -i, m. *tributary*
stīpendium, -i, n. *yearly tribute, soldier's pay, campaign*
sto, 1, steti, statum, *stand, am anchored, remain, abide by, cost*
stolidus, adj. *thick-headed, stupid*
strāgēs, -is, f. *destruction*
strēnuus, adj. *prompt, energetic*
strepitus, -ūs, m. *noise, clash*
strepo, 3, -ui, -itum, *resound, am deafened*
stringo, 3, strinxi, strictum, *draw (sword), graze, press together*
studium, -i, n. *zeal, desire*
stultitia, -ae, f. *stupidity*
stultus, adj. *foolish*
stupor, -ōris, m. *astonishment*
stuprum, -i, n. *violation*
suādeo, 2, suāsi, suāsum, *urge, advise*
suāsor, -ōris, m. *adviser, supporter (of a law)*
sub, prep. *under, close to, about*
subdo, 3, -didi, -ditum, *apply*
subdūco (dūco), **3,** *withdraw, lead up to, haul up*
subeo (eo), **4,** *approach, undergo*
subitō, adv. *suddenly*
subitus, adj. *sudden*
sublātus, see **tollo**

submitto (mitto), 3, *send up*
submoveo (moveo), 2, *drive off*
subsidium, -i, n. *reserve, assistance*
subsisto, 3, -stiti, -stitum, *halt, resist*
subtraho (traho), 3, *remove, pull out*
subveho (veho), *bring up*
succēdo (cēdo), 3, *approach, take the place of, succeed*
succenseo (censeo), 2, *bear ill-will*
successus, -ūs, m. *success*
succīdo, 3, -cīdi, -cīsum, *cut from behind, hamstring*
succumbo, 3, -cubui, -cubitum, *yield, succumb*
sūdo, 1, *drip, sweat*
sufficio, 3, -fēci, -fectum, *supply, substitute, suffice*
suffrāgium, -i, n. *voting-tablet, vote*
suillus, adj. *belonging to swine*
sum, esse, fui, defect. *exist, am*
summa, -ae, f. *chief power, command, general engagement, sum*
summus, adj. *highest, utmost, top of*
sūmo, 3, sumpsi, sumptum, *take, take up, exact*
super, prep. and adv. *above, besides*
superbus, adj. *proud, arrogant*
supericio, 3, -iēci, -iectum, *throw upon, exaggerate*
superincubo, 1, *lie upon*
superior, -ōris, adj. *higher, previous, superior*
supero, 1, *overcome, am abundant, cross, remain*
superquam, adv. *besides*
supersto, 1, *stand over*
supersum (sum), irreg. *survive, remain*
supervacāneus, adj. *superfluous*
supervenio (venio), 4, *come in addition*
suppedito, 1, *supply, am in store*
supplēmentum, -i, n. *reinforcements*
supplicātiō, -ōnis, f. *public prayer*
supplicium, -i, n. *public prayer, entreaty, punishment*

supplico, 1, *pray*
supprimo (premo), 3, *sink, check*
suprā, prep. and adv. *above*
surgo, 3, surrexi, surrectum, *rise*
suspensus, adj. *doubtful, in suspense*
sustineo, 2, -tinui, -tentum, *uphold, withstand, endure*
suus, adj. *his, their, one's own, special*

T. stands for *Titus*, **Ti.** for *Tiberius*
tabernāculum, -i, n. *tent*
tacitus, adj. *silent, unspoken*
taedium, -i, n. *weariness, disgust*
taeter, -tra, -trum, adj. *horrible, dreadful*
talentum, -i, n. *talent (of money)*
tālis, adj. *such*
tam, adv. *so*
tamen, adv. *however, but*
tamquam, conj. *as if, just as*
tandem, adv. *at last*
tango, 3, tetigi, tactum, *touch, reach, strike (by lightning)*
tantum, adv. *so much, only*
tantummodo, adv. *only*
tantus, adj. *so much, so great*
tantusdem, adj. *equally large*
tardē, adv. *slowly*
tardus, adj. *slow*
tectum, -i, n. *roof, building*
tego, 3, texi, tectum, *cover, protect, hide*
tegumentum, -i, n. *cover, case*
tēlum, -i, n. *missile weapon, javelin*
temerārius, adj. *rash*
temere, adv. *rashly, at random*
temeritās, -ātis, f. *recklessness*
tempestās, -ātis, f. *time, weather, storm*
templum, -i, n. *temple*
tempto, 1, *test, try*
tempus, -oris, n. *time, opportunity*
tendo, 3, tetendi, tentum and tensum, *stretch, go, encamp, strive*
tenebrae, -ārum, f. pl. *darkness*
teneo, 2, tenui, tentum, *hold, reach*
tenor, -ōris, m. *course*

tentōrium, -i, n. *tent*

tenuis, adj. *thin, slender, paltry*

tergum, -i, n. *back, rear (of army)*

terminus, -i, m. *boundary*

tero, 3, trīvi, trītum, *rub, tread, waste (time)*

terra, -ae, f. *earth, land*

terreo, 2, *frighten*

terrestris, adj. *terrestrial, land*

terribilis, adj. *terrifying*

terror, -ōris, m. *terror, panic*

tertius, numer. adj. *third*

testis, -is, c. *witness*

testor, 1, dep. *call to witness*

timeo, 2, *fear*

timidus, adj. *timid*

timor, -ōris, m. *fear*

tīrō, -ōnis, m. *recruit*

titulus, -i, m. *inscription, title of honour*

toga, -ae, f. *civilian robe*

togātus, -i, m. *civilian*

tolerābilis, adj. *bearable*

tolero, 1, *endure, tolerate*

tollo, 3, sustuli, sublātum, *raise, remove, destroy*

torpidus, adj. *stupefied, paralysed*

torridus, adj. *parched*

tot, indecl. adj. *so many, as many*

totiens, adv. *so often, as often*

tōtus, adj. *whole*

trādo, 3, -didi, -ditum, *hand over, hand down*

trādūco (dūco), 3, *lead across, transfer*

traho, 3, traxi, tractum, *draw, drag, attract, delay*

trāicio, 3, -ieci, -iectum, *bring over, cross*

trans, prep. *across, beyond*

transcendo, 3, -di, -sum, *cross, surpass, board*

transdūco, see trādūco

transeo (eo), 4, *cross, desert*

transfero (fero), 3, *transfer*

transfīgo (fīgo), 3, *pierce*

transfuga, -ae, c. *deserter*

transfugium, -i, n. *desertion*

transgredior, 3, -gressus, dep. *cross*

transitiō, -ōnis, f. *desertion*

transitus, -ūs, m. *passage, crossing*

transmitto (mitto), 3, *convey across, transfer, pass across*

transversus, adj. *cross, transverse (of roads)*

trecēni, -ae, -a, pl. numer. adj. *three hundred each*

trecenti, -ae, -a, pl. numer. adj. *three hundred*

tremo, 3, -ui, -itum, *tremble, tremble at*

trepidātiō, -ōnis, f. *confusion, panic*

trepidē, adv. *hurriedly*

trepidus, adj. *alarmed, disturbed*

trēs, tria, pl. numer. adj. *three*

triārii, -ōrum, m. pl. *third line of legion, veterans*

tribūnal, -is, n. *judgment seat*

tribūnus, -i, m. *tribune*

trīduum, -i, n. *space of three days*

triens, -entis, m. *a third part*

trīgintā, indecl. numer. adj. *thirty*

tristis, adj. *sad, gloomy*

trīticum, -i, n. *wheat*

trucīdo, 1, *slaughter*

tū, pron. *thou*

tueor, 2, tuitus, dep. *watch, guard*

tum, adv. and conj. *then, next, moreover*

tumultuārius, adj. *irregular, disorderly*

tumultus, -ūs, m. *riot, rebellion, uproar*

tumulus, -i, m. *killock*

tunica, -ae, f. *tunic, undergarment*

turba, -ae, f. *crowd*

turbo, 1, *confuse, rout*

turma, -ae, f. *troop, squadron*

turpiter, adv. *shamefully*

turris, -is, f. *tower*

tūtō, adv. *safely*

tūtor, 1, dep. *protect*

tūtus, adj. *safe*

tuus, adj. *thy, thine*

ubi, adv. *where, when, whenever*

ubīque, adv. *everywhere*

ullus, adj. *any*

ulterior, -ōris, adj. *further*

ultimus, adj. *farthest, last*

ultrā, prep. and adv. *beyond*

umbilīcus, -i, m. *navel, waist*

umerus, -i, m. *shoulder*

ūmor, -ōris, m. *damp*

umquam, adv. *ever*

unde, adv. *whence*

undētrīgintā, indecl. numer. adj. *twenty-nine*

undique, adv. *from all sides, everywhere*

ūnicus, adj. *one and only, unique*

ūnīversus, adj. *whole, universal, combined*

ūnus, adj. *one, individual, only*

urbānus, adj. *belonging to the city, polite*

urbs, -is, f. *city*

urgeo, 2, ursi, *push, beset, follow close*

ūro, 3, ussi, ustum, *burn*

usquam, adv. *anywhere*

usque, adv. *as far as, up to*

ūsus, -ūs, m. *use, possession, profit*

ut, utī, conj. *as, when, that, though, how!*

uter, -tra, -trum, pron. *which of two?*

uterque, utraque, utrumque, pron. *each of two*

ūtilis, adj. *useful*

utinam, adv. *would that...!*

utique, adv. *at any rate*

ūtor, 3, ūsus, dep. *use*

utrimque, adv. *on both sides*

utrum, interr. adv. *whether?*

vādo, 3, -si, -sum, *go, rush*

vadum, -i, n. *ford, shoal*

vagē, adv. *widely, everywhere*

vagor, 1, dep. *wander, cruise*

vagus, adj. *wandering*

validus, adj. *strong*

vallis, -is, f. *valley*

vallum, -i, n. *rampart*

vānus, adj. *empty, vain, deceptive*

variē, adv. *with varying results*

vario, 1, *vary, change, differ*

varius, adj. *spotted, changeable*

vās, vāsis, n. *vessel, equipment*

vastitās, -ātis, f. *devastation*

vasto, 1, *lay waste*

-ve, conj. *either, or*

vectīgālis, adj. *paying taxes, tributary*

vegetus, adj. *vigorous*

veho, 3, vexi, vectum, *carry, ride, sail, travel*

vel, conj. *either, or; even*

vēlōcitās, -ātis, f. *rapidity*

velut, velutī, *just as, for example, considering*

vendo, 3, -didi, -ditum, *sell*

venio, 4, vēni, ventum, *come*

ventus, -i, m. *wind*

veprēs, -is, f. *thorn-bush*

vēr, vēris, n. *spring, first-fruits*

verber, -is, n. *whip, scourging, blow*

verbum, -ī, n. *word, order*

vērē, adv. *truly, actually*

vereor, 2, dep. *revere, fear*

vergo, 3, *incline, face towards*

vēritās, -ātis, f. *truthfulness, facts, truth*

vernus, adj. *belonging to spring*

vērō, adv. *but, indeed*

verso, 1, *move about, work upon*

verto, 3, verti, versum, *turn, overturn, change*

vērum, -i, n. *the truth*

vērus, adj. *true, reasonable*

vescor, 3, dep. *feed upon*

vestālis, adj. *devoted to Vesta*

vester, -tra, -trum, adj. *your*

vestibulum, -i, n. *porch, court-yard*

vestīgium, -i, n. *footprint, trace*

vestīmentum, -i, n. *garment*

vestio, 4, *clothe, cover*

vestis, -is, f. *clothing, robe*

veterānus, adj. and noun, *veteran*

veto, 1, vetui, vetitum, *forbid*

vetus, -eris, adj. *old*

vetustās, -ātis, f. *age, ancient times*

via, -ae, f. *road, way, manner*

viāticum, -i, n. *travelling money*

viātor, -ōris, m. *traveller, summoner*

vicem, vicis, f. *turn, change, fortune*; **in vicem**, *by turns*

vīcēni, -ae, -a, pl. numer. adj. *twenty each*

vīcīnus, adj. *neighbouring, resembling*

victima, -ae, f. *victim, sacrifice*

victor, -ōris, m. *conqueror*; as adj. *victorious*

victōria, -ae, f. *victory*

victus, -ūs, m. *provisions*

vīcus, -i, m. *village, suburb*

vidēlicet, adv. *namely, evidently*

video, 2, vīdi, vīsum, *see, care for*

videor, 2, vīsus, dep. *seem, seem good to*

vigeo, 2, *flourish, am strong*

vigilia, -ae, f. *wakefulness, watch, sentinel*

vigintī, indecl. numer. adj. *twenty*

vīlis, adv. *cheap, common, despised*

villa, -ae, f. *country-house, farm*

vincio, 4, -xi, -ctum, *bind*

vinco, 3, vīci, victum, *conquer, prevail*

vinculum, -i, n. *chain, tie, obligation*

vīnea, -ae, f. *vineyard*

vir, viri, m. *man, husband*

virga, -ae, f. *twig, rod*

virgultum, -i, n. *bush, brushwood*

virtūs, -ūtis, f. *courage, merit, virtue*

vīs, vim, vī, f. *force, quantity*; pl. **vīrēs**, vīrium, *strength*

viscus, -eris, n. (usually pl.) *internal organs of body; heart*

vīso, 3, vīsi, vīsum, *visit, explore*

vīta, -ae, f. *life*

vitiōsus, adj. *faulty*

vitium, -i, n. *fault, flaw*

vīvo, 3, vixi, victum, *live*

vīvus, adj. *alive*; **ad vīvum**, *to the quick*

vix, adv. *scarcely*

vixdum, adv. *scarcely yet*

vōciferātiō, -ōnis, f. *outcry, shout*

vōciferor, 1, dep. *shout, exclaim*

voco, 1, *call, summon, call out for*

volgō, see **vulgō**

volgus, see **vulgus**

volo, velle, volui, 3, defect. *wish, wish for, decree*

voluntārius, -i, m. *volunteer*; as adj. *voluntary*

voluntās, -ātis, f. *will, free-will, eagerness*

volvo, 3, volvi, volūtum, *roll, form circle*

vorāgō, -inis, f. *whirlpool, abyss*

vōs, pl. of tū, *you, ye*

vōtum, -i, n. *vow, prayer*

voveo, 2, vōvi, vōtum, *vow, devote*

vulgō, adv. *publicly*

vulgo, 1, *publish, spread abroad*

vulgus, -i, n. *common people, crowd*

vulnero, 1, *wound*

vulnus, -eris, n. *wound*

vultus, -ūs, m. *look, features*

INDEX OF WORDS MENTIONED IN THE NOTES.

[The numbers refer to chapter and section.]

subjunctive of repeated acts **1** 7,
   38 3
  indef. **7** 5, **11** 2
  potential **54** 11
  hypothetical **59** 10
  in assertions **59** 3
  in indignant questions **59** 18
  in 2nd pers. sing. in general
    remarks **8** 12, **61** 10
  with *priusquam* of past facts **8** 1
submovere **56** 1
subsidia **47** 6
super **7** 11, **56** 2
supero **25** 12
superquam **1** 14
supplicatio **1** 15
supplicia **57** 5

taeter **9** 8
tamen **1** 5
tantadem **49** 15
tantum confirmatory **27** 4
tenor **15** 1
titulus **31** 11
toga **26** 1
togati **23** 3
triarii **5** 7
tribunal **30** 8

unicus **14** 9, **27** 3
unus **42** 3
unus with superlative **22** 8
usu capere **44** 6
ut elliptically in prayers **53** 10;
  with *sum* **2** 4
ut = 'considering' **5** 1
  = 'as was natural' **21** 4
  with concessive subj. **25** 2
  repeated **11** 4
  definitive **5** 7, **28** 6
ut si **50** 9
ut vero **14** 3
utique **7** 11

variari **60** 3
vectigalis **54** 1
velut **3** 12, **17** 4
verius **19** 11, **53** 8
ver sacrum **9** 10
versare **25** 17
vestales **57** 2
via fornicata **36** 8
viator **11** 5
vitio creari **33** 11
vitiosus **34** 10
volvere orbem **29** 5

INDEX OF PROPER NAMES.

[The numbers refer to chapter and section.]